John Wallace
Writings

Edgehill Publications

NEWPORT, RHODE ISLAND

John Wallace: Writings

Published in the United States by Edgehill Publications, 200 Harrison Avenue, Newport, RI 02840

Library of Congress Cataloging-in-Publication Data

Wallace, John, 1931–
  [Selections.   1989]
  John Wallace : Writings.—1st ed.
     p.   cm.
  ISBN 0-926028-00-6 : $16.95
     1.   Alcoholism.   I. Title.   II. Title: Writings.
RC565.W2925   1989   89-83897
  362.29′2—dc20   CIP

To Muriel Zink, John Newsom,
Doug Chalmers, and Susan Mardon—
for one shining moment.

Table of Contents

Preface

I first started talking about alcoholism in early 1962. Up until that time, I don't believe I had ever used the word. To be sure, I often talked about drunks, drinking, getting drunk, smashed, loaded and acting crazy, but alcoholism, nary a peep out of me on that subject. What came over me in early 1962 I really can't say. I was working on a PhD in Psychology at Northwestern University in Evanston, Illinois and all of a sudden I began asking rather basic questions, none of which I could answer in any coherent fashion. What is an alcoholic, I wondered? How could a person tell if he was one? Didn't you have to get drunk everytime you picked up a drink to be an alcoholic? What if you drank only beer? You know, that sort of thing. I was baffled by this strange disease, fascinated by it, and wanted to know more. Needless to say, my thinking on the subject was more than a bit muddled. During this early period there wasn't a hint of promise or any indication at all that my thinking would lead anywhere. The possibility that I might actually write something down about alcoholism that others might regard as significant seemed remote.

Sometime in the Spring of 1963, I began dropping in on meetings of one of the better known self-help groups in America. For the first time in my life I heard sober alcoholics talking about what it had been like, what had happened, and what it was like now. I had, of course, talked with many alcoholics before in my life in bars, nightclubs, dance halls, and universities. But these "wet" alcoholics were not sober. In fact, they had no idea at all what sobriety was all about.

After six months of hanging around this famous self-help group, I moved to the West Coast to Stanford University in Palo Alto where I began my first professorship. Once in California, it didn't take me long to forget the few ideas that I had picked up from the sober alcoholics in Evanston. In 1964, I had my undergraduate lab students perform an alcohol-free experiment on alcohol. I was actually quite proud of this experiment since it showed to my satisfaction that most of the effects of alcohol on behavior were caused not by the drug alcohol, but by expectations people held toward the drug. In one memorable lecture to a group of undergraduates at Stanford, I expounded on my theory that people who called themselves alcoholics were people who had somehow been duped into believing that they would lose control over their drinking once they started to drink. If you could persuade them to give up this belief then they could drink like other people. One of the undergraduates took issue with me and said her mother was an alcoholic and it didn't matter what her mother believed since she'd get drunk anyway once she started to drink.

I began talking to my heavy drinking friends about their beliefs and expectations and how they could keep on drinking but stop getting drunk and making messes of their lives if they would just change their beliefs about alcohol and what they expected from it. My friends were enthusiastic about these ideas but they continued to get drunk and make messes of their lives anyway. I concluded that there was nothing wrong with my theory. My friends just wouldn't change their beliefs and expectations. I came to the further conclusion that my friends were alcoholic because they wanted to be. Otherwise, why would they continue to get drunk and make messes of their lives? I reasoned that it was only 1964 and I was probably on the right track but way ahead of my time.

In 1964, I also became enamored of the concept of controlled intoxication. I spoke fondly of this alternative to either complete abstinence or controlled, social drinking. Choose your level of intoxication I told my alcoholic friends. Pick out how drunk you want to get and stay right there. No need to get too drunk, just drunk enough. Once again, my alcoholic friends were very accepting of my thinking. And why not? To them, complete abstinence was unthinkable and controlled, social drinking seemed pointless. Why drink if you can't get drunk, they asked and applauded my fresh insights and creative alternatives. All they would have to learn to do was just say no—no thanks, I'm drunk enough!

From the summer of 1964 to the fall of 1966, I continued to urge my alcoholic friends to keep trying to achieve controlled intoxication. By this time, I was even trying it myself. Unfortunately, while we continued to be enthusiastic, none of us seemed to be able to get the knack of it. Somehow or another, we always managed to go too far— to pass out at a dinner party, get arrested on the freeway for drunken driving, or start a nasty argument at home. I concluded that my concept of controlled intoxication still had merit but that my friends and I needed more time to perfect it.

My wife at that time was not at all enthusiastic about the concept of controlled intoxication. In fact, when I explained to her how an alcoholic could actually choose his level of intoxication, she rolled her eyes, threw up her hands, and rushed off to a meeting of that other well-known self-help group. I was surprised to discover she had been going to these meetings for sometime and had her own thoughts about alcoholism, none of which agreed with mine. By the winter of 1967, our ideas about alcoholism clashed so violently that she gave me an ultimatum—straighten out your thinking or else. I considered her ultimatum unfair since I didn't threaten to throw her out of the house if she didn't straighten out her thinking about alcoholism. Anyway, I went along with her and started dropping in again on meetings of that well-known self-help group. This time things seemed to make sense to me and I stayed. That was over twenty years ago.

Since December of 1967, my thinking about alcoholism has undergone considerable change. Surprisingly, my most creative ideas about alcoholism and alcoholics were the first to go. Choosing your level of intoxication no longer appeared feasible, nor did stamping out loss of control by changing the beliefs and expectations of alcoholics about alcohol while urging them to drink. Instead, I began talking about the disease model of alcoholism, about genetics and neurotransmitters, biological risk factors, higher powers, and spiritual growth. I came to believe that abstinence was not only feasible for alcoholics but actually desirable. While continuing to teach at the University of California, Irvine, I took a clinical job at South Coast Community Hospital in South Laguna, California. Here I began treating alcoholics in a clinical team consisting of Muriel Zink, CAC, Dr. John Newsom, Dr. Douglas Chalmers and Susan Mardon, MSW. This was a wonderful group to be in. Muriel, John, Doug, and Susan were smart, caring, dedicated people with lots of enthusiasm and good ideas. The concept of interdisciplinary team treatment of alcoholics was just catching on and we were filled with energy, excitement, and hope for the future. I learned much from my colleagues and my patients at South Coast Community Hospital. I began to write out of my experiences in treating alcoholics and my writing took on that sense of conviction that flows from immersion in the real world. During this time I wrote papers about the tactics and defenses alcoholics employed and how therapists could use these to their advantage. I wrote about practical techniques for changing alcoholic behavior, doing group psychotherapy, and the nature of alcoholism. In 1974, I left Southern California for New York where I treated alcoholics at the old Hospital for Joint Diseases and Medical Center on famous 125th Street in Harlem. Here I found other colleagues who taught me about alcoholism among Blacks and Hispanics. Jim Salley, Frank English, and Jerry Weaver not only became my teachers but my life long friends.

Over the years, I worked in a rural outpatient clinic, various inpatient programs, State government, universities, and as a consultant to the Federal government. Today, largely because of the encouragement of Chet Kirk and Frank Fanella, I am the Director of Treatment at Edgehill Newport in Newport, Rhode Island.

This book is a record of my twenty years of work in the field of alcoholism. Included are papers on psychotherapy, behavior modification, treatment evaluation, children of alcoholics, brain chemistry, Alcoholics Anonymous, controlled drinking research, and models of alcoholism. My arguments with the traditionalists in the field of behavioral psychology are also included as well as my papers on the politics of alcoholism. A number of these papers were either unpublished or published in journals inaccessible to people working clinically in the field. In weeding out the pieces I wanted to include in this collection, I was quite surprised to see just how much I had written about alcoholism. Despite all these words, however, a great deal is still unknown. Alcoholism remains a mystery and there is much yet to understand. In recent years we have accepted the challenges of new patients and new problems. And we have developed fresh theories and methods. I hope this book will not only provide the reader with a view of where we have been, but where we are now and our paths into the future.

John Wallace
Newport, Rhode Island
January 20, 1989

Acknowledgments

"Myths and Misconceptions About Alcoholics Anonymous." Copyright © 1984 by John Wallace. Appeared in *About AA: A Newsletter for Professional Men and Women,* Spring 1984. Reprinted here courtesy of Alcoholics Anonymous.

"Ideology, Belief, and Behavior: Alcoholics Anonymous As A Social Movement." Copyright © 1983 by John Wallace. This chapter appeared in *Etiologic Aspects of Alcohol and Drug Abuse* (1st Edition) edited by Edward Gottheil, Keith Druley, Thomas Skoloda, and Harold Waxman, 1983. Reprinted here courtesy of Charles C. Thomas, Publisher, Springfield, Illinois.

"Alcoholism Counselor Burnout." Copyright © 1981 by John Wallace. Appeared as the proceeding of a conference sponsored by the New York State Division of Alcoholism and Alcohol Abuse.

"Smoke Gets in our Eyes: Professional Denial of Smoking." Copyright © 1986 Pergamon Press. Appeared in *Journal of Substance Abuse Treatment,* Vol. 3, 1986. Reprinted here courtesy of Pergamon Press, plc.

"The Importance of Aftercare in Alcoholism Treatment." Copyright © 1989 John Wallace.

The following short pieces appeared at various times in the *Link,* the Edgehill Newport, Inc. Alumni Newsletter. "Studies in Prestigious Journals Invalidate Controlled Drinking for Alcoholics," "Sobriety is More than Not Drinking," "Cocaine and Sudden Death," "Hope, Love, and Faith: Foundations of Sobriety," "A Letter to a Recovering Family," "Stress, Alcoholism and Relapse," "The Hidden Menace of Designer Drugs," "Controlled Drinking is not for Alcoholics," "Letting Go," "Realistic Expectations about Recovery," "When More is not Enough," "Recovery, People, Places, and Things," "Studies in Brain Chemistry Confirm Disease Concept of Alcoholism," and "Minding Ourselves." Copyright © 1989 John Wallace.

I am particularly grateful to Chester H. Kirk, Al D'Amico, Kenneth Kirk, and Frank Fanella of Edgehill Newport, Inc. for their support of this project.

I am also indebted to my secretary, Teresa L. Haas, for her considerable assistance in preparing this collection for publication.

I especially want to thank the Professional Staff of Edgehill Newport, Inc. for all that I have learned from them over the past seven years.

Part I

The Nature of Alcoholism

Alcoholism from the Inside Out: A Phenomenological Analysis

The first thing any knowledgeable person is likely to say about alcoholics is that they are a highly varied collection of human beings. The second thing is that alcoholics have some things in common. The paradox, however, is only a seeming one. When we remember that the outward expression of alcoholism can be influenced by sex, age, race, class, and culture, it is not surprising to find differences among groups of alcoholic persons. However, when we look more closely at the alcoholic experience and dig beneath the obvious surface differences, it soon becomes apparent that there are *common* elements as well.

In writing this chapter on the inner world of alcoholism, I have chosen to concentrate on these common elements that make up the alcoholic experience. However, the differences among alcoholics must also be considered if we are to make any sense of the nature of this phenomenon. Accordingly, my discussion begins with a brief review of the many differences among alcoholics and the suggestions that have been made to account for these.

EXTERNAL VIEW OF ALCOHOLISM: VARIABILITY AMONG ALCOHOLICS

Viewed from the outside, the alcoholic experience is characterized by seemingly endless variety. The differences among alcoholics are so numerous that one hesitates to speak of a single, unified "alcoholic experience." Alcoholics come in all shapes, sizes, colors, sexes, occupations, levels of intelligence, states of mental health, and income levels.

Contrary to all popular stereotypes, alcoholics do not even drink alike, nor do they share a single, common life history. Some alcoholics drink daily; others drink in episodic patterns, staying "dry" for intervals between drinking binges. Some drink enormous quantities of alcoholic beverages; others consume relatively little. Certain alcoholics will drink only beer or wine; others only distilled spirits such as bourbon and Scotch. In terms of life careers, the patterning of the disease is equally variable, appearing very early in the lives of some people and later in the lives of others. There are persons who claim to have started drinking alcoholically from their very first drink; many others report that they drank for a number of years before crossing over the "invisible line" that separates "social drinking" from alcoholic drinking.

When we examine the consequences of alcoholic drinking, variability is once again the rule. There is no single set of consequences apparent in the external lives of alcoholics. Not all alcoholics become insane, go to jail, or die as a consequence of continued drinking. Many alcoholics finish out their lives without ever seeing the inside of a "drunk tank," a mental institution, or a detoxification ward in a hospital.

Even in Alcoholics Anonymous (AA), an organization that actively strives for a sense of unity and identification among all alcoholics, members can be heard to remark about their inability to identify with some fellow alcoholics because their patterns of drinking and life histories were simply too foreign to their own.

Typologies and the Problem of Variability

Faced with the many surface differences among alcoholics, some authorities in the field have questioned the assumption that alcoholism is a single, unified disease process. This problem of one or many is not peculiar to alcoholism but is encountered frequently in the health sciences. For example, is cancer a single disease entity, or must we speak of a group of diseases called the cancers? Similarly, must we speak of *the alcoholisms* rather than alcoholism?

Jellinek,[7] a pioneer in the scientific analysis of alcohol use and abuse, pointed the way toward a study of the alcoholisms in his typology, which consisted of five types. Drawing on the Greek alphabet, Jellinek called these types of alcoholism Alpha, Beta, Gamma, Delta, and Epsilon.

Jellinek based his typology on several underlying dimensions. The first of these is a dimension involving *psychologic versus physiological dependence.* Alpha alcoholism is thought to be a matter of pure psychological dependence on alcohol, whereas Gamma and Delta alcoholisms are believed to involve increased tissue tolerance, adaptive cell metabolism, and physiological dependence, evidenced by the appearance of withdrawal symptoms on the cessation of drinking.

A second underlying dimension in Jellinek's types concerns *inability to abstain from drinking versus loss of control over drinking.* The Delta alcoholic cannot abstain from drinking, whereas the predominant feature of Gamma alcoholism is loss of control over the drinking. These two concepts seem closely related but are distinguishable. The Delta alcoholic is the so-called steady-state drinker, one who has learned to regulate dose and frequency so that an even "glow" of intoxication is maintained throughout the day. The Gamma alcoholic shows some evidence of ability to abstain on given occasions but cannot control the intake of alcohol once the drinking has started. Gamma alcoholics were thought by Jellinek to be the most prevalent type in American society and also the most commonly found type among the members of AA.

Jellinek's third dimension is a frequency-of-drinking dimension involving *daily versus episodic drinking.* The Epsilon or periodic drinker does not drink daily but is subject to unpredictable "binges" or "sprees." After days, weeks, and even months of complete abstinence, the Epsilon alcoholic erupts into a furious round of drinking that lasts for periods of several days to several weeks.

Jellinek's final dimension, *physical health versus disease,* seems the least satisfactory of his efforts to develop a useful typology of alcoholism. His fifth type, Beta alcoholism, is characterized by nutritional deficiency diseases associated with alcoholic drinking. But since physical disease, either dietary in origin or linked directly to high levels of alcoholic consumption, are common in all types of alcoholism, Beta alcoholism is not readily distinguishable as an independent type.

Although Jellinek's typology is of definite interest and value, it does not resolve the problem of variability among alcoholics in a satisfactory manner. The categories suggested by Jellinek are neither precisely defined nor sufficiently independent. For example, while psychological and physiological dependence are surely involved in alcoholism, both are likely to be present in varying degrees in the majority of alcoholics. It is, in fact, difficult to imagine the development of physiological dependence in a given drinker without the development of psychological dependence as well.

Discussions of efforts to construct a useful typology of alcoholism are present in more recent works as well.[5,8,10,11,14]

PHASES OF ALCOHOLISM: A SECOND APPROACH TO VARIABILITY

In addition to typologies, the problem of variability has been dealt with by considering alcoholism as a single disease characterized by different *phases*. According to a phase theory, all alcoholics pass through identifiable stages of the disease. Differences among alcoholics are to be expected, since the patterning of the disease varies as a function of point of progression.

Once again, Jellinek[6] has influenced our thinking with regard to the progression of alcoholism. Jellinek's model of progression consists of a unidimensional process involving four phases. Phase I, the pre-alcoholic phase, is characterized by the use of alcohol to relax and to deal with the everyday tensions and anxieties of life. Unfortunately, continued drinking for these purposes leads to a gradual increase in physiological tolerance for the drug, and the person must drink larger quantities and more frequently to achieve the same subjective effects.

Phase II, the early alcoholic phase, is ushered in by the experience of a blackout—a brief period of amnesia occurring during or directly after a drinking episode. Early alcoholism is characterized by the following experiences: (1) further blackouts, (2) sneaking of drinks, (3) growing preoccupation with drinking and drinking situations, (4) defensiveness about drinking with attendant increased rationalization of it, and (5) feelings of guilt about drinking, resulting in the increased use of denial as a defense mechanism.

In phase III, the crucial phase, frank addiction is thought to occur. Physiological dependence is now clearly in evidence, and the person loses control over his drinking. Job loss, marital conflict, separation and divorce, general interpersonal difficulties, and increased aggressive behavior are apparent. The individual becomes willing to risk everything he has struggled for to continue drinking.

Phase IV alcoholism is the chronic phase of the illness. It is at this point that the alcoholic experiences many of the horrors associated with alcoholism as it is traditionally understood. Advanced liver disease may appear in the form of alcoholic cirrhosis of the liver. Polyneuropathy, cardiomyopathy, pancreatitis, hypertension, tachycardia, central nervous system damage, anemia, muscle and bone disease, skin diseases, and oral cancers may occur either singly or in varying combinations. With abrupt termination of drinking, the person may experience frightening hallucinations, violent tremor, severe agitation, paranoid episodes, and a host of other psychiatric symptoms. Severe depressions, manic acting out, a pervasive sense of futility and hopelessness, suicidal thoughts and impulses, panic episodes, dread, and self-loathing are commonly encountered in the later stages of alcoholism.

Although Jellinek's four-phase model of progression has been widely accepted, Albrecht[1] has pointed out that there is no compelling reason to accept Jellinek's as the only model imaginable or, for that matter, the correct one. Indeed in a truly representative sample of the total population of alcoholics, a uniform and unidimensional progression of the disease may not be apparent at all. Jellinek's studies were conducted with members of AA, a highly selected sample of the alcoholic population. Recent research by Park,[9] for example, suggested some confirmation of aspects of Jellinek's model of progression but disconfirmation of other aspects. At the moment the precise nature of the progression of alcoholism is in question. Although there are undoubtedly a number of alcoholics who fit the Jellinek model, there are probably a large number who do not conform to it at all.

Still Other Approaches to the Problem of Variability

Perhaps the simplest approach to the problem of variability is to pretend that it does not exist and that each alcoholic is very much like every other alcoholic. On the positive side, this solution does yield all the tactical therapeutic advantages associated with any *ideology*. By forcing a unified picture of alcoholism—even when it does not square with the facts—a sense of unity, solidarity, and identification can be fostered among members of therapeutic communities. Unfortunately, the negative side of such forced unity and identification is the great likelihood of collective projection and the development of delusional communities that may "turn off" as many prospective members as they succeed in attracting. In addition, such communities, as a consequence of ideological blindness, may attract "pseudoalcoholics," many of whom require forms of treatment and rehabilitation other than those appropriate to true alcoholics.

An equally simple solution to the problem of variability is to take the opposite extreme—to regard each and every alcoholic as an absolutely unique case. Although such fervid individualism may also have great ideological appeal, especially to those drawn to the "do your own thing" rhetoric, it too suffers serious limitations. If each alcoholic is totally unlike every other alcoholic, knowledge of alcoholism in any general sense is not possible. Moreover, nothing can be gained from studying alcoholics, since by definition nothing can be generalized from one case to another.

Phenomenological Analysis and the Experience of Being an Alcoholic

Perhaps the solution to the problem of variability among alcoholics lies in recognition of the limitations of varying frames of reference or points of view. When we adopt an "objective," external view of alcoholism, we see large differences and precious little similarity. But if for a moment we concern ourselves with the *inner world of alcoholism*—with the view from *inside out* rather than outside in—what might we discover?

When we adopt the frame of reference of the alcoholic himself and attempt to understand his experience of the disease, we are engaged in an analysis called *phenomenological*. In this type of analysis we are concerned with the world not as it might be described "objectively" but with the world as experienced by the person himself. We must, so to speak, crawl inside the skin of the other, look at the world as he looks at it, feel with him as he experiences the happenings of his life. In short, we must develop the ability to *empathize,* to imagine the world as it appears to another and not as it appears to us. We must, in effect, put aside our own frame of reference and be willing to enter into that of another to see how he makes sense of his experiences and reacts to them.

For 2 decades now I have spent a great deal of my life trying to understand the inner world of alcoholism by listening to alcoholics talk about themselves, their disease, their lives, and the happenings of the alcoholic experience. In countless AA meetings I have listened to the joyous voices of recovering alcoholics telling and retelling the almost mythic tale of psychological death and resurrection. On the detoxification wards I have stood in the gray early morning light that is not light at all and listened to the voices of anxiety, despair, futility, hopelessness, meaninglessness, and self-pity. In group psychotherapy sessions in clinics and hospitals I have listened to the bewildered and confused voices earnestly seeking to understand this baffling disease called alcoholism. At 3 o'clock in the morning when the bars have closed and the late, late show has gone and given back the loneliness, I have listened to the voices of *anything*—panic, desperation, agitation, silliness, anger, accusation, craziness, hilarity, foolishness, futility, despair—at the other end of the telephone.

In years of listening I have heard many voices of alcoholism. I fear that I have not always understood, but I have gained some insights about the experience of being an alcoholic person. In reading these, the reader should bear in mind the following. First, I make no claims to having discovered immutable laws true for *all* alcoholics. The truths I think I know about alcoholics appear to me as regularly recurring themes among alcoholic people with whom I have worked. Second, by concerning myself with the inner world of alcoholism, I am not adopting a particular hypothesis with regard to the "cause" of alcoholism. I do not wish to imply that alcoholism is "caused" by psychological factors, nor any other reductionistic, "nothing but" primary circumstance. My own thinking on the problem is very much in line with the contemporary view of alcoholism as a multidimensional phenomenon involving physiological, neurophysiological, psychological, societal, cultural, and spiritual dimensions. Finally I do not regard phenomenological analysis as being opposed to or incompatible with other methods of inquiry that proceed from a different perspective. I consider it as complementary to, rather than in conflict with, other ways of coming to know.

The Alcoholic's Epistemological Quandary

The inner world of the alcoholic is characterized by great confusion. He does not understand what is happening to him or why. He may know that something is terribly wrong with his life, but for a variety of reasons he cannot connect his growing feelings of discomfort, anxiety, and unfulfillment to his use of alcohol. Moreover, he is unable to see the relationship between his drinking and the undesirable events starting to take place in his life.

In accounting for the alcoholic's seeming lack of understanding of the relationship between his drinking and his troubles, we professionals quickly jump to the conclusion that the alcoholic is using the defense mechanism of *denial*. Alcoholism is considered by many to constitute "a disease of denial," that is, a disease process worsened by the patient's unconscious refusal to see what is happening to him. However, although something like a denial process probably does take place in alcoholism, not all the alcoholic's inability to grasp the relationship between his drinking and his unhappy state of affairs can be accounted for by this concept. My reasons for saying this should become clearer as we look more closely at the alcoholic's epistemological quandary—his difficulties in coming to know about himself.

The first factor that enters into the alcoholic's epistemological quandary is the massive uncertainty of the drinking history itself. *The alcoholic did not get drunk each and every time he drank, nor did he experience negative happenings on each drinking occasion.* The vast majority of alcoholics can point to periods in their lives and occasions on which they drank without mishap of any kind. Many report periods of moderate social drinking before the onset of alcoholic drinking. Some may report a return to moderate drinking for *brief periods* or even fairly lengthy periods after an interval of alcoholic drinking has occurred. Of course, in the latter cases the majority cannot sustain the moderate drinking and eventually lapse once again into frequent intoxication. The point is that the alcoholic himself is often terribly confused by the on-again, off-again nature of his problem. He cannot predict with certainty where a drink will lead him. This intermittent or probabilistic quality of negative feedback in the drinking history has been overlooked by students of alcoholism.

The second factor in the epistemological dilemma is the incongruity of the alcoholic's recalled images of early, pleasant mild intoxication and the immediate perceptions of the present ugly realities of extreme intoxication and its consequences. Any alcoholic worth his salt remembers the "glow" that alcohol once brought. Oh, the alcoholic "glow" of yesteryear! The gentle warmth spreading throughout the body, relaxing the muscles, unwinding the busy mind clock, releasing one from the inevitability of tomorrow, making everything possible, and subtly changing perception, feeling, and cognition. One should not underestimate the power of these early positive experiences with alcohol. Their continued hold on the alcoholic, even years after his drinking has led him from one disaster to another, is uncanny. By using detailed life history inquiries in psychotherapy, I have been able to show in alcoholic after alcoholic a simple, common characteristic: the alcoholic persists in trying to recapture the early "glow" experience with alcohol long after it has ceased entirely, in some instances 20 to 30 years later. This incongruity between illusory images from the past and those of present reality contributes much to the inner confusion of the alcoholic.

The third factor giving rise to the epistemological quandary is the *disjunctive* nature of the category "alcoholism." Concepts or categories, as we know from the work of Bruner, Goodnow, and Austin,[2] can be either conjunctive or disjunctive. A conjunctive category is one in which the defining attributes must be jointly present for any individual to qualify for membership. For example, to be in the category "registered voter" one must be at least 18 years of age, be a citizen, and meet certain residency requirements. A disjunctive category, on the other hand, is one in which rules of membership require the presence of *all, any combination of some,* or *any one* of the defining attributes. Since "alcoholism" is precisely such a disjunctive concept, it yields many confusing and complex instances. For example, a person may be classified as an alcoholic if he (1) has had several blackouts, (2) has experienced personality change while drinking, (3) has had delirium tremens, or (4) has experienced any one or combination of these.

As my own research with Sechrest[13] has shown, disjunctive categories are in general exceedingly difficult to grasp—far more so than conjunctions. Human beings do not take naturally to disjunctive categories and, in fact, tend to see things in terms of simple congruencies. In understanding the disjunctive category of "alcoholism," learning the concept is extremely difficult, especially for the alcoholic himself. Consider the task facing him. He must review his history, weigh the evidence, and decide whether he fits the category "alcoholism." Given the widespread human tendency to think in terms of conjunctive categories, he naturally applies this concept to his own self-diagnostic problem. He is likely to say something like this: "Well, I do drink fairly often, but since I drink only beer, I'm not an alcoholic." Implicitly, he is using a conjunctive concept of alcoholism and is really saying, "Alcoholics drink often and drink hard liquor. I drink often, but I never touch hard liquor; therefore I'm not an alcoholic."

In actuality, however, what the alcoholic is often being asked to see—in clinics, rehabilitation homes, hospitals, and AA—is that he must deal with a fairly confusing, seemingly contradictory, disjunctive concept. Moreover, this complicated category is being thrown at him at a time when he is not thinking too clearly anyway. He keeps trying to force it all back into a simple conjunction with which he can deal, but the therapist will not let him. When the alcoholic says, "Yes, but I never had a seizure, and I never went to jail, and I never stole money for a drink, and I never . . . ," the therapist usually concludes that his client is filled with denial and will not admit to and surrender to the facts of his alcoholism. Unfortunately, what the therapist fails to see is that the alcoholic may not be denying his alcoholism at all—he may be massively confused by the perplexing, self-categorizing problem before him.

The fourth factor entering into the epistemologic quandary is that not only is the category "alcoholism" a disjunctive one, it is one in which the attributes stand in a complicated, probabilistic relationship to the category. No "symptom" of alcoholism stands in a simple one-to-one relationship to the larger category. An experience of a blackout, for example, may point toward a diagnosis of alcoholism but does not indicate it with certainty. To complicate matters even further, the significance of any one symptom varies as a function of the presence or absence of still other symptoms. A single occurrence of a blackout in the absence of other symptoms does not have the significance of a blackout in the context of one or more other symptoms of alcoholism.

Because of these complex, probabilistic relationships of attributes to category membership, confusion may consequently result. For example, pseudoalcoholism and alcoholism may be confused. It is important to remember that a person may show a period of alcohol abuse during which one or several symptoms of alcoholism may be evident, but he may still not fit the category. As the research of Cahalan, Cisin, and Crossley[3] has shown, individual drinking patterns do vary over the course of a lifetime. Although it is true that a pattern of problem drinking once established tends to persist, it is clear that *some* individuals are able to reverse this pattern. In other words, although alcoholism is indeed a steadily deteriorating disease, *alcohol abuse* need not be. Unfortunately, the two categories are not conceptually or operationally distinct for all possible cases.

A final factor concerns *social comparison information* available to the drinking person. The theory of social comparisons, a general social-psychological theory developed by Festinger,[4] reminds us that people develop normative ideas about their own behavior by watching others. And what is it that the alcoholic sees when he looks out at the world? The answer is, of course, drinking—and a great deal of it too. Regardless of social class or position, the alcoholic is surrounded by people who drink. Some drink far less than he does, but there are always others who seem to drink far more. *No matter how excessive his drinking has become and how disastrous the consequences, the alcoholic can always find others who seem to be in far worse shape than he.* The social comparisons conclusion is obvious: "These other people—the ones whose drinking seems far worse than mine—these are the alcoholics, not me.' Complicating the social comparisons judgment even further is the alcoholic's observation that these other people neither consider themselves alcoholic, nor do they go to clinics, rehabilitation programs, or AA. Then why should he? The answer is, of course, he should not. His drinking is not really that bad.

These, then, are five factors that make up the epistemological quandary of the alcoholic and make it difficult for him to understand his own experience.

In actuality the epistemological quandaries of the alcoholic himself are perfect mirror images of the quandaries that confront the thoughtful professional engaged in alcoholism treatment and research. How ironic then that when the alcoholic complains that he is uncertain that he fits the category, we jump quickly to the conclusion that he is *denying* his "alcoholism," but when the alcoholism research specialist complains of lack of rigorous definition and measurement, we nod our heads in agreement and lapse into vague statements about the complexities involved in "scientific knowing." In other words, viewing the *alcoholic's experience* from our point of view and not his, we see in him an unconscious, defensive process; but viewing *our experience* in attempting to understand the alcoholic, we see in ourselves an epistemological problem common in scientific inquiry.

Phenomenological analysis, then, has led us to the first serious rival hypothesis to the concept of denial. Looking at the alcoholic experience from the point of view of the alcoholic himself raises the strong possibility that the characteristic "blindness" of the alcoholic involves much more than that implied by an unconscious, automatic, and defensive distortion of the facts. The inner confusion of the alcoholic suggests a person caught in the web of a complex epistemological problem.

THE ALCOHOLIC'S NEVER INVALIDATED HYPOTHESIS

Even though the person may come to categorize himself as an alcoholic, his epistemological problems are far from over. He may "know" that he is an alcoholic, but for many persons, labeling oneself an alcoholic does not lead to an immediate end to drinking. Acceptance of the label "alcoholism" is not the same thing as acceptance of the *fact* of alcoholism and all that it implies.

Having labeled himself an alcoholic, a person may conclude that he must change something about his drinking, but not the drinking itself. He may switch from one beverage to another, change the time and pattern of his drinking, decide to drink only on a full stomach, drink only when he is feeling happy, stay away from certain bars, drop certain friends, get a divorce, change jobs, move, and make other changes. However, the fact that he should abstain from alcohol entirely does not occur to him. Despite disastrous outcomes of such experimentation, the person may continue drinking. Arrests, convictions, confinements, hospitalizations, divorces, job loss, automobile accidents, convulsions, and threats of serious medical complications may interrupt the drinking for brief periods, but the person, in seeming defiance of all that is rational, will return once again to his old pattern.

Viewed externally, the alcoholic's behavior seems driven by a terrible, self-destructive urge. But viewing the alcoholic's behavior internally, from his perspective, we are led to a very different notion: *the alcoholic is in the grip of a powerful hypothesis that can never be invalidated completely. He believes that if he searches long enough and hard enough, he will find a way to control and enjoy his drinking.* This fundamental delusion lies at the very heart of alcoholism, and until it is fully understood and accepted, the person is vulnerable to continued drinking. However, even after he does understand and accept it, he will never be entirely free of it; the controlled-drinking hypothesis is never invalidated completely. Although the recovering alcoholic finally accepts the near certain *probability* that he can never again control his drinking, the *possibility* that he might under some set of ideal circumstances remains with him even after many years of abstinence from alcohol.

I do not mean that the obsession with alcohol continues to plague the recovering alcoholic for the remainder of his life. That unhappy state of affairs is not the case, since the compulsion to drink eventually is removed, especially in sober alcoholics participating in a program of recovery such as AA. Nor do I wish to imply that recovering alcoholics continue to entertain consciously and deliberately the possibility of a return to controlled drinking. For the most part, recovering alcoholics with some years of sobriety talk and act as though they cannot ever drink in a controlled fashion, but the controlled-drinking hypothesis, although weakened, remains an elusive possibility. The pilot light of alcoholism, so to speak, is never extinguished, even though the fire is out.

The recovering alcoholic's *belief system* about himself in relation to alcohol is not cast in stone. Like any other set of personal beliefs, it waxes and wanes in strength of conviction. Members of AA have long recognized this fact. They speak of thinking that is "on the beam," and of "stinking thinking." When a recovering alcoholic's thinking is "on the beam," he shows all the attitudes, emotions, and beliefs associated with secure, comfortable sobriety. When the thinking turns "stinking," he has started to show once again the patterns of thought and action associated with active alcoholism.

For many recovering alcoholics, perhaps the majority of them, the best protection against a reactivation of the controlled-drinking hypothesis is an action-oriented life program in which involvement with other recovering persons is possible. Activities may include membership in programs such as AA, participation in governmental and private organizations concerned with alcoholism, charitable and volunteer work, and professional service.

THE CHEMICAL SPLIT: THE ALCOHOLIC'S IDENTITY PROBLEM

In addition to not knowing what is wrong with him, the alcoholic very often does not know *who he is*. As one recovering alcoholic put it, "When I was drinking, I was so mixed up inside I could have posed for a group portrait!" Identity confusion is a regularly occurring theme among alcoholics. Almost invariably, recovering alcoholics regard their "drinking personalities" as radically different from their "sober personalities." As a rule, the drinking personalities are cast in terms of negative or socially undesirable characteristics. Alcoholics, in attempting to describe this dual personality structure, make metaphoric use of *The Strange Case of Dr. Jekyll and Mr. Hyde*, Robert Louis Stevenson's class tale of the good doctor who transforms himself into a vicious, brutal creature with secret concoctions of his own invention.

The alcoholic identity problem is a direct outcome of the repeated assaults of intoxicated thoughts and actions on the basic system of beliefs, values, and attitudes that constitute the primary or "sober" personality. Because his actions when intoxicated are so markedly discrepant with his primary personality, the alcoholic experiences ever-increasing identity confusion. In a sense he is caught in a state of massive, painful cognitive dissonance. His private and most cherished beliefs about himself are constantly contradicted by the facts of his overt, intoxicated actions.

THE INNER WORLD OF FEELINGS: THE COMMON GROUND OF ALCOHOLISM

Despite the great variations in the external facts of alcoholic careers, alcoholic people do identify with one another. There is a common bond among alcoholics, especially among recovering alcoholics, that even the most naive observer cannot help but discern. This sense of identification of one alcoholic with another has its roots in the inner world of feelings and emotions. Anguish is anguish, no matter the origin.

The progression of the disease of alcoholism leaves in its wake a residue of feelings and emotions from which few if any true alcoholics manage to escape completely. *Remorse, guilt, shame,* and *self-hatred* form a group of inner feelings that are much in evidence in any collection of alcoholic people. The self-esteem of the alcoholic is literally shattered. Despite the surface picture of grandiosity, excessive self-confidence, and narcissism evident in some alcoholics, the facts are usually to the contrary. Beneath the confident exterior, the alcoholic is typically a frightened person, overflowing with self-doubt and self-loathing. Usually it takes many years of complete sobriety for him to overcome guilt feelings and a negative self-image. In some cases these may continue in disguised forms, even though the recovering alcoholic himself may insist that he has finally freed himself from irrational guilt about his alcoholic past. Underlying guilt and low self-esteem are evidenced by such traits as lack of self-assertion, striving for perfection, inordinate need for approval from others, compulsive patterns of overwork, permitting oneself to be used and manipulated by others, and neglect of self-interest.

Feelings of *loneliness, alienation,* and *apartness from others* are also found routinely among alcoholic people. A recovering alcoholic woman expressed it perfectly when she said, "Back then, during my drinking days, I felt like I was in a glass telephone booth looking out at the other people, and when I dialed the number, I kept getting a busy signal." Alcoholics truly are people who can feel lonely in a crowd. Even when they appear lively, sociable, and outgoing at a cocktail party, this is usually a chemical facade. Without the social lubricant of alcohol, many become quiet, inward, and withdrawn.

It is often the case that alcoholics feel absolutely unique, different from others. These feelings of uniqueness of personality and life situation accentuate and contribute to the alcoholic's alienation from others and estrangement from self as the disease progresses.

Depression and feelings of hopelessness, futility, and *a pervasive sense of meaninglessness in life* further complicate the inner world of alcoholics. It is not surprising to find feelings such as these in alcoholic people when we remember that alcohol is classified in psychopharmacology as a *nonselective general depressant.* In structure and/or effect on the central nervous system, alcohol is indistinguishable from other CNS depressants such as ether, diazepam (Valium), chlordiazepoxide (Librium), and phenobarbital. The direct negative effects of alcohol on mood are well known to anybody who has worked closely with alcoholics in detoxification and rehabilitation programs. A transient depression that yields quickly to brighter spirits as detoxification proceeds is commonly seen in hospital recovery programs. In truth, although they are usually totally unaware of it, alcoholics are often depressed because they drink large quantities of a depressant drug. For some alcoholics, however, depression may not be transient but indicative of an affective disorder. In these cases, treatment must be directed to the affective disorder as well as to the alcoholism.

Feelings of hopelessness, futility, and meaninglessness in life are practically the sine qua non of the inner experience of alcoholism. In my opinion they reflect the spiritual emptiness of the alcoholic and his growing awareness that something of fundamental importance is missing from his life. Alcoholics speak of this inner emptiness as that "hole-in-the-gut feeling." In trying to fill this emptiness, many pursue obsessions in addition to alcohol. However, such things as compulsive sexuality, material goods, money, fame, power, and fortune rarely do the job.

The Greeks had a word for the God within—*en theos*. The English word "enthusiasm" derives from it. From my experience in working with alcoholics, I am now thoroughly convinced that the inner emptiness must be replaced with enthusiasm, whatever its source. Although some people do recover from active alcoholism without undergoing some sort of spiritual transformation, I am of the strongly held opinion that to ignore the inner, spiritual condition of the majority of alcoholics is to neglect one of the most critical common elements of the disease.

ALCOHOLIC TACTICS: EMERGENT COPING DEVICES

In response to the disease, the alcoholic develops a number of tactics that enable him to cope with the deepening experience of alcoholism. Although these coping devices are often cast in terms of classic defense mechanisms, I prefer to think of them as tactics and to distinguish these tactics from defense mechanisms for a number of reasons. First, the motivational bases for them seem much broader than that of the anxiety avoidance associated with defense mechanisms. Although anxiety is surely associated with alcoholism, I do not regard anxiety (or anxiety reduction) as the principal cause of alcoholism. Second, alcoholic tactics seem more readily accessible to conscious awareness than to deeply unconscious and automatic mechanisms of defense. In the hands of a highly skilled therapist, for example, an alcoholic patient can be brought to see his use of tactical denial in an amazingly short period of time. Third, defense mechanisms are generally thought to be aspects of the neuroses and to constitute, along with certain behaviors, symptoms of underlying psychological disorders. I neither regard alcoholism as one of the neuroses, nor do I regard alcoholism and the coping tactics associated with it as symptoms of anything other than themselves. Alcoholism is the disease. Alcoholic coping tactics are predictable *outcomes* of it. Finally, in the classic view, defense mechanisms should be removed if change is to be expected. Paradoxically, in alcoholism therapy the very same tactics that the alcoholic used to maintain his drinking can be put to good advantage in helping him to achieve and maintain abstinence in the early stages of treatment.

Tactical denial is probably one of the more common devices employed by alcoholics. This tactic is evidenced by characteristic "blindness" to the impact of alcohol on one's health, work, reputation, and social relations in general. It is also indicated in the alcoholic's refusal to admit that he has lost control and drinking has become a problem for him. He may, on occasion, deny drinking entirely or minimize the amount of his drinking. In recognizing tactical denial, however, care must be taken to distinguish it from epistemological confusion. As I have discussed earlier, the alcoholic may be ignorant of what is happening to him.

Another tactic is *rationalization.* This tactic is revealed in the alcoholic's efforts to make his continued drinking appear reasonable to himself and others. The alcoholic always has reasons for taking a drink, and these may appear sensible and, in fact, logical—especially to a person thoroughly naive about alcoholism. The alcoholic will say that he needs alcohol to relax or to get to sleep at night. Perhaps he drinks because of the tragic loss of a loved one. Sometimes it is because he is a sensitive person in a cruel and dehumanizing world. The business he is in may require him to drink, or he lives in a heavy-drinking neighborhood. He is misunderstood, underrated, abused, divorced, married, happy, or sad. He has lost a lot of money or made a lot of money. The list is endless. In actuality, a therapist working with alcoholics must get one fundamental rule firmly in mind if he expects to be of any help at all. *Although there are thousands of excuses for an alcoholic to take a drink, in the final analysis there are no valid reasons for him to do so.* Like all human beings, alcoholic people will suffer pain, grief, sorrow, and misfortune. However, unlike other persons, alcoholics must learn to suffer misfortune and to deal with life's inevitable problems without resorting to the temporary use of sedating chemicals to get them through. For the nonalcoholic person, pain and suffering may be little more than a nuisance. For the alcoholic these need to be seen as stepping-stones to further growth. Each time that he does not drink in a problematic situation, the alcoholic's inner resources are strengthened.

Blame assignment is yet another tactic that alcoholics are prone to use in coping with their disease and its consequences. Husbands, wives, parents, bosses, police officers, judges, the "system," and society are at fault in the eyes of many alcoholics. Blaming everybody and everything *except alcohol* for their miseries, drinking alcoholics fail to see the obvious.

Well-meaning friends are often drawn into the alcoholic's delusional construction of the world, lending support to it unwittingly. One or more lovers may prove necessary in the alcoholic's constant struggle against the "cold, unfeeling, and uncaring spouse" to whom he attributes all his unhappy feelings and shortcomings. Some alcoholics are so skillful in the use of blame assignment tactics that they manage to pack *their spouses* off to psychiatrists or psychologists for treatment of *their* emotional difficulties.

Psychologists, psychiatrists, and physicians are not immune to the artful blame assignment tactics of alcoholics. Failing to recognize and appreciate the facts of an alcoholic problem in their clients, some professionals may find themselves becoming a part of the problem rather than an aid to its solution. Physicians may prescribe minor tranquilizers, such as diazepam and chlordiazepoxide, inadvertently contributing to the development of a second drug dependence. Psychologists and psychiatrists may succeed in doing little more than giving the alcoholic a sophisticated repertoire of "psychological reasons" to support and maintain his drinking. In some instances psychotherapists have unwittingly exacerbated the resentments of drinking alcoholics, encouraged further acting out of destructive impulses, and worsened already critically bad family situations by operating on the mistaken assumption that alcoholics, like neurotics, need to "get their feelings out" or "get in touch with their anger and express it." I know of instances in which psychotherapists ignorant of alcoholism have given alcoholic beverages to their clients during therapy sessions in the belief that this practice would "cut through the guilt feelings the alcoholic has about his drinking!"

Tactical denial, rationalization, and blame assignment are but three of the tactics that alcoholics develop in response to their disease. I have discussed other common alcoholic tactics.[12]

SUMMARY

My search for the common elements in the alcoholic experience has led me to an examination of the inner world of alcoholism. Although external, "objective" analyses have revealed numerous differences among alcoholic people, phenomenological analysis suggests unity and similarity. The reader may naturally demand to know which of the two approaches to inquiry into alcoholism leads to the "truth." The answer is, of course, both. In the human behavioral sciences, truth is constrained by the perspective taken or the *paradigms* with which scientific workers operate. A paradigm is the unconscious set of beliefs, values, opinions, intuitions, conventions, assumptions, and choices that enter into virtually all scientific theories of human behavior. By choosing to focus on the world as experienced by the alcoholic person, I have adopted a given paradigm within which to search for the meaning of the alcoholic experience. As a consequence, my knowledge about alcoholics is surely constrained and limited by my paradigm as well. I do not for a moment pretend that I have discovered universal laws true to alcoholic persons everywhere. What I have done is to listen carefully to several thousands of alcoholics trying to make sense out of *their* experience of alcoholism. Hopefully, I have reported their observations and conclusions faithfully and accurately.

REFERENCES

1. Albrecht, G.L.: The alcoholism process: a social learning viewpoint. In Bourne, P.G., and Fox, F., editors: Alcoholism: progress in research and treatment, New York, 1973, Academic Press, Inc.
2. Bruner, J.S., Goodnow, J.J., and Austin, G.A.: A study of thinking, New York, 1956, John Wiley & Sons, Inc.
3. Cahalan, D., Cisin, I.H., and Crossley, H.M.: American drinking practices: a national survey of behavior and attitudes, monograph no. 6, New Brunswick, N.J., 1969, Rutgers Center for Alcohol Studies.
4. Festinger, L.A.: A theory of social comparison processes, Human Relations 7:117–140, 1954.
5. Jacobson, G.R.: The alcoholisms, New York, 1976, Human Sciences Press, Inc.
6. Jellinek, E.M.: Phases of alcohol addiction, Q. J. Stud. Alcohol 13:673–684, 1952.
7. Jellinek, E.M.: Disease concept of alcoholism, New Haven, Conn., 1960, United Printing Service.
8. Kissin, B.: Theory and practice in the treatment of alcoholism. In Kissin, B., and Begleiter, H., editors: The biology of alcoholism, vol. 5, New York, 1977, Plenum Press.
9. Park, P.: Developmental ordering of experience in alcoholism, Q. J. Stud. Alcohol 34:473–488, 1973.
10. Schuckit, M.A.: The use of alcoholic subtype diagnoses in the U.S. Navy, Dis. Nerv. Sys. 35(12):563–567, 1974.
11. Schuckit, M.A., and Morrissey, E.R.: Alcoholism in women: some clinical and social perspectives with an emphasis on possible subtypes. In Greenblatt, M., and Schuckit, M.A., editors: Alcoholism problems in women and children., New York, 1976, Grune & Stratton, Inc.
12. Wallace, J.: Tactical and strategic use of the preferred defense structure of the recovering alcoholic, New York, 1975, National Council on Alcoholism.
13. Wallace, J., and Sechrest, L.: Relative difficulty of conjunctive and disjunctive concepts. J. Psychol. Stud. 12:97–104, 1961.
14. Wanberg, K.W., and Horn, J.L.: Alcoholism symptom patterns of men and women. Q. J. Stud. Alcohol 31:40–60, 1970.

Alcoholism: Is a Shift in Paradigm Necessary?

Perhaps no human problem has been as richly and extensively described in ethnographic, clinical and phenomenological terms as has alcoholism. In the past century, a basic paradigm has emerged. This paradigm suggests the following: alcoholism is a heritable disease, the expression of which may be modified by host and environmental factors; the disease is characterized by inconsistent control over drinking behavior and behavior while drinking; it is complicated by psychological and biomedical consequences of alcohol consumption that vary in nature and severity.

Despite extensive description, however, not all persons would agree that this emergent paradigm is either useful or based upon reliable information.

Rohan [1], for example, doubts the very existence of alcoholism and believes "the term, 'alcoholism', is merely a convenient shorthand label for selected events involving alcohol use and damage, not the name of an actual entity" (p. 31).

Pattison and Kaufman [2] repeat Pattison, Sobell, and Sobell's [3] earlier criticisms of the "assumptions" that they believe underlie a "unitary model of alcoholism." According to these authors, "substantial and serious contravening evidence" derived from empirical scientific research can be marshalled against all of these "assumptions." They doubt that there is a "unitary phenomenon that can be identified as alcoholism" and disbelieve that "alcoholics are essentially different from nonalcoholics." They do not agree that alcoholics have lost control over their drinking, and are apparently persuaded that alcoholism is a temporary, reversible "syndrome" rather than a permanent, irreversible disease.

In effect, Pattison, Kaufman, Sobell, and Sobell hold viewpoints that are not incompatible with those of many, if not most, psychologists and psychiatrists who see alcoholism as a behavior problem, "symptom complex" or "escape mechanism" [4].

Data bearing upon the reconceptualization of alcoholism do, of course, continue to appear. Whether such data now require a radical shift in basic paradigm is clearly a matter of scientific debate. As in many fields of scientific inquiry, recent empirical studies in alcoholism are characterized by considerable uncertainty, inconsistency, incompleteness, and either no attempt at replication or failure to replicate. Moreover, data cautioning against a fundamental shift in paradigm continue to appear. In this paper, several issues concerning the necessity for a shift in paradigm are explored.

CAN ALCOHOLISM BE DIAGNOSED RELIABLY AND VALIDLY

Rohan's [1] assertion that alcoholism is a "label" and not an "entity" is, of course, an instance of radical nominalism. Whether the assertion is merely a restatement of a general philosophical doctrine or an attempt at meaningful scientific statement is not readily discernible. Perhaps an alternative question that might be capable of empirical investigation is as follows: "Can alcoholism be diagnosed reliably in the sense that different observers using the same set of criteria can agree upon its presence or absence?"

The answer to this question is clearly in the affirmative. In fact, as Helzer et al. [5] have demonstrated, the diagnosis of alcoholism may more reliably be made by psychiatrists than any other psychiatric diagnosis. In a study of the reliability of the Feighner criteria from which the DSM-III criteria were developed, Helzer and his colleagues showed that psychiatrists displayed *far* greater agreement with each other when diagnosing alcoholism than when diagnosing any other psychiatric condition. While a mean overall reliability index, Kappa (K), of .52 was obtained, *alcoholism* had a K of .70. By way of contrast, *mania* had a K of only .26 while *phobic neurosis* was somewhat better with a K of .51, and *depression* reached a K of .62.

Landeen et al. [6] showed that even a simple self-report screening device with high face validity (and, hence, high potential for faking) could identify alcoholics with great accuracy. In a sample of alcoholics in advanced stages of the disease, the brief Michigan Alcoholism Screening Test correctly identified 95% of the alcoholics. The Diagnostic errors were only four false negatives. Similar highly satisfactory results were obtained by Jacobson [7,8] using a psychometrically refined version of the National Council on Alcoholism Criteria for the diagnosis of alcoholism.

Despite Rohan's doctrinaire questioning and Pattison and Kaufman's ideological misgivings, it is apparent that the presence or absence of alcoholism can be determined reliably by psychiatrists and validly as well. As Helzer et al. [5] demonstrated, psychiatrists and other interviewers not only correctly identified 91% of previously diagnosed alcoholics, they were able to identify 97% of the non-alcoholics. The only other diagnosis which came close to alcoholism in terms of validity was depression. But while interviewers correctly identified 85% of the diagnosed depressives, they incorrectly identified 25% of the non-depressives as depressives.

Sophisticated evidence for a biochemical profile diagnostic method has been reported recently by Eckardt and colleages [9]. Automated multiple analyses of γ-glutamyl transpeptidase (GGT) and mean corpuscular volume (MCV) as well as 24 other biochemical and hematologic variables were conducted. GGT and MCV together correctly identified 36% of the alcoholics and 94% of the non-alcoholics. Profile analysis of the 24 Laboratory tests correctly identified 98% of the alcoholics and 100% of the non-alcoholics.

Accurate discriminations of 98% of the alcoholics and 95% of the non-alcoholics were obtained from 10 clinical tests. These were as follows: alkaline phosphatase, urea nitrogen, total bilirubin, carbon dioxide, serum glutamic pyruvic transaminase, sodium, chloride, phosphorus, total protein, and serum oxalocetic transaminase.

In commenting on the development of the DSM-III, Robins [10] has stated the case for the diagnosis of alcoholism well. "It is remarkable, given these logical difficulties, the assembling of symptoms from grossly different conceptual realms, and the reported unreliability of alcoholics as historians, that the diagnosis of alcoholism by symptom self-report is repeatedly found to be one of the most valid and reliable of the psychiatric diagnoses" (p. 53).

Is Alcoholism Reversible?

The possibility that alcoholics following treatment might be able to resume normal, social, moderate, attenuated, controlled, or non-problem drinking continues to interest persons. Large numbers of drinking alcoholics and considerably smaller numbers of behavioral scientists seem particularly attracted to this possibility.

Spontaneous remission of unknown frequency and duration does occur in alcoholism as it does in many other diseases. Precisely how many alcoholics may experience spontaneous remission of their disease and for how long are questions for which solid scientific evidence does not yet exist. Clinical workers and long-time members of Alcoholics Anonymous insist that if it occurs at all, spontaneous remission occurs at levels too insignificant to be of much import.

The most controversial aspect of the findings from the widely discussed 1976 report by Armor, Polich, and Stambul [11] was not that spontaneous remission occurred at all in alcoholism since repetition of that common observation would be trivial. Rather, the finding that did arouse considerable skepticism concerned the very high numbers of persons (22%) who were reported to have experienced spontaneous remission in the form of "normal drinking." The many substantial and serious methodological problems that characterized this research by three Rand Corporation social scientists who were largely unfamiliar with the nature of treatment of alcoholism further increased skepticism on the part of clinicians and more experienced clinical researchers. Despite the efforts of the Rand Corporation authors to discount the impact of such serious problems as a total loss of 9,000 subjects out of an initial admissions sample of 11,500 and a subject loss rate of approximately 40% in a second study, criticism of the research continued. Wallace [12] for example, reanalyzed the 1976 data and showed that not only were the samples biased on outcome, but that the patterning of various sample bias estimates revealed internal contradictions in the data that could be explained most readily by invalid measurement of normal drinking.

In effect, all of the remission data, abstention and normal drinking, reported by the Rand authors were inaccurate and could not be generalized to any alcoholic population.

While the first Rand studies were seriously marred by sampling and measurement errors, they were unimpressive for still another reason: an extremely short-term window on drinking behavior of only 30 days. Fortunately, the 1980 study by Polich, Armor, and Braiker [13] did permit observations on the frequency of long-term nonproblem drinking following treatment and an uncorrected long-term nonproblem drinking rate of 7% was reported. Taking into account the authors' data on invalid measurements of consumption and some likelihood of incorrect initial diagnoses, a rate of long-term nonproblem drinking of 4% in the 1980 study seems a more realistic estimate.

A long-term nonproblem drinking rate of 4% is consistent with recent data reported by Pettinati et al. [14]. Pettinati and her colleagues conducted a four year follow-up in which patients were assessed each year following treatment. The follow-up rate in this study was extraordinary in that it was 100%! Only 3% of the followed patients reported being able to drink with no life-adjustment problems over the four year period.

A rate of nonproblem drinking of 4% at follow-up is of no practical significance in the treatment of alcoholism at this time since a clinical decision upon admission to assign all patients an abstention goal would be appropriate 96% of the time. On the other hand, given the most complex of multivariate methods, the attempt to predict which of the 4% of patients could succeed at nonproblem drinking would result in *incorrect* clinical decisions well over 50% of the time.

Serious problems of lack of confirmation have been reported recently with regard to another major study concerned with controlled or nonproblem drinking in alcoholics. Sobell and Sobell [15] treated some alcoholic patients with a controlled drinking goal and followed them after treatment. A subsequent third year follow-up of the same patients was conducted by Caddy et al. [16].

Chalmers [17] provided extensive methodological criticism of the research by Sobell and Sobell including the important observation that most of the "functioning well days" of the controlled drinking subjects were attributable to abstinent days and not controlled drinking days during the follow-up period. In effect, Chalmers pointed out that care must be taken to distinguish controlled drinking as a *treatment goal* in this research and controlled drinking as actual behavior during follow-up. If Chalmers is correct in his criticisms, then the research by Sobell and Sobell may show the paradoxical result that, for this sample, abstention during follow-up was more likely to be produced by attempts to teach controlled drinking during treatment rather than abstention.

More serious, however, is the recent report by Pendery et al. [18] that provided virtually no confirmation of controlled drinking in this sample. In a careful subsequent follow-up of the patients treated by Sobell and Sobell, Pendery and her colleagues found that the vast majority of these patients could not be classified as controlled drinkers. Of 20 patients treated with a controlled drinking treatment goal, 19 patients showed subsequent histories on re-interview that were consistent with multiple relapses into alcoholic drinking, re-hospitalization, serious alcohol-related illnesses, death, or total abstention.

There are, of course, other studies that have reported remissions of some type or another in alcoholics. Pattison, Sobell and Sobell [3], for example, have alluded to a substantial body of evidence comprising 74 "scientific studies." In a later book by Sobell and Sobell [19], six additional studies were added to the original list of 74.

When this body of putative evidence in favor of controlled drinking is examined, one is impressed not only by the astonishingly wide variation in reported outcomes, but by the equally wide variation in scientific rigor, comprehensiveness, and methodological sophistication. Of these "scientific studies," several are anecdotal, two are case studies, one is a newspaper report from the *Los Angeles Times,* several refer to Japanese interest, now over a decade ago, in the chemical cyanamide, some are survey research studies of questionable methodological adequacy, a number are either unpublished dissertations or papers presented at conferences, many are outcome studies characterized by common methodological problems ubiquitous to outcome research in alcoholism, and five are papers that refer to work conducted by Pattison, Sobell and Sobell themselves.

While there are studies in this collection which require serious attention, it would be misleading for anyone to advertise the entire collection as constituting "strong" scientific evidence in favor of controlled drinking as a viable treatment goal. Moreover, it is statistically meaningless to "average" the results of this uneven collection, and misleading to promulgate this average as a reliable estimate of a population value [19].

In short, to argue that alcoholism is a temporary, reversible condition and that alcoholics can engage successfully in normal, social, moderate, controlled or nonproblem drinking following treatment is to advocate that a *cure* for alcoholism has been found. All such claims, even those purporting to apply to "some" alcoholics if not all must be taken as seriously as any claims of cure in medicine and should be judged accordingly. At present levels of scientific knowledge, alcoholism can be treated and often arrested but not cured. The possibility of enduring spontaneous remissions of unknown but likely low frequency simply cannot be used ethically to advocate treatment goals aimed at cure at the present time.

With regard to the question of the reversibility of alcoholism, the following questions are critical:

1. How many alcoholics can be expected to succeed in nonproblem drinking following treatment?
2. Over what periods of time can such behavior be sustained?
3. Do we have reliable and valid methods for differentiating very small numbers of alcoholic patients who might succeed from the large numbers of persons who are highly likely to fail?
4. Are the nature and levels of risk involved in attempts at nonproblem drinking by alcoholics known with reasonable degrees of certainty?
5. Do we have reliable and valid methods for producing normal drinkers out of alcoholics?

Solid scientific evidence bearing upon these five critical questions is not yet at hand.

Is Alcoholism Progressive?

Whether or not alcoholism *per se* is a progressive disease is probably not answerable in any scientific sense at present. The biomedical and psychosocial *consequences* of alcoholism do, of course, intensify for many alcoholics over time. Alcohol-related illnesses of the cardiovascular, nervous, and digestive systems may appear and worsen over the course of the disease. Divorce, financial and legal difficulties, and problems in parenting and other important interpersonal relationships may occur.

However, whether these many negative happenings in the lives of alcoholics are attributable to changes in the disease itself or in other factors is not clear. As time passes, alcoholics grow older, change jobs and careers, marry and divorce, suffer further illnesses and disorders, and so forth. These many changes in host and environment that characterize lives in progress are intricately related to the disease *per se*, often in complex and poorly understood ways. It is possible, for example, that tolerance to alcohol may decline in mid and later life. And it is possible that the stresses of divorce, death of a spouse, or loss of a job may seriously reduce the alcoholic's ability to resist the disease.

Although earlier research reported by Jellinek [20] and subsequently partially replicated by Park [21] on a different population did suggest a uniform course, it has been pointed out by Albrecht [22] that the Jellinek model is not the only one imaginable. As recent studies on the natural history of alcoholism have suggested [13,14], the course of alcoholism may be more variable than previously realized.

Part of the difficulty with the progressive disease concept seems to lie with the way in which it is formulated. Casting the problem in global terms does not encourage the examination of the course of particular biomedical and psychosocial consequences over time. A focus on specific consequences can lead to clear-cut results.

Robins et al. [23], for example, have provided a useful model of investigation. In a study of hospitalized, employed male alcoholics, data were obtained that showed a relationship between symptom frequency and length of drinking history, with frequency covarying inversely with symptom severity. It was obvious in these data that the more rare an alcoholism symptom, the longer the drinking history necessary to produce it. Delirium tremens, for example, occurred in only 7% of the sample and was associated with a median drinking history of 30 years. On the other hand, a self-report by the patient that he "felt he drank too much" occurred in 53% of the sample and was associated with a median drinking history of 17 years.

In short, it is probably more useful to trace the development of specific biomedical and psychosocial outcomes over time than to posit a single, uniform course. It is likely that when the progression of alcoholism is construed in this manner, both consistency and inconsistency appear. Moreover, it is probable that multiple paths into alcoholism exist. In many instances, florid states of the disease may appear early in the developmental history while in other cases, several decades of increasingly problematic drinking may precede the onset of symptoms too dramatic to be ignored by self and others.

Is Some Disease Concept Viable?

Advocates for and critics of a disease concept of alcoholism both seem to imply that a single disease concept is at issue and can be proven or disproven by available data. In actuality, neither proof nor disproof of the role of numerous possible biological factors in the etiology of alcoholism can be advocated in any absolute sense at this time. Data pointing to the importance of particular biological factors are now available as are data implicating psychological and sociocultural factors. Available data from any one of these domains cannot be used either to confirm or disconfirm possible etiological factors drawn from the other domains. Rather, a multifactorial etiology seems necessary.

In addition to a multifactorial etiology, alcoholism may be characterized by multiple pathways of origin. At present, any or all of the following models are possible pathways involving biological factors.

1. Genetic factors inexorably unfold in the life of the individual and culminate in alcoholism regardless of psychological or sociocultural events.

2. Genetic factors predispose to alcoholism but particular patterns of psychological and sociocultural factors are necessary for the disease to become manifest.

3. Alcoholism is a consequence of certain drinking patterns rather than a cause of these. In this case, drinking alters the body and these bodily changes result in more drinking leading to further physical changes, and so on.

4. Psychological and sociocultural factors interact with bodily changes produced by drinking to produce negative psychosocial consequences and further bodily changes. The stresses associated with negative psychosocial consequences interact with these alcohol-induced bodily changes to produce more drinking, and so on.

These four models do not exhaust the possibilities since additional pathways of origin that involve biological factors can be imagined readily. At present, it is not possible to choose among these models, one or more may be true and all may be necessary to provide a complete account of alcoholism.

But whatever the resolution of this problem of possible multiple etiological factors and pathways of origin, it is now apparent that biological factors cannot be ignored.

Numerous studies in animals on the pharmacogenetics of alcohol preference, consumption, and effects of hypnotic doses reveal that hereditary influence is ubiquitous [24]. Selective breeding in mice and rats has been accomplished and strain differences are well documented.

Human genetic studies [25,26,27] conducted internationally indicate that the sons of alcoholics have at least a three-time greater risk of becoming alcoholics than the sons of non-alcoholics. This increased risk was found in studies where social learning effects were *absent,* and was not further increased in studies where both genetic and social learning effects were jointly present. In addition, the rate of concordance for alcoholism in identical twins is 60% and 30% in fraternal twins. Moreover, young men with alcoholism in first degree family members metabolize alcohol differently than men without such family histories. Higher associated levels of acetaldehyde and less behavioral impairment after three drinks have been noted in young men with alcoholism in first degree family members [27].

A recent study of patients with and without familial histories of alcoholism revealed numerous differences [28]. Patients with familial histories showed more severe symptomatology of alcoholism, more antisocial behavior, worse academic and social performance in school, unstable employment histories and more severe physical symptoms related to alcohol.

In a recent study of Gabrielli et al. [29], young sons of alcoholic fathers showed high frequency EEG activity (above 18 Hz). Hence, fast EEG activity, which is a heritable characteristic and is frequently found in adult alcoholics, has been found in the EEG records of the 11–13-year old sons of alcoholics. Since alcohol is known to slow brain activity, alcoholics may be persons who learn to reduce genetically determined fast brain wave activity by self-medication with alcoholic beverages.

Numerous studies have centered on the effects of alcohol on brain neurotransmitters and the possible effects of neurotransmitter systems on drinking behavior. Serotonin (5-HT) metabolism is apparently altered by alcohol and lesions of neuron systems containing

5-HT result in increased preference for alcohol in rats [30]. On the other hand, alcohol intake in rats can be suppressed by administration of a 5-HT precursor, 5-Hydroxytryptophan (5-HTP).

Alcohol preference may be related to norepinephrine levels (NE). When neuron systems of the rat containing NE are lesioned by a neurotoxin infused directly into the cerebral ventricle, suppression of preference for alcohol is observed [31].

In the past decade, considerable interest has developed in the possible role of acetaldehyde-biogenic amine combinations. Acetaldehyde, the first metabolic intermediary of alcohol, in combination with various biogenic amines yields a family of substances called tetrahydroisoquinolines (TIQs). For example, dopamine plus acetaldehyde yields salsolinol. Dopamine plus dopaldehyde yields tetrahydropapaveroline (THP), an alkaloid that is a morphine precursor.

Administration of TIQs to animals has been shown to increase preferences for ethanol solutions. Myers and his colleagues [32,33], for example, have shown that in rats and monkeys when THP is infused into the cerebral ventricles, preferences for astonishingly high concentrations of ethanol (40%) can be established. Moreover, it appears that such preferences are irreversible.

Blum and his associates [34] have hypothesized that alcohol and opiate addiction may be linked by morphine precursors formed by alcohol-biogenic amine condensation products. In effect, alcoholism may be related to the brain's production of various TIQs. The following findings support an alkaloid isoquinoline role in alcoholism:

1. THP and salsolinol interact with opiate receptor sites;
2. Elevated THP levels in patients entering alcoholism treatment have been noted;
3. Apparently irreversible preferences for very high concentrations of ethanol can be induced in animals by infusions of THP into the cerebral ventricles.

In summary, research on biological etiological factors has reached a level of sophistication that renders the question of whether or not alcoholism is a disease nonproductive, if not absurd. On the basis of available data, biological factors can be seen as entering into both the etiology and maintenance of alcoholism. Attention and debate should now be directed toward further clarification of the roles of neuropharmacology, neuroanatomy, pharmacogenetics, bioelectric phenomena, and psychobiology in an effort to determine precisely what kind of a disease (or diseases) alcoholism is, what further biological factors are associated with its origins and maintenance, and what kinds of interventions may finally cure the disease rather than arrest it.

NEEDED: A MEANINGFUL BIOPSYCHOSOCIAL MODEL

Neither a simplistic disease model of alcoholism nor a simplistic behavioral model is likely to resolve complex questions concerning the origins, maintenance, and treatment of alcoholism. Biological, psychological, and sociocultural factors are clearly involved in alcoholism. The disease is obviously biopsychosocial [35].

But while it has become more or less fashionable to consider alcoholism a biopsychosocial phenomenon, very difficult questions remain to be addressed. How may variables drawn from each of the domains of biology, psychology, and culture be conceptualized such that coherent, meaningful, and scientifically useful multivariate models can be conceived, developed and tested? At present, it is difficult to see how micro level variables concerned with alternative pathways for 5-HT metabolism in the presence of ethanol can be conceptualized as interacting with macro systems involving cross-cultural differences in sanctions against alcohol misuse.

In short, the development of a meaningful biopsychosocial model of alcoholism involves more than the demonstration that biological, psychological and sociocultural factors in isolation are involved in the disease. Interactions between and among variables drawn from these various domains constitute the difficult and as yet largely unexamined problems of data and imagination. Wallace [36] provided an early attempt to develop one such model.

IS A SHIFT IN PARADIGM NECESSARY?

Despite ideological postures that deny the very existence of alcoholism [1], question its irreversibility [2,3,11,15,16,37,38] and attempt to minimize or deny biological factors in its origins as well as its consequences [2,3,39], it is apparent that the basic paradigm that has given coherence and direction to research and treatment for the past three decades need not be abandoned. While particular elements of this basic paradigm require continuing reformulation as new information is generated from research in areas such as psychobiology, neuropharmacology, pharmacogenetics, and behavioral genetics, a radical shift in paradigm does not appear justified on strictly empirical grounds at the present time.

References

1. W.P. Rohan, "The concept of alcoholism: assumptions and issues", in *Encyclopedic Handbook of Alcoholism*, E.M. Pattison and E. Kaufman, editors, Gardner Press, New York, 1982, pp. 31–39.
2. E.M. Pattison and E. Kaufman, "The alcoholism syndrome: definitions and models," in *Encyclopedic Handbook of Alcoholism*, E.M. Pattison and E. Kaufman, editors, Gardner Press, New York, 1982, pp. 3–30.
3. E.M. Pattison, M.B. Sobell, and L.C. Sobell, *Emerging Concepts of Alcohol Dependence*, Springer, New York, 1977.
4. W.J. Knox, "Attitudes of psychiatrists and psychologists toward alcoholism," in *Medicine, Law, and Public Policy*, N. Kittrie, H. Hirsch, and G. Wegner, editors, AMS, New York, 1975.
5. J. Helzer, L. Robins, J. Croughan, and A. Welner, "Renard diagnostic interview: Its reliability and validity with physicians and lay interviewers," *Archives of General Psychiatry*, Vol. 38, 1981, 393–398.
6. R. Landeen, A. Aaron, and P. Breer, "A multipurpose self-administered drinking problem questionnaire," in *Currents in Alcoholism*, Vol. 1, F. Seixas, editor, Grune & Stratton, New York, 1977.
7. G. Jacobson, *The Alcoholisms: Detection, Diagnosis, and Assessment*. Human Sciences Press, New York, 1976.
8. G. Jacobson, D. Niles, D. Moberg, E. Manderhr, and L. Dusso, "Identifying alcoholic and problem-drinking drivers: Wisconsin's field test of a modified NCA criteria for the diagnosis of alcoholism," in *Currents in Alcoholism*, Vol. 6, M. Galanter, editor, Grune & Stratton, New York, 1979.
9. M. Eckardt, R. Ryback, R. Rawlings, and B. Graubard, "Biochemical diagnosis of alcoholism: A test of the discriminating capabilities of -glutamyl transpeptidase and mean corpuscular volume," *Journal of the American Medical Association*, Vol. 246, 1981, pp. 2707–2710.
10. L.N. Robins, "The diagnosis of alcoholism after DSM-III," in *Encyclopedic Handbook of Alcoholism*, E.M. Pattison and E. Kaufman, editors, Gardner Press, New York, 1982, pp. 40–54.
11. D. Armor, J. Polich, and H. Stambul, *Alcoholism and Treatment*, Rand Corporation, Santa Monica, 1976.
12. J. Wallace, "Alcoholism and Treatment revisited," *World Alcohol Project*, Vol. 1, 1979, pp. 3–18.
13. J. Polich, D. Armor, and H. Braiker, *The course of Alcoholism: Four Years After Treatment*, Rand Corporation, Santa Monica, 1980.
14. H. Pettinati, A. Sugerman, N. DiDonato, and H. Maurer, "The natural history of alcoholism over four years after treatment," *Journal of Studies on Alcohol*, 1982, Vol. 43, pp. 201–215.
15. M. Sobell and L. Sobell, "Individualized behavior therapy for alcoholics," *Behavior Therapy*, 1973, Vol. 4, pp. 49–72.
16. G. Caddy, H. Addington, and D. Perkins, "Individualized behavior therapy for alcoholics: A third year independent double-blind follow-up" *Behavior Research and Therapy*, 1978, Vol. 16, pp. 345–362.
17. D. Chalmers, "The alcoholic's controlled drinking time," *World Alcohol Project*, 1979, Vol. 1, pp. 18–28.
18. M. Pendery, I. Maltzman, and L.J. West, "Controlled drinking by alcoholics? New findings and a reevaluation of a major affirmative study," *Science*, 1982, Vol. 217, pp. 169–175.

19. M. Sobell and L. Sobell, *Behavioral Treatment of Alcohol Problems,* Plenum, New York, 1978.

20. E.M. Jellinek, *Disease Concept of Alcoholism,* New Haven, United Printing Service, 1960.

21. P. Park, "Developmental ordering of experience in alcoholism," *Quarterly Journal of Studies on Alcohol,* 1973, Vol. 34, pp. 473–488.

22. G. Albrecht, "The alcoholism process: A social learning viewpoint," in Bourne, P.G. and Fox, F. (eds) *Alcoholism: Progress in Research and Treatment,* New York, Academic Press, 1973.

23. L. Robins, P. West, and G. Murphy, "The high rate of suicide in older white men: A study testing ten hypotheses," *Social Psychiatry,* 1977, Vol. 12, pp. 1–20.

24. G. McClearn, "Genetic studies in animals," *Alcoholism: Clinical and Experimental Research,* 1981, Vol. 5, pp. 447–448.

25. D. Goodwin, F. Schulsinger, N. Moller, L. Hermansen, G. Winokur, and S. Guze, "Drinking problems in adopted and nonadopted sons of alcoholics," *Archives of General Psychiatry,* 1974, Vol. 31, pp. 164–169.

26. L. Kaij, *Alcoholism in Twins,* Almqvist and Wiksell, Stockholm, 1960.

27. M.A. Schuckitt, "The genetics of alcoholism," *Alcoholism: Clinical and Experimental Research,* 1981, Vol. 5, pp. 439–440.

28. R. Frances, S. Timm, and S. Bucky, "Studies of familial and nonfamilial alcoholism," *Archives of General Psychiatry,* 1980, Vol. 37, pp. 564–566.

29. W. Gabrielli, S.A. Mednick, J. Volavka, V.E. Pollock, F. Schulsinger, and T. Itil, "Electroencephalograms in children of alcoholic fathers," *Psychophysiology,* 1982, Vol. 19, pp. 404–407.

30. R.D. Myers and C.L. Melchoir, "Alcohol and alcoholism: Role of serotonin", in *Serotonin in Health and Disease,* W.B. Essman, editor, New York, Spectrum, 1977, pp. 373–430.

31. R.D. Myers, "Psychopharmacology of Alcohol," *Annual Review of Pharmacology and Toxicology,* 1978, Vol. 18, pp. 125–144.

32. R.D. Myers, "Tetrahydroisoquinolines in the brain: the basis of an animal model of alcoholism," *Alcoholism: Clinical and Experimental Research,* 1978, Vol. 2, pp. 145–154.

33. R.D. Myers, M.L. McCaleb, and W.D. Ruwe, "Alcohol drinking induced in the monkey by tetrahydropapaveroline (THP) infused into the cerebral ventricle," *Pharmacology, Biochemistry, and Behavior,* 1982, Vol. 16, pp. 995–1000.

34. K. Blum, M. Hamilton, M. Hirst, and J. Wallace, "Putative role of isoquinoline alkaloids in alcoholism: A link to opiates," *Alcoholism: Clinical and Experimental Research,* 1978, Vol. 2, pp. 113–120.

35. J.A. Ewing, "Alcoholism—Another biopsychosocial disease," *Psychosomatics,* 1980, Vol. 21, pp. 371–372.

36. J. Wallace, "Compulsive drinking: A biopsychosocial model," unpublished manuscript, Edgehill Newport, Newport, R.I. 02840.

37. O.F. Pomerleau, "Current behavioral therapies in the treatment of alcoholism," in *Encyclopedic Handbook of Alcoholism,* E.M. Pattison and E. Kaufman, editors, Grune & Stratton, New York, 1982, pp. 1054–1067.

38. P.E. Nathan and D.W. Briddell, "Behavior assessment and treatment of alcoholism," in *The Biology of Alcoholism,* B. Kissen and H. Begleiter, editors Vol. 5, *Treatment and Rehabilitation of the Chronic Alcoholics,* New York, Plenum, 1977.

39. P.E. Nathan, G.A. Marlatt, and T. Loberg, editors, *New Directions in Behavioral Research and Treatment,* New York, Plenum, 1978.

Part II

Treatment

Working with the Preferred Defense Structure of the Recovering Alcoholic

INTRODUCTION

Within the past five years, substantial progress has been made in understanding the origins of alcoholism, the factors that maintain it, and the methods by which it can be treated. Both alcoholism specialists and general mental health professionals have come to construe the disease as biopsychosocial in nature (Ewing, 1983; Tarter, 1983; Wallace, 1978). Most important, alcoholism is now widely recognized as an illness requiring specialized interventions and expertise. Methods useful with other clinical populations may have little direct application in the treatment of alcoholism and may, in fact, result in undesirable outcomes for the alcoholic patient.

In this chapter, I shall attempt to describe a theoretical framework for psychotherapy with alcoholics. This framework constitutes a modal or typical approach to alcoholism therapy, but does not preclude individualized treatments as well. As we have come to appreciate, both the commonality and individuality evident among alcoholics in treatment must be addressed. Accordingly, the general approach to alcoholism psychotherapy presented here, while focusing on commonality, is intended to be consistent with a multimodality approach to treatment.

A sophisticated disease concept of alcoholism does not ignore psychological and sociocultural factors. Whereas biological factors are clearly involved in the origin and maintenance of the disease, psychological and sociocultural factors play important roles as well. The naive question "Is alcoholism a disease or a learned problem of behavior?" is now properly construed as inadequate to address the complexity of the illness. More pertinent questions of etiology might very well concern issues involving a triangulation of pharmacogenetics, neurochemistry, and culture, for example, "How do family histories interact with particular brain peptide levels in individuals drawn from cultures varying widely in drinking styles, customs, and practices?"

Biological Factors Are Primary. Recent research clearly implicates biological factors in the etiology and maintenance of alcoholism. Numerous studies in animals on the pharmacogenetics of alcohol preference, consumption, and effects of hypnotic doses reveal that hereditary influence is substantial (McClearn, 1981). Selective breeding in mice and rats has been achieved and strain differences have been shown.

Human genetic studies (Goodwin, Schulsinger, Moller, Hermansen, Winokur, and Cuze, 1974; Kaij, 1960; Schuckitt, 1981) conducted internationally indicate that the sons of alcoholics have at least a three times greater risk of becoming alcoholics than the sons of non-alcoholics. This increased risk was found in studies where social learning effects were *absent* and was not further increased in studies where both genetic and social-learning effects were jointly present. In addition, the rate of concordance for alcoholism in identical twins is 60% and 30% in fraternal twins. Moreover, young men with alcoholism in first degree family members metabolize alcohol differently than men without such family histories. Higher associated levels of acetaldehyde and less behavioral impairment after three drinks have been noted in young men with alcoholism in first degree family members (Schuckitt, 1981).

A recent study of patients with and without familial histories of alcoholism revealed numerous differences (Frances, Timm, and Bucky, 1980). Patients with familial histories showed more severe symptomatology of alcoholism, more antisocial behavior, worse academic and social performance in school, unstable employment histories, and more severe physical symptoms related to alcohol.

In a recent study by Gabrielli, Mednick, Volavka, Pollock, Schulsinger, and Itil, 1982, young sons of alcoholic fathers showed a high frequency EEG activity (above 18 Hz). Hence, fast EEG activity which is an inheritable characteristic and is frequently found in adult alcoholics has been found in EEG records of the 11–13 year-old-sons of alcoholics. Since alcohol is known to slow brain activity, alcoholics may be persons who learn to reduce genetically determined fast brain wave activity by self-medication with alcoholic beverages. Recent work by Bohman, Sigvardsson, and Cloninger (1981), indicates that female alcoholism is also partially genetically determined. In a study of female adoptees in Sweden, a 3-fold increase in subsequent alcoholism was found in adopted females whose biological mothers were alcoholic. For males, a crossfostering analysis revealed a 9-fold increase in male adoptees whose biological fathers were alcoholic (Cloninger, Bohman, and Sigvardsson, 1981).

Numerous studies have centered on the effects of alcohol on brain neurotransmitters and the possible effects of neurotransmitter systems on drinking behavior. Serotonin (5-HT) metabolism is apparently altered by alcohol and lesions of neuron systems containing 5-HT result in increased preference for alcohol in rats (Myers and Melchoir, 1977). On the other hand, alcohol intake in rats can be suppressed by administration of a 5-HT precursor, 5-Hydroxytryptophan (5-HTP).

Alcohol preference may be related to norepinephrine levels (NE). When neuron systems of the rat containing NE are lesioned by a neurotoxin infused directly into the cerebral ventricle, suppression of preference for alcohol is observed (Myers, 1978a).

In short, these studies on neurotransmitter systems suggest that alcoholism may be related to particular biochemical events in the brain.

In the past decade, considerable interest has developed in the possible role of aldehyde-biogenic amine combinations. Acetaldehyde, the first metabolic intermediary of alcohol, along with other adelhydes, in combination with various neurotransmitters yields a family of substances called tetrahydroisoquinolines (TIQs). For example, dopamine plus acetaldehyde yields salsolinol. Dopamine plus dopaldehyde yields tetrahydropapaveroline (THP), an alkaloid that is a morphine precursor.

Administration of TIQs to animals has been shown to increase preferences for ethanol solutions. Myers and his colleagues (Myers, 1978b; Myers, McCaleb, and Ruwe, 1982) for example, have shown that in rats and monkeys when THP is infused into the cerebral ventricles, preferences for astonishingly high concentrations of ethanol (40%) can be established. Moreover, it appears that such preferences are irreversible. These results are remarkable since monkeys do not naturally prefer alcohol to water. Also, the concentrations of ethanol are very high.

Blum, Hamilton, Hirst, and Wallace (1978) have hypothesized that alcohol and opiate addiction may be linked by morphine precursors formed by alcohol-biogenic amine condensation products. In effect, alcoholism may be related to the brain's production of various TIQs. The following findings support an alkaloid isoquinoline role in alcoholism.

1. Elevated THP levels in patients entering alcoholism treatment have been noted.
2. THP and salsolinol interact with opiate receptor sites, that is, these isoquinolines appear to be similar to opiates.
3. Apparently irreversible preferences for *very high* concentrations of ethanol can be induced in animals by infusions of THP into the cerebral ventricles.

These findings clearly implicate biological factors in the origin of alcoholism. Moreover, research such as this on biological factors has reached a level of sophistication that renders the question of whether or not alcoholism is a disease non-productive, if not absurd.

The Psychological Perspective. If biological factors play a primary role in the etiology and maintenance of alcoholism, how may psychological factors be construed? While psychological factors may act to some extent as *antecedent* conditions for the development of alcoholism, it is probable that they act largely as significant *consequences* of the disease. Withdrawal symptoms, for example, are clearly outcomes, rather than causes, of alcoholism. Low self-esteem, denial, poor frustration tolerance, depression, and anxiety may also be outcomes of the disease. Most important, however, is the fact that these physical and psychological outcomes can serve to maintain the disease and complicate recovery.

Psychological interventions with alcoholics can lead to satisfactory results if therapists are able to recognize the typical psychological outcomes of alcoholism and to work with them effectively in early, middle, and late stages of psychotherapy. In effect, the typical psychological outcomes can be viewed as learned coping strategies.

In the following pages, a case is presented for working with these learned coping strategies of alcoholics. This does not imply that these learned coping strategies are the cause of alcoholism. Rather, they are seen as important psychological outcomes of the disease and constitute important factors in the maintenance of active alcoholism. My arguments shall include the following major ideas:

1. Alcoholics can be described in terms of a preferred defense structure. This preferred defense structure (PDS) need not be construed at all in terms of the classical language of defense mechanisms. The alcoholic PDS can be thought of as a collection of skills or abilities—tactics and strategies, if you will—for achieving one's ends.
2. Therapy with alcoholics, as it is currently practiced, too often attempts to remove the alcoholic PDS instead of utilizing it effectively to facilitate the achievement of abstinence. Thera-

peutic efforts that confront the alcoholic PDS prematurely and too heavily will increase, rather than reduce, the probability of further drinking.

3. Recovery programs successful in producing abstinence, such as Alcoholics Anonymous, partially owe their success to the intuitive recognition of the fact that the alcoholic PDS is to be protected and capitalized on rather than confronted and radically altered.

4. Paradoxically, the very same defenses that the alcoholic used to maintain his drinking can be used effectively to achieve abstinence.

5. Equally paradoxically, the very same defenses that enabled the alcoholic to drink, as well as achieve abstinence, must ultimately be removed if long-term sobriety is to be maintained. However, in many cases such growth must take place over periods of time ranging from two to five years of abstinence.

6. Alcohol therapy must be viewed as a *time-dependent* process. A particular therapeutic intervention for a recently drinking alcoholic may be entirely inappropriate for one who has managed to achieve several years of sobriety and vice-versa.

THE PREFERRED DEFENSE STRUCTURE (PDS) OF THE RECOVERING ALCOHOLIC

For my purposes, I have assumed that an alcoholic PDS exists and that it is the *outcome* of alcoholism, not an antecedent condition. In the following, I do not mean to suggest a single, unvarying profile—one that is characteristic of each and every alcoholic drinker. I am assuming, however, that *some* of these are found in *some* combinatorial pattern in virtually every alcoholic drinker at *some* point in his drinking and recovery from alcoholism.

Denial. Enough has been written about denial as a major defense in alcoholism as to require very little in the way of further elaboration here. What has *not* been observed, however, is that aside from the obvious destructive nature of denial in matters concerned with drinking, denial is not without merit. Tactical denial or, if you will, *deliberate* denial of certain life difficulties or problems is a useful and extremely valuable temporary adjustive and coping device. In the case of the alcoholic well-practiced in such behavior, denial as a general tactical mechanism should not be discarded totally. That would be rather like throwing out the baby with the bath water.

But, of course, the recovering alcoholic must stop denying the impact of alcohol upon his major life concerns. That is an obvious truism in alcoholism therapy that need not be altered. Simply because that statement is true, however, it does not follow that the recovering alcoholic must immediately, thoroughly, and completely root out all evidence of denial generally in his personality and behavior. First of all, he can't. Second, he rather likes the tactic of denial—he should, he's leaned heavily upon it for years. Third, at some level or another, he recognizes that tactical denial is a coping strategy he simply cannot do without.

In any case, the important point is as follows: alcoholism may very well be referred to aptly as "the merry-go-round of denial." If my analysis is correct, however, with regard to denial generally, the alcoholic is going to keep going round and round, *long after his drinking stops.* And the very worst thing a therapist could ever possibly do is try to jam the mechanism and block the use of tactical denial entirely.

Projection. While much has been written about *disowning* projection (the tendency to attribute unwanted and unacceptable aspects of self to others), there has been very little appreciation of other types of projection in the field of alcoholism. This is most surprising since *assimilative* projection is perhaps the most outstanding characteristic of both drinking and sober alcoholics. Assimilative projection is the tendency to assume that others are very much like oneself and to perceive them as such. Negative or socially unacceptable impulses and traits need not be seen in others. In fact, much of assimilative projection involves many desirable and socially admirable characteristics. As we shall see, the tendency toward assimilative projection has great significance, both for the illusion and substance of identification and also for the understanding of therapeutic communities.

All-or-None Thinking. It is often the case that the alcoholic will exhibit a strong preference for certainty. Judgments of people, events, and situations are often extreme. Decision-making does not often seem to take into account the realistically probable. Decision rules are often inflexible, narrow in scope, and simplistic. Perceived alternatives are few, consisting largely of yes-no, go-no go, black-white, dichotomized categories. It is in this sense that the thinking is said to be "all or none" in character. This aspect of the alcoholic PDS has obvious implications for the nature of persuasive communications in therapy as well as for the manner in which information is structured and presented.

In general, it is my experience with alcoholics in a variety of therapeutic contexts that they prefer large amounts of structure. While the drinking alcoholic may certainly appear to prefer uncertainty and unpredictability bordering on chaos, the recovering alcoholic seems to like things to move along in a fairly predictable and structured manner. Meetings of AA, for example, are certainly among the most structured of social encounters.

The qualities of all-or-none thinking, preference for highly certain communications, simple decision-making rules, restricted choices, and highly structured social encounters all have obvious implications for the conduct of therapy and the structuring of therapeutic environments.

Conflict Minimization and Avoidance. Although their behavior while drinking may suggest otherwise, alcoholics do not like interpersonal conflict, nor do they handle it well; nor do they thrive in competitive relationships. As others have suggested, alcoholics do best in relationships characterized by complementarity rather than competition. Complementary relationships are those based upon satisfaction of reciprocally balanced needs. For example, a dominant person and submissive person would constitute a complementary relationship. These attributes concerning conflict minimization and conflict avoidance have obvious implications for both the nature and depth of therapeutic confrontation with the alcoholic. Confrontation tactics should be used by only the most skillful of therapists and only at carefully selected times in the therapeutic process. Angry and hostile confrontation with the alcoholic client is rarely, if ever, appropriate. Moreover, the group therapist working with alcoholics should exercise extreme caution in utilizing the resources of the group to confront a resistant member.

Rationalization. As anybody with only a passing acquaintance with alcoholism can testify readily, alcoholics are often masters of rationalization. Many have developed the art and science of wishful thinking to its ultimate form of expression. They have had to. Anybody who can continue to drink in the face of the steadily accumulating disastrous consequences of active alcoholism must surely have learned a trick or two in order to make his drinking appear perfectly reasonable to himself and to others. But, as we have already seen with denial, rationalization can be a useful tactic in dealing with otherwise difficult situations, anxiety-laden happenings, and guilt-provoking personal actions.

After years of making the procuring and drinking of alcohol his number one priority, the alcoholic understands very well how ultimate priorities can be maintained. Paradoxically, it is a relatively straightforward shift from rationalizing drinking to rationalizing other less than desirable behaviors *with sobriety*. That is, in the early stages of abstinence, the recovering alcoholic may quickly discover that while drinking was a crutch, sobriety is an even better one!

"Why, I can't do that, I might get drunk!" "I had to choose between her and my sobriety." In essence, the recovering alcoholic may discover that he has a freedom of personal action that few others can enjoy. But such rationalization can be an invaluable tactic in avoiding the reexperiencing of painful emotional clues that previously served as triggers to drinking, for example, guilt, remorse, anxiety, resentment, and anger. Eventually, of course, the recovering alcoholic must face up to his *sober* rationalizations. However, the word to be stressed in that sentence is *eventually*. What the alcoholic very definitely does not need early in his sobriety is a therapist who moves too rapidly.

Self-Centered Selective Attention. Alcoholics, for the most part, tend to look at things from a single perspective—*theirs*. Even in some alcoholics with considerable sobriety, there is often a curious lack of true empathy, a seeming inability to grasp the position of the other. This is not to say that alcoholics are "selfish." The facts are often to the contrary. But an alcoholic can be generous to a fault and still show extreme self-centeredness. As used here the term *self-centered selective attention* refers to the fact that alcoholics tend to be obsessed with self, to perceive the happenings around them largely as they impinge upon self. They attend selectively to information relevant to self, ignore other information not relevant to self, screen out information that is discrepant with their views of themselves, and distort other information that does not fit their preferred self-image.

In a very real sense, alcoholics are often resistant to feedback from others as well as from their own life experiences. This characteristic "blindness" can prove severely distressing and, in fact, maddening to those whose lives are linked to the alcoholic in important ways. It is often the case that drinking alcoholics (as well as recently sober ones) can maintain views of reality in the face of even massively disconfirming feedback. Faced with these obvious contradictions, the therapist may feel that it is his responsibility to apply immediate corrective feedback. Unfortunately, with the alcoholic client that is surely the very worst thing that the therapist could do. One must never forget that the characteristic blindness of the alcoholic is there for reasons, that it is dynamically linked to chronically low self-esteem, feelings of worthlessness, guilt, fear, and what might otherwise prove to be overwhelming anxiety. It is not that the therapist and his client are uninterested in the "truth," whatever that might be. It is really more a matter of *when* "truths" get revealed and also what "truths" need to be invented if the client is to get sober.

Preference for Nonanalytical Modes of Thinking and Perceiving. It often seems to be the case that alcoholics are influenced more by the emotional persuasive appeal than the "rational." Leadership styles that are likely to work with the alcoholic are often charismatic, inspirational, and "spiritual." It is not that alcoholics cannot operate in logical-analytical modes. That would be patently false since alcoholics are as capable as nonalcoholics in approaching matters in a linear, logical, and analytical manner.

Passivity versus Assertion. Although the intoxicated individual may often appear aggressive, assertive, and even frankly hostile, it is often the case that the alcoholic in the initial stages of abstinence prefers passivity over active coping as a general adjustive strategy. Assertion and active coping tend to bring the person into normal conflict with others, and, as we have seen, alcoholics do not thrive in situations characterized by conflict, competition, and win-lose outcomes. In fact, it is precisely in these situations that they tend to pick up a drink.

In actuality, despite the surface picture, the preferences of the alcoholic are for a general life attitude of passivity rather than active assertion.

Obsessional Focusing. Alcoholics are, for the most part, intense people, and, as nearly everyone knows, they are often obsessed people. Intense obsession is no stranger to the alcoholic. In addition to the obsession with alcohol during periods of active drinking, it is not uncommon to find obsessions with work, money, success, sexuality, and so forth. Contrary to popular stereotype, the alcoholic, sober and drinking, is often so obsessed with work as to fully deserve the label "workaholic."

In general, the alcoholic seems to prefer a state characterized by a moderate-to-high activation level. Witness the enormous amounts of stimulating drugs, for example, caffeine and nicotine, consumed by sober alcoholics. Even the so-called states of serenity of many sober alcoholics are intensely focused states of moderate-to-high activation rather than low.

The therapeutic problem in alcoholism therapy is not to alter directly this level of intense obsession, but to *redirect* it. Along these lines, it is interesting to note how the obsession with alcohol, previous drinking, and sobriety continues in the *sober* alcoholic. Recovering alcoholics in AA, for example, often seem obsessed with their programs, with meetings, and with alcoholism generally. Curiously, this same obsession with the problem is what enables them to remain sober when previously it served to maintain drinking.

In essence, the problem in alcoholism therapy is not to reduce obsessional energy, an often impossible task, but to switch the focus of the obsession.

TACTICAL AND STRATEGIC USE OF THE PDS

In the preceding material, I described the alcoholic PDS and hinted at how it might be used effectively to help the alcoholic client achieve abstinence. I do not wish to imply that the above is an exhaustive description of the PDS. However, the major features of that structure have now been considered. We are in a position now to restate the central thesis of this chapter. An alcoholic preferred defense structure exists. It is not only ineffectual but therapeutically disastrous to confront this structure prematurely. The therapist knowledgeable about alcoholics will turn this structure to the advantage of his client and himself by selectively reinforcing and encouraging the defenses of the alcoholic client. The central problem in therapy with the alcoholic is learning how to swing the PDS into the service of abstinence rather than continued drinking.

Eventually, the alcoholic preferred defense structure must be dealt with directly if real changes in personality are to be achieved. When and to what extent such changes should be attempted, however, depends upon characteristics of individual alcoholics as well as upon years of continuous sobriety. In my opinion, in the majority of recovering alcoholics, such changes should not be attempted until several years of sobriety have been achieved.

The therapeutic task in alcoholism therapy at the early stages of abstinence differs radically from that of other psychotherapies. The role of the therapist is not to expose, confront, and modify the defenses of the alcoholic client. Rather, the role of the therapist is to teach the alcoholic client how to use these very defenses to achieve and maintain abstinence. Denial, rationalization, projection, and so forth have for too long been construed in moralistic terms by psychotherapists. In actuality, such mechanisms are perfectly acceptable *tactics* when used deliberately and selectively for particular purposes. In the case of the alcoholic, these tactics have become part of a preferred defense structure throughout years of alcoholic drinking. For a therapist to try to remove these is equivalent to trying to force water to flow uphill.

Little therapeutic imagination is required to see how tactics such as denial and rationalization can be used effectively with the recovering alcoholic. Once the denial and rationalization associated with drinking have been confronted and dealt with, the recovering alcoholic typically is faced with many very real and difficult life problems. A list of these may serve to remind us of the intolerable internal and external stressors the recovering alcoholic may be required to face. He may have to deal with very serious malfunctions of physical health. His marital situation may remain complicated for many years after his last drink. His finances are often in alarmingly poor condition. He may have alienated everybody who ever meant anything to him. He may be facing nontrivial legal and criminal proceedings, unemployment, disturbed interpersonal relationships, parent-child complexities of unbearable proportions, personal emotional problems of serious dimensions, and so on. What can we do for the person in, not one serious life crisis, but a host of them all at once? It is precisely here that variants of denial and rationalization become important. Through direct tuition, we can help the alcoholic to the position that things will work out if he just will stay sober, that even though his life is complicated at the moment, at least he is sober, that sobriety is his number one priority, and so on and so forth. In other words, we as therapists are appealing to his preferred use of denial and rationalization to give him a toehold on abstinence.

Similarly, by appealing to the alcoholic's preference for assimilative projection, we can get him to identify with other persons whose problems seem to center around something called "alcoholism." If the alcoholic comes to construe himself in these terms, then all of the benefits that can flow from such a self-attribution are his. The label "alcoholic" or "alcoholism" provides the person with a convenient explanatory system for much of his behavior. Moreover, by listening to the experiences of others who make the same self-attribution and who also conveniently explain their behavior by this attribution, the person has a ready source of social reinforcement for his changing belief system. Furthermore, he is now open to considerable positive social influence. And he has been given the key to dealing with otherwise overwhelming anxiety, remorse, guilt, and confusion. In addition, by fixing his lifeline in terms of two clearly demarcated points (i.e., when you were drinking and now that you are sober), we have provided the client with reference points for a belief system that includes the possibility of dealing with the negativity of previous behavior and the possibility of hope for desired future behaviors.

In a very real sense, helping the client to achieve a self-attribution of "alcoholic" and, hence, an explanatory system for his behaviors is a central role of the therapist. It should not be done directly. In fact, the guiding principle of work at this phase of therapy should be, "as little external force as necessary for the attribution to be made." If the therapist literally tries to force the attribution upon the client, one of two things will happen: The client will become defiant and reject the therapist's attribution, or the client will publicly acquiesce but privately disagree.

Psychotherapy with the client at this point is very much the teaching of an "exotic belief." The often heard phrase, "your life was a mess because you were drinking, you weren't drinking because your life was a mess," and the many variants of this phrase are, in actuality, efforts to teach the client the convenient fiction that his problems are entirely attributable to alcoholism. If it enables the client to (1) explain his past behavior in a way that gives him hope for the future, (2) cope with his guilt, anxiety, remorse, and confusion, and (3) provide himself with a specific behavior (staying sober) that will change his life in a desired direction, then the assertion is valuable in early treatment. *The therapist must remember that the recovering alcoholic has a lifetime of sobriety in which to gradually recognize the fact that not all of his personal and social difficulties can be attributed to alcoholism.* In the meantime, the therapist can make very good use of assertions that have their basis in denial and rationalization. In effect, the therapeutic task is one of helping the client to construct a belief system. The fact that this belief system may at the beginning of sobriety contain strong elements of denial and rationalization should not trouble us. One must remember that the recovering alcoholic in initial stages of sobriety is faced with so many serious life problems that he will need a healthy dose of denial and rationalization if he is to survive at all.

MIDDLE AND LATE PHASE TREATMENT

Whereas a supportive psychotherapy that respects the learned coping strategies of the person in the early stages of abstention is important, it is equally important that middle and late phase treatment be increasingly more intense. Alcoholics, in order to achieve a comfortable and secure sobriety, must begin to abandon these learned coping strategies in exchange for open, nondefensive, and authentic relationships with self and others. Of course, anxiety is often the price that patients must pay for psychological growth, insight into self, and awareness of feelings. One does not become whole without discomfort.

In middle and later stages of psychotherapy, it is extremely important for both the therapist and the patient to risk manageable degrees of anxiety in order for insight into self and others to increase and for growth to continue. Normally, however, these more intensive therapeutic efforts with alcoholics should not be attempted before one year of sobriety has been achieved. Ideally, they should be begun within two to five years of continuous sobriety.

Summary and Conclusions

Throughout this chapter, I have argued for the existence of learned coping strategies (a preferred defense structure) in the alcoholic client. I have further maintained that traditional and even contemporary psychotherapies are largely inappropriate for the recovering alcoholic precisely because they have failed to recognize the value of this alcoholic preferred defense structure. Therapeutic ideologies that consist largely of disguised moralistic stances concerning certain behaviors called "defenses" are likely to do more harm than good in the early stages of treatment.

The central problem in early alcoholism therapy is not one of exposing, uncovering, and modifying the alcoholic PDS. The central problem is one of discovering ways of swinging the PDS into the service of achieving and maintaining sobriety.

Finally, we psychotherapists need to construe alcoholism therapy as a time-dependent process. We must begin to understand that entirely different therapeutic behaviors are called for in various stages of the long recovery period from active alcoholism.

References

Blum, K., Hamilton, M., Hirst, M., and Wallace, J. Putative role of Isoquinoline alkaloids in alcoholism: A link to opiates. *Alcoholism: Clinical and Experimental Research*, 1978, 2, 113–120.

Bohman, M., Sigvardsson, S., and Cloninger, C. R. Maternal inheritance of alcohol abuse: Cross-fostering analysis of adopted women. *Archives of General Psychiatry* 1981, *38*, 965–969.

Cloninger, C. R., Bohman, M., and Sigvardsson, S. Inheritance of alcohol abuse: Cross-fostering analysis of adopted men. *Archives of General Psychiatry*, 1981, *38*, 861–868.

Ewing, J. A. Alcoholism—another biopsychosocial disease. *Psychosomatics*, 1980, *21*, 371–372.

Frances, R., Timm, S., and Bucky, S. Studies of familial and nonfamilial alcoholism. *Archives of General Psychiatry*, 1980, *37*, 564–566.

Gabrielli, W., Mednick, S. A., Volavka, J., Pollock, V. E., Schulsinger, F., and Itil, T. Electroencephalograms in children of alcoholic fathers. *Psychophysiology*, 1982, *19*, 404–407.

Goodwin, D., Schulsinger, F., Moller, N., Hermansen, L., Winokur, G., and Guze, S. Drinking problems in adopted and nonadopted sons of alcoholics. *Archives of General Psychiatry*, 1974, *31*, 164–169.

Kaij, L. *Alcoholism in twins*. Almqvist & Wiksell: Stockholm, 1960.

McClearn, G. Genetic studies in animals. *Alcoholism: Clinical and Experimental Research*, 1981, *5*, 447–448.

Myers, R. D. and Melchoir, C. L. Alcohol and alcoholism; Role of Serotonin. In W. B. Essman, *Serotonin in Health and Disease.* New York: Spectrum, 1977.

Myers, R. D. Psychopharmacology of Alcohol. *Annual Review of Pharmacology and Toxicology,* 1978, *18,* 125–144. (a)

Myers, R. D. Tetrahydroisoquinolines in the brain: the basis of an animal model of alcoholism. *Alcoholism: Clinical and Experimental Research,* 1978, *2,* 145–154. (b)

Myers, R. D., McCaleb, M. L., and Ruwe, W. D. Alcohol drinking induced in the monkey by tetrahydroparaveroline (THP) infused into the cerebral ventricle. *Pharmacology, Biochemistry, and Behavior,* 1982, *16,* 995–1000.

Schuckitt, M. A. The genetics of alcoholism. *Alcoholism: Clinical and Experimental Research,* 1981, *5,* 439–440.

Tarter, R. E. The causes of alcoholism: A biopsychosocial analysis. In E. Gottheil, K. Druley, T. Skoloda, and H. Waxman (Eds.), *Etiological aspects of alcohol and drug abuse.* Springfield, Ill: Charles C Thomas, 1983.

Wallace, J. *Compulsive drinking: A Biopsychosocial model.* Unpublished manuscript, 1978. Edgehill Newport, Newport, Rhode Island 02840.

Critical Issues in
Alcoholism Therapy

INTRODUCTION

The Ancients recognized that life is often a matter of choosing a safe course between two equally hazardous alternatives. Navigators operating off the coast of Italy were cautioned to find the narrow passage between Scylla, the rock, and Charybdis, the whirlpool, since sailing too close to either meant certain disaster.

This metaphor for danger on the left *and* on the right is still meaningful, especially so for psychotherapy with the alcoholic client. As some psychotherapists are beginning to realize, making choices in psychotherapy is tricky business. Too often, choice results in exchanging one unsatisfactory state of affairs for another.

In the present chapter, I will show that alcoholism psychotherapy consists of a number of strategic choices in the presence of multiple Scyllas and Charybdises—multiple hazardous alternatives.

DENIAL VERSUS PREMATURE SELF-DISCLOSURE

The Scylla of denial is a well-charted hazard in alcoholism therapy. Therapists working with alcoholics are so familiar with their client's unwillingness (or inability) to see the facts of the drinking and its consequences that nothing further need be added here.

What is not appreciated, however, is the corresponding Charybdis of premature self-disclosure. In working with alcoholics, we must realize that denial is there for a purpose. It is the glue that holds an

This chapter appeared in Practical Approaches to Alcoholism Psychotherapy, 2nd Edition, 1985, edited by Sheldon Zimberg, John Wallace, and Sheila Blume. Reprinted by permission of Plenum Press.

already shattered self-esteem system together. And it is the tactic through which otherwise overwhelming anxiety can be contained.

In psychotherapy generally, anxiety is often the price that is paid for increments in self-awareness and disclosure to others. Unfortunately, in alcoholics, anxiety is also one of the more important inner cues or "triggers" for drinking. It follows then that the most difficult task in alcoholism therapy is to lessen the denial and encourage increased self-awareness and disclosure while simultaneously keeping anxiety at minimal levels. This means that the alcoholism therapist must be content with a gradually deepening self-awareness in his client rather than demanding sudden, dramatic "breakthroughs." Moreover, the therapist must insure a therapeutic context in which high levels of support are available as the client uncovers aspects of self and discloses these to others.

GUILT VERSUS SOCIOPATHY

Among recovering alcoholics, guilt requires careful therapeutic management. Like anxiety, guilt can operate as a powerful inner trigger for continued drinking. Both therapists and recovering alcoholics recognize this fact and, as a consequence, strive to minimize guilt or avoid it entirely. In fact, the excessive moralism surrounding alcoholism historically, and still prevalent in some quarters, leads many persons to take the extreme position that guilt serves no useful psychological or social function.

But while it is undeniably true that many lives have been wrecked by excessive guilt, it is equally true that as many have been lost in the chaos resulting from the absence of a sharply defined set of values and a developed individual conscience.

Normal guilt serves a highly useful function. It acts as an important feedback signal to the person that his actions are no longer in harmony with his central, core beliefs and values. A therapist who attempts to eliminate guilt of this nature is doing his client an ultimate disservice. And the recovering alcoholic who refuses to acknowledge normal guilt may find himself caught in an ever-increasing spiral of rationalization and further self-deception.

Irrational guilt, or "neurotic guilt," is of course another matter. Guilt of this nature serves no useful purpose. Moreover, it often leads to paradoxical effects, serving to maintain the actions that produced it. In the drinking alcoholic, irrational guilt over drinking may trigger further drinking, leading to yet more drinking, and so on. This familiar pattern constitutes a cycle—the *guilt-alcohol abuse vicious cycle*. Once caught in it, the alcoholic can spin from one drunk to another.

But, while irrational guilt can snare the drinking alcoholic, the absence of normal guilt in the recovering alcoholic and a determined refusal to assume responsibility for his actions does not bode well for recovery either.

In alcoholism psychotherapy, neither irrational guilt nor sociopathic values are to be encouraged. Instead, the alcoholic client must come to see that while he need not feel guilty for becoming an alcoholic, nor for previous actions while intoxicated, he is responsible: responsible for doing something now and in the future about his disease, for his present actions, and for meeting the complications stemming from his past in an honest, fair, and just manner.

SELF-BLAME VERSUS BLAMING OTHERS

Blaming is closely associated with excessive guilt in alcoholics. Typically, the alcoholic swings radically from blaming others to blaming self. He may hold his spouse responsible for his drinking, his parents, children, friends, employers, or even "society." Well-meaning but misguided friends and associates of the alcoholic will often help him to make erroneous blame assignments.

But at other times the alcoholic will go to the other extreme—heaping abuse upon himself. When the self-punishment becomes too painful to bear, he will once again attribute his drinking and its associated miseries to external agents.

As with the guilt-alcohol abuse cycle, the alcoholic may find himself caught in a *blame-assignment cycle.* Blaming others will not work since this perception of cause arouses resentment, still another critically important inner trigger for continued drinking. But blaming self leads once again to irrational guilt and to further lowering of self-esteem, and these too result in further drinking.

For the alcoholic caught in the blame-assignment cycle, there seems to be no way out. But there is an obvious alternative and the effective alcoholism therapist knows how to make good use of it; *attributions of cause can be made to the disease of alcoholism.* If he must place blame somewhere, the alcoholic can blame the disease of alcoholism. Obviously not all of the client's difficulties are attributable to his alcoholism. But in the early stages of abstinence and treatment, tactical use of this attribution can be very effective.

Despite its recent critics, the disease concept of alcoholism continues to be superior to any available competing theoretical formulation. Its advantages are as follows:

1. It provides the patient with a simple, easy to grasp explanation of his perplexing and seemingly inexplicable condition.

2. It gives the client the means to reconstruct his past, cope with the present, and plan his future without being overwhelmed by irrational guilt.

3. It enables the patient to reduce the free-floating anxiety associated with a previously unlabeled and, hence, cognitively unstructured, terrifying life situation.

4. It facilitates the client's decision to remain abstinent rather than continue futile attempts to maintain controlled drinking.

5. It reduces the social stigma growing out of the irrationally moral conception of alcoholism.

6. Extensive community and clinical experience have shown that recovering alcoholics who accept the disease concept are more likely to achieve sobriety and, more important, *maintain* it over longer periods of time than alcoholics who do not.

7. Recent scientific findings point directly to significant biological factors in the etiology of alcoholism (Wallace, 1983).

Rebellion versus Compliance

Therapists working with alcoholics must be prepared to deal with two frequently encountered patterns of client behavior—rebellion and compliance. Neither of these patterns is associated with continued sobriety.

The rebellious client is a formidable challenge to the therapist's skill and patience. Overtly or passively aggressive, this client rejects efforts to help him. He is hypercritical of the therapist, his information, and his therapeutic techniques. Argumentative, negative, and closed-minded, the client is very often preoccupied with finding faults with the treatment center, therapists, and staff rather than with making therapeutic progress.

The dynamics of the rebellious client are quite apparent. If he can force others to adopt a hostile, rejecting, and punitive attitude toward him, then he is "justified" in keeping others at a distance; that is, his own hostility is appropriate. And he is also "justified" in resuming his alcoholic drinking.

An easy-going, matter-of-fact approach is the correct way to proceed with the openly rebellious client. The therapist should monitor his own actions and attitudes, taking care not to allow reciprocal hostility and rejection to develop on his part. The therapist can then avoid giving the rebellious client the "excuse" that he is looking for to drink.

Compliance, although not as overtly challenging to the therapist, is a more insidious pattern than open rebellion. The compliant client is agreeable, pleasant, and seemingly cooperative. In in-house hospital programs, he is usually "model patient" on the ward, quick to agree with virtually anything treatment staff suggests or recommends.

Unfortunately, compliance is not the same thing as the *inner belief and attitude change* necessary for sobriety to be achieved and maintained. The compliant alcoholic client is the patient who, after arousing great expectations in his therapist, will promptly shatter these by getting drunk on the day he leaves the hospital.

In working with either rebellious or compliant clients, the therapist should adhere to the following central principle: *Employ the least amount of external therapeutic force necessary to achieve belief and attitude change.*

I refer to this principle as the *principle of least justification.* It recognizes that the ultimate goal of alcoholism psychotherapy is a self-governing human being with strong inner convictions and controls. If too much external control is applied during treatment, then the source of sobriety is seen as external and the justification for its continuance remains *outside* the client.

Derivations from the principle of least justification make it clear why strong confrontation tactics are questionable in alcoholism psychotherapy. In the case of the rebellious alcoholic, such forceful therapeutic tactics give the client exactly what he is seeking: an external agent as the locus of control and sobriety against whom he can continue to react.

In the case of the compliant alcoholic, strong confrontation tactics will simply yield more compliance. In the presence of the therapist and in the context of the treatment situation, the compliant alcoholic will appear obedient. But once these external constraints are removed, the compliant alcoholic will drink.

Whatever the therapeutic tactics, it is clear that neither rebellion nor mindless compliance is the desired goal of alcoholism psychotherapy. Surrender to the facts of the alcoholism and acceptance of them are the desired alternatives. These are the keys to a long-term, contented sobriety.

ACTING-OUT VERSUS REPRESSION

Impulse control and expression of feelings are particularly troublesome for the alcoholic. When drinking, his behavior is likely to be unpredictable, spontaneous, and impulsive. Moreover, at that time his feelings are close to the surface and easily aroused. Anger, affection, sorrow, self-pity, depression, aggressiveness, sexuality, and so forth are readily evoked in the drinking alcoholic.

But when he stops drinking, this picture of poor impulse control and hyperemotionality changes radically. When abstinent, the "dry" alcoholic swings to the opposite extreme. He shows rigid defenses, tight control over his impulses, flat emotionality, and compulsivity rather than spontaneity. Moreover, he usually resists therapeutic efforts designed to open up areas of feeling.

The fact that the "dry" alcoholic clings to repressive adaptive tactics is not surprising. He has been out of control, not only in his drinking, but usually in his social behavior as well. As a consequence, therapeutic techniques that require the "dry" alcoholic to give up control even temporarily are often difficult to employ. The alcoholic is likely to resist these. In the early stages of abstinence, the recalled images of prior loss of control are too vivid, disgusting, and terrifying for the alcoholic to relax his grip upon himself. Incapable of "letting go," he is likely to keep a tight rein on feelings, actions, and attitudes. Early on in treatment, the therapist should respect these rigid boundaries in his client and not try to breach them prematurely.

Although there are clear advantages in easy-going and moderate therapeutic tactics in the early stages of abstinence, in the long run the recovering alcoholic should be helped to get in touch with his feelings. He must learn to have feelings when *sober*, not only when drinking. The trick, of course, is to help him to realize that simply *because he has feelings and impulses, he need not act them out.*

Neither uncontrolled acting-out nor repression is the desired goal of alcoholism psychotherapy. Rather, the client should be helped to see that awareness and acceptance of feelings and impulses will enrich a sober life, not diminish it.

In dealing with feelings and impulses, however, the therapist is advised to move cautiously, with great care, perceptiveness, and sensitivity. Timing is all-important and the therapist who must have dramatic release of feelings and explosive acting-out of impulses early in the treatment process might better seek these high-intensity experiences with nonalcoholics in group-encounter settings.

Obsession with the Past versus Refusal to Consider It

If permitted by the therapist, some alcoholics will ruminate endlessly over the past and report its happenings in great detail. In group-therapy settings, this form of alcoholic behavior tends to drive other clients to distraction. In handling this type of client, the therapist must gently but firmly insist that he focus on the present.

On the other hand, therapists will encounter the opposite: clients who refuse to talk about their pasts at all. Refusal to consider the past is as dangerous for the alcoholic as wallowing in it. As the saying goes "the man who dwells in the past will lose one eye, but the man who forgets his past will lose both eyes."

The desired alternative here involves the learning of several important attitudes. First, the alcoholic must come to accept his past *precisely as it happened.* It will not do for him to engage in retrospective rationalization, nor in distortion or minimization of the facts.

Second, the recovering alcoholic must *own* his past. It is his and not anybody else's. Assigning blame to others for all that happened simply will not do.

Third, the alcoholic client must come to see that his past, faced honestly and squarely, is his most valuable tool in helping himself and others. The past is there to be learned from, not shoved aside so that the same disastrous mistakes can be repeated over and over. In helping the alcoholic client come to terms with his past, it is useful to remember Albert Ellis' thought: "It is not so much what has happened to a person that is important, but what a person tells himself about what has happened." Obviously alcoholic clients can tell themselves many different things about their pasts. Some of these accounts can be helpful. Others can be hazardous. Part of the therapist's task is to help the client choose those constructions of the past that hold the greatest promise for a future of sober, contented living.

Fourth, the recovering alcoholic must accept the likelihood that past events may continue to affect his present life situation. In some cases, the effects of prior active alcoholism may be long delayed. Marriages may fail, jobs may be lost, and health problems may develop even years after the drinking has ceased.

The therapist can be an invaluable aid in helping his client see that events once set in motion may have to proceed to their natural conclusions. The recovering alcoholic may not like these delayed costs of his prior drinking. He may rail bitterly against the injustice of it all, especially since he has been sober for several years or more. While the recovering alcoholic has every right not to like such delayed costs, he must nevertheless learn to accept them.

It is clear that neither obsession with the past nor refusal to acknowledge it is the correct attitude or behavior for the recovering alcoholic. An informed therapist will see that his client learns appropriate alternatives. But as with all things in alcoholic therapy, such learnings take time. The therapist should not permit his client to rush headlong into a detailed examination of his past mistakes. Rather, he will encourage a pattern of gradual realization and deepening acceptance.

INDISCRIMINATE DEPENDENCY
VERSUS STUBBORN INDEPENDENCE

In discussing interpersonal dependency, we usually pose the question in terms of whether or not one should be "dependent" or "independent." But since human lives are necessarily intertwined in complex ways, it is misleading to cast the issue in these terms. We are all dependent upon one another in varying degrees. The important questions that rarely get asked are as follows:

1. Upon *whom* should I be dependent?
2. For *what*?
3. At what *costs*?

Indiscriminate dependency on others *or* a stubborn, self-defeating pattern of independence is commonly encountered among both drinking and abstinent alcoholics. Neither pattern is appropriate.

In the case of indiscriminate dependency, the alcoholic client is remarkably adept at attracting people who are all wrong for him. Hoping to satisfy love, affectional, sexual, and friendship needs, he very often ends up in destructive relationships with people who are "toxic" for him. The pain and misery of such relationships can take the recovering alcoholic back to drinking more readily than any single, traumatic event.

Not only must the recovering alcoholic develop a discriminating attitude in his basic love relationships, but he must also come to see that a certain degree of selectivity is indispensable in all of his interpersonal and social relationships. Since we must all depend to some degree upon others for *information* about ourselves, others, and events in which we are involved, we must exercise judgment in seeking advice and counsel from others. Too often, drinking and recovering alcoholics seek out others whose perceptions and constructions of reality are even more distorted than their own. Even in therapeutic communities such as Alcoholic Anonymous, a recovering alcoholic can manage to find somebody who will tell him precisely what he needs to hear in order to hold on to attitudes, beliefs, and actions harmful to himself and others.

While indiscriminate dependency is likely to complicate the alcoholic's life further, the answer does not lie in stubborn independence.

People need people. And in the case of the alcoholic, the need is even more intense. For too many alcoholics, the belief that they could solve their problem by themselves has led them from one drinking disaster to another. While there surely is some small number of alcoholics who were successful in stopping drinking by themselves, for the majority this has not been possible.

The development of discriminating dependency upon others is the proper therapeutic course with regard to this particular Scylla and Charybdis. The alcoholic client must learn that in social relationships generally, *discriminating trust* is in order. He need not practice general mistrust of others, nor must he avoid relationships of all kinds. The point is that in relationships that really matter to him, he must be clear about the person in whom he places his trust, the things he expects from the relationship, and the costs he may be paying for whatever it is he receives.

COMPULSIVE SOCIALIZING VERSUS ALIENATION

Closely related to the issue of dependency is the issue of compulsive socializing versus alienation. Therapists working with alcoholics must be aware that while alienation is a clearly undesirable alternative, the development of compulsive socializing is to be avoided as well. Certainly the recovering alcoholic should attend group-therapy sessions and meetings of Alcoholics Anonymous. But as sobriety lengthens, the therapist should not continue to encourage excessive dependency upon himself, treatment centers, clinics, or other groups. Although the recovering alcoholic will continue to need therapeutic contacts for many years, these should not become the totality of his existence. The goal of rehabilitation should be a normal life—one in which the concerns of family, friendships, work, play, and continuing recovery activities should be in balance.

Just as the alienated alcoholic needs to reach out more to others, the compulsively social alcoholic needs to learn to be *alone* without feeling *lonely*. He needs to learn how to use small amounts of anxiety and discomfort as stimuli for further growth rather than rushing off after immediate relief from these in the warm bath of group support and security. In the early stages of abstinence, it is correct for the therapist to encourage the uncomfortable client to use the telephone or get to an AA meeting. But in later stages, some of this anxiety should be capitalized upon as motivation for deeper self-exploration and further changes in attitudes, beliefs, and actions.

Precisely because it works so well in reducing felt discomfort, group affiliation takes on the properties of a powerful reinforcer. And, as experience has shown, it is a reinforcer that many alcoholics cannot do without if sobriety is to be achieved and maintained. But like many good things in life, group affiliation can become excessive and, in time, detrimental to the total pattern of growth of the person. While a degree of compulsivity in meeting attendance is important in the first one to five years of sobriety, these activities should not preclude a balanced life in later years. *Choice,* not compulsion, should be the ultimate goal of long-term treatment of the recovering alcoholic.

Pain and discomfort are indeed dangerous triggers for drinking early in sobriety, but we must not forget that they are also the necessary motivating conditions for deep inner changes. Therapists who persist in assuming responsibility for their client's feelings of well-being as treatment progresses are making a fundamental error. The recovering alcoholic must learn to "sit still and hurt" when it is necessary to do so. In the long run, he must learn that only he can do something about his inner emotional and spiritual condition.

PERFECTIONISM VERSUS INFERIORITY

Alcoholics are often snared on one of the extremes of perfectionism or inferiority. In some cases, the same individual can fluctuate back and forth between the two. In perfectionism, the client can make himself miserable by trying to do the impossible. Mistakes of any kind are to be avoided at any cost, dress and grooming must be impeccable, performance consistently superior, and behavior beyond reproach. Nobody could possibly sustain such unrealistically high standards, but the perfectionistic alcoholic client will try. Moreover, he is likely to make everybody else miserable by forcing, either explicitly or implicitly, his unreasonable expectations on those around him.

The dynamics of striving after perfection in the recovering alcoholic are readily apparent. This pattern stems directly from the client's low self-esteem, poor self-regard, and self-doubting. A thoroughgoing perfectionism is often the alcoholic's way of coping with these negative self-perceptions and attitudes. Since even one imperfection or mistake is likely to arouse the underlying self-dislike, the alcoholic strives to avoid any at all.

Such all-or-none judgmental attitudes toward self are self-defeating. The perfectionistic alcoholic either grits his teeth and bears up under a tight, nervous, harassed sobriety or returns to drinking. Once drinking, his previous pattern of perfectionism swings back and forth between frank expressions of inferiority, self-doubting, and self-hatred on the one hand and grandiosity on the other.

Grandiosity, a commonly encountered phenomenon among drinking alcoholics, is but a variant of striving after perfection. Its dynamics are also to be understood in terms of low self-esteem. If the alcoholic feels that his inner person is a "small" human being, then the outer person is likely to be portrayed as a "big" one.

If the Scylla of perfectionism and the Charybdis of inferiority are to be avoided, then the therapist must steer a steady course toward a differentiated, realistic self-image in his client. The client's strengths and weaknesses must be explored honestly and realistically. He must be counseled to see that self-acceptance and positive self-regard are not only possible in the presence of self-imperfections, but highly desirable. Moreover, the unrealistic nature of his all-or-none thinking about self and its negative consequences must be made clear.

Perhaps most important, the therapist should facilitate the view that personal shortcomings are either problems capable of solution *or* unchangeable conditions that must be *accepted*. It simply will not do to permit the client to try to maintain the impossible fiction that he is "perfect." Nor will it do to allow him to hate himself.

But neither can the therapist permit his client to "cop out" with the rationalization that whatever he does is acceptable simply because he is a recovering alcoholic! A convenient fiction like that one may be in order in the very early stages of abstinence, but in the long run, if sobriety is to be maintained, such childish personal and social attitudes must yield to more mature and responsible ones. Maturity, whatever else it may mean, is knowing the price of things—not only the prices one must pay for one's own actions, but those that *others* must pay for them as well.

SELF-OBSESSION VERSUS OBSESSION WITH OTHERS

Throughout years of alcoholic drinking, alcoholics tend to become highly self-centered. *Self-centeredness* as used here does not mean *selfishness*. Alcoholics can be very generous people but still be highly self-centered. Self-centeredness in this sense refers to the alcoholic's highly subjective perceptions and his tendency to focus his attention back upon himself.

Self-centeredness can lead quite naturally to obsession with self. When this happens, the alcoholic can make himself miserable by ruminating over his past and present life situations. Minor problems are blown up and out of proportion and transformed into seemingly insoluble difficulties. Worry, anxiety, impatience, depression, agitation, and intolerable frustration are the unfortunate outcomes of obsession with self.

Counselors who understand the alcoholic obsession with self will rightly encourage the client to stop being so concerned with self by placing his attention on another person. The alcoholic is often advised to try to help others if only as a form of therapy for himself. But, while the alcoholic should be encouraged to shift his attention from self to others at certain points in the recovery process, therapists should be aware that this practice can lead dangerously close to the Charybdis of obsession with others to the neglect of self.

It is not uncommon to find recovering alcoholics who have become so obsessed with others that they seem to have lost any sense of self-hood and an individuated identity. Recovering alcoholics who work professionally in the field are particularly vulnerable to the dangers of losing self in the demands of helping others, as are active AA sponsors who overextend themselves by agreeing to work with far too many newcomers to their program.

The way out of this particular dilemma is for the therapist and his client to keep in mind that the solution is not an either/or one. Neither obsession with self nor obsession with others is the goal of treatment. While each extreme is tactically useful at various points in recovery, the therapist should help his client to achieve a balance between his own needs and those of others. This requires teaching the client the difficult skill of holding both his own point of view and that of others in mind simultaneously.

It is unfortunate that many have misconstrued the nature of the concept of therapeutic community. Individual uniqueness need not be sacrificed so that community may be achieved. Identification with others does not require one to give up precious aspects of self not shared with others. In fact, a true therapeutic community does not stamp out individuality but encourages and enhances it by providing the necessary social-emotional support for its growth. A stable, clear, and strong self-identity firmly grounded in community is the ideal outcome in alcoholism therapy.

PESSIMIST VERSUS POLLYANNA

Alcoholics will often show extreme expectations. Some tend to focus upon adverse aspects, conditions, and possibilities or to expect the worst possible outcome. Others swing the other way, adopting an irrepressible optimism that can only be shored up with massive denial. In fact, the "denial high" or "pink cloud" is routinely found among alcoholics in early stages of recovery.

Extreme expectations of either kind—pessimistic or optimistic—

should not be encouraged by the therapist. Unrealistically high expectations lead inevitably to the frustration of disconfirmation. And the pain of frustration can lead to drinking. It is even possible that some alcoholics will deliberately choose high levels of expectation so that failure may be insured and a subsequent return to drinking justified.

Recovering alcoholics should be counseled to face life realistically, not in terms of highly improbable outcomes. Neither the Scylla of cynicism and pessimism nor the Charybdis of irrepressible optimism is the long-term desired goal in alcoholism therapy.

SUMMARY

Alcoholism psychotherapy is frequently undertaken and evaluated without a clear sense of the critical issues involved. Treatment programs are developed and launched with only the vaguest notions about "helping the alcoholic," trying some "behavioral therapy," using didactic lectures, transactional analysis, psychodrama, and so on and so forth. This is all rather like putting the cart before the horse.

Theories of treatment should proceed from a clear understanding of the nature of the alcoholic client, his characteristics, the dilemmas he faces, and the choices he has to make.

This chapter has attempted to provide a systematic view of psychotherapy with the alcoholic by exposing the critical issues. It has argued for a theory of psychotherapy that consists of a number of strategic choices. Moreover, it has shown that these choices during the long recovery from alcoholism must be made in the presence of multiple Scyllas and Charybdises—multiple hazardous alternatives. In each case, not only have I identified the hidden dangers at each choice-point, but I have also tried to indicate the most reasonable compromise. I hope this analysis of the critical issues involved in treating alcoholics will be of assistance in the invention of methods and techniques *specific* to the disease of alcoholism.

REFERENCES

Wallace, J. Alcoholism: Is a shift in paradigm necessary? *Journal of Psychiatric Treatment and Evaluation*, December, 1983.

Behavioral Modification Methods as Adjuncts to Psychotherapy

INTRODUCTION

Behavioral modification methods are a collection of techniques useful in attempting to change behavior directly without reference to assumed underlying motivational factors. For the most part, these methods have their roots in modern theories of learning. However, they can be used effectively despite one's theoretical or ideological persuasion. They are not tied exclusively to a simplistic, learned behavior model of alcoholism that excludes biological factors, nor are their uses restricted to efforts to teach alcoholics how to control their drinking. Behavioral methods can be used in helping alcoholics to achieve initial abstention from alcohol and an eventual self-fulfilling sobriety.

In this chapter I will discuss the relevance of the behavioral modification tradition for psychotherapy of alcoholism. Along with accepted methods, I will discuss techniques of my own invention that have evolved directly from the practical business of alcoholism treatment. Total behavioral treatment approaches, such as aversion therapy, are not considered.

For many alcoholics, drinking is a greatly overlearned behavior. It is associated with many physical and social cues or stimuli. As a consequence, the *initiation* of drinking is under widespread external stimulus control. Drinking can begin in numerous situations in which the alcoholic has no conscious intention of drinking and, on occasion, cannot even remember when he actually started. Generalized habit-pattern-disruption techniques are designed to increase the alcoholic's awareness of situational determinants of his drinking and other behaviors.

Practicing the Opposite. In this method the alcoholic patient is directed to reverse the order and nature of his typical activities. He is asked to shave first in the morning if he had previously showered first and then shaved. He is instructed to leave and enter his bed from the right side if his typical pattern was to do so from the left. He is encouraged to perform simple activities like teeth brushing with his left hand rather than his right.

In general, the focus in this method is to concentrate upon simple, usual activities rather than the more complex ones. Its purpose is to stimulate awareness of habitual ways of approaching and responding to typical situations. It is designed to promote the general outlook that the patient is actively and purposively engaged in changing his life. It also serves as an aid to emerging discriminations in the patient with regard to old ways of doing things and new ways.

Substitute Activities. The patient is encouraged to seek out alternative activities that do not involve drinking or drinking environments. If there was an identifiable temporal pattern to the patient's drinking, substitute activities are devised for these time periods. For example, a female patient sober for several months could not understand why she continued to feel agitated, anxious, and depressed. A careful analysis of her prior drinking revealed that her drinking usually began on Friday afternoons and continued on into the weekend. A further analysis revealed that her negative feelings in sobriety usually centered around Fridays and weekends. She was counseled to develop a schedule of enjoyable activities that did not involve drinking starting at Friday afternoon and carrying on through the weekend. After following this temporal rearrangement of her typical activities, she reported positive changes in mood, tension level, and general outlook.

Disruption of Typical Social Activities and Relationships. Because of the potency of previous social situations and relationships to perpetuate drinking, efforts are made to restructure the patient's social behaviors. He is counseled to stay away from old drinking situations and old drinking "buddies." Bars, poolrooms, night clubs, taverns, homes of friends who continue to drink heavily or alcoholically, and other such situations are to be avoided. For the alcoholic who drank "on the street," activities that place him in support systems that do not involve heavy drinking are located. Alcoholics will often resist such suggestions. They will try to remain sober while continuing to associate with actively alcoholic or heavily drinking friends. In some cases they will try to hang out in old drinking haunts, drinking soft drinks rather than beer, wine, or liquor. In most instances these continued associations with persons and places from the alcoholic past eventuate in a return to dangerous drinking.

Following the Drunk Through. Alcoholics rarely consider the likely negative consequences when initiating a given drinking episode. When I question patients as to what they had been thinking about when they decided to drink, various answers are forthcoming. Many patients say, "Nothing, I just wanted to drink." Others answer that they "wanted to get comfortable." "I wanted to get a glow on," is a common response along with "I wanted to get a little high."

Following the drunk through is a technique in which the delayed negative consequences of drinking are imagined along with the initial positive ones. Typically, I ask the patient to imagine himself in his own movie. I ask him to imagine vividly the entire drinking episode in terms of its serial progression from initial drinking to the finish. At each stage of the exercise, the patient is asked to pay close attention to his feelings.

This technique is similar but not identical to the formal behavioral modification procedure known as *covert sensitization* (Cautela, 1966). Covert sensitization is an attempt to condition imagined aversive stimuli to an imagined situation in which drinking might commence. Following the drunk through is not a conditioning procedure; it is an attempt to give the alcoholic a conceptual tool through which he can simulate the likely temporal arrangement of events and consequences of drinking. It is, in effect, an attentional-shifting device, one that forces the alcoholic beyond the initial positive expectations to awareness of delayed negative consequences. In this sense, the exercise is an attempt to disrupt the temporal sequencing of cognitive and behavioral events.

Attendance at Meetings of Alcoholics Anonymous. Efforts should be made to have the patient at least try out AA on an experimental basis. Patients should never be forced directly into such matters, but the therapist should be willing and able to counter usual misconceptions, prejudices, and distortions of fact about AA. Attendance at AA meetings is, in effect, a behavioral change in the life of the alcoholic of significant proportions. Going to such meetings alters his typical schedule of activities, enables him to make new friendships, exposes him to a host of social supports and reinforcements, and permits him to gather information about other alcoholics and the disease of alcoholism very directly. In many respects AA itself is a behavioral change program in that it advocates practical methods of achieving and maintaining sobriety in the context of a community social-support network. *Positive reinforcement* (social recognition and status for staying sober), *social modeling* (the accessibility of role models and their behaviors for learning how to stay sober), *desensitization* (anxiety and guilt reduction through sharing of common experience, laughter and general merriment over past alcoholic behaviors, and a general atmosphere of social acceptance), and *cognitive behavioral change* (cognitive restructuring of self, behavior, and alcoholism) are aspects of AA that are most congruent with modern versions of behavior therapy.

DISCRIMINATING SOBER VERSUS ALCOHOLIC BEHAVIORS

Research has not generally supported the notion that an "alcoholic personality" exists and predates the onset of active alcoholism. Whether such a personality exists in isolation from the alcoholic experience itself is probably unknowable. It is more fruitful to think of the many commonalities apparent among alcoholics as *common outcomes* of alcoholism rather than as antecedent conditions. Along with sharing commonalities with other alcoholics in terms of outcomes, each alcoholic may also be seen as possessing unique responses to the disease and the particular form it has taken in his own life. It is useful in psychotherapy with the alcoholic to focus on both common and unique outcomes of alcoholism in terms of a collection of attitudes, feelings, beliefs, and behaviors that must be discriminated and contrasted with some alternative collection. In this sense, then, it is useful to talk about a drinking personality and a sober one. Techniques for sharpening this discrimination are important tools in the psychotherapist's repertoire of change methods.

Writing a Behavioral Inventory of Drinking. The simple act of helping the patient to write a behavioral inventory of his drinking is an effective means of sharpening the discrimination between alcoholic behaviors and sober ones. The patient is instructed to begin with his first remembered drinking episode, to write down exactly the circumstances and his actions, and to list the overt consequences. In this inventory no attempt is made to establish motivations for drinking or to gain insights into reasons for drinking. The writing is purely behavioral in the sense that it focuses entirely on situations, actions, and consequences. It is usual to proceed forward in time either in single years or blocks of years covering significant drinking episodes and periods from the beginning of the drinking up until the present. In the group context the therapist can use the patient as informant and write down the more significant details of the drinking history on a chalkboard so that these may be shared with all group members. In the group setting the behavioral inventory of drinking can be a dramatic technique, one loaded with sudden awarenesses and feelings. In a sense it is similar to the behavioral technique known as *flooding,* in which the patient is confronted with a rather massive stimulus configuration concerning a feared object, a lost loved one, or an anxiety-provoking situation. Many alcoholics have never viewed their drinking histories as a whole, but rather as fragmented and partial recollections. When confronted with the massive facts of their past behaviors, they are often visibly startled and provoked to new levels of awareness. And in the group setting this reaction is intensified. Of course the decision to utilize this technique in the group setting is dependent upon a number of factors—the patient's ego strength, trust in other group members, levels of guilt and anxiety, and so forth.

In addition to aiding discrimination between the alcoholic person and the sober one, this technique fosters an important temporal distinction. The patient is invited to consider his *past* and to differentiate it from his *present.* In a sense the behavioral inventory of drinking is one way for the patient to "punctuate" his life—to place a period or marker at a given point and to separate this from the present and the possibility of an alternative future. The idealized self-image or sober personality is seen as an open-ended and permeable self-construct capable of growth and change over time.

Cognitive Behavioral Sharpening. In this technique the patient is invited to have a conversation with himself. It is particularly effective in the group setting and is in fact a method I have derived from Gestalt group therapy (Perls, 1969).

The patient is given his choice of which of two chairs to sit in to begin the exercise. After choosing he is asked to announce which of his persons—the sober one or the alcoholic one—is seated in that particular chair. He is then asked to consider the other chair as containing his other person and then told to begin a conversation with the hypothetical other. In my experience patients rarely refuse the exercise and enter into it willingly. I am careful to keep reminding the patient of the distinction that is represented by the spatial separation of the chairs. I say such things as "O.K., the sober you is sitting in this chair, the other you is over there."

The patient is asked for a description of the sober person. After he has given this, he is asked to move across the space and to seat himself in the other chair. Once he is there, I ask, "Who is in this chair?" I then ask the patient to describe the drinking person. I then instruct the patient to return to the original chair, and again I remind him of who is in the first chair. Often the reminder is in the form of a question: "Now who is in this chair?" I ask the patient to talk to the other person, the hypothetical drinking person, with regard to such things as intentions, plans, wants, wishes, and aspirations. The situation is then reversed and the patient talks from the perspective of the drinking person to the hypothetical sober one. The patient is encouraged to continue his conversation, moving back and forth between the chairs throughout the exercise.

The purpose of this exercise is to sharpen and clarify the inner conflict commonly encountered in patients early in their recovery. The patient quickly realizes that he wants both to drink and to stay sober and, moreover, he is a mass of other contradictory impulses, attitudes, feelings, goals, intentions, and beliefs. The exercise provides the structure in which the patient can freely verbalize these contradictory response tendencies.

This exercise also reveals the clarity and strength of the patient's discrimination between his alcoholic person and his sober one. While the patient is encouraged to *own* both collections of behaviors, he is also encouraged to maintain a sharp, clear distinction between two different response repertoires, life styles, and modes of being in the world. In my experience a patient capable of doing this is taking a necessary though not sufficient first step toward continued sobriety. Patients who show great confusion and are unable to maintain the simple cognitive-spatial distinctions demanded have not yet achieved the identity separation necessary.

Naming the Alcoholic Person. A simple but often effective technique is to invite group members to name their alcoholic person. Patients by and large take to this activity with enthusiasm and quite a bit of fun. The names that they give their drinking personalities are informative. A proper, elderly female alcoholic who drank mostly at home labeled her alcoholic person "Honey West." "Big Slick," "Tarzan," "Don Juan," "F. Scott Fitzgerald," "Crazy Horse," "Pug Nacious," and "Lonely Sam" are some of the names I have collected from alcoholics to describe their drinking persons. These of course reflect the self-perceptions of the drinking alcoholics. Aside from diagnostic interest, this naming process can be used effectively as a further technique to sharpen sober-drinking distinctions.

In a group context, once all members have named their drinking personas and shared these with the group, I divide them into pairs. Each member of the pair interviews the other's drinking persona and explores the meanings behind the name. Finally, each member of the pair reports back to the group the things he has discovered about the other's drinking persona. This leads to a general sharing of present feelings and perceptions of various members by the entire group and the manner in which these present perceptions contrast with the material from the interviews.

RESOLVING THE ALCOHOLIC IDENTITY CRISIS

Very often alcoholic people enter therapy with a serious crisis of identity. This identity confusion is the result of the repeated assault of intoxicated thoughts, feelings, and actions upon the primary or sober personality. The alcoholic is often in a painful state of cognitive dissonance, a predictable outcome of repeated circumstances wherein private, cherished *beliefs* about self are contradicted by public intoxicated *actions*. Techniques to resolve such problems of identity are available.

Fixed-Role Therapy. A technique that I have found useful is one that I have derived from George Kelley's invention (1955), fixed-role therapy. I have found it particularly useful in broadening the patient's behavioral repertoire, inventing sets of complex role performances, and salvaging valuable and positive aspects of the drinking personality that might otherwise be suppressed, devalued, or discarded completely. It is particularly valuable in cases in which the patient construes the drinking personality in totally negative terms and the sober one in impossibly perfect and positive terms. One alcoholic female with whom I worked, for example, persisted in construing her drinking personality as a "whore" and her sober one as a "nun." The tensions generated by this obviously unworkable self-construction contributed to relapse after relapse. A description of this case may illustrate fixed-role therapy.

In the group context I asked the patient to describe her dichotomized self-construction. Her drinking person was described as promiscuous, lively, selfish, exciting, sexy, witty, fun-loving, happy-go-lucky, and devil-may-care. Her sober self was described as dull, boring, plodding, serious, responsible, frigid, thoughtful, caring, religious, and guilt-ridden. With the help of feedback from group members, the patient came to see that her drinking personality contained many positive qualities, while her sober personality as she had constructed the role showed many negative ones.

She was asked to consider a *third* complex set of role constructs and behaviors for herself that combined the best of both possible identities. With the help of group members, the patient constructed a new role identity for herself. During the next week, she consciously tried to act out the role in her social interactions. This *behavioral enactment* led to *feedback* in the real world, which was then considered in group therapy again. The patient, other group members, and the therapist discussed *role fit*—the extent to which the patient felt capable of enactment of the original prescribed role. The results of this scrutiny of role fit led to *role modification* in which the possible behaviors from the original role were retained and the impossible or difficult modified. Armed with a new set of behaviors and supporting self-cognitions, the patient again tried a period of behavioral enactment in the real world with resulting feedback. Once again role fit and role modification were discussed in group and further modifications were developed.

Fixed-role therapy, then, can be seen as a process in which ideal role constructs and behaviors are discovered and then tested in continuous cycles of behavioral enactment, feedback, appraisal of role fit, and role modification.

Positive Reinforcement of Sober Actions, Attitudes, and Values. From a behavioral perspective, it is entirely legitimate for the therapist to reinforce patterns of behavior, attitudes, and values consistent with sobriety. Care must of course be exercised here since such therapist behaviors could be construed by the patient as manipulative, patronizing, controlling, and possibly even demeaning. Social reinforcements, however, are not only a matter of specific utterances, phrases, or other tangible behaviors and material goods; they are also defined by the manner in which they are administered in the larger context of symbolic meanings that grow out of the interaction. I usually genuinely share in the patient's amazement and delight in his newfound ability to stay sober. When he reports specific decisions reached or situations handled sober, I ask him to consider how he might have handled these while drinking. I then ask him to consider what these sober experiences tell him about who he really is, what he is really like, and what he seems to want out of life after all. All of these occasions are used to support the patient's growing self-identity as a competent, responsible, and *sober* person.

In the beginning of therapy, I support *any* self-categorizations by the patient that realistically appraise his problems with alcohol. "Problem-drinker," "in trouble with alcohol," "potential alcoholic," and "possible alcoholic" are typical labels that patients apply to self. I invite the patient to explore more deeply these self-categorizations and the implications of each. In the majority of successful therapies, the patient does eventually arrive at a self-categorization of "alcoholic." Some authorities regard this labeling process as relatively unimportant, while others think it possibly destructive to the patient's progress. Although at the tactical level I do not make an issue of how the patient labels himself, I do not regard the process or the substance of labeling of self an "alcoholic" as unimportant or countertherapeutic. Construing self as "alcoholic" is an important new identity for the patient, one that will enable him to reconstruct his past along different conceptual lines, reexamine his present, and plan his future actions accordingly. In some patients the role identity of "sober alcoholic" is all that they have to cling to in lives beset by unbelievable complexity, devoid of opportunity, and surrounded on all sides by the wreckage of the past. It is, in fact, the only thing that gives meaning to the past, makes the present bearable, and promises hope for the future.

When self-categorizations as "alcoholic" begin to appear in the patient, I support, encourage, and elaborate these in terms of what they represent—an emergent, new, and in some cases exciting self-identity with terribly important implications for the immediate and future well-being of the person.

In some treatment centers and AA groups, material reinforcers are formally distributed at various stages of sobriety. Certificates, tokens of various colors coded to indicate months of sobriety achieved, pins, rings, and other such items are awarded. While I have no idea of the effectiveness of such devices, I have observed them to be meaningful to some patients, who seem to require tangible and fairly immediate indications of progress. Other patients, however, regard such things as trivial in their recovery programs. Still other patients appear to avoid them altogether.

Reinforcement procedures have been used successfully by Hunt and Azrin (1973) and Pickens (1979).

METHODS FOR ACHIEVING RELAXATION

Patients often complain of difficulty in achieving a relaxed state in sobriety. Tension, anxiety, and insomnia are commonly encountered. Methods for dealing with these are available.

Progressive Relaxation. Techniques for deep muscle relaxation derived from work by Jacobson (1974) are of some use for certain alcoholics. In this approach, relaxation is viewed as a response and the skills associated with it trainable. Basic to this approach is the learning of a discrimination between a state of muscle tension and a state of tension. For example, the patient is first instructed to clench his fist, hold it, and feel the tension that results. He is then instructed to suddenly release the tension and note the bodily cues and sensations associated with relaxation. Various muscle groups of the body are progressively tensed and relaxed and the associated cues discriminated. The patient's breathing is also manipulated through a series of commands to inhale, hold the breath, and then exhale slowly. The breathing exercises are also an aid to the learning of the discrimination between states of tension and relaxation. Through a systematic application of these procedures, the patient learns to bring the relaxation response under self-control. A complete description of progressive relaxation therapy is beyond the scope of this chapter. Fortunately, however, a variety of taped programs suitable for both clinic and home practice are available from commercial sources (Procter, 1975).

In my experience with systematic relaxation programs with alcoholic patients, I have had mixed results. Progressive relaxation requires discipline, determination, and home practice in between clinical sessions. While these methods are often greeted with an initial burst of enthusiasm, many patients quickly find them boring and uninteresting. More seriously, a large number will not sustain practice outside the clinical setting.

Biofeedback Techniques. A variety of biofeedback devices is now available for use with alcoholic patients. As with many novel treatments, fairly extraordinary claims accompanied the early introduction of these techniques (Birk, 1973). Mushrooming enthusiasm for these devices seemed at times to suggest a popular fad rather than considered scientific judgment. Despite the application of biofeedback techniques to a wide variety of disorders and clinical evidence for their effectiveness, controlled, large-sample research is lacking. What evidence we do have suggests some optimism and some pessimism. Sterman's (1973) research on *sensory-motor rhythm* (a 12–15 Hz rhythm recorded from sensory-motor cortical areas) is a model of rigorous research. His findings indicate that biofeedback control of rhythm can dramatically reduce seizures in patients previously uncontrolled by even extreme medication regimens.

Schwartz and Shapiro's (1973) studies of biofeedback control of essential hypertension indicate caution but some promise as well. Paradoxical results have been reported in the long-term application of finger temperature control of the treatment of migraine. Excellent results have been reported with regard to EMG (electromyograph) feedback for generalized muscle relaxation and control of tension headaches.

With regard to alcoholism *per se,* the research literature on biofeedback techniques is suggestive of promise but not definitive. Studies have been largely anecdotal, very-small-sample experimental research, or methodologically problematic. In one study by Steffen (1975), a small number of alcoholic subjects did show reduced muscle action potentials following EMG therapy, but did not differ in number of drinks ordered after treatments. Studies on alpha rhythm (8–12 Hz rhythm recorded from dominant occipital area) by Passini, Watson, Dehnel, Herder, and Watkins (1977) suggest that biofeedback control of alpha production may reduce certain kinds of anxiety while leaving others unaffected.

In my experience with selected alcoholic patients, I have found EMG feedback to be an effective procedure for training muscle relaxation. My clinical work with the EMG was confined to an inpatient 21-day treatment-program context. Under these conditions, regular sessions could be scheduled and carried out. Training always began with electrode placement on the frontalis muscle and was then generalized to other locations. In some instances I used the technique simply as a dramatic illustration to a patient that he could in fact, relax without resorting to alcohol or other chemicals. In others I used the procedure as a part of a therapeutic interview in which biofeedback data were introduced to counter the patient's continued denial of affect-laden material. In still other cases I systematically taught the patient the skills of relaxation. On one occasion, with a patient who complained that he could not fall asleep under any circumstances, I employed the following procedure:

I put the patient to bed in his room, covered him with a blanket, and hooked him up to the EMG with electrode placement on the frontalis. I explained the nature of the feedback signals and what they meant, set the feedback signal volume control low, and left the room. I returned 20 minutes later to find the patient asleep! I promptly woke him up and asked him to explain the meaning of his behavior. He was clearly astonished that he had fallen asleep so easily and that he had done so without alcohol or sleeping medications. This incident not only changed the way in which he construed his insomnia problem but also led to a high level of motivation to pursue a systematic training program of EMG therapy. Moreover, this experience increased the patient's motivation in other treatment modalities as well.

While my experiences with EMG biofeedback training were generally positive, I found alpha training of limited value. In the context of a 21-day, multimodal inpatient treatment program, alpha training proved too complex a procedure. Moreover, despite early enthusiasm, patients seemed to tire quickly of the disciplined attention required. Finally, a number of my patients seemed to show appreciable baseline alpha production *prior* to treatment. In these cases *magnitude* rather than frequency seemed to be the problem since low-magnitude 8–12 Hz waves were noted in the records. The research literature is inconsistent on this point, with some investigators reporting a preponderance of beta activity (fast waves) in alcoholics while others report no differences between alcoholics and nonalcoholics in baseline alpha production. Still others report slight differences but very large overlap between distributions for alcoholics versus nonalcoholics.

Despite inconsistent findings, biofeedback devices are clearly worthy of continued investigation in alcoholism therapy. Control of sensory-motor rhythm might prove of value in dealing with seizures during withdrawal as well as chronic seizure disorders in recovered alcoholics. As is well documented, the incidence of hypertension is higher among alcoholics than among nonalcoholics (Klatsky, Friedman, Abraham, Siegelaub, and Gerard, 1977). This chronic hypertension must of course be differentiated from the transient elevation of blood pressure routinely noted in many alcoholics in the early stages of withdrawal and treatment. Biofeedback procedures involving blood-pressure control are certainly worthy of further investigation in alcoholism therapy. Finger temperature devices (thermistors) may have application in the treatment of migraine in particular alcoholics, while EMG feedback therapy may prove of worth in the treatment of tension headaches in selected alcoholic patients in addition to achieving reduced muscle tension generally in such patients.

Breathing, Meditation, and Self-Commands. In helping alcoholics to achieve relaxed states, it is sometimes useful to consider a variety of techniques that involve breathing, meditation, and self-commands.

Alcoholic patients sometimes show difficulty with irregular breathing patterns and particularly hyperventilation. I have found it useful to teach patients to consciously slow their breathing and to moderate it in terms of rhythmic patterns. Breathing in to a count, holding to a count, and then exhaling gradually is one way to accomplish this. On occasion, I have asked agitated and excited patients to bring their breathing into "sync" with my own. Concentration on breathing helps to achieve relaxation in two ways. First, it acts as an attentional-focusing device that distracts the patient from ruminating over anxiety-provoking material. Second, a deliberate change of the breathing to slow, rhythmical patterns reduces the effects of lowered carbon dioxide levels in the blood that sometimes occurs with fast irregular breathing patterns. In cases of frank hyperventilation, I not only teach the patient breathing techniques, I instruct him on how to breathe into a paper bag fitted over his nose and mouth. This procedure increases the percent carbon dioxide in the inhaled air.

Various meditation techniques have shown some value for inducing relaxed states in selected alcoholic patients (Benson and Wallace, 1972). Transcendental meditation is the more popular of these with some evidence available for judging its effectiveness. And, of course, meditation has long been a recommendation of one of the steps to recovery in Alcoholics Anonymous.

Self-commands are useful devices for reinstating relaxed states. During relaxation, the patient is taught to associate certain self-produced cues with the relaxed state. In tense situations he can attempt to partially reinstate the relaxed condition by evoking these cues or self-commands. Typical self-commands are as follows: *calm; easy does it; slow down; relax.* In some cases, entire phrases can be used. The serenity prayer popular in Alcoholics Anonymous is a useful self-command. I have observed alcoholics using the following to good advantage: *This too shall pass. Don't make a big deal of this. Keep it simple. What difference does any of this make anyway? Let go and let God!*

FEAR-REDUCTION PROCEDURES

Recovering alcoholics often show numerous fears. These can involve such simple things as driving a car to more complex matters of "rejection" and "failure."

Systematic Desensitization Procedures. Introduced by Mary Cover Jones (1924) in the earlier part of this century and further elaborated by Joseph Wolpe (1958), Arnold Lazarus (1971), Marvin Goldfried and Gerald Davison (1976), and many others, systematic desensitization is a technique presumably based upon learning theory. The idea behind systematic desensitization therapy is quite simple: a person cannot be anxious and relaxed at the same time. As a consequence, if the person can be made to make a relaxation response in the presence of a feared object or situation, the usual fear response will be inhibited or blocked. The trick, of course, is in getting the patient to make the relaxation response in a situation that normally arouses fear. This is accomplished in two ways. First, the patient is taught deep relaxation techniques. Second, the feared object is analyzed in terms of what is called a *hierarchy*. The hierarchy is formed from the many components of a complex physical or social stimulus configuration. Each component is scaled from low to high according to its anxiety- or fear-eliciting properties.

Elements low in the hierarchy are dealt with first. In a deeply relaxed state, the patient is asked to imagine vividly the element lowest in associated fear. For example, a person fearful of dogs might be asked to first image a piece of fur. When the patient is able to relax in the presence of this real or imagined element low in the hierarchy, a second element higher in the hierarchy is introduced. Gradually, the patient is exposed to all of the elements in the hierarchy until he is able to maintain relaxation in the presence of the feared object. By systematically pairing the relaxation response with elements of increasing potency, the fear is thought to undergo extinction.

Apparently logical, the model is not without its theoretical problems. Recent research has indicated that fear desensitization can occur without explicit instruction in relaxation. Moreover, fear reduction has been reported through methods that proceed from an entirely opposite position: a sudden and rather massive bombardment of the patient with all aspects of the feared situation (flooding).

Bearing in mind these issues of underlying theoretical principles, it is still possible to recommend systematic desensitization for particular patients. After all, subsequent research has not shown that the technique does not work; it has shown that the technique does work, but probably not for the reasons its proponents have claimed.

Behavioral Rehearsals and Enactments. People in general devote an enormous amount of time to fear rehearsal. Alcoholics are no exception. Fear rehearsal is indicated by phrases of the "what if" variety: What if this should happen? What if that should happen? What would I do if she should decide to leave me, if my boss should fire me, if my kid should get sick? and so on. Moreover, it is intriguing to note that many people spend most of their imaginative energies rehearsing failure rather than success.

A variety of methods can be brought to bear upon these related matters of fear rehearsal and failure preparation. Perhaps one of the simplest and most ingenious techniques is Albert Ellis' cognitive behavior elaboration of the feared situation (1962). Ellis invites the patient to consider the "worst possible thing that could happen." Then he asks realistic questions such as, "What would you do then?" or "What do you imagine would happen then?" In many cases either the patient discovers that he has the resources to cope with even the most disastrous of circumstances he can imagine or he realizes that the situation has been blown out of proportion.

Direct efforts to alter typical fear and failure rehearsals are also in order. The patient is asked to imagine himself as capable, confident, and successful rather than incapable, filled with self-doubts, and a failure. With regard to specific situations facing him, the patient is asked to imagine himself vividly in the forthcoming situations. Various response alternatives are discovered and these are rehearsed mentally. Throughout, emphasis is placed upon positive thinking, and any indications of this type of thinking are reinforced by the therapist. Negative thinking is either ignored by the therapist or actively confronted and discouraged. The patient is encouraged to visualize himself in specific situations, but instead of concentrating upon the possibility of failure, he is instructed to see himself performing competently and successfully.

Behavioral enactments are role-playing devices that simulate the conditions under which the patient is required to perform. These simulations may range from simple two-party interactions to more complex arrangements such as psychodrama and group role-playing. Group role-playing enables the therapist to use *social modeling* procedures. In these, the patient observes competent role models performing alternative responses to difficult social situations. These enactments of real-life situations can be conducted in such a way as to increase the probability of successful role performances by the patient in forthcoming events.

In a sense, fear and failure rehearsals can take place only in a person tyrannized by the future. Just as some persons allow themselves to become victims of their biographies, others permit themselves to become victims of biographies yet to be written. In the alcoholic patient, future focusing or dwelling in the psychological future can be dangerous business. The emphasis in AA upon taking life 24 hours at a time is intelligent, realistic to a point, and effective. *Time binding* is an important idea that the alcoholism therapist can use to advantage. By continuously reinforcing cognitive activity centered on the psychological present and discouraging excessive future focusing, the therapist may be able to disrupt self-defeating patterns of fear and failure rehearsal.

ALTERING ATTITUDES TOWARD SELF

Problems of low self-esteem are a common outcome of active alcoholism. Feelings of inferiority, disliking of self, and the extremes of self-hatred and loathing are common in alcoholism. These are among the most difficult characteristics to change. In certain cases these may continue to plague the recovering alcoholic even years after sobriety has been achieved.

Assertive-Behavior Training. According to Miller (1978), the less assertive the alcoholic, the more alcohol he or she is likely to consume. Training in being more assertive may not only give the patient appropriate behaviors to use in his self-interest but may produce generalized effects upon self-esteem and other cognitions about self (Materi, 1977).

In my clinical experience with alcoholic patients, I have found them to possess very limited repertoires of assertive and aggressive responses. Quite typically the patient's repertoire consists of extremely mild aggressive responses and intense hostility, the latter erupting only when the patient is intoxicated. There are, of course, exceptions. Some patients, drunk or sober, respond habitually with high-level aggressive responses and intense hostility. In these cases, assertive behavior training must be approached with caution, since the problem is one of reducing aggression, not increasing it. In still other cases, highly aggressive behaviors simply do not occur—drunk or sober.

But for the majority of alcoholics with whom I have worked, the problem has been one of developing mild to moderate levels of aggressive responding. The emphasis is upon developing a series of such responses of varying levels of intensity, reducing the necessity for either open hostility or complete suppression of anger.

Training in assertion can take place in groups specifically organized for this purpose. In general group-therapy contexts, the therapist can capitalize upon spontaneous events to conduct a brief assertive-behavior training session. Such training can also be accomplished in individual psychotherapy sessions.

Assertive responses can constitute specific actions or verbalizations. Actions may include such things as breaking off a destructive relationship, confronting an unfair or unrealistic supervisor, refusing to do something one really does not want to do, asking for a salary increase, pursuing a love affair, or confronting a neighbor over objectionable behaviors. Verbalizations may include such things as leveling about one's feelings, stating what one will and will not permit, making demands, and giving warnings.

Self-Rewards. In dealing with low self-esteem it is sometimes helpful to encourage the patient to set up a schedule of self-rewards. Self-rewards not only increase the probability that desirable patterns of behavior will be maintained but are symbolic gestures to the patient that he regards himself as fully deserving of such things and worthy of receiving them.

Behavioral Actions in the Real World. Self-esteem can scarcely be considered in isolation from the real-life behaviors of the patient. While some of the patient's negative self-regard is grist for the analytic mill, some of it is clearly a function of his actual behaviors outside the clinical setting. As a therapist, I do not take the position that everything my patient does is simply more material for analysis. I sharply confront destructive behaviors that are not in the patient's interests. With patients who persist in acting out reprehensible behaviors in their real-life situations, I very often say something like the following: "Of course you feel negative about yourself. How could you feel otherwise given the facts of your present behavior?" Such statements are clear indications to the patient that psychotherapy is not a procedure to make him feel good and to assuage his realistic guilt as he continues to make messes of his own and other people's lives. Psychotherapy is about *change*—change in attitudes, cognitions, feelings, and *behavior*.

In helping recovering alcoholics feel good about themselves, I frequently ask them to begin doing things that will support positive self-regard. I generally suggest that each day the patient make it a point to do one small thing for somebody else. As a general rule, I try to encourage the patient to bring his private behavior into line with his public behavior. In my experience, alcoholics do not feel good about themselves nor do they maintain their sobriety when their private lives are characterized by dishonesty, deception, and deceit.

Finally, with regard to increasing self-esteem in alcoholics, I find the ideas of AA concerning the making of amends helpful. For certain patients who cannot comfortably accept their past behaviors, I encourage them to become willing to make amends for these and, when realistic, to do so. Of course, one must first appraise the potential sadism of the recipients of such amends as well as the masochistic potential of the patient! Nothing is to be gained from a situation that further damages the self-esteem of the patient or invites him to engage in further intropunitive behavior.

Self-Management Methods. Miller (1979) and Meichenbaum (1977) have discussed self-management training as a means of changing maladaptive coping skills. In self-management training, a number of components are used. A patient is first provided with a cognitive framework for engaging in a self-management activity. He is taught self-monitoring as a means of arriving at an accurate and useful self-evaluation. Consistent with the cognitive and self-monitoring frameworks, change procedures are introduced. These change procedures are: (1) Learning relaxation techniques; (2) exposing of maladaptive elements in the patient's belief system; (3) changing inappropriate cognitive styles; (4) altering the relationships between cues and behavioral consequences; (5) generalizing newly learned self-management skills to the real-world (Neuman, 1983).

It is unfortunate that behavioral methods have come to be associated with controlled drinking (e.g., Sobell and Sobell, 1978; Pattison Sobell, and Sobell, 1977). As shown throughout this chapter, behavioral methods can be employed for a variety of purposes in helping alcoholics get sober. Methods such as desensitization, reinforcement, covert conditioning, self-management, biofeedback, relaxation training, and assertion training can be extremely useful tools for the clinician treating patients in the early phases of sobriety. Azrin (1976), for example, has shown how reinforcement theory can be applied in a community setting. Studies in blood alcohol discrimination by Nathan (1983) and his colleagues, although largely of theoretical interest, may eventually lead to practical application. Neuman (1983) suggests possibilities for behavioral therapy in conjunction with "physiological aids" and Christian psychological approaches.

Miller (1979, 1983) has discussed behavioral methods that may help certain problem drinkers moderate their consumption of alcoholic beverages and avoid negative consequences of consumption. Whether Miller's methods would work with alcoholics is not evident from the data he presents nor the literature he reviews.

The scientific literature on controlled, attenuated, moderate, or social drinking among alcoholics has not been characterized by the rigor, objectivity, methodological sophistication, and soundness one normally expects of treatment interventions that involve high risk to patients (Wallace, 1983,a,b). Whereas some proponents of controlled drinking persist in casting the debate in a "science versus ideology" dichotomy, the available scientific evidence indicates that caution rather than advocacy is in order. Further studies on controlled or nonproblem drinking goals has raised doubts about the feasibility of these goals for alcoholics. Pendery, Maltzman, and West's (1983) failure to confirm Sobell and Sobell's (1973) earlier work on controlled drinking has raised serious questions concerning the scientific adequacy of much of the data in this area. Although the work by Armor, Polich, and Stambul is still cited by some as scientific evidence for controlled drinking by large numbers of alcoholics following treatment, subsequent research by these same authors (Polich, Armor, and Braiker, 1980) reported a long-term, sustained nonproblem drinking rate of only 7%. Corrected for several sources of error, this rate is more likely 4% and agrees closely with a long-term nonproblem drinking rate of 3% recently reported by Pettinati and her colleagues (1982).

A long-term nonproblem drinking rate of 3% is of no practical importance in alcoholism treatment at this time. With treatment centers now reporting long-term abstention rates of better than 50% (e.g., Patton, 1979), the ethical and scientific choice is quite clear: *Until convincingly demonstrated otherwise, abstention remains the only practical course for alcoholics wishing to avoid the awesome personal, social, psychological, medical, and spiritual costs of this disease.*

SUMMARY

In this chapter, I have tried to show the relevance of behavioral modification procedures to alcoholism psychotherapy. Variants of the following have been presented: Habit pattern disruption techniques; cognitive behavioral change methods; relaxation, assertion, and biofeedback training; reinforcement, desensitization, and self-management approaches.

With regard to the continuing debate involving abstention versus controlled drinking, it was pointed out that behavioral methods and indeed behavioral psychology, need not be restricted to controlled drinking treatment goals. Behavioral methods can serve as very useful adjuncts to psychotherapy in the service of helping alcoholics achieve abstention and maintain sobriety.

REFERENCES

Armor, D. J., Polich, J. M., and Stambul, H. B. *Alcoholism and treatment.* Santa Monica: Rand Corporation, 1976.

Azrin, N. H. Improvement in the community reinforcement approach to alcoholism. *Behavior Research and Therapy,* 1976, *14,* 339–348.

Benson, H., and Wallace, K. R. Decreased drug abuse with transcendental meditation: A study of 1,862 subjects. In C. Zarafonetis (Ed.), *Drug abuse proceedings of the international conference.* Philadelphia: Lea and Febiger, 1972.

Birk, L. *Biofeedback: Behavioral medicine.* New York: Grune and Stratton, 1973.

Cautela, J. R. Treatment of compulsive behavior by covert sensitization. *Psychological Record,* 1966, *16,* 33–41.

Davies, D. L. Normal drinking in recovered alcohol addicts. *Quarterly Journal of Studies on Alcohol,* 1962, *23,* 94–104.

Ellis, A. *Reason and emotion in psychotherapy.* New York: Lyle Stuart, 1962.

Goldfried, M. R., and Davidson, G. C. *Clinical behavior therapy.* New York: Holt, Rinehart, & Winston, 1976.

Hunt, G. H., and Azrin, N.H. A community reinforcement approach to alcoholism. Behavior Research and Therapy, 1973, *11,* 91–104.

Jacobson, E. *Progressive relaxation.* Chicago: University of Chicago Press (Midway Reprint), 1974.

Kelly, G. *The psychology of personal constructs* (Vol. 2). New York: W. W. Norton, 1955.

Klatsky, A. L., Friedman, G. D., Abraham, B., Siegelaub, A. B., and Gerard, M. J. Alcohol consumption and blood pressure. *Annals of the New York Academy of Sciences,* 1977, *296,* 1194–2000.

Lazarus, A. A. *Behavior therapy and beyond.* New York: McGraw-Hill, 1971.

Materi, M. Assertiveness training: A catalyst for behavior change. *Alcohol Health and Research World,* 1977, *1,* 23–26.

Meichenbaum, D. *Cognitive-behavioral modification: An integrative approach.* New York: Plenum Press, 1977.

Miller, P. M. Behavior therapy in the treatment of alcoholism. In G. A. Marlatt, and P. E. Nathan (Eds.), *Behavioral approaches to alcoholism.* New Brunswick, N.J.: Center for Studies on Alcohol, 1978.

Miller, W. R. Problem drinking and substance abuse: Behavioral perspectives. In N. A. Kraseneger (Ed.) *Behavioral analysis and treatment of substance abuse.* Research

Monograph Series, No. 25, Washington, D.C.: National Institute on Drug Abuse, 1979.

Nathan, P. E., and Bridell, D. W. Behavior assessment and treatment of alcoholism. In B. Kissin and H. Begleiter (Eds.), *The biology of alcoholism, Vol. 5, Treatment and rehabilitation of the chronic alcoholic.* New York: Plenum Press, 1977.

Neuman, J. K., Behavior therapy of substance abuse: An overview and discussion of future directions. In E. Gottheil and D. Kruley (Eds.), *The etiologic aspects of alcohol and drug abuse.* Springfield, Ill.: Charles C Thomas, 1982.

Passini, F. T., Watson, C. G., Dehnel, L., Herder, J., and Watkins, B. Alpha wave biofeedback training in alcoholics. *Journal of Clinical Psychology*, 1977, *33*, 292–299.

Pattison, E. M., Sobell, M. B., and Sobell, L. C. *Emerging concepts of alcohol dependence.* New York: Springer, 1977.

Patton, M. *Validity and reliability of Hazelden treatment follow-up data.* Center City, Minnesota: Hazelden Educational Services, 1979.

Pendery, M., Maltzman, I., and West, L. J., Controlled drinking by alcoholics? New findings and a reevaluation of a major affirmative study. *Science,* 1982, *217,* 169–175.

Perls, F. S., *Gestalt therapy verbatim.* Lafayette, La.: Real People Press, 1969.

Pettinati, H., Sugerman, A., DiDonato, N., and Maurer, H., The natural history of alcoholism over four years after treatment. *Journal of Studies on Alcohol,* 1982, *43,* 201–215.

Pickens, R. A behavioral program for treatment of drug dependence. In N. A. Kraseneger (Ed.), *Behavioral analysis and treatment of substance abuse.* Research Monograph Series No. 25, Washington, D.C.: National Institute on Drug Abuse, 1979.

Polich, M. J., Armor, D. J., and Braiker, H. B. *The course of alcoholism: Four years after treatment.* ADM 281-76-0006 Santa Monica, California: Rand Corporation, 1980.

Proctor, J. *Relaxation procedures.* New York: Biomonitoring Applications, 1975. (Cassette recording.)

Schwartz, G. E., and Shapiro, D. Biofeedback and essential hypertension. In L. Birk (Ed.), *Biofeedback: Behavioral medicine.* New York: Grune and Stratton, 1973.

Sobell, L. C., and Sobell, M. B. Individualized behavior therapy for alcoholics. *Behavior Research and Therapy,* 1973, *4,* 49–72.

Sobell, L. C., and Sobell, M. B. *Behavioral treatment of alcohol problems: Individualized therapy and controlled drinking.* New York: Plenum Press, 1978.

Sterman, M. B. Neurophysiological and clinical studies of sensorimotor EEG biofeedback training. In L. Birk (Ed.), *Biofeedback: Behavioral medicine.* New York: Grune and Stratton, 1973.

Steffen, J. J. Electromyographically induced relaxation in the treatment of chronic alcohol abuse. *Journal of Consulting and Clinical Psychology,* 1975, *43,* 275.

Wallace, J. Ideology, belief, and behavior: Alcoholics anonymous as a social movement. In E. Gottheil and K. Druley (Eds.), *The etiologic aspects of alcohol and drug abuse.* Springfield, Ill.: Charles C Thomas, 1982.

Wallace, J. Alcoholism: Is a shift in paradigm necessary? *Journal of Psychiatric Treatment and Evaluation,* December, 1983.

Wolpe, J. *Psychotherapy by reciprocal inhibition.* Stanford: Stanford University Press, 1958.

Treatment

Data from a number of sources indicate that alcoholism treatment services and numbers of people in treatment continue to increase (Harwood et al. 1985; Noble 1985). American Hospital Association (1978, 1984) survey data indicate that total alcoholism and other drug dependency treatment units increased from 465 in 1978 to 829 in 1984 (78 percent), while total in-hospital alcoholism and other drug dependency beds increased from 16,005 to 25,981 for the same 6-year period (62 percent). The largest increase was in the private for-profit sector, where the number of units increased by 347 percent and the number of in-hospital beds increased by 392 percent from 1978 to 1984. These data are summarized in table 1.

Harwood et al. (1985) report comparative data on the ownership of services for 1978 and 1984 (see figure 1). By 1984, State and local governments owned 20 percent of 25,981 beds (a decrease of 20 percent), while investor-owned, for-profit beds increased from 5 percent in 1978 to 15 percent in 1984. Nongovernment, nonprofit control increased from 31 percent in 1978 to 44 percent in 1984. A total of 289,933 patients was estimated to be in alcoholism treatment on September 30, 1982 (NDATUS 1983), with 203,469 of these in alcoholism specialty units (see table 2). On September 28, 1984, 540,411 patients were in treatment in both alcohol only and combined alcohol and other drug dependency units. Of these, 40,786 (8 percent) were in an inpatient facility, 51,976 (10 percent) in a residential setting, and 447,649 (82 percent) were active outpatients (USDHHS 1984).

In 1984 there were approximately 34,148,000 discharges from short-stay hospitals. Of these, approximately 1,086,000 (3.2 percent) had an alcohol-related diagnosis. By 1990, the number of persons in treatment is estimated to increase by 8 percent, on the basis of projections of the 1982 National Drug and Alcohol Treatment Utilization Survey data. Most of this increase is estimated to be accounted for by almost 22,000 men and women, 21 through 44 years old.

TABLE 1. Hospital units and beds for alcoholism and other drug dependency

	1978		1984		Difference		% Change 1978 to 1984	
Type of hospital	Units	Beds	Units	Beds	Units	Beds	Units	Beds
Federal	97	3,884	130	5,159	33	1,275	+34.0	+33.0
State and local	133	6,356	149	5,299	16	−1,057	+12.0	−17.0
Not for profit	205	4,952	416	11,520	211	6,568	+103.0	+133.0
For profit	30	813	134	4,003	104	3,190	+347.0	+392.0
Total	465	16,005	829	25,981	364	9,976	78.0	62.0
Average bed per unit		34.4		31.0				

SOURCE: Modified from *Hospital Statistics*, 1978 and 1984 editions.

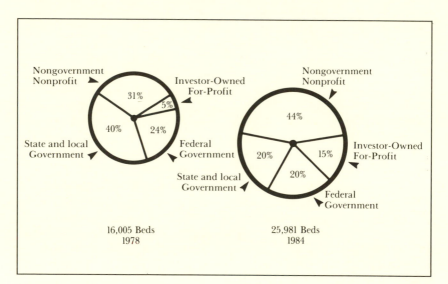

FIGURE 1. Control of hospital beds with services for alcoholism and other drug dependency.
SOURCE: Harwood et al. 1985.

DIAGNOSIS, NOMENCLATURE, AND CONCEPTUALIZATION

The *Fifth Special Report to the U.S. Congress on Alcohol and Health* (USDHHS 1984) covered recent developments in nomenclature and diagnosis. In that report, attention was given to the third edition of the *Diagnostic and Statistical Manual of Mental Disorders* (American Psychiatric Association 1980) as well as to work on the International Classification of Diseases sponsored jointly by the U.S. Alcohol, Drug Abuse, and Mental Health Administration and the World Health Or-

TABLE 2. Number of clients in treatment, budgeted capacity, and utilization rate for drug abuse and alcoholism treatment units

Type of unit	Number of clients	Budgeted capacity	Utilization rate (percent)
Drug abuse units			
Drug abuse only units	137,076	146,046	93.9
Combined units			
(Drug abuse portion)	36,403	50,243	72.3
Total	173,479	196,289	88.3
Alcoholism units			
Alcoholism only units	203,469	241,260	84.3
Combined units			
(Alcoholism portion)	86,464	103,955	83.2
Total	289,933	345,215	84.0

SOURCE: National Drug and Alcoholism Treatment Utilization Survey, September 1983.

ganization (World Health Organization 1982). This chapter does not review this work discussed in the *Fifth Special Report* but concentrates on further advances in conceptualization.

Both the *Fourth Special Report* (USDHHS 1981) and the *Fifth Special Report* (USDHHS 1984) emphasized the heterogeneity evident within and between populations of persons with drinking problems. The *Fourth Special Report* (USDHHS 1981, p. 29) noted, "These many variations in alcohol-related problems suggest that no single concept will suffice for adequate description. Categories such as alcoholism, alcohol abuse, alcohol dependence, problem drinking, and alcohol-related disabilities are of definite although limited value. Each is useful for certain purposes and certain populations, but none can represent adequately the full range of problems associated with alcohol consumption in American society."

An historical perspective readily informs us that variability among persons with alcohol-related problems, including those diagnosed as alcoholics, has been appreciated for many years. Jellinek (1960) in his classic study, *The Disease Concept of Alcoholism,* proposed a classification system consisting of five types of alcoholics. Moreover, a careful reading of the major publications of Alcoholics Anonymous (AA) (Alcoholics Anonymous World Services 1953, 1976) reveals early explicit concern with "types" of alcoholics and differences among people so labeled. Numerous early theorists and researchers have discussed the variability among alcoholics (e.g., Clinebell 1956; Jellinek 1960; Partington and Johnson 1969). While there has been interest in variability among alcoholics, systematic formal research has begun only recently (e.g., Wanberg and Horn 1970).

In addition to variability among persons with alcohol-related problems, the multidimensional nature of these problems has also been recognized for some time. With regard to alcoholism, Ewing (1980), Tarter (1983), and Wallace (1985a) have all independently discussed elements of an interactive biopsychosocial model of alcoholism in which biological, behavioral, and sociocultural factors are considered essential for understanding etiology, pathogenesis, course, maintenance, and treatment.

This traditional view of alcoholism and alcohol-related problems as varied and multidimensional is explored further in this chapter in terms of recent developments. The chapter begins with a focus on continued efforts to define and assess the heterogeneity within and between populations of persons with alcohol-related problems. Also, the implications of such heterogeneity for the treatment of alcoholics are explored. Other issues concerning treatment are examined throughout the chapter.

DEVELOPMENT OF THE ALCOHOL DEPENDENCE SYNDROME

In a series of studies, Wanberg and Horn and their colleagues (Horn and Wanberg 1969; Wanberg and Horn 1970, 1983; Horn et al. 1974, 1984; Wanberg et al. 1977) identified a multiple-syndrome diagnostic model through factor analytic techniques. Working with an initial item pool and larger samples, these authors succeeded in constructing the Alcohol Use Inventory. This instrument, consisting of 147 items and 16 scales, defines 6 dimensions that form patterns of alcohol use. In effect, Wanberg and Horn take the position that alcoholism is not a unitary phenomenon and that multiple syndromes are necessary to describe persons with alcohol-related problems.

Working with the Alcohol Use Inventory, Skinner (1981) developed the Alcohol Dependence Scale. Four scales from the Alcohol Use Inventory make up Skinner's Alcohol Dependence Scale: (1) loss of behavioral control, (2) psychophysical withdrawal symptoms, (3) psychoperceptual withdrawal symptoms, and (4) obsessive-compulsive drinking style. Skinner, in effect, through factor analytic techniques, identified a general factor that measures, in part, the alcohol dependence syndrome as outlined by Edwards and Gross (1976).

Hodgson et al. (1978) defined an alcohol dependence syndrome in terms of the following elements: (1) narrowing of the drinking repertoire, (2) salience of drink-seeking behavior, (3) increased tolerance to alcohol, (4) repeated withdrawal symptoms, (5) relief drinking, (6) compulsion to drink, and (7) readdiction liability.

The usefulness of the alcohol dependence syndrome concept lies in its potential for differentiating among people with alcohol-related problems with regard to severity of dependence. The hope of such differentiation, of course, is that it may lead eventually to meaningful predictions concerning individual treatment planning, individualized treatment interventions, and improved treatment outcome.

Research with the Severity of Alcohol Dependence Questionnaire (Edwards 1986), an instrument derived directly from the alcohol withdrawal syndrome concept, has yielded empirical findings of significance. Stockwell et al. (1983) were able to provide evidence for one element of the syndrome, "narrowing of the drinking repertoire." Topham (1983) showed that degree of dependence was related to the speed with which sweating, shaking, craving, and morning drinking returned after relapse. Several studies have demonstrated relationships between measured level of dependence and desire for a drink, rapidity with which drinks are consumed, quantity of drinking, resistance to placebo-expectancy effects, and perception of withdrawal symptoms as cues for drinking (Hodgson et al. 1979; Rankin et al. 1980, 1982; Stockwell et al. 1982).

With regard to predicting resistance to abstinence as a treatment goal, Skinner and Allen (1982) found that all patients scoring high on the Alcohol Dependence Scale considered themselves to be alcoholics, and virtually all did not believe that they could cut down to a few drinks a day. In contrast, the majority of patients who scored low on alcohol dependence did not believe they were alcoholic and did believe they could cut down to a few drinks a day.

With regard to coexisting psychopathology, Skinner and Allen (1982) found significant relationships between scores on the Alcohol Dependence Scale and a host of measures of psychopathology. Two studies (Smail et al. 1984; Stockwell et al. 1984) found relationships between alcohol dependence scores and phobic anxiety. These studies suggest that clinicians should be alert to other problems as alcohol dependence increases.

The relationship of alcohol dependence to treatment goals is of interest. Edwards et al. (1983) reported that virtually all patients followed over an 11-year period who scored moderate to high on the measure of alcohol dependence could not engage successfully in nonproblem drinking.

Vaillant (1983), in the context of a longitudinal study that spanned many years, observed that appearance of only a small number of dependence symptoms predicted failure at moderate or nonproblem drinking. Polich et al. (1981), in their analysis of the Rand Corporation followup data, concluded that their results were consistent with

Edwards' emphasis on alcohol dependence and suggested that non-problem drinking decreased as the severity of dependence increased.

Perhaps the relationship between severity of dependence and treatment goals is best summarized by Miller and Hester (1980, p. 102): "The picture that emerges is clear: individuals who will become successful controlled drinkers show less resemblance to the classic diagnostic picture of alcoholism. They have fewer problems related to drinking and have had them for a shorter period of time, have fewer symptoms and less family history of alcoholism, and drink less."

OTHER APPROACHES TO HETEROGENEITY OF PROBLEM DRINKERS

As mentioned earlier, Skinner (1981), through factor analysis of the Alcohol Use Inventory, identified an alcohol dependence factor. Skinner also identified three other factors: (1) perceived benefits of drinking (the person believes that alcohol facilitates social and mental functioning), (2) marital discord (drinking problems are intimately associated with marital difficulties), and (3) polydrug abuse (illicit drug use along with a gregarious drinking style). These factors correlate with clinic attendance, physical symptoms, and psychosocial problems.

Morey et al. (1984) through cluster analysis identified three types of drinkers as determined by severity of their alcohol problem, psychopathology, cognitive functioning, and social adjustment. Type A, early-stage problem drinkers, had evidence of drinking problems but not major symptoms of alcohol dependence. Type B, with affiliative, moderate alcohol dependence, were more socially oriented and tended to drink daily. Type C, schizoid, with severe alcohol dependence, were socially isolated binge drinkers with the most severe symptoms of alcoholism. This typology may well predict resistance to abstinence as a treatment goal, because Type A patients (early-stage problem drinkers) believed that they could cut down on their drinking and that moderation was a desirable goal. However, it is difficult to identify Type A patients. Types B and C believed that they could not cut down and that abstinence would be the only successful approach. For a compendium of diagnostic instruments, interested readers are referred to Lettieri et al. (1985). Babor and Lauerman (1986) have provided a comprehensive review of the numerous other systems for classifying alcoholics that have been proposed.

VARIABILITY WITH REGARD TO OTHER DRUG ABUSE

Drug use and abuse among alcoholic treatment populations has increased sharply over the past decade. Sokolow and his colleagues

(1981), in a study of 1,340 alcoholics in 17 New York State alcoholism treatment centers, found current other drug use in 46 percent of the patients. Freed (1973), in a review of the literature from 1925 to 1972, concluded that 20 percent of alcohol-dependent persons also use other addictive drugs. By 1977, however, a review by Carroll et al. suggested that between 60 and 80 percent of alcoholics use other drugs. Hesselbrock et al. (1985) found a lifetime incidence of other drug abuse in 45 percent of male primary alcoholics and 38 percent of female alcoholics. Schuckit (1985), in a study of the 577 alcoholics admitted to the San Diego Veterans Administration Medical Center between 1982 and 1984, found that 11 percent of the patients had a diagnosis of primary drug abuse and secondary alcoholism. Of Schuckit's primary alcoholic admissions, 53 percent had used marijuana, 23 percent stimulants, 14 percent cocaine, and 11 percent depressants.

These findings have important implications for clinical staffs who treat alcoholics. Clinical staffs must be prepared to alter their perceptions of and actions toward alcoholics who abuse other drugs because studies have shown that these patients are more impaired both physically and psychologically than are alcoholics who do not abuse other drugs. Schuckit (1985) reported many more childhood antisocial problems among primary drug abusers who abused alcohol than among primary alcoholics. Moreover, these patients showed more psychiatric hospitalizations, depressions, suicide attempts, and visits to mental health workers. Alcoholism counselors working with polydrug abuse alcoholic patients need to be alert to the increased likelihood of other serious problems and the necessity for individualized treatment interventions directed toward these.

Obviously, alcoholic patients who abuse other drugs will require information in treatment different from that given persons who do not abuse drugs. Given the high rates of other drug abuse in current treatment populations, lectures are essential on such topics as drug synergy; half-lives (amount of time necessary to metabolize one-half of initial dose); cross-tolerance; drug classifications; and effects on brain, lungs, heart, and other body systems and organs.

Because drugs can be more readily brought into alcoholism treatment centers and consumed there, numerous alcoholism treatment centers have implemented drug use detection systems.

PSYCHIATRIC DISORDERS AMONG ALCOHOLIC TREATMENT POPULATIONS

Alcoholic treatment populations vary considerably with regard to psychiatric problems. Halikas et al. (1983), through use of a systematic, structured interview, found evidence for psychiatric problems in 50 percent of a sample of 71 female alcoholics. The most common diagnosis was affective disorder, with 24 percent showing unipolar disorder and 4 percent showing bipolar affective disorder. Ten percent of the patients had anxiety disorders of some kind. In addition, 6 percent had shown psychotic symptoms prior to treatment.

Hesselbrock and her colleagues (1985) also found high levels of psychiatric problems in alcoholism treatment patient samples. In her studies, 18 percent of the men and 38 percent of the women were seen as depressed, while 15 percent of the men and 29 percent of the women showed phobias. Five percent of the men and 9 percent of the women met criteria for panic disorder. Bedi and Halikas (1985) found a lifetime rate of affective disorder of 43 percent in alcoholic females and 29 percent in males.

In addition to influencing primary treatment, variations in primary diagnostic groups among alcoholics in treatment have implications for outcome results and planning for aftercare. Schuckit (1985) found that the best outcome results for a sample of 577 Veterans' Administration hospital patients were for primary alcoholics (78 percent of the sample), and the worst results were for primary antisocial personalities (7 percent of the sample.) Primary antisocial personalities were younger, less well educated, and more likely to have reported secondary affective episodes, suicide attempts, and psychiatric hospitalizations. These people also reported patterns of drug abuse almost as intense as primary drug abusers. At followup, primary antisocial personalities with secondary alcoholism showed the worst outcome of any group; they had higher rates of police- and drug-related problems, using a weapon while drunk, and living on the streets. These results for primary, antisocial personality patients indicate that individualized treatment planning and interventions in both primary alcoholism treatment and aftercare must be the rule if outcome results are to be improved.

With regard to personality characteristics of alcoholics, Nerviano and Gross (1983) have summarized research in this area in terms of seven subtypes: (1) a chronic severe distress group, (2) passive aggressive sociopaths, (3) antisocial sociopaths, (4) acute reactive depressives, (5) a mixed-character dysphoric group, (6) a paranoid alienated group, and (7) a severely neurotic psychophysiological group. Some support for Nerviano and Gross' typology was provided by Bartsch and Hoffman (1985), who performed a cluster analysis on responses of alcoholics to the Millon Clinical Multiaxial Inventory.

Recognition of the variability in personality characteristics among alcoholics may have important implications for the clinical management of patients within given treatment programs as well as for patient assignment to treatment interventions, programs, and facilities. Moreover, post-treatment followup of certain types of patients may be more difficult—for example, patients who are younger, single, and of lower occupational status (Billings et al. 1985).

Because alcohol is a neurotoxin, it is not surprising to note that studies have shown neuropsychological deficits among alcoholism treatment populations and social drinkers (e.g., Parker and Noble 1977; Ryan et al. 1980). These findings of impaired neuropsychological functioning have implications for the manner in which information is learned, stored, and retrieved by patients in treatment for alcoholism. Butters and Cermak (1980) have pointed to the possibility that long-term alcoholics may not spontaneously generate effective learning and memory strategies. Tarter and Parsons (1971) have demonstrated that alcoholics show difficulty on neuropsychological tests requiring concept formation and shifts in cognitive sets. These findings concerning learning, memory, and concept formation strategies may have important implications for how information is presented to alcoholics in lectures, group therapies, films, books, and other formats commonly employed in alcoholism treatment facilities. McCrady and Smith (1986) have recently explored implications of neuropsychological deficits for alcoholism treatment. Becker and Jaffe (1984) have shown impaired memory for treatment-relevant information in male alcoholics in inpatient treatment. Eckardt and Martin (1986) recommend that the cognitive capabilities of alcoholics be considered in the formulation of treatment plans, because there is evidence of brain dysfunction in a high proportion of detoxified alcoholics without organic brain syndrome and this makes neuropsychological assessment an important part of the overall clinical evaluation of alcoholic patients. However, the impact of cognitive impairment on alcoholism treatment outcome is not well understood at this time, and further research is needed in this area.

THERAPEUTIC MODALITIES, CONTEXTS, AND METHODS

Although necessarily limited by cost-effectiveness considerations, alcoholism treatment has become increasingly multimodal and multidisciplinary. As is generally recognized, a comprehensive system of services is essential if the varying treatment needs of alcoholics are to be met. This comprehensive system of services includes at least the following: detoxification; inpatient rehabilitation; outpatient services, including clinic, day hospital, and partial hospital services; family treatment; aftercare; residential or supervised living services; and sobering-up services. These categories of service are not mutually exclusive.

DETOXIFICATION

Research over the past decade has continued to show that detoxification can be accomplished in a variety of ways. Depending on the severity of withdrawal, the course of detoxification may be managed either medically or nonmedically. It is generally accepted that patients experienceing severe withdrawal symptoms and patients suffering from coexisting illnesses such as serious cardiac disease, hypertension, seizure disorders, and overt psychotic reactions will require medical management of detoxification in a medical setting. For patients experiencing mild to moderate withdrawal symptoms without coexisting medical problems, however, numerous studies suggest that detoxification may be accomplished safely in a nonmedical setting and without medication for a large number of alcoholics (e.g., O'Briant et al. 1976/1977; Whitfield et al. 1978; Smith 1980; Den Hartog 1982; Diesenhaus 1982; Naranjo et al. 1983).

Gordis and Sereny (1981) argue that the important question concerning withdrawal and its management really relates to the possible impact of the withdrawal experience on successful outcome of rehabilitation treatment. These authors assert, "Withdrawal is but a small first step in rehabilitation. If the quality of withdrawal is unrelated to retention in treatment and successful rehabilitation, then it can be judged on cost and safety alone. If long-term outcome is somehow related to the withdrawal experience, then the cost of withdrawal treatment alone is a minor point" (Gordis and Sereny 1981, p. 44).

Unfortunately, as Gordis and Sereny point out, evidence is generally lacking on the possible relationship between withdrawal experience and subsequent success in modifying drinking behavior. One study (Fagan and Mauss 1978) did find that one-third of a predominantly socioeconomically deprived population did accept referral for rehabilitation treatment following detoxification. Smart and Gray (1978b) found that receiving medical evaluation and medication was related to acceptance and continuation in treatment as an outpatient. This effect was evident for lower middle-class and lower-class alcoholics. Reed and Mandell (1979), however, found no relationship between administration of chlordiazepoxide during withdrawal and completion of a 7-day hospital-based program.

With respect to alcoholics of higher socioeconomic classes, virtually nothing certain is known about the quality of withdrawal experience and subsequent modification of drinking behavior.

Studies are also needed of physician prescribing rules and behaviors within medical detoxification settings. Such studies are likely to reveal differences in the manner in which medical practitioners use psychoactive drugs in alcohol withdrawal. Some physicians appear to administer benzodiazepines or sedatives to all admissions to an alcoholism facility. Others seem to use medications only for patients experiencing severe withdrawal symptoms. Still others give medications mainly to prevent the onset of delirium tremens or to avoid seizures. Some may prescribe in order to make patients more comfortable during withdrawal in the belief that this action will increase the likelihood that patients will remain in the facility and accept rehabilitation treatment following detoxification. Obviously, empirical studies of differing physician motivations, beliefs, attitudes, and prescribing rules are needed to clarify the actual behavior of medical practitioners in medical detoxification settings. Surprisingly little is known with certainty as to what physicians actually do in such settings.

PHARMACOTHERAPIES

There have been no dramatic developments in the pharmacotherapy of alcoholism since publication of the *Fourth Special Report* and *Fifth Special Report* (USDHHS 1981, 1984). Although pharmacotherapeutic agents of various kinds have continued to be used as adjuncts for limited purposes, no specific, successful pharmacotherapy for altering long-term drinking behavior in alcoholics exists.

The complex issue of the effectiveness of disulfiram (Antabuse) was treated in considerable detail in both the *Fourth* and *Fifth Special Reports* (USDHHS 1981, 1984). The interested reader is urged to consult these documents. In general, however, as these reports make clear, disulfiram is no longer recommended for use alone in treating alcoholism, but it may be used as an adjunct to a comprehensive treatment regimen (Kwentus and Major 1979). As studies have shown, the effectiveness of disulfiram may be related to patient characteristics including age, motivation to remain sober, compulsivity, and ability to form dependent relationships. Moreover, in controlled studies disulfiram, when shown to be effective, has generally demonstrated only a small to modest effect. The usefulness of disulfiram, however, may be simply as a short-term influence over the decision to remain abstinent while the patient seeks to establish an initial program of recovery. Disulfiram for some patients may, in effect, constitute a way to "buy time" while they become further involved in treatment, pursue aftercare plans, or make contacts with self-help programs.

It is also possible that the willingness to take disulfiram is only a corollary of a strong motivation to quit drinking, and that individuals who are willing to take the drug daily would be likely to have a successful treatment outcome even if they did not take it.

The effectiveness of voluntary use of disulfiram in promoting abstinence has been challenged by a recent controlled, randomized, study involving 605 alcoholic men in nine clinics (Fuller et al. 1986). The patients were divided into three groups of about 200 men, and each group was randomly assigned to one of three treatment protocols: disulfiram in a pharmacologically effective dose plus counseling; dilsulfiram in an ineffective dose plus counseling; and counseling alone. Patients receiving disulfiram were told so, but they did not know whether they were receiving the effective or the ineffective dose, and, until the study was concluded, neither did the investigators. Thus this part of the study was "double-blinded" to avoid bias, and both disulfiram groups were presented with the same psychological threat of a disulfiram-alcohol interaction if they resumed drinking. After discharge from the hospital, the patients in all three groups were interviewed at regular intervals over a period of a year. Blood and urine alcohol tests were done during these followups to corroborate the patient's own reports of their alcohol consumption and compliance with Antabuse therapy. No significant differences were found in the three groups in percentage of total abstainers, time to first drink, employment, or social stability. Among the patients who drank, however, those receiving the pharmacologically effective dose of disulfiram reported significantly fewer drinking days than those receiving the ineffective dose. The investigators concluded that, although disulfiram in a pharmacologically effective dose did reduce the frequency of drinking in men who could not remain abstinent, it made no contributions to sustained abstinence, delay of relapse, employment, and social stability beyond those provided by counseling alone.

Various methods have been tried with some success to increase patient compliance and, hence, disulfiram effectiveness. Azrin et al. (1982) reported a successful behavioral disulfiram assurance program that involved role playing and communication skills for some patients and a behavior therapy package for others. Liebson et al. (1978), working with heroin addicts who had secondary alcoholism, made receipt of methadone contingent upon disulfiram compliance. This procedure did result in higher rates of compliance. Wilson et al. (1984), as well as others, have employed subcutaneous disulfiram implants with improved compliance. Unfortunately, as Miller and

Hester (1980) point out, serum blood levels with implants are unpredictable as are disulfiram/ethanol reactions. As a consequence, early enthusiasm for implants based upon positive initial outcome results in uncontrolled studies must be viewed cautiously.

Although initial reports of the effectiveness of lithium carbonate in alcoholism treatment indicated promise (Kline et al. 1974), subsequent research has provided mixed results. Pond et al. (1981) did not find reductions in drinking in alcoholics to whom lithium had been administered.

More recently, Fawcett et al. (1984) evaluated lithium carbonate therapy in a group of 84 volunteers who had also received other treatments for 3 weeks in two hospital alcoholism treatment programs, as well as attended AA during aftercare. Results did favor a group of patients who complied with the lithium medication regimen and showed blood levels at or above minimum therapeutic level (≥ 0.4 m/q/L). These compliant patients with therapeutic blood levels of lithium were more likely to be abstinent at 6-month followup intervals than were all other groups studied.

Although the Fawcett et al. (1984) study is definitely of interest, it must be interpreted with caution. First, the numbers of patients in the four groups studied were small. By the 18-month followup, the results for the compliant patients with therapeutic blood levels of lithium were based on only eight patients. For noncompliant placebo controls, the number of patients at the 18-month followup was only seven. Second, there was a very high rate of major depression in these subjects, much higher than one expects to find in samples of alcoholics. At intake, 67 percent of the patients met criteria for major depression, and 88 percent met criteria for lifetime diagnoses of major depression. Moreover, 57 percent showed a lifetime course of recurrent unipolar depression. Obviously, these results for lithium, if reliable, may be applicable only to alcoholic patients with coexisting bipolar or unipolar affective disorder.

AVERSIVE THERAPY

Presumably based on classical conditioning procedures in which conditioned stimuli are repeatedly paired with unpleasant unconditioned stimuli, aversion therapies have been used with specific treatment populations. In the case of alcoholism, conditioned stimuli are the sights, smells, and tastes of alcoholic beverages, while the unconditioned stimuli have been nausea-producing drugs (chemical aversion therapy) or electric shock (electric aversion therapy).

Results concerning the efficacy of chemical aversion therapy have been both encouraging and discouraging (Lemere and Voegtlin 1950), poor to fair (Neubuerger et al. 1981), modest (Neubuerger et al. 1981), and good (Wiens et al. 1976; Wiens and Menustik 1983). As with most other approaches to alcoholism treatment, characteristics of patients undergoing chemical aversion therapy are important predictors of success. As a rule, patients who do well following chemical aversion therapy are married, socially stable, and of middle-class or higher socioeconomic status; they also have intact jobs and sufficient motivation to stay sober to expose themselves to an unpleasant treatment experience. The discouraging results referred to in the study by Lemere and Voegtlin (1950) were obtained with "charity" cases, while the poor to fair results of Neubuerger et al. (1981) were associated with Medicare status, low socioeconomic class, and low educational level. Wiens and Menustik (1983) have demonstrated the increased efficacy of aversion therapy as a result of periodic booster treatments in aftercare.

Although chemical aversion therapy appears to be effective with highly motivated, good prognosis patients, electrical aversion therapy for alcoholics has not shown equivalent promise (e.g., Ewing 1984). In fact, Miller and Hester (1980, p. 36), following a review of the literature on electrical aversion therapy and abstinence, concluded that "electrical aversion therapy appears to be relatively ineffective in comparison to alternative methods."

Neither chemical aversion therapy nor electrical aversion therapy can be construed in terms of classical conditioning as originally proposed. The procedure seems to result in taste aversion rather than in a classically conditioned emotional or nausea response. In addition to chemical and electrical aversive therapy, a type of aversive therapy called covert sensitization therapy has been studied. In this procedure, verbally guided images concerning alcohol and drinking are associated with imagined nausea, vomiting, and other unpleasant experiences. Miller and Hester (1980, p. 42) point out that while the procedure is promising, present "research data are inadequate to reach firm conclusions regarding covert sensitization." However, numerous studies reviewed by Miller and Hester indicate that covert sensitization is more effective than no treatment. Nathan and Briddell (1977, pp. 340–341), however, have concluded that "aversive conditioning—electrical, chemical, or covert—has not been proven effective *in isolation* as a means of modifying or eliminating excessive drinking. When tested for therapeutic efficacy by themselves, neither electrical nor covert aversion led to significant changes in drinking behavior on either a short-term or long-term basis.

BEHAVIOR THERAPY

In addition to aversive therapies, other behavior therapy methods have been utilized. Some of these methods are as follows: behavioral self-control training including blood alcohol discrimination training (teaching people to perceive accurately the level of alcohol in their bloodstream), video tape self-confrontation, relaxation training, systematic desensitization, extinction, social skills training, operant conditioning procedures including a community-reinforcement method, and cognitive-behavioral methods. Two comprehensive reviews of studies on these procedures are available to the interested reader. An early review by Nathan and Briddell (1977) and a recent review by Miller and Hester (1980) have provided summaries of research on these methods. In general, results suggest promise for some of these methods and problems with others. In particular, Hunt and Azrin's (1973) work on community-reinforcement approaches has shown interesting results. In Hunt and Azrin's study, two groups of alcoholics were studied. The experimental group received help from an experienced behavioral clinician in the community. The help consisted of assistance in finding employment, improvement in family and marital relations, enhancement of social skills, and restructuring of reinforcing social skills. The control group received standard hospitalization milieu therapy only. Results showed that the community-reinforcement group showed less time drinking, unemployed, away from home, or institutionalized than the control group. These results, however, were based upon only eight subjects in each condition.

Relaxation training and systematic desensitization in isolation appear to have little value in alcoholism treatment, but are probably effective as adjuncts for certain patients. A small effect of video tape confrontation is offset by a high patient dropout rate. Results with blood alcohol discrimination (Vogler 1982; Vogler and Bartz 1982) suggest that while it is of theoretical interest, it is of little practical importance in the treatment of alcoholism at this time. Behavioral self-control therapy, however, has received consistent support in a number of studies with certain types of problem drinkers. Investigations into cognitive-behavioral methods are presently underway.

COUNSELING AND PSYCHOTHERAPY

Although individual and group counseling and some form of "psychotherapy" are widespread in the modern treatment of alcoholics, little is known with certainty about these procedures. Traditional dynamic psychotherapy has not been regarded as a treatment of choice for alcoholics, but it may be a useful adjunct for the treatment of co-existing psychopathology in some alcoholics. Treatment relies heavily on group methods (e.g., Blume 1985). McCrady and Sher (1983) have provided a recent comprehensive review of research on patient and treatment variables.

In contrast to classical, dynamic, insight-oriented psychotherapy, alcoholism counseling is directive, supportive, reality centered, focused on the present, short term, and oriented toward real world behavioral changes. Counselors vary in the importance they place on feelings expressed by the patients during therapy sessions. Counselors also differ in the degree of confrontation they use or will use with resistant patients. Some counselors will use aggressive or even hostile confrontations with patients, while others regard such therapist behaviors as counterproductive (Wallace 1985b).

Although the benefits derived from confrontation with alcoholic patients may not be consistently productive, evidence exists that sharing information about the patient's condition in a realistic, straightforward, and nonthreatening manner may be beneficial. Kristenson et al. (1983) reported that persons given test results showing elevated liver enzymes associated with heavy drinking did modify their behavior accordingly. At followups lasting as long as 5 years, informed patients had lower mortality, incidence of illness and hospitalization, and absenteeism than a group of controls.

Although reviews of the effectiveness of psychotherapy (e.g., Hill and Blane 1967) and of psychological treatments (Emrick 1975) are often cited as disappointing, careful examination reveals that these reviews appear to have had little to do with the effectiveness of individual psychotherapy. Much of Hill and Blane's review appears to have dealt with studies concerning larger program evaluations, with group therapy, or with poorly and incompletely described treatment modalities that may have had little to do with individual psychotherapy as such. As Cartwright (1981) has pointed out, Emrick's review dealt largely with studies of medical and behavioral therapies including drug therapies, hypnosis, and aversive conditioning. One-quarter of the studies dealt with total program evaluation; less than 10 concerned group and marital counseling. Since few of Emrick's studies dealt with individual psychotherapy, empirical studies bearing directly on individual and group counseling or "psychotherapy" should be considered a high priority. Many programs include considerable amounts of individual counseling.

A study by McLachlan (1974) is a clear example of the type of research needed in this area of study. McLachlan investigated the degree of correspondence between the patient's conceptual level and the therapist's conceptual level. At level 1, the lowest conceptual level, persons are poorly socialized, egocentric, impulsive, and cognitively simple. At level 2, they are dependent on authority, compliant, and concerned with rules. At level 3, they are independent, questioning, and self-assertive. Persons at the highest conceptual level are interdependent, empathic, and cognitively complex. Patients were designated as either matched or mismatched to their group therapists in terms of measured conceptual level. Hence, a level 1 patient was considered matched when he got a therapist with a similar conceptual level and mismatched if he got a therapist at the highest conceptual level. The results clearly favored the matched patients, who showed a 70 percent recovery rate (abstinence), versus mismatched patients, who showed a 50 percent recovery rate.

Cartwright (1981) has discussed the fact that only a small fraction of studies of alcoholism treatment have dealt with the therapist's perspective. He cites the early study by Ends and Page (1957) as one of a few that actually compared different therapeutic perspectives. Ends and Page compared groups treated by Mower's two-factor learning theory therapy, client-centered therapy, psychoanalytic therapy, and social discussions. The poorest outcome was for two-factor learning theory; the best outcome was for client-centered therapy. Psychoanalytic therapy was second, and social discussion third.

Pomerleau et al. (1978) compared behavioral self-control training to insight-oriented psychotherapy and found a significant total improvement rate of 72 percent at 12-month followup in the behavioral group versus 50 percent in the insight-oriented group.

Brandsma et al. (1980) compared patients randomly assigned to rational behavior therapy, insight-oriented therapy, AA, or an untreated control group. Both treated groups and AA participants had better outcomes than the untreated controls, and the treated groups did slightly better than the AA members. In a review of group therapy with alcoholics, Brandsma and Pattison (1986) found some evidence for effectiveness. However, abstinence or improvement rates varied from a low of 15 percent to a high of 53 percent.

An earlier paper by Rosenburg et al. (1976) is of interest. Working with counselor trainees, these investigators were able to show large differences in ability to keep patients in treatment. Differences were attributable to therapist behaviors because the characteristics of the patients of the successful counselors did not differ from the characteristics of patients of the unsuccessful counselors. What is needed is an extension of this study in which differences between successful and unsuccessful counselors are examined as well. Valle (1981), for example, has shown that when counselors are compared on levels of interpersonal functioning, counselors with higher levels of functioning have patients who show fewer relapses, fewer relapse days, and less use of alcohol during 2 years after treatment.

Given the crucial role that counselors and therapists of various therapeutic perspectives play in the treatment of alcoholism, it is evident that considerably more empirical study of counselor behaviors, styles, attitudes, beliefs, and personality characteristics is needed in the field of alcoholism treatment.

ALCOHOLICS ANONYMOUS

Programs such as Alcoholics Anonymous, Al-Anon, and Alateen continue to provide critically needed, community-based support services for alcoholics and their families. While Alcoholics Anonymous is a program for alcoholics, Al-Anon is a separate program for the spouses, parents, adult children, siblings, and other concerned persons whose lives are closely tied to alcoholics. Alateen is a program for the teenage children of alcoholics. Large numbers of alcoholics achieve sobriety and maintain it for many years through Alcoholics Anonymous alone. Others recover through a combination of professional treatment services and membership in AA. Precisely how many people recover through AA alone or AA in conjunction with professional treatment services is not known with certainty. However, there is evidence that attendance at AA meetings is positively correlated with the maintenance of abstinence (Gordis et al. 1981; Polich et al. 1981; Pettinati et al. 1982; Vaillant 1983).

Pettinati et al. (1982), in a 4-year followup study of 225 alcoholics treated in an inpatient program, found that regular attendance at AA meetings was significantly related to abstinence. Other posttreatment interventions were not related to abstinence. Vaillant et al. (1984), in an 8-year longitudinal study of 100 alcoholics, found a "striking association" between attendance at AA meetings and continued recovery.

An approach to evaluating the effectiveness of certain AA concepts in a treatment context has been provided by Alford (1980). Studying 56 alcoholic patients (27 men and 29 women) in an AA-oriented inpatient treatment setting, Alford found that 58 percent were abstinent at 6 months following treatment. This study, of course, provides only a partial test of AA effectiveness because it is addressed to AA concepts as applied in a treatment setting and not to the fellowship of AA.

Although many anecdotal reports attest to the effectiveness of AA, at present its effectiveness has not been scientifically documented (Glaser and Ogborne 1982; Miller and Hester in press). Conducting controlled evaluations of AA is difficult because of methodological problems. Research is hampered by the voluntary and informal nature of AA, absence of membership lists, and poor documentation; existing studies suffer from inadequate baseline assessment and followup (Glaser and Ogborne 1982). Many of the existing studies have evaluated AA not by itself but as one element of a complex treatment program, making it difficult to determine AA's independent contribution to outcome (Miller and Hester 1980).

A review of the literature on outcomes in AA suggests an abstinence rate between 26 percent and 50 percent at 1 year, which compares favorably with the results of other approaches (Miller and Hester 1980). AA may be optimal for a certain type of alcoholic; future research needs to identify the type of person for whom AA is the best approach (Glaser and Ogborne 1982).

AA membership changes continue to be reported through the fellowship's triennial survey. In the 1983 survey (AA World Services 1984), worldwide membership was reported as 1,351,793. U.S. membership was reported as 630,679, up from 476,000 in 1980. The percentage of women in the 1983 survey remained constant since 1980 at 30 percent. The proportion of people 30 years old and under increased from 14.7 percent in 1980 to 20 percent in 1983. The proportion of people reporting counseling agencies and treatment facilities as responsible for referral to their first AA meeting continues to rise from 19 percent in 1977 to 26 percent in 1980 to 31 percent in 1983. Finally, more persons with drug problems in addition to their alcohol problems are entering AA (31 percent of the membership).

Prior to the introduction of formal treatment programs for family members, the spouses, parents, and children of alcoholics had nowhere to turn for help, advice, and support other than Al-Anon and Alateen. Spouses of alcoholics, particularly wives, were often regarded as neurotic and treated inappropriately in the mental health system. The stress of living with or near active alcoholism was not recognized, and psychological problems of spouses were regarded as intrapsychic in origin and treated accordingly. Due to the efforts of Al-Anon, attention came to be focused on family members as well as on the alcoholic within the family system.

Without question, AA, Al-Anon Family Groups, and Alateen are fellowship programs that have played and will continue to play major roles in community responses to alcoholism.

MARITAL AND FAMILY THERAPY

Alcohol problems affect and are affected by the patient's family situation. Marital and family therapy includes a variety of therapeutic techniques used by clinicians who share a conviction that disturbed family life plays a significant role in individual pathology and that treating the family will produce positive change. In some approaches, treatment targets not only the drinking and drinking-related behaviors of the patient but also the patterns of family communication and interaction.

Therapeutic approaches that involve the family have given encouraging results (Moos and Moos 1984), and controlled studies of marital or family therapy for alcoholics have found moderately better short-term outcomes than individual approaches (McCrady et al. in press). Alcoholics treated in joint hospitalization programs with their spouses showed more improvement after 4 years than did patients treated only with individual therapy or with joint therapy sessions with their spouses, but the differences were not significant (McCrady et al. 1982). At 4 years the subjects from the three groups were similar with respect to periods of abstinence, drinking history, and use of hospitalization and aftercare resources. Whereas more than three-fourths of the subjects showed short-term inprovement at 6 months, less than one-third functioned consistently well over the 4 years. Findings suggest that a certain subpopulation of married alcoholics may benefit from intensive conjoint involvement and that involvement of the spouse may have an important short-term impact but no particular long-term advantage over individual treatment. In general, these studies by McCrady et al. (1986) and Moos and Moos (1984) have strongly supported the hypothesis that family dysfunction appears to be the result of alcoholism rather than the cause of it.

In another study comparing couples groups (in which the husband had begun outpatient alcoholism counseling) with individual treatment (O'Farrell et al. 1985), the behavioral marital therapy group had improved marital adjustment compared with couples in interactional therapy and individuals treated alone, although differences in drinking behavior were not statistically significant. However, the husbands in the behavior marital therapy group had fewer alcohol-involved days during treatment.

A recent study by McCrady et al. (1986) has compared the effectiveness of different types of spouse involvement in alcoholism treatment. Alcoholics and their spouses were treated as outpatients with minimal spouse involvement, alcohol-focused spouse involvement, or alcohol-focused spouse involvement plus marital therapy. Although all subjects markedly reduced their drinking and reported increased life satisfaction, the best outcome was found in the marital therapy group. Alcoholics in this group improved more quickly, relapsed more slowly, were more likely to stay in treatment, and had better marital satisfaction.

A new approach under development, unilateral family therapy (Thomas and Santa 1982), is directed toward changing the behavior of an uncooperative family member by working with and providing therapeutic assistance to a cooperating member as a mediator.

In the past decade, clinicians have come to recognize family members as primary patients deserving of treatment in their own right, and not simply as adjuncts to treatment of the alcoholic. Modern treatment of spouses and children recognizes that the stress of living in an alcoholic family situation can, in some instances, have devastating effects upon the emotional and psychological health of family members. These problems must be addressed therapeutically whether or not alcoholic family members recover. Treatment of spouses, dependent children, and adult children of alcoholics have become central therapeutic issues; demand is increasing for therapeutic services for these groups independent of alcoholism treatment per se.

With growing recognition of the need for treatment of family members, regardless of the course of alcoholism in the alcoholic family member, evaluation of family therapy must begin to address questions other than the impact of such therapy on the drinking behavior of the alcoholic.

FACTORS AFFECTING TREATMENT OUTCOME

The outcome of alcoholism treatment is a complex issue, one that involves many difficult questions. Emrick and Hansen (1983) point out that the outcome of treatment can be influenced by any and all of the following: patient characteristics, sample selection and attrition, patient experiences outside of and after treatment, duration of followup, type of outcome variables examined, analysis and interpretation of data, and a host of scientific methodological problems related to the conduct of outcome research (e.g., Emrick 1982; Emrick and Hansen 1985). Given these many sources of variability in treatment outcome results, it is not surprising to find striking differences in reported outcome statistics in the alcoholism treatment literature. When patients, programs, staffs, goals of treatment, community environments, definitions of successful outcomes, and conduct of research differ, it is obvious that no single outcome statistic could possibly describe the results of alcoholism treatment interventions.

Despite the complex issues involved in the evaluation of treatment, there is growing consensus that alcoholism treatment does work (Saxe et al. 1983). And in some instances, with particular patient populations treated with particular methods, it works very well indeed. Increasing recognition of the effectiveness of treatment has led investigators to pose more sophisticated questions: For whom does alcoholism treatment seem not to work well and why? Can treatment results be improved for people who respond poorly to present treatments? Is it possible to match patients to treatment and increase effectiveness by doing so? Is alcoholism treatment cost-effective? These questions are considered in the following discussion of treatment outcome.

Patient Characteristics as Factors in Outcome

Numerous studies have demonstrated the significance of patient characteristics in predicting outcome of treatment. As a rule, patients who are married, stably employed, free of severe psychological impairments, and of higher socioeconomic status respond most favorably to treatment (e.g., Baekeland 1977; Gibbs and Flanagan 1977; Neubuerger et al. 1981; McLellan et al. 1983a). Gibbs and Flanagan (1977), in a review of 45 studies involving 55 different treatment groups, found several characteristics that were frequently but not always related to positive outcome. These were steady work history, marriage or cohabitation, higher status occupation, history of AA contact prior to treatment, higher social class, fewer arrests, and type of occupation regardless of status.

That such patient characteristics can influence treatment outcome is evident in a comparison of results for two programs serving very different populations. Patton (1979), in a followup study of employed, well-educated, largely middle- to upper middle-class alcoholics treated at the Hazelden Treatment Center in Minnesota, found a combined abstention and improvement rate of 92 percent. At 18 months following treatment, 62 percent of the sample reported complete abstention from alcohol for the entire 18-month period. Over the 18-month followup period, the followup response rate was 75 percent. Consideration of major possible sources of error in the Hazelden outcome suggests a lower bound of 50 percent for the 18-month abstention rate. In effect, the reported 62 percent abstention rate in Patton's study may be an overly optimistic estimate.

Gordis et al. (1981), working with a far more difficult patient population in which 71 percent were unemployed at the time of admission, 17 percent were on public assistance, and 50 percent had been treated for alcoholism elsewhere, reported an abstinence rate of 32 percent at 1 year. In contrast to the 75 percent followup rate at 18 months achieved by Patton (1979), Gordis et al. (1981) found that 45 percent of their patients were lost to followup before 30 days. Such dramatic differences in outcome results for these two programs serving very different populations are probably attributable to population rather than program differences. Costello (1980), for example, found a large correlation between scores on a measure of the treatment difficulty posed by patients and outcome of treatment. Treatment difficulty was a combined measure of social, biological, psychological, and drinking variables. The more difficulty patients experienced in all these areas of functioning, the less likely they were to respond favorably to alcoholism treatment.

In summary, differences in response to treatment are often more readily attributable to the characteristics of patients served than to differences in program content.

CONTEXTS, INTENSITY, AND LENGTH OF TREATMENT

It has long been recognized that not all alcoholics require formal treatment for alcoholism in order to recover. Many achieve recovery through community resources such as AA and other self-help groups, organized religions, and other means. As pointed out earlier, the 1983 survey of the membership of AA (Alcoholics Anonymous World Services 1984) reported that approximately 30 percent of its members come to the program through referral from counseling services and treatment facilities. This may mean that many members of AA may establish initial programs of abstinence without formal, professional treatment services. Precisely how many members of AA achieve initial abstinence without professional help of any kind is not known with certainty.

Just as alcoholics do not always need formal treatment to recover, those treated for alcoholism do not always require intensive treatment or longer-term inpatient treatment (Longabaugh et al. 1983). To define which alcoholics require more intensive treatment through inpatient or outpatient programs, or longer-term inpatient treatment, however, will require further research on treatment outcome.

A number of studies have involved comparisons of inpatient care with outpatient care (Pittman and Tate 1972; Wanberg et al. 1974; Mosher et al. 1975; Wilson et al. 1978). Other studies have compared inpatient care to less intensive forms of treatment such as partial hospitalization (Longabaugh et al. 1983) and day clinic (McLachlan and Stein 1982). Edwards et al. (1977) and Orford et al. (1976) have compared patients receiving intensive outpatient treatment to patients given advice only.

With the exception of Wanberg et al. (1974), studies of treatment context have not yielded differences in outcomes between patients treated in inpatient settings versus outpatient, partial hospitalization, and day clinic settings.

While these studies do show consistent results, there are both methodological and interpretive issues that indicate that conclusions and implications must be drawn cautiously. When continuous abstinence (the most scientifically rigorous measure of successful outcome) is examined, interpretation of the majority of these studies is complicated by high relapse rates. In the Mosher et al. (1975) study at 6-month followup, 82 percent of the outpatients had relapsed (i.e., failed to sustain abstinence) versus 77 percent of the inpatients. Wilson et al. (1978) reported relapse rates of 74 percent for both inpatients and outpatients at 15-month followup. Pittman and Tate (1972) reported relapse rates of 71 percent for outpatients and 78 percent for inpatients at 12-month followup. Stein et al. (1975) reported 4-month followup relapse rates of 64 percent for outpatients and 57 percent for inpatients. (It is important to note that Stein et al.'s (1975) relapse rates do not necessarily reflect sustained abstinence since they are based upon the numbers of patients in various outcome categories at each followup period. Hence, a patient categorized as abstinent at 4-month followup could be drinking pathologically at 13-month followup and vice versa.) McLachlan and Stein (1982) reported relapse rates of 67 percent for both outpatients and inpatients at 12-month followup. Longabaugh et al. (1983) reported 6-month relapse rates of 57 percent with these rising to 77 percent at 24-month followup (Fink et al. 1985). Edwards et al. (1977) reported that brief advice was presumably as effective as intensive treatment, but at 2-year followup (Orford et al. 1976), the relapse rate was 100 percent. As Orford et al. (1976) reported, the majority of men regardless of whether they had been in the "advice" or the treatment group drank within a few weeks of their initial consultation. By 12-month followup, all but 8 of the 95 men had returned to drinking, and by the 2-year followup only 2 of 95 men showed sustained abstention with these 2 returning to drinking shortly thereafter. Given the 100 percent relapse rate in this study, the conclusion that the Edwards et al. (1977) study showed that brief "advice" is as effective as intensive treatment is unwarranted. Rather, the Edwards et al. (1977) study showed that *neither* advice nor intensive treatment was effective in the hands of these particular clinicians when effectiveness was defined in terms of the rigorous measure of sustained, continuous abstention from alcohol following treatment.

In general, the relatively high relapse rates observed in the majority of the particular treatment programs and populations utilized in these studies of different treatment contexts raise serious problems of interpretation. When neither treatment program being compared is particularly effective, it is not possible to draw meaningful generalizations about comparative *cost-effectiveness,* for other inpatient treatment programs and treatment populations in which successful outcomes of 50 percent or more have been reported (e.g., Patton 1979; Laundergan 1982; Neubuerger et al. 1982; Wiens and Menustik 1983; Pickens et al. 1985). As Schuckit et al. (1986, p. 151) have cautioned, "However, even after these—[many]—factors are determined, it is still possible that findings from one population (e.g., veterans, the military, outpatients, skid row groups, court referred people) will not generalize to another."

With regard to questions concerning length and intensity of treatment, some studies appear to show no difference while others find effects favoring longer treatment. Numerous studies have not shown differences in treatment outcome as a result of length of treatment (e.g., Willems et al. 1973; Mosher et al. 1975; Page and Schaub 1979; Miller and Hester 1980, 1986; Emrick 1982; Powell et al. 1985).

Conversely, Welte et al. (1981) evaluated 756 patients at 3 and 8 months after inpatient treatment and found that patients who stayed in inpatient treatment longer were more likely to be abstaining or drinking less at followup. This improvement was greater among patients of low social stability. Bromet and Moos (1977) found that longer lengths of stay appeared to decrease rehospitalizations in three of five alcoholism treatment facilities studied.

In a subsequent study, Finnel et al. (1981) found significant positive correlations between length of stay in a halfway-house setting and abstinence, alcohol consumption, and rehospitalization at followup. Positive correlations between length of treatment and successful outcome have been reported by Armor et al. (1976), Smart (1978), and Smart and Gray (1978a). Kish et al. (1980) reported statistically significant differences at followup in sustained abstinence between alcoholic men with shorter stays and those with longer stays. Men who had stayed for shorter periods in an inpatient treatment setting had significantly more drinking episodes at followup (59 percent) than did men with longer stays (35 percent). Kish and Herman (1971) found differences in outcome associated with longer stays at the 1-year followup but not at the 2-year followup.

With regard to questions of context of treatment, length of stay, and intensity of treatment, it is likely that no general answer can be given. The considerable variability evident among alcoholics in psychiatric occupational, marital, family, psychological, and general social functioning indicates that variable lengths of stay will probably prove necessary. As pointed out previously, some alcoholics and problem drinkers will require no formal treatment, others may show improvement with minimal treatment (e.g., Miller and Baca 1983; Buck and Miller in press), others may require relatively brief stays in inpatient settings, and still others will require stays of a month or more in inpatient treatment if stable recovery is to be achieved. Research directed toward discovering explicit clinical criteria that can be used to determine how long individual patients will need to stay in inpatient and outpatient programs is needed.

PATIENT-TREATMENT MATCHING

Given the necessity for a comprehensive system of alcoholism services and the need for variable lengths of stay in facilities offering such services, it does not appear fruitful to continue to pose questions in terms of one service versus another (e.g., inpatient versus outpatient) or one length of stay versus another (e.g., minimal treatment versus longer-term treatment). The considerable heterogeneity among alcoholic persons suggests that a person with one set of personal and situational characteristics may respond favorably to one type of treatment or setting but unfavorably to another. Such possible differential response to varying treatments has led to an interest in patient-treatment matching (Miller and Hester in press).

In the broadest meaning of the term, matching of patients to treatments occurs when individual treatments are administered in an effort to alleviate problems identified through clinical assessments. Many alcoholism treatment programs, including those that offer a single, common core program to all patients, provide this type of patient-treatment matching. Hence, depressed patients in a typical alcoholism rehabilitation program are usually referred for psychiatric evaluation and, if necessary, for treatment with antidepressant medications. Patients who show a bipolar depression in addition to their alcoholism are stabilized with lithium as they complete their alcoholism rehabilitation program. Similarly, patients with anxiety disorders may be given relaxation training, desensitization therapy, or appropriate medications (e.g., low-dose antidepressant therapy in the case of panic disorder). Formal research on patient characteristics and response to treatment is an attempt to improve on this type of clinical patient-treatment matching by giving it a more rigorous empirical basis.

Formal research on patient-treatment matching may involve one or more of the following treatment components: therapeutic process, treatment regimen, treatment format, treatment setting, and treatment philosophy. Conceptual issues in patient-treatment matching have been discussed by Glaser (1980), Glaser and Skinner (1981), Finney and Moos (1986).

Research on patient characteristics and response to particular treatments has provided interesting hypotheses but is still far from conclusive. Moreover, many of the characteristics that have been related to one treatment in a particular study are clearly related to other treatments in other studies. For example, there have been a number of studies of patient characteristics and response to disulfiram treatment. These studies have shown that favorable responders tend to be older, socially stable, less depressed, more motivated, married, and more compulsive (Baekeland et al. 1971; Fuller and Roth 1979; Azrin et al. 1982). Unfortunately, many, if not most, of these characteristics have been shown to be related to favorable response to *any* treatment, not just disulfiram therapy. For example, patients responding well to other drug aversion therapy are also older, socially stable, married, and motivated. The same set of patient characteristics describes favorable responders to inpatient rehabilitation treatment (e.g., Welte et al. 1981).

In order to show that particular characteristics are *differentially* related to different treatments, it is necessary to vary patient characteristics and treatments simultaneously. That is, one must study the responses of patients with varying characteristics to two or more treatments. These differential patient-treatment matching studies are rare. However, McLellan and his colleagues have contributed several studies in this regard.

In the first study, McLellan et al. (1983a) studied the responses to treatment of 460 alcohol-dependent and 282 drug-dependent patients treated in 6 different programs in the Veterans' Administration treatment network during 1978. The six programs were as follows: (1) Alcohol Therapeutic Community (60-day inpatient), (2) Fixed-Interval Drinking Decisions, (3) Combined Alcohol and Drug Program (60-day inpatient for alcoholics and drug addicts treated together), (4) Alcohol Outpatient, (5) Drug Abuse Therapeutic Community, and (6) Methadone Maintenance. When data were analyzed in terms of an addiction severity index, no significant differences were found. However, use of a measure of severity of psychiatric disturbance developed in an earlier study (McLellan et al. 1980) resulted in several interesting patient-treatment matches. Although patients with low severity of psychiatric problems did well in either inpatient or outpatient programs, patients with high severity of psychiatric problems did poorly no matter what treatment they received. The most interesting findings concerned those with middle-range severity of psychiatric problems. For patients with midrange psychiatric problems who also had greater employment or family problems, outpatient treatment led to worse outcomes than inpatient treatment. Patients with midrange psychiatric problems who also had legal problems tended to do less well in the two inpatient programs.

In a later prospective study, McLellan et al. (1983b) matched patients to their six treatment programs on the basis of findings from their first retrospective study. Using measures of psychiatric severity as well as measures of employment, family, and medical severity, the investigators succeeded in matching 53 percent of a new sample of 510 alcohol- and drug-dependent patients to appropriate treatments. Of the remaining 47 percent of the patients, 27 percent were mismatched to the appropriate treatment program because of lack of bed availability, 13 percent were mismatched because of the patient's refusal to accept a particular program assignment, and 7 percent of the mismatches stemmed from simple assignment errors or clinical staff disagreement with research decisions to assign patients to particular treatment programs.

The effects of matching patients to appropriate treatments were evident in some of McLellan et al.'s outcome measures. Matched alcohol-dependent patients from the low and midrange psychiatric severity groups were rated as significantly more motivated for treatment, stayed in treatment longer (60 days versus 50 days), and had a higher proportion of favorable discharges than did mismatched patients (33 irregular discharges versus 43 irregular discharges). Moreover, the matched alcohol-dependent patients showed significantly better 6-month outcomes concerning employment, medical condition, drug use, legal status, and family relations. In all, matched alcohol-dependent patients showed better outcomes on 17 of 19 followup comparisons.

In summary, the work by McLellan et al. (1980, 1983a, b) demonstrated two things. *First, even without patient-treatment matching procedures, alcoholism treatment was effective.* Alcohol-dependent patients who stayed in treatment for at least 15 days showed decreases of 67 percent in their drinking, reductions of 38 percent in family problems, reductions of 61 percent in psychiatric problems, and an increase of 92 percent in earned income 6 months after treatment. *Second, effec-*

tiveness of treatment was improved by matching patients to the most appropriate treatments. The overall outcome of the matched patients (averaged across all criteria) was 19 percent better than that of the mismatched patients.

With regard to severity of impairment, hypotheses concerning length of stay have also been proposed. One might expect that more severely impaired alcoholics would do better in longer term treatment programs. However, one direct test of the hypothesis that alcoholics who are more severely impaired neuropsychologically would respond better to longer lengths of stay was not confirmed (Walker et al. 1983). And in McLellan et al.'s (1983a, b) studies, alcoholics who were severely impaired psychiatrically did poorly in all types of treatment programs studied.

Despite these early discouraging findings, it is possible that as more is learned about alternative counseling and learning strategies with more severely impaired alcoholics (particularly the neuropsychologically impaired), new treatment methods developed specifically for this group may enhance outcomes (e.g., Goldman et al. 1985; McCrady and Smith 1986).

AFTERCARE SERVICES

It is widely accepted among alcoholism treatment professionals that aftercare services are a critical component of comprehensive alcoholism treatment services. A continuum of care including aftercare services is considered essential because of the relatively long period of recovery that many alcoholics appear to need and the high probability of relapse noted among alcoholics who leave treatment systems early. Walker et al. (1983) provide some empirical support for these traditional views of alcoholism treatment professionals. In a study of 245 male veterans grouped according to neuropsychiatric functioning, Walker and his colleagues found the strongest relationships were between aftercare involvement and treatment outcome. Patients who attended weekly aftercare groups for 9 months following hospitalization were three times more likely to remain abstinent than patients who dropped out of aftercare (70.2 percent versus 23.4 percent). These results are consistent with Costello's review of 23 2-year followup studies. The provision of an aggressive outpatient followup or aftercare was one of seven characteristics that distinguished successful from unsuccessful programs (Costello 1975). Further correlational analysis by Costello (1980) also supported clinicians' views on the importance of aftercare services.

Cronkite and Moos (1984), in a study of 332 alcoholic patients, found a tendency for more married men to have received outpatient aftercare than unmarried men (50 percent versus 41 percent). Unmarried women, in contrast, were more likely to have received outpatient aftercare than were married women (68 percent versus 44 percent). For men, receiving aftercare services was associated with better outcomes. Only 28 percent of the married men who had relapses had participated in outpatient aftercare, and 54 percent of the married men who did not suffer relapses had received outpatient aftercare.

In general, then, available data do support the traditional view of the importance of aftercare services in alcoholism treatment. With regard to length of aftercare services, Siegel et al. (1984a) tracked 325 alcoholic patients who had received inpatient treatment. Patients were followed for a period of 2 years in terms of how much outpatient aftercare they had used during this time and if they had been readmitted to inpatient services. Patients who had received either no outpatient services or an average of up to 5.4 months aftercare were more likely to be readmitted to inpatient care than patients receiving longer periods of aftercare.

Cost Analyses of Alcoholism Treatment

What do alcoholism services cost relative to other problems in the mental health sector? Siegel et al. (1984b) have reported comparative costs of services to alcoholics and other mental health patients in suburban Rockland County, New York. A group of 315 patients with a primary diagnosis of alcoholism was compared with a group of 516 patients with nonalcoholic psychiatric diagnoses with regard to services for a 2-year period. Although alcoholics represented the largest single diagnostic group in the cohort studied (39 percent), the cost of their care was only 22 percent of the total cost. Alcoholics had lower costs because they used cumulatively fewer inpatient days and received fewer days of the most costly outpatient services of full-day treatment. Siegel et al. (1984b, p. 504) concluded, "On the average, the cost to treat severe alcoholic patients is less than half the cost to serve nonalcoholic patients."

Costello and Hodde (1981) raised questions about how costs are distributed among system components and among individuals. Inpatient treatment accounted for 73 percent of the costs generated by 100 socially unstable men and women patients to a comprehensive alcoholism treatment system, but only 5 patients accounted for 48 percent of the total inpatient treatment costs of $297,150 over the 4-year period (1972–1976). In fact, these 5 patients accounted for 38 percent of the total treatment system costs of $406,060. Two of these five patients were still in an inpatient setting after 4 years and had generated costs of $29,585 and $31,025, respectively. The most costly patient accounted for $53,560 in less than 3 years before being transferred to a nursing home. Costello and Hodde (1981, p. 91) concluded not only that costs were not distributed equally over patients, but also that for this population of socially unstable alcoholics, "outpatient service and aftercare were extremely difficult to implement."

Still another question arising from cost analyses of alcoholism treatment concerns cost-benefit analysis. Do the benefits derived from treating alcoholics balance or offset the costs? A large number of studies reviewed by Jones and Vischi (1979) justify an affirmative response to the question of cost-benefit analysis in alcoholism treatment. Brock and Boyajy (1978) reported a 40 percent reduction in outpatient care utilization after alcoholism treatment while Sherman et al. (1979) found a 27 percent reduction in inpatient and outpatient medical care costs at Kaiser Permanente in Southern California. Hunter (1978), in a study of the Arizona Health Plan, found reductions in posttreatment care costs. With regard to dollar savings, Hayami and Freebori (1981), in the context of a health maintenance organization (HMO), estimated a savings of $0.40 for every $1.00 spent on treatment. Holder and Hallan (1978), in a study of the health benefits program of the California Public Employees Retirement system, found an annual savings of $84 per person following alcoholism treatment initiation. The authors followed a group of 90 alcoholics and their families from the same health insurance program and reported an average annual reduction in total health care costs of $864 per person (Holder and Hallan 1981).

Holder and colleagues (1985) examined the impact of alcoholism treatment on overall health care utilization and costs for individuals and families filing claims with the Aetna Life Insurance Company under the Federal Employees Health Benefit Program. On the average, families with at least one member filing a claim for alcoholism treatment during calendar years 1980–1983 used health care services and incurred costs at a rate about twice that of a comparison group consisting of a random sample of families who filed no alcoholism claims during that period. Average monthly health care costs for the two groups over this period were $210 per person and $107 per person, respectively.

The study also found a gradual rise in the overall health care costs and utilization for alcoholics during the 3 years preceding alcoholism treatment, with the most dramatic increase occurring in the 6 months before treatment. Total monthly costs increased from about $150 per month 2 years prior to treatment to an average of more than $450 per month during the 6 months prior to treatment and $1,370 in the final pretreatment month.

After alcoholics started treatment, their health care costs dropped significantly and eventually reached approximately the level that existed several years prior to treatment. Their total monthly costs averaged $294 during the first 6 months after treatment and declined to an average of $190 per month by 2.5 to 3 years after treatment. The most significant drop in health care costs occurred for treated alcoholics under the age of 45.

Using a variety of forecasting techniques, the project estimated that the average alcoholic's treatment cost could be offset by reductions in other health care costs within 2 to 3 years following the start of treatment.

Although sufficient empirical data are available to show that alcoholism treatment makes good sense from a cost-benefit perspective, data bearing on cost-effectiveness are less easily interpreted. At a micro level of analysis in which alternative treatments such as inpatient and outpatient care are delivered in a single hospital setting, it is reasonable to conclude that the costs associated with feeding and housing patients will be lower in particular outpatient treatment programs in comparison with particular inpatient programs.

However, because large health care systems' results may not mirror results at the level of the individual hospital, it is not possible to predict with certainty the impact of variations at the individual hospital level on large health care systems. For example, because inpatient and outpatient treatment may stand in a *complementary* rather than *substitutive* relationship at the large health care system level, increases in the provision of outpatient services could increase both the quality and the cost of care (Freiberg 1977). Hence, although outpatient costs are generally accepted as lower than inpatient costs, it does not necessarily follow that changing the mix of outpatient to inpatient services in all large health care systems will automatically result in substantial reductions in cost per unit of equivalent effectiveness. Numerous studies cited by Freiberg (1977) do not show reduced system costs as outpatient services are increased.

Despite these cautions, however, it is clear that alcoholism treatment not only is effective (Gottheil 1985), but also—because it has been shown to reduce total health care costs—probably constitutes an approach to cost containment generally in health care systems. Studies of cost-effectiveness are as yet inconclusive, but promising leads have been uncovered, particularly with regard to recent studies of patient-treatment matching (e.g., McLellan et al. 1983a, b). If treatment costs can be reduced and treatment effectiveness increased through patient-treatment matching, alcoholism treatment will show further gains in cost-effectiveness.

POSTTREATMENT ENVIRONMENT AND MAINTENANCE OF GAINS

The posttreatment environment, especially family characteristics and work settings, is important in the recovery process and may enable some alcoholics to attain essentially normal patterns of functioning. Moos and Finney (1983) designed strategies to recognize the extent of environmental factors external to treatment and their effect on treatment outcome. Environmental stressors, coping responses, and social resources had as much influence on the recovery process as did patients' treatment experiences and characteristics at intake combined, and posttreatment functioning of recovered alcoholics was similar to that of nonalcoholic control subjects (Moos et al. 1981; Billings and Moos 1983). Information from systematic assessments of extra-treatment factors may help increase the effectiveness of treatment by identifying situations that increase the risk of relapse and by suggesting changes in coping patterns, family settings, and work settings.

Overall, about two-thirds of treated alcoholics improve, although reported success rates depend on whether the outcome indicator is abstinence, improved but not abstinent, or some other indicator (Saxe et al. 1983). One estimate of average short-term responses to treatment is that one-third of those treated become abstinent and one-third are improved but not abstinent (Miller and Hester 1980). Rates of abstinence at 1 year after treatment, a commonly used evaluative measure, typically range from 25 percent to 50 percent (Nathan in press). The lower rates are seen in poorly motivated, older, unemployed chronic alcoholics who are often in public treatment facilities. Higher rates are found among well-motivated, younger, employed, subchronic alcoholics treated in private facilities. At 3 years after treatment, the rates are generally half or less of the 1-year rates (Nathan in press).

Vaillant et al. (1983) have reported the results of an 8-year followup of a prospective study of alcoholism treatment. The duration of this study is twice that of any other prospective study in the literature. Subjects were 100 inpatients who received 1 to 9 days of counseling and education and who attended AA meetings. At 8 years or at the time of death, 29 percent had achieved stable abstinence of at least 3 years' duration, 24 percent had intermittent alcoholism, and 47 percent had continuing serious alcohol problems. Premorbid social stability and sustained abstinence were major factors in good psychosocial outcome at 8 years, and premorbid social stability and AA attendance were independent contributors to sustained abstinence. The investigators suggest that these data and those from other longitudinal studies indicate that factors other than professional treatment itself have substantial effects on long-term outcome.

Marlatt (1984) has developed various cognitive assessment and intervention procedures designed to prevent relapse during the recovery or maintenance phase. These procedures emphasize the personal responsibility of alcoholics for their behavior and teach them techniques for coping with high-risk situations and dealing with urges and cravings. Research designed to test the theories underlying these procedures is under way.

A serious difficulty with many posttreatment assessment studies is their reliance on self-reports regarding alcohol consumption by the subjects. A study by Orrego et al. (1979) suggests that such reports should be regarded with much skepticism. From their study of outpatients with alcoholic liver disease, these investigators concluded that self-reports are very unreliable. Alcohol measurements were made on urine samples mailed by the 37 subjects daily for up to 6 months in order to check on the accuracy of their self-reports during periodic personal interviews. Patients who had alcohol in their urine were successful 52 percent of the time in convincing their physician that they had not been drinking, and 25 percent of patients with alcohol in their urine denied drinking at every interview. Only 17 percent of patients who had been drinking were consistently truthful about it. The investigators concluded that the personal interview should not be used to separate populations of abstainers and nonabstainers in the followup of alcoholic patients.

TREATMENT GOALS

Abstinence from alcohol as well as from other psychoactive drugs has been regarded as a major goal of treatment. Not only are today's treatment populations urged to abstain from drinking, they are also counseled to avoid minor tranquilizers; hallucinogens; central nervous system stimulants such as cocaine, amphetamines, and caffeine; narcotics; and all nonselective general depressant drugs. Of course, alcoholics with coexisting mental illnesses may be required to take medications directed at these additional problems, such as antidepressants, lithium, and phenothiazines. As a rule, however, alcoholism treatment is directed toward producing patients who neither drink alcohol nor take psychoactive drugs.

While there have been numerous reports of reduced drinking among some persons treated for alcoholism (e.g., Pattison et al. 1977), the case for questioning abstention as a desired goal of alcoholism treatment has rested upon a small number of highly influential studies. The study by Davies (1962), for example, has been regarded as a classic paper in this area by proponents of nonabstinence treatment goals and has been cited frequently. Davies reported that 7 "alcohol addicts" out of 93 patients sampled returned to sustained "normal drinking" over a period of 7 to 11 years. Edwards (1985), however, reinvestigated the fate of Davies' subjects and found that the majority of them could not be considered to be "normal drinkers," either during Davies' original followup or thereafter. The evidence gathered by Edwards indicated that five of Davies' seven subjects experienced significant drinking problems throughout the initial and subsequent followup periods, and that three of the five subjects also used psychotropic drugs heavily. The two remaining men (one of whom was never severely dependent on alcohol) did engage in trouble-free drinking over the entire period. In effect, only 2 percent of Davies' original sample of 93 patients appeared to be able to "return to normal drinking," and the evidence suggests that one of these two subjects was probably misdiagnosed because he was never severely dependent on alcohol.

A study by Vaillant (1983) provides a perspective on attempts by alcoholics to drink. This was a longitudinal study (1940–1980) on the natural history of alcoholism, using subjects in Harvard Medical School's Study of Adult Development. Vaillant reported that nonproblem drinking is not predictive of a favorable long-term outcome. Vaillant noted that when middle-aged alcoholics who had required detoxification attempted to return to asymptomatic drinking, their situation was analogous to driving a car without a spare tire—disaster was usually only a matter of time.

Finney and Moos (1981) reported on 131 patients who returned to their families after treatment in 1 of 5 residential, abstinence-oriented alcoholism treatment programs. Within the first 6 months, 36 had relapsed. Another 37 who had tried to drink moderately within 6 months of alcoholism treatment had a significantly higher relapse rate at the 2-year followup mark than did those who abstained for at least 6 months before beginning moderate drinking. Given the very high mortality rates for those alcoholics who continue to misuse alcohol, relapse is a most serious outcome (Barr et al. 1984).

Studies of inpatients given a broad-spectrum, moderation-oriented program in addition to hospital treatment have not yielded positive findings. Foy et al. (1984) studied 62 chronic alcoholics receiving broad-spectrum behavioral treatment for alcoholism as inpatients at a Veterans' Administration Medical Center. The subgroup of 30 that received additional training in nonproblem drinking skills had significantly fewer abstinent days and more abusive drinking days at 6 months' followup than did the 32 not given this training.

In another recent report, Helzer et al. (1985) examined the 5- to 7-year outcome for 1,289 diagnosed alcoholics (confirmed by record review) treated as inpatients or outpatients. Of the 83 percent of the sample who were followed, 1.6 percent were considered to be moderate drinkers (up to six drinks a day), 15 percent had become totally abstinent, and 4.6 percent were mostly abstinent with occasional drinking. The investigators point out that the subjects were, however, likely to have been advised to stop drinking rather than to moderate their drinking. Helzer et al. concluded that the evolution to stable moderate drinking appears to be a rare outcome among alcoholics treated at medical or psychiatric facilities.

Pettinati et al. (1984) studied psychological functioning, as measured by the Minnesota Multiphasic Personality Inventory, in 61 alcoholics before they underwent inpatient treatment at 4 years' followup. Psychological functioning was most improved in those who maintained abstinence for a long time, compared with those who were abstinent with slips and those who were periodic drinkers. The investigators note that virtually no rehospitalization or subsequent treatment occurred among those who were able to maintain consistent and complete abstinence. Moreover, only 3 percent of the patients studied were able to engage in nonproblem drinking throughout the followup period.

In general, the bulk of clinical and scientific evidence appears to support the interpretation that once significant physical dependence has occurred; the alcoholic no longer has the option of returning to social drinking (Kissin and Hanson 1985); hence, abstinence is the most appropriate goal for alcoholic persons.

SUMMARY

Alcoholism treatment services have increased in the 6 years from 1978 to 1984. More than 500,000 persons were reported to be in treatment on September 28, 1984, with 40,786 (8 percent) in an inpatient setting, 51,976 (10 percent) in a residential setting, and

447,649 (82 percent) as active outpatients. State and local government control of in-hospital treatment units decreased by 17 percent, while for-profit ownership of such units increased by 392 percent. Other drug abuse, alcohol or drugs, was recorded as a discharge diagnosis on 1.13 million (2.7 percent) of all discharges from short-term hospitals in 1983.

Continuing attention is being paid to the heterogeneity apparent among alcoholics, and various attempts to develop concepts and measurements appropriate to such heterogeneity have been apparent. The alcohol dependence syndrome concept has been researched extensively. Possible applications of this concept involve approaches to individualized treatment planning.

There have been no dramatic changes in pharmacotherapy for alcoholics. Interest continues in possible uses of disulfiram with some alcoholics as an adjunct to more comprehensive treatment. Lithium carbonate may constitute a useful therapy for some alcoholics, mainly those with coexisting affective disorder.

Detoxification of alcoholics can be accomplished safely and effectively in both social settings and medical settings. Severity of alcohol dependence and withdrawal symptoms, general medical condition, psychiatric features, and other factors determine which setting for detoxification is most appropriate.

Studies of inpatient and outpatient treatment indicate that some alcoholics do not require inpatient treatment. Patient-treatment matching, with patients assigned to different treatments on the basis of various characteristics that are correlated with outcome, continues to be of considerable interest. However, studies of inpatient and outpatient treatment indicate that it is not yet clear as to which alcoholics require inpatient treatment and which require outpatient treatment.

With regard to cost issues, the costs of treatment should be viewed in light of the current $117 billion total economic care costs for alcoholism and problem drinking. All treatment expenditures, including a substantial portion for treatment of the medical consequences of alcoholism, are estimated at $15 billion a year. Alcoholism treatment is effective for many persons. Favorable cost-benefit ratios that show reduced general health care expenditures in treated alcoholics indicate that alcoholism treatment is an effective means of containing health care costs throughout the health care system.

A problem that permeates all studies of treatment is the validity of self-reports. Research is needed to develop objective and reliable markers of treatment outcome.

Studies of treatment goals indicate that abstention from alcohol and other psychoactive drugs continues to be the most reasonable treatment goal for diagnosed alcoholics in light of current scientific and clinical information.

REFERENCES

Alcoholics Anonymous World Services. *Alcoholics Anonymous*. New York: Alcoholics Anonymous World Services, 1953.

Alcoholics Anonymous World Services. *Twelve Steps and Twelve Traditions*. New York: Alcoholics Anonymous World Services, 1976.

Alcoholics Anonymous World Services. *1983 Survey of the Membership*. New York: Alcoholics Anonymous World Services, 1984.

Alford, G.S. Alcoholics Anonymous: An empirical outcome study. *Addictive Behaviors* 5:359–370, 1980.

American Hospital Association. *Hospital Statistics, 1978 Edition: Data from the American Hospital Association 1977 Annual Survey*. Chicago: American Hospital Association, 1984.

American Hospital Association. *Hospital Statistics, 1984 Edition: Data from the American Hospital Association 1983 Annual Survey*. Chicago: American Hospital Association, 1984.

American Psychiatric Association. *Diagnostic and Statistical Manual of Mental Disorders* (DSM III). 3d ed. Washington, D.C.: American Psychiatric Association, 1980.

Armor, D.J.; Polich, J.M.; and Stambul, H.B. *Alcoholism and Treatment*. Santa Monica, Calif.: Rand, 1976.

Azrin, N.H.; Sisson, R.W.; Meyers, R.; and Godley, M. Alcoholism treatment by disulfiram and community reinforcement therapy. *Journal of Behavior Therapy and Experimental Psychiatry* 13:105–112, 1982.

Babor, T.F., and Lauerman, R.J. Classification and forms of inebriety: Historical antecedents of alcoholic typologies. In: Galanter, M., ed. *Recent Developments in Alcoholism*. Vol. IV. New York: Plenum Publishing Corp., 1986. pp. 113–114.

Baekeland, F. Evaluation of treatment methods in chronic alcoholism. In: Kissin, B., and Begleiter, H., eds. *The Biology of Alcoholism*. Vol. V. *Treatment and Rehabilitation of the Chronic Alcoholic*. New York: Plenum Publishing Corp., 1977. pp. 385–440.

Baekeland, F.; Lundwall, L.; Kissin, B.; and Shanahan, T. Correlates of outcome in disulfiram treatment of alcoholism. *Journal of Nervous and Mental Diseases* 153:1–9, 1971.

Barr, H.L.; Antes, D.; Ottenberg, D.J.; and Rosen, A. Mortality of treated alcoholics and drug addicts: The benefits of abstinence. *Journal of Studies on Alcohol* 45:440–452, 1984.

Bartsch, T.W., and Hoffman, J.J. A cluster analysis of a million clinical multiaxial inventory (MCMI) profiles: More about a taxonomy of alcoholic subtypes. *Journal of Clinical Psychology* 4:707–713, 1985.

Becker, J.T., and Jaffe, J.H. Impaired memory for treatment-relevant information in inpatient men alcoholics. *Journal of Studies on Alcohol* 45:339–343, 1984.

Bedi, A., and Halikas, J.A. Alcoholism and affective disorder. *Alcoholism: Clinical and Experimental Research* 9:133–134, 1985.

Billings, A.G.; Cronkite, R.C.; and Moos, R.H. Difficulty of follow-up and posttreatment functioning among depressed patients. *Journal of Affective Disorders* 6:9–16, 1985.

Billings, A.G., and Moos, R.H. Psychosocial processes of recovery among alcoholics and their families: Implications for clinicians and program evaluators. *Addictive Behaviors* 8:205–218, 1983.

Blume, S.B. Group psychotherapy in the treatment of alcoholism. In: Zimberg, S.; Wallace, J.; and Blume, S.B., eds. *Practical Approaches to Alcoholism Therapy.* 2d ed. New York: Plenum Publishing Corp., 1985. pp. 73–85.

Brandsma, J.M.; Maultsby, M.C.; and Welsh, R.J. *The Outpatient Treatment of Alcoholism: A Review and Comparative Study.* Baltimore, University Park Press, 1980.

Brandsma, J.M., and Pattison, E.M. The outcome of group psychotherapy with alcoholics: An empirical review. *American Journal of Drug and Alcohol Abuse* 11:151–162, 1986.

Brock, C.B., and Boyajy, T.G. *Group Health Association of America Study: Alcoholism Within Prepaid Group Practice HMOs.* Report to NIAAA No. 5H8AA01745. Washington, D.C.; Supt. of Docs., U.S. Govt. Print. Off., 1978.

Bromet, E., and Moos, R.H. Environmental resources and the posttreatment functioning of alcoholic patients. *Journal of Health and Social Behavior* 18:326–338, 1977.

Buck, K., and Miller, W.R. Minimal intervention in the treatment of problem drinkers: A controlled study, in press.

Butters, N., and Cermak, L.S. *Alcoholic Korsakoff's Syndrome: An Information-Processing Approach to Amnesia.* New York: Academic Press, 1980.

Carroll, J.F.; Malloy, F.E.; and Kendrick, F.M. Drug abuse by alcoholics and problemdrinkers: A literature review and evaluation. *American Journal of Drug and Alcohol Abuse* 4:317–341, 1977.

Cartwright, A.K.J. Are different therapeutic perspectives important in the treatment of alcoholism? *British Journal of Addiction* 76:347–361, 1981.

Clinebell, H. *Understanding and Counseling the Alcoholic.* New York: Abingdon Press, 1956.

Costello, R.M. Alcoholism treatment and evaluation. In search of methods. II. Collation of two-year follow-up studies. *International Journal of the Addictions* 10:857–867, 1975.

Costello, R.M. Alcoholism aftercare and outcome: Cross-legged panel and path analyses. *British Journal of Addictions* 75:49–53, 1980.

Costello, R.M., and Hodde, J.E. Cost of comprehensive alcoholism care for 100 patients over 4 years. *Journal of Studies on Alcohol* 42:87–93, 1981.

Cronkite, R.C., and Moos, R.H. Sex and marital status in relation to the treatment and outcome of alcoholic patients. *Sex Roles: Journal of Research* 11:93–112, 1984.

Davies, D.L. Normal drinking in recovered alcohol addicts. *Quarterly Journal of Studies on Alcohol* 23:94–104, 1962.

Den Hartog, G.L. *A Decade of Detox: Development of Non-hospital Approaches to Alcohol Detoxification—A Review of the Literature.* Substance Abuse Monograph Series. Jefferson City, Mo.: Division of Alcohol and Drug Abuse, 1982.

Diesenhaus, H. Current trends in treatment programming for problem drinkers and alcoholics. In: National Institute on Alcohol Abuse and Alcoholism. *Prevention, Intervention, and Treatment: Concerns and Models.* Alcohol and Health Monograph No. 3. DHHS Pub. No. (ADM) 82–1192. Washington, D.C.: Supt. of Docs., U.S. Govt. Print. Off., 1982. pp. 219–290.

Eckardt, M.J., and Martin, P.R. Clinical assessment of cognition in alcoholism. *Alcoholism: Clinical and Experimental Research* 10:123–127, 1986.

Edwards, G. A later follow-up of a classic case series: D.L. Davies's 1962 report and its significance for the present. *Journal of Studies on Alcohol* 46:181–190, 1985.

Edwards, G. The alcohol dependence syndrome: A concept as stimulus to enquiry. *British Journal of Addiction* 81:171–183, 1986.

Edwards, G.: Duckitt, A.; Oppenheimer, E.; Sheehan, M.; and Taylor, C. What happens to alcoholics? *Lancet* 2:269–271, 1983.

Edwards, G., and Gross, M.M. Alcohol dependence: Provisional description of a clinical syndrome. *British Medical Journal* 1:1058–1061, 1976.

Edwards, G.; Orford, J.; and Egert, S. Alcoholism: A controlled trial of "treatment" and "advice." *Journal of Studies on Alcohol* 38:1004–1031, 1977.

Emrick, C.D. A review of psychologically oriented treatment of alcoholism. II. The relative effectiveness of different treatment approaches and the effectiveness of treatment versus no treatment. *Journal of Studies on Alcohol* 36:88–108, 1975.

Emrick, C.D. Evaluation of alcoholism psychotherapy methods. In: Pattison, E.M., and Kaufman, E., eds. *Encyclopedic Handbook of Alcoholism.* New York: Gardner Press, 1982. pp. 1152–1169.

Emrick, C.D., and Hansen, J. Assertions regarding effectiveness of treatment for alcoholism: Fact or fantasy? *American Psychologist* 38:1078–1088, 1983.

Emrick, C.D., and Hansen, J. Thoughts on treatment evaluation methodology. In: McCrady, B.S.; Noel, N.E.; and Nirenberg, T.D., eds. *Future Directions in Alcohol Abuse Treatment Research.* DHHS Pub. No. (ADM) 85–1322. Washington, D.C.: Supt. of Docs., U.S. Govt. Print. Off., 1985. pp. 137–172.

Ends, E.J., and Page, C.W. A study of three types of group psychotherapy with hospitalized male inebriates. *Quarterly Journal of Studies on Alcohol* 18:263–277, 1957.

Ewing, J.A. Alcoholism: Another biopsychosocial disease. *Psychosomatics* 21:371–372, 1980.

Ewing, J.A. Electric aversion and individualized imagery therapy in alcoholism: A controlled experiment. *Alcohol* 1:101–104, 1984.

Fagan, R.W., and Mauss, A.L. Padding the revolving door: An initial assessment of the Uniform Alcoholism and Intoxication Treatment Act in practice. *Social Problems* 26:232–247, 1978.

Fawcett, J.; Clark, D.C.; Gibbons, R.D.; Aagesen, C.S.; Pisani, V.D.; Tilkin, J.M.; Sellers, D.; and Strutzman, D. Evaluation of lithium therapy for alcoholism. *Journal of Clinical Psychiatry* 45:494–499, 1984.

Fink, E.B.; Longabaugh, R.; McCrady, B.M.; Stout, R.L.; Beattie, M.; Authelet, A.R.; and McNeil, D. Effectiveness of alcoholism treatment in partial versus inpatient settings: Twenty-four-month outcomes. *Addictive Behavior* 10:235–248, 1985.

Finney, J.W., and Moos, R.H. Characteristics and prognoses of alcoholics who become moderate drinkers and abstainers after treatment. *Journal of Studies on Alcohol* 42:94–105, 1981.

Finney, J.W., and Moos, R.H. Matching patients with treatments: Conceptual and methodological issues. *Journal of Studies on Alcohol* 47:122-134, 1986.

Finney, J.W.; Moos, R.H.; and Chan, D.A. Length of stay and program component effects in the treatment of alcoholism: A comparison of two techniques for process analysis. *Journal of Consulting and Clinical Psychology* 49:120–131, 1981.

Foy, D.W.; Nunn, L.B.; and Rychtarik, R.G. Broad-spectrum behavioral treatment for chronic alcoholics: Effects of training controlled drinking skills. *Journal of Consulting and Clinical Psychology* 52:218–230, 1984.

Freed, E.X. Drug use by alcoholics: A review. *International Journal of the Addictions* 8:451–473, 1973.

Freiberg, L. "Alternatives to Inpatient Care." Paper presented at the Conference on Health Care Financing at the Center for Public Law and Service of the University of Alabama, April 29–30, 1977. (Available from Medical Economics Department, National Association of Blue Shield Plans.)

Fuller, R.K.; Branchey, L.; Brightwell, D.R.; Derman, R.M.; Emrick, C.D.; Iber, F.L.;

James, K.E.; Lacoursiere, R.B.; Lee, K.K.; Lowenstam, I.; Maany, I.; Neiderhiser, D.; Nocks, J.J.; and Shaw, S. Disulfiram treatment of alcoholism: A Veterans Administration cooperative study. *Journal of the American Medical Association* 256: 1449–1455, 1986.

Fuller, R.K., and Roth, H.P. Disulfiram for the treatment of alcoholism: An evaluation in 128 men. *Annals of Internal Medicine* 90:901–904, 1979.

Gibbs, L., and Flanagan, J. Prognostic indicators of alcoholism treatment outcome. *International Journal of the Addictions* 12:1097–1141, 1977.

Glaser, F.B. Anybody got a match? Treatment research and the matching hypothesis. In: Edwards, G., and Grant, M., eds. *Alcoholism Treatment in Transition*. London: Groom Helm, 1980. pp. 178–186.

Glaser, F.B., and Ogborne, A.C. Does A.A. really work? *British Journal of Addiction* 77:123–129, 1982.

Glaser, F.B., and Skinner, H.A. Matching in the real world. In: Gottheil, E.; McLellan, A.T.; and Drucy, K.A., eds. *Matching Patient Needs and Treatment Methods in Alcoholism and Drug Abuse*. Springfield, Ill.: Thomas, 1981. pp. 295–324.

Goldman, M.S.; Klisz, D.K.; and Williams, D.L. Experience-dependent recovery of cognitive functioning in young adults. *Addictive Behaviors* 10:169–176, 1985.

Gordis, E.; Dorph, D.; Sepe, V.; and Smith, H. Outcome of alcoholism treatment among 5,578 patients in an urban comprehensive hospital-based program: Application of a computerized data system. *Alcoholism: Clinical and Experimental Research* 5:509–522, 1981.

Gordis, E., and Sereny, G. Controversy in approaches to alcoholism. In: Rosender, V.M., and Rothschild, M.A., eds. *Controversies in Clinical Care*. New York: SP Medical and Scientific Books, 1981. pp. 37–55.

Gottheil, E. Introduction. In: Lettieri, D.J.; Sayers, M.A.; and Nelson, J.E., eds. *Summaries of Alcoholism Treatment Assessment Research*. DHHS Pub. No. (ADM) 85–1379. Washington, D.C.: Supt. of Docs., U.S. Govt. Print. Off., 1985.

Halikas, J.A.; Herzog, M.A.; Mirassou, M.M.; and Lyttle, M.D. Psychiatric diagnoses among female alcoholics. In: Galanter, M., ed. *Currents in Alcoholism*. Vol. VIII. New York: Grune and Stratton, 1983. pp. 283–291.

Harwood, H.J.; Rachal, J.V.; and Cavanaugh, E. Length of stay in treatment for alcohol abuse and alcoholism: National estimates for short term hospitals, 1983. Submitted as draft to NIAAA, 1985.

Hayami, D.E., and Freebori, D.K. Effect of coverage in the use of an HMO alcoholism treatment program, outcome and medical care utilization. *American Journal of Public Health* 71:1133–1144, 1981.

Helzer, J.E.; Robins, L.N.; Taylor, J.R.; Carey, K.; Miller, R.H.; Combs-Orme, T.; and Farmer, A. The extent of long-term moderate drinking among alcoholics discharged from medical and psychiatric treatment facilities. *New England Journal of Medicine* 312:1678–1682, 1985.

Hesselbrock, M.H.; Meyer, R.E.; and Keener, J.J. Psychopathology in hospitalized alcoholics. *Archives of General Psychiatry* 42:1050–1055, 1985.

Hill, M.J., and Blane H.T. Evaluation of psychotherapy with alcoholics: A critical review. *Quarterly Journal of Studies on Alcohol* 28:76–104, 1967.

Hodgson, R.; Rankin, H.; and Stockwell, T. The concept of craving and its measurement. *Behavior Research and Therapy* 17:379–387, 1979.

Hodgson, R.; Stockwell, T.; Rankin, H.; and Edwards, G. Alcohol dependence: The concept, its utility and measurement. *British Journal of Addiction* 73:339–342, 1978.

Holder, H.D.; Blose, J.G.; and Gasiorowski, M.J. *Alcoholism Treatment Impact on Total Health Care Utilization and Costs: A Four-Year Longitudinal Analysis of the Federal*

Employees Health Benefit Program with Aetna Life Insurance Company. Chapel Hill, N.C.:H-2, Inc., 1985.

Holder, H.D., and Hallan, J.B. The California pilot program to provide health insurance coverage for alcohol treatment—1 year after. Chapel Hill, N.C.: H-2, Inc., 1978.

Holder, H.D., and Hallan, J.B. Medical care and alcoholism treatment costs and utilization: A five-year analysis of the California pilot project to provide health insurance coverage for alcoholism. Chapel Hill, N.C.: H-2, Inc., 1981.

Horn, J.L.; Skinner, H.A.; Wanberg, K.; and Foster, F.M. *Alcohol Dependence Scale ADS.* Toronto: Addiction Research Foundation, 1984.

Horn, J.L., and Wanberg, K.W. Symptom patterns related to excessive use of alcohol. *Quarterly Journal of Studies on Alcohol* 30:35–38, 1969.

Horn, J.L.; Wanberg, K.W.; and Foster, F.M. *The Alcohol Use Inventory—AUI.* Denver, Colo.: Center for Alcohol-Abuse Research and Evaluation, 1974.

Hunt, G.M., and Azrin, N.H. The community-reinforcement approach to alcoholism. *Behavior Research and Therapy* 11:91–104, 1973.

Hunter, H. *Arizona Health Plan Cost-Benefit Study.* Report to NIAAA No. 5H84AA01745. Washington, D.C.: Supt. of Docs., U.S. Govt. Print. Off., 1978.

Jellinek, E.M. *The Disease Concept of Alcoholism.* Highland Park, N.J.: Hillhouse Press, 1960.

Jones, K.R., and Vischi, T.R. Impact of alcohol, drug abuse, and mental health treatment on medical care utilization: A review of the research literature. *Medical Care* 17 (Supplement), 1979.

Kish, G.B.; Ellsworth, R.B.; and Woody, M.M. Effectiveness of an 84-day and a 60-day alcoholism treatment program. *Journal of Studies on Alcohol* 41:81–85, 1980.

Kish, G.B., and Herman, H.T. The Fort Meade alcoholism treatment program: A followup study. *Quarterly Journal of Studies on Alcohol* 32:628–635, 1971.

Kissin, B., and Hanson, M. Integration of biological and psychological interventions in the treatment of alcoholism. In: McCrady, B.S.; Noel, N.E.; and Nirenberg, T.D., eds. *Future Directions in Alcohol Abuse Treatment and Research.* DHHS Pub. No. (ADM) 85–1322. Washington, D.C.: Supt. of Docs., U.S. Govt. Print. Off., 1985. pp. 63–103.

Kline, N.S.; Wren, J.C.; Cooper, T.B.; Varga, E.; and Canal, O. Evaluation of lithium therapy in chronic and periodic alcoholism. *American Journal of the Medical Sciences* 268:15–22, 1974.

Kristenson, H.; Ohlin, H.; Hulten-Nosslin, M-B.; Trell, E.; and Hood, B. Identification and intervention of heavy drinking in middle-aged men: Results and follow-up of 24–60 months of long-term study with randomized controls. *Alcoholism: Clinical and Experimental Research* 7:203–209, 1983.

Kwentus, J., and Major, L.F. Disulfiram in the treatment of alcoholism: A review. *Journal of Studies on Alcohol* 40:428–446, 1979.

Laundergan, J.C. The outcome of treatment: A comparative study of patients 25 years old and younger and 26 years and older admitted to Hazelden in 1979. Center City, Minn.: Hazelden Foundation, 1982.

Lemere, F., and Voegtlin, W.L. An evaluation of the aversion treatment of alcoholism. *Quarterly Journal of Studies on Alcohol* 11:199–204, 1950.

Lettieri, D.J.; Sayers, M.A.; and Nelson, J.E., eds. *Summaries of Alcoholism Treatment Assessment Research.* DHHS Pub. No. (ADM) 85–1379. Washington, D.C.: Supt. of Docs., U.S. Govt. Print. Off., 1985.

Liebson, I.A.; Tommasello, A.; and Bigelow, G.E. A behavioral treatment of alcoholic methadone patients. *Annals of Internal Medicine* 89:342–344, 1978.

Longabaugh, R.; McCrady, B.; Fink, E.; Stout, R.; McAuley, T.; Doyle, C.; and McNeil, D. Cost-effectiveness of alcoholism treatment in partial vs. inpatient settings: Six-month outcomes. *Journal of Studies on Alcohol* 44:1049–1071, 1983.

Marlatt, G.A. Cognitive assessment and intervention procedures for relapse prevention. In: Marlatt, G.A., and Gordon, J.A., eds. *Relapse Prevention: Maintenance Strategies for Addictive Behavior Change.* New York: Guilford Press, 1984. pp. 201–279.

McCrady, B.S.; Moreau, J.; Paolino, T.J., Jr.; and Longabaugh, R. Joint hospitalization and couples therapy for alcoholism: A four-year follow-up. *Journal of Studies on Alcohol* 43:1244–1250, 1982.

McCrady, B.S.; Noel, N.E.; Abrams, D.B.; Stout, R.L.; Nelson, H.F.; and Hay, W. Comparative effectiveness of three types of spouse involvement in outpatient behavioral alcoholism treatment. *Journal of Studies on Alcohol* 47:459–467, 1986.

McCrady, B.S., and Sher, K.J. Alcoholism treatment approaches: Patient variables, treatment variables. In: Tabakoff, B.; Sutker, P.B.; and Randall, C.L., eds. *Medical and Social Aspects of Alcohol Abuse.* New York: Plenum Publishing Corp., 1983. pp. 309–373.

McCrady, B.S., and Smith, D. Implications of cognitive impairment for the treatment of alcoholism. *Alcoholism: Clinical and Experimental Research* 10:145–149, 1986.

McLachlan, J.F.C. Therapy strategies, personality orientation and recovery from alcoholism. *Canadian Psychiatric Association Journal* 19:25–30, 1974.

McLachlan, J.F.C., and Stein, R.L. Evaluation of a day clinic for alcoholics. *Journal of Studies on Alcohol* 43:261–272, 1982.

McLellan, A.T.; Luborsky, L.; Woody, G.E.; and O'Brien, C.P. An improved diagnostic instrument for substance abuse patients: The Addiction Severity Index. *Journal of Nervous and Mental Disorders* 168:26–33, 1980.

McLellan, A.T.; Luborsky, L.; Woody, G.E.; O'Brien, C.P.; and Druley, K.A. Predicting response to alcohol and drug abuse treatments. *Archives of General Psychiatry* 40:620–625, 1983a.

McLellan, A.T.; Woody, G.E.; Luborsky, L.; O'Brien, C.P.; and Druley, K.A. Increased effectiveness of substance abuse treatment: A prospective study of patient-treatment "matching." *Journal of Nervous and Mental Disease* 171:597–605, 1983b.

Miller, W.R., and Baca, L.M. Two-year follow-up of bibliotherapy and therapist-directed controlled drinking training for problem drinkers. *Behavior Therapy* 14:441–448, 1983.

Miller, W.R., and Hester, R.K. Treating the problem drinker: Modern approaches. In: Miller, W.R., ed. *The Addictive Behaviors: Treatment of Alcoholism, Drug Abuse, Smoking and Obesity.* Oxford: Pergamon Press, 1980. pp. 11–141.

Miller, W.R., and Hester, R.K. Inpatient alcoholism treatment: Who benefits? *American Psychologist* 41:794–805, 1986.

Miller, W.R., and Hester, R.K. Matching problem drinkers with optimal treatments. In: Miller, W.R., and Heather, N., eds. *Treating Addictive Behaviors: Processes of Change.* New York: Plenum Publishing Corp., in press.

Moos, R.H., and Finney, J.W. The expanding scope of alcoholism treatment evaluation. *American Psychologist* 38:1036–1044, 1983.

Moos, R.H.; Finney, J.W.; and Chan, D.A. The process of recovery from alcoholism. I. Comparing alcoholic patients and matched community controls. *Journal of studies on Alcohol* 42:383–402, 1981.

Moos, R.H., and Moos, B.S. The process of recovery from alcoholism. III. Comparing functioning in families of alcoholics and matched control families. *Journal of Studies on Alcohol* 45:111–118, 1984.

Morey, L.C.; Skinner, H.A.; and Blashfield, R.K. A typology of alcohol abusers: Correlates and implications. *Journal of Abnormal Psychology* 93:408–417, 1984.

Mosher, V.; Davis, J.; Mulligan, D.; and Iber, F.L. Comparison of outcome in a 9-day and 30-day alcohol treatment program. *Journal of Studies on Alcohol* 36:1277–1281, 1975.

Naranjo, C.A.; Sellers, E.M.; Chater, K.; Iversen, P.; Roach, C.; and Sykors, K. Nonpharmacologic intervention in acute alcohol withdrawal. *Clinical Pharmacology and Therapeutics* 34:214–219, 1983.

Nathan, P.E. Alcoholism treatment outcome: Current methods, problems, and results. *Journal of Consulting and Clinical Psychology*, in press.

Nathan, P.E., and Briddell, D.W. Behavioral assessment and treatment of alcoholism. In: Kissin, B., and Begleiter, H., eds. *The Biology of Alcoholism*. Volume V. *Treatment and Rehabilitation of the Chronic Alcoholic.* New York: Plenum Publishing Corp., 1977. pp. 301–349.

National Drug and Alcoholism Treatment Utilization Survey, NIAAA Comprehensive Report. USDHHS, PHS, ADAMHA. Rockville, Md.: NIAAA, 1983.

National Institute on Alcohol Abuse and Alcoholism. Characteristics of alcoholism services in the United States—1984. Data from the September 1984 National Alcoholism and Drug Abuse Program Inventory. Washington, D.C.: Supt. of Docs., U.S. Govt. Print. Off., 1986.

Nerviano, V., and Gross, W. Personality types of alcoholics in objective inventories. *Journal of Studies on Alcohol* 44:837–851, 1983.

Neubuerger, O.W.; Hasha, N.; Matarazzo, J.D.; Schmitz, R.E.; and Pratt, H.H. Behavioral-chemical treatment of alcoholism: An outcome replication. *Journal of Studies on Alcohol* 42:806–810, 1981.

Neubuerger, O.W.; Miller, S.I.; Schmitz, R.E.; Matarazzo, J.D.; Pratt, H.; and Hasha, N. Replicable abstinence rates in an alcoholism treatment program. *Journal of the American Medical Association* 248:960–963, 1982.

Noble, J. "Profile of the U.S. Alcoholism Treatment Capacity, Funding and Trend Data." Paper presented at Alcohol Drug Problems Association Conference, Austin, Tex., March 11, 1985.

O'Briant, R.; Petersen, N.W.; and Heacock, D. How safe is social setting detoxification? *Alcohol Health and Research World* 1:22–27, 1976/1977.

O'Farrell, T.J.; Cutter, H.S.G.; and Floyd, F.J. Evaluating behavioral marital therapy for male alcoholics: Effects on marital adjustment and communication from before to after treatment. *Behavior Therapy* 16:147–167, 1985.

Orford, J.; Oppenheimer, E.; and Edwards, G. Abstinence or control: The outcome for excessive drinkers two years after consultation. *Behavior Research and Therapy* 14: 409–418, 1976.

Orrego, H.; Blendis, L.M.; Blake, J.E.; Kapur, B.M.; and Israel, Y. Reliability of assessment of alcohol intake based on personal interviews in a liver clinic. *Lancet* II:1354–1356, 1979.

Page, R.E., and Schaub, L.J. Efficacy of a three-versus-five week alcohol treatment program. *International Journal of the Addictions* 14:697–714, 1979.

Parker, E.S., and Noble, E.P. Alcohol consumption and cognitive functioning in social drinkers. *Journal of Studies on Alcohol* 38:1224–1232, 1977.

Partington, J.T., and Johnson, F.G. Personality types among alcoholics. *Quarterly Journal of Studies on Alcohol* 30:21–34, 1969.

Pattison, E.M.; Sobell, M.B.; and Sobell, L.C. *Emerging Concepts of Alcohol Dependence.* New York: Springer, 1977.

Patton, M. Validity and reliability of Hazelden treatment follow-up data. City Center, Minn.: Hazelden Educational Services, 1979.

Pettinati, H.M.; Sugerman, A.A.; DiDonato, N.; and Maurer, H.S. The natural history of alcoholism over four years after treatment. *Journal of Studies on Alcohol* 43: 201–215, 1982.

Pettinati, H.M.; Sugerman, A.A.; and Maurer, H. Psychological changes in abstaining and drinking alcoholics. *Digest of Alcoholism Theory and Application* 3:15–19, 1984.

Pickens, R.W.; Hatsukami, D.K.; Spicer, J.W.; and Svikis, D.S. Relapse by alcohol abusers. *Alcoholism: Clinical and Experimental Research* 9:244–247, 1985.

Pittman, D.J., and Tate, R.L. A comparison of two treatment programs for alcoholics. *International Journal of the Addictions* 18:183–193, 1972.

Polich, J.M.; Armor, D.; and Braiker, H.B. *The Course of Alcoholism: Four Years After Treatment.* New York: Wiley & Sons, 1981.

Pomerleau, O.; Pertschuk, M.; Adkins, D.; and Brady, J.P. A comparison of behavioral and traditional treatment for middle income problem drinkers. *Journal of Behavioral Medicine* 2:187–200, 1978.

Pond, S.M.; Becker, L.E.; Vandervoort, R.R.; Phillips, M.; Bowler, R.M.; and Peck, C.C. An evaluation of the effects of lithium in the treatment of chronic alcoholism. I. Clinical results. *Alcoholism: Clinical and Experimental Research* 5:247–251, 1981.

Powell, B.J.; Penick, E.C.; Read, M.R.; and Ludwig, A.M. Comparison of three outpatient treatment interventions: A twelve-month follow-up of men alcoholics. *Journal of Studies on Alcohol* 46:309–312, 1985.

Rankin, H.; Hodgson, R.; and Stockwell, T. The behavioural measurement of alcohol dependence. *British Journal of Addiction* 75:43–47, 1980.

Rankin, H.; Stockwell, T.; and Hodgson, R. Cues for drinking and degrees of alcohol dependence. *British Journal of Addiction* 77:287–296, 1982.

Reed, J.R., and Mandell, W. Chlordiazepoxide and dropping out of a detoxification service. *Journal of Studies on Alcohol* 40:719–722, 1979.

Rosenburg, C.N.; Gerrein, J.R.; Mandhar, V.; and Leetick, J. Evaluation of training of alcoholism counselors. *Journal of Studies on Alcohol* 37:1236–1246, 1976.

Ryan, C.; Butters, N.; Montgomery, K.; Adinolfi, A.; and DiDario, B. Memory deficits in chronic alcoholics: Continuities between the intact alcohol and alcoholic Korsakoff patient. In: Begleiter, H., and Kissin, B., eds. *Alcohol Intoxication and Withdrawal.* New York: Plenum Publishing Corp., 1980. pp. 701–718.

Saxe, L.; Dougherty, D.; Esty, K.; and Fine, M. *Health Technology Case Study 22: The Effectiveness and Costs of Alcoholism Treatment.* Washington, D.C.: U.S. Congress, Office of Technology Assessment, 1983.

Schuckit, M.A. The clinical implications of primary diagnostic groups among alcoholics. *Archives of General Psychiatry* 42:1043–1049, 1985.

Schuckit, M.A.; Schwei, M.G.; and Gold, E. Prediction of outcome in inpatient alcoholics. *Journal of Studies on Alcohol* 47:151–155, 1986.

Sherman, R.M.; Reiff, S.; and Forsythe, A.B. Utilization of medical services by alcoholics participating in an outpatient treatment program. *Alcoholism: Clinical and Experimental Research* 3:115, 1979.

Siegel, C.; Alexander, M.J.; and Lin, S. Severe alcoholism in the mental health sector. II. Effects of service utilization on readmission. *Journal of Studies on Alcohol* 45: 510–516, 1984a.

Siegel, C.; Haugland, M.A.; Goodman, A.B.; and Wanderling, J. Severe alcoholism in the mental health sector. I. A cost analysis of treatment. *Journal of Studies on Alcohol* 45:504–509, 1984b.

Skinner, H.A. Primary syndromes of alcohol abuse: Their measurement and correlates. *British Journal of Addiction* 76:63–76, 1981.

Skinner, H.A., and Allen, B.A. Alcohol dependence syndrome: Measurement and validation. *Journal of Abnormal Psychology* 91:199–209, 1982.

Smail, P.; Stockwell, T.; Canter, S.; and Hodgson, R. Alcohol dependence and phobic anxiety states. I. A prevalence study. *British Journal of Psychiatry* 144:53–57, 1984.

Smart, R.G. Do some alcoholics do better in some types of treatment than others? *Drug and Alcohol Dependence* 3:65–75, 1978.

Smart, R.G., and Gray, G. Minimal, moderate, and long-term treatment for alcoholism. *British Journal of Addiction* 73:35–38, 1978a.

Smart, R.G., and Gray, G. Multiple predictors of dropout from alcoholism treatment. *Archives of General Psychiatry* 35:363–367, 1978b.

Smith, B.J. Comprehensive treatment for alcoholics: A systems approach in Colorado. Colorado Division of Alcohol and Drug Abuse, 1980.

Sokolow, J.D.; Welte, J.; Hynes, B.A.; and Lyons, J. Multiple substance use by alcoholics. *British Journal of Addiction* 76:147–158, 1981.

Stein, L.I.; Newton, J.R.; and Bowman, R.S. Duration of hospitalization for alcoholism. *Archives of General Psychiatry* 32:247–252, 1975.

Stockwell, T., Hodgson, R.; Rankin, H.; and Taylor, C. Alcohol dependence, beliefs, and the priming effect. *Behavior Research and Therapy* 20:513–522, 1982.

Stockwell, T.; Murphy, D.; and Hodgson, R. The severity of alcohol dependence questionnaire: Its use, reliability, and validity. *British Journal of Addiction* 78:145–155, 1983.

Stockwell, T., Smail, P.; Hodgson, R.; and Canter, S. Alcohol dependence and phobic anxiety states. II. A retrospective study. *British Journal of Psychiatry* 144:58–63, 1984.

Tarter, R.E. The causes of alcoholism: A biopsychosocial analysis. In: Gottheil, E.; Druley, K.; Skoloda, T.; and Waxman, H., eds. *Etiological Aspects of Alcohol and Drug Abuse.* Springfield, Ill.: Thomas, 1983. pp. 173–201.

Tarter, R.E., and Parsons, O.A. Conceptual shifting in chronic alcoholics. *Journal of Abnormal Psychology* 77:71–75, 1971.

Thomas, E.J., and Santa, C.A. Unilateral family therapy for alcohol abuse: A working conception. *American Journal of Family Therapy* 10:49–58, 1982.

Topham, A. "Alcohol Dependence and Craving." Unpublished Ph.D. thesis, University of London, 1983.

U.S. Department of Health and Human Services. *Fourth Special Report to the U.S. Congress on Alcohol and Health.* DeLuca, J.R., and Wallace, J., eds. DHHS Pub. No. (ADM) 81–1080. Washington, D.C.: Supt. of Docs., U.S. Govt. Print. Off., 1981.

U.S. Department of Health and Human Services. *Fifth Special Report to the U.S. Congress on Alcohol and Health.* DHHS Pub. No. (ADM) 84–1291. Washington, D.C.: Supt. of Docs., U.S. Govt. Print. Off., 1984.

Vaillant, G.E. *The Natural History of Alcoholism.* Cambridge, Mass.: Harvard University Press, 1983.

Vaillant, G.E.; Clark, W.; Cyrus, C.; Milofsky, E.S.; Kopp, J.; Wulsin, V.W.; and Mogielnicki, N.P. Prospective study of alcoholism treatment. Eight-year follow-up. *American Journal of Medicine* 75:455–463, 1983.

Vaillant, G.E.; Clark, W.; Cyrus, C.; Milofsky, E.S.; Kopp, J.; Wulsin, V.W.; and Mogielnicki, N.P. Follow-up of alcoholics eight years after inpatient treatment. *Digest of Alcoholism Theory and Application* 3:5–9, 1984.

Valle, S.K. Interpersonal functioning of alcoholism counselors and treatment outcome. *Journal of Studies on Alcohol* 42:783–790, 1981.

Vogler, R.E. Successful moderation in a chronic alcohol abuser. In: Hay, W., and Nathan, P., eds. *Clinical Case Studies in the Behavioral Treatment of Alcoholism.* New York: Plenum Press, 1982. pp. 185–205.

Vogler, R.E., and Bartz, W.R. *Better Way to Drink.* New York: Simon and Schuster, 1982.

Walker, R.D.; Donovan, D.M.; Kivlahan, D.R.; and O'Leary, M.R. Length of stay, neuropsychological performance, and aftercare: Influences on alcohol treatment outcome. *Journal of Consulting and Clinical Psychology* 51:900–911, 1983.

Wallace, J. Predicting the onset of compulsive drinking in alcoholics: A biopsychosocial model. *Alcohol* 2:589–595, 1985a.

Wallace, J. Working with the preferred defense structure of the recovering alcoholic. In: Zimberg, S.; Wallace, J.; and Blume, S. *Practical approaches to Alcoholism Psychotherapy.* 2d ed. New York: Plenum Publishing Corp., 1985b. pp. 23–25.

Wanberg, K.W., and Horn, J.L. Alcoholism symptom patterns of men and women: A comparative study. *Quarterly Journal of Studies on Alcohol* 31:40–61, 1970.

Wanberg, K.W., and Horn, J.L. Assessment of alcohol use with multidimensional concepts and measures. *American Psychologist* 38:1055–1068, 1983.

Wanberg, K.W.; Horn, J.L.; and Fairchild, D. Hospital versus community treatment of alcoholism problems. *International Journal of Mental Health* 3:160–176, 1974.

Wanberg, K.W.; Horn, J.L.; and Foster, F.M. A differential assessment model for alcoholism: The scales of the alcohol use inventory. *Journal of Studies on Alcohol* 38:512–543, 1977.

Welte, J.; Hynes, G.; Sokolow, L.; and Lyons, J.P. Effect of length of stay in inpatient alcoholism treatment on outcome. *Journal of Studies on Alcohol* 42:483–491, 1981.

Whitfield, C.L.; Thompson, G.; Lamb, A.; Spencer, V.; Pfeifer, M.; and Browning-Ferrando, M. Detoxification of 1,024 alcoholic patients without psychoactive drugs. *Journal of the American Medical Association* 239:1409–1410, 1978.

Wiens, A.N., and Menustik, C.E. Treatment outcome and patient characteristics in an aversion therapy program for alcoholism. *American Psychologist* 38:1089–1096, 1983.

Wiens, A.N.; Montague, J.R.; Manaugh, T.S.; and English, C.J. Pharmacological aversive counterconditioning to alcohol in a private hospital: One year followup. *Journal of Studies on Alcohol* 37:1320–1324, 1976.

Willems, P.J.A.; Letemendia, F.J.J.; and Arroyave, F. A two-year followup study comparing short and long stay inpatient treatment of alcoholics. *British Journal of Psychiatry* 122:637–648, 1973.

Wilson, A.; Blanchard, R.; Davidson, W.; McRae, L.; and Maini, K. Disulfiram implantation: A dose response trial. *Journal of Clinical Psychiatry* 45:242–247, 1984.

Wilson, A.; White, J.; and Lange, D.E. Outcome evaluation of a hospital-based alcoholism treatment programme. *British Journal of Addiction* 73:39–45, 1978.

World Health Organization. *Diagnosis and Classification of Mental Disorders and Alcohol and Drug-Related Problems.* Summaries of working papers from an international conference, Copenhagen, Denmark, April 1982.

Six-Month Treatment Outcomes in Socially Stable Alcoholics: Abstinence Rates[1]

Baekeland (1977) called attention to the differences among alcoholic treatment populations and pointed to the important role of social stability in moderating recovery rates. In his review of the English-language literature, Baekeland noted recovery rates ranging from 32% to 68% for socially stable alcoholics. For socially unstable patients, improvement rates ranged downward from 18%.

Alcoholism treatment outcomes are also related to numerous factors other than patient characteristics. Treatment variables and extratreatment factors have been seen as predicting outcomes (Nathan & Skinstad, 1987). In women, the number of life problems and the number of supportive relationships are significantly related to outcome (MacDonald, 1987). Schuckit (1985) found outcomes of alcoholism treatment to vary considerably as a function of primary and secondary diagnoses. Billings and Moos (1983) have reported that three extra-treatment domains account for as much of the variance in outcome as do treatment variables and patient characteristics combined. In effect, alcoholism treatment settings, extra treatment factors, and treatment populations vary considerably. As a consequence, no single outcome statistic is likely to prove sufficient for describing treatment outcomes. Obviously, varying treatment outcome rates are needed to describe outcomes for heterogeneous patients, different treatment settings, and variable life situations.

But while the facts of heterogeneity among alcoholics, treatment settings, and life situations are most apparent, the implications of such heterogeneity are not always appreciated when recovery rates are discussed. Longabaugh (1986), for example, in a discussion of heterogeneity among alcoholics and the need for patient-treatment match-

[1]This study was done in collaboration with Dwight McNeill, David Gilfillan, Karen MacLean, and Frank Fanella.

133

ing, is pessimistic about the robustness of present treatment methods. He has stated, "moreover, when the effectiveness of any and all treatments are compared with no treatment, the modest incremental effectiveness of the former over the latter suggests that our existing treatment armamentarium is not very robust" (Longabaugh, 1987, p. 2). The question here, of course, is not whether alcoholism treatment is or is not robust in some general sense, but rather, *for whom is it robust and for whom is it not robust?*

Given the many factors that can complicate recovery from alcoholism, important factors such as social stability versus instability cannot be ignored. In fact, one might argue that since negative extra-treatment factors are largely absent or greatly reduced in socially stable treatment populations, such populations might well be considered optimal for testing the effectiveness of alcoholism treatment *per se.* Unfortunately, socially stable treatment populations have been the exception and not the rule in studies of alcoholism treatment effectiveness. Few studies of socially stable populations are apparent in the alcoholism treatment literature. Hence, it is possible that a portion of the pessimism about treatment effectiveness stems from the fact that researchers have focused upon difficult but accessible treatment populations, rather than on representative populations.

The present study, then, should be viewed as an attempt to provide further information about an infrequently studied population—socially stable alcoholics treated in a modern, multimodal, specialized, private, freestanding, for-profit, alcoholism treatment center.

The study focuses on a sample of socially stable alcoholics and follows them for a six-month period following treatment. In subsequent papers we will report on one-year, eighteen-month, and two-year periods following treatment with the same sample. The present paper concentrates on the subject of abstinence rates. Subsequent papers will deal with other aspects of the data obtained on this cohort.

METHOD

SUBJECTS

Patients had to meet the following criteria to be eligible for the study:

1. They met NCA criteria for the diagnosis of alcoholism, and/or had drug abuse/dependence diagnoses, required inpatient care, and had restorative potential;
2. They were transferred from the medical detoxification and evaluation unit to a rehabilitation unit, which indicated that medical,

psychiatric, detoxification, and self-care problems, if any, were sufficiently managed so that the patient could participate fully in the rehabilitation program;

3. They were married and residing with their spouses, and had no plans for separating; and
4. They had sufficient resources to pay for treatment (virtually all had third-party insurance coverage for the treatment of alcoholism).

All patients who were married and had completed at least 21 days of treatment during the period of October 1985 through September 1986 were eligible for inclusion in the study ($N = 802$). Every odd-numbered admission was selected to be considered for the sample ($N = 380$). This list of case numbers and associated admission dates was computer generated and sorted in order of admission date on a weekly basis. The interviewer selected patients to be interviewed in sequential order from the top to the bottom of the list to the extent that he could accommodate interviews in a given week. Of the 380 odd-numbered admissions, he interviewed 257. Hence, the sampling frame was 32% of all married patients who had completed 21 days of treatment. Patients were interviewed during the third week of treatment and evaluated as to whether they fit the inclusionary criteria. Of those interviewed, 65 were excluded because they did not reside with their spouses (44), did not subsequently finish treatment (10), or were not actually married (11). At this initial meeting, the interviewer explained the purposes of the study, the nature of the patient's participation in the study, the need for permission to contact a significant other, and the risks involved. The patient was then asked to give informed consent to participation in the study. Eleven (6%) of the eligible patients refused to participate in the study. Following this, the patient was interviewed to measure pretreatment functioning (to be described in a later section). All of these patients (except one who died before the six-month followup) who subsequently were discharged regularly comprised the study cohort to be followed for two years. There were 181 patients who agreed to participate in the study. Characteristics of the study sample are included in Table 1.

There were no statistically significant differences between the study completers and the nonresponders on any of the patient characteristics displayed in Table 1.

TREATMENT PROGRAMS

Edgehill Newport is a 160 bed, freestanding alcoholism treatment center. The treatment program at Edgehill Newport is multimodal

TABLE 1 Characteristics of the Study Sample (N = 181)

	N	%
Age: < 30 years	38	21
31–40	51	28
> 40	92	51
Sex: Male	130	72
Female	51	28
Education: High school grad	143	79
Employed: Full-time or part-time	132	73
Marital status: Married	181	100
Resides with: Spouse	181	100
Primary addiction: Alcohol	116	64
Polydrug	65	36
Spouse involved in family treatment	65	36
Previous AA	81	45

with both individual and common elements. Medical, psychological, psychosocial, and psychiatric assessments are followed by individualized treatment planning. Medical detoxification is used as needed. Depending upon their individual treatment plans, patients receive some appropriate form of group and/or individual therapy/counseling daily. All patients receive daily educational experiences including lectures, films, and bibliotherapy. Medications are used sparingly, with pharmacotherapy directed almost entirely at coexisting problems (e.g., antidepressants, lithium, phenothiazines). A small number of patients receive disulfiram. All patients receive some form of activity/recreation therapy and all are expected to become familiar with the basic concepts, procedures, and meetings of A.A., N.A., and Al-Anon. When appropriate, patients and significant others are treated in an intensive weekend family program for three weekends. All patients receive aftercare planning and aftercare placement in transition group meetings, outpatient counseling and therapies of various kinds, and/or self-help groups.

The philosophy of the program is based upon the position that alcoholism is a *biopsychosocial* disease and that biological, psychological, and sociocultural factors enter into its etiology and maintenance. The principle treatment goal is abstinence from alcohol and all unauthorized psychoactive chemicals.

DATA-COLLECTION PROCEDURES, INSTRUMENTS AND VARIABLES

Procedures. After giving consent for their participation and for permission to contact a significant other, patients were interviewed during their third week of treatment by a trained research assistant, using the Edgehill Newport Family Outcome and Health Care Utilization Inventory (described below).

Subsequently, they were contacted every 30 days for a telephone interview which focused on substance use, changes in family and work status, and use of health care and support services.

After gaining the patient's consent, study staff contacted the significant other in order to introduce him or her to the project. Significant others were informed of the nature of the study, the patient's consent to participate in the study, and the patient's consent to have the significant other participate in data collection. They were then asked to participate. Following the obtaining of their consent, significant others were interviewed over the telephone getting measures of the patient's functioning prior to treatment and covering the same areas of content as in the interviews with patients. They were contacted every two months thereafter.

Measures: The Edgehill Family Outcome & Health Care Utilization Inventory. These instruments were administered to patients in a personal interview at baseline to measure key variables for the six months prior to treatment. Key outcome variables were tracked at each monthly contact. The instrument contains items that provide sociodemographic, clinical history, and substance use/dependence profiles of the patient in addition to assessments of the patient's functioning in major (and measurable) areas. Some of the measures were selected from preexisting instruments. Additional items were added.

1. *Measures of Alcohol and Drug Use/Dependency:* Days abstinent, type and frequency of substances used, substance use pattern, total abstinence continuously from discharge, and currently at time of assessment.
2. *Measures of Functioning in Major Areas:* Work functioning, including number of days worked, promotion/demotion, disability, occupational level, loss of job, job satisfaction; family functioning, including quality of spouse and child relationships; legal issues including arrests and days in prison.
3. *Measures of Health Care Utilization:* Number of days in hospital for general medical, psychiatric, and alcoholism rehabilitation. Visits to physician, emergency department, psychiatrist, counseling, outpatient medical.
4. *Attendance and Quality of Participation in AA/NA:* Number of meetings attended and the quality as judged by whether patient has told story, attended a 12-step meeting, spoken at a 12-step meeting, performed a task at a meeting, chaired a meeting, done 12-step work.

5. *Patients Response to Treatment:* This is a 37-item scale that measures the levels of denial, subjective distress, and attitude towards constructive treatment engagement during the patient's
   third week of treatment (Wallace, 1986). Also included was a
   scale for recording the counselor's assessment of patient's commitment to recovery. This included prognostic judgments on the
   patient's commitment to abstinence, to AA attendance, to general health, and to family support (Wallace, 1986). Treatment
   groups attended and whether members of patient's family attended the family program were noted.
6. *Clinical History:* This included a substance use/dependence profile, psychiatric and alcoholism treatments, history of alcoholism
   in current family and family of origin, DSM-III diagnosis, and
   the alcoholism dependency scale (Edwards et al., 1977).
7. *Sociodemographic Data:* This included age, gender, marital status,
   whom the patient resides with, education, occupation, referral
   source, and payment source.

All of the above items were covered during the baseline interview.
Items (1), (2), and (3) were tracked every month during the telephone
interview. The correspondent baseline interview and follow-up interviews were basically the same as the patient interviews.

RESULTS

The initial number of subjects in the study was 181; one patient
expired. At six-month follow-up, the study research team located 169
subjects for a follow-up rate of 94%.

COLLATERAL VERIFICATION

Significant-other information was available for 98% of the located
patients at the six-month follow-up interview. The concordance rate
for subject and collateral on the outcome variable "current" abstinence at six-months was 86%. For the 24 pairs that were discordant
on this variable, our decision rule was to always use the more conservative rating. That is, if one member of the discordant pair said that
the subject was not abstinent, then we used the not-abstinent datum in
the analysis. In 60% of the discordant pairs, we used the collateral's
datum rather than the patient's. In 40% of the discordant pairs, we
used the subject's datum rather than the collateral's. Our intent in
using collateral information was to arrive at the most accurate state-

ment of the patient's status. It should be noted that our conservative approach produces a negative bias in the results relative to the many studies that use only the subjects' reports regardless of conflicting collateral data. Overall, the agreement rate between subjects and collaterals in this study was very high.

TYPES OF PATIENTS IN SAMPLE

Included in the initial sample were the following types of chemically dependent patients: (1) alcoholics (64%); (b) alcoholic/polydrug abuse or dependent patients (36%). Polydrug patients were those who were assessed as currently (within 6 months) abusing or dependent on any psychoactive substance in addition to alcohol. The decision on whether to classify as polydrug abuse or dependent was based on medical, nursing, and counselor assessments, interview material, and information from significant others. Different patterns of quantity and frequency of drug use for different psychoactive substances were employed as operational definitions of abuse and dependence. These criteria for the various drugs are available from the authors.

TOTAL SAMPLE ALCOHOL ABSTINENCE

Results will be presented separately for the total sample, for the two subgroups, and also for both alcohol and drug abstinence. For all patients the rates of continuous abstention (no drinking at all) for the entire six-month period following treatment was 61%. When the definition of abstinence was broadened to include a single drinking episode contained within a single day out of the 180 days following treatment, then the total abstinence rate rose by 4% to 65%. An additional 7% of the patients were currently abstinent at six months, although they had not maintained continuous abstention for all six months. The mean period of abstention for this group was 4.2 months. Hence, a total of 72% of the located patients currently were abstinent at the time of follow-up. "Currently abstinent" was operationally defined as abstinent during the month prior to the six-month interview.

COMBINED ALCOHOL AND DRUG ABSTINENCE

When both alcohol and other drugs are considered, 57% of the total sample had not drunk or taken any drug since leaving treatment.

An additional 4% had had one brief, contained return to drinking or drug use for a single day during the entire 180 day period, yielding a total combined alcohol and drug abstinence rate of 61%. An additional 7% were currently abstinent yielding a total currently-abstinent rate of 68%.

DRINKING AND COMBINED ALCOHOL/DRUG ABSTINENCE FOR ALCOHOLIC ONLY PATIENTS

Of the two types of patient groups, alcoholic patients had the highest continuous abstinence rate. Sixty-four percent of the patients were alcohol dependent only and did not report abuse or dependence on any other drug. Of these patients, 66% were continuously abstinent from alcohol during the entire 180-day period following treatment. These alcoholic-only patients also showed a combined drinking and drug abstinence rate of 66%. In short, 66% of the alcoholics had not drunk since leaving treatment, and 66% had neither drunk nor used drugs.

Of these alcoholic patients, a full 77% were currently abstinent at the time of follow-up.

DRINKING AND COMBINED ALCOHOL/DRUG ABSTINENCE RATES FOR ALCOHOLIC/POLYDRUG PATIENTS

Patients who showed problems with both alcohol and drugs comprised 36% of the initial sample. These patients showed a continuous drinking abstinence rate of 52% for the six-month period since leaving treatment. They also showed a continuous drug abstinence rate of 66% six months following treatment. Of these patients, fully 77% were currently abstinent from drugs at the time of follow-up.

OTHER OUTCOME MEASURES

Inpatient Days Used—Seven percent of the sample were hospitalized after treatment (for any disorder) compared to 24% during the six months before admission ($x^2 = 15$; $p < .01$). The mean days hospitalized for the sample were 3.1 before and 1.0 after ($t = 2.95$; $p < .01$).

Outpatient Utilization was the same before and after treatment, with 80% of the sample having at least one visit.

Employment—The unemployment rate (of those employable)

TABLE 2 Six-Month Total Abstinence by Frequency of AA/NA Attendance

	Low	Medium	High	Total
Abstinent	45 (50%)	19 (58%)	32 (71%)	96
Not Abstinent	46	14	13	73
Total	91	33	45	169

Note. Test for linear trend in proportions: $z = 2.34$; $p < .05$.

dropped from 12% to 8%, pretreatment to posttreatment. The mean number of days lost from work for any reason other than planned vacation during the six-months before and after treatment changed from 21.9 to 16.8 ($t = 1.63$; $.05 < p < .1$). In terms of job satisfaction, 45% of the sample felt that their satisfaction with work during the six months after treatment relative to the six months before had stayed the same, 50% felt that it had gotten better, and 5% felt that it had gotten worse.

Marital and Child Relationships—Concerning marital satisfaction, 38% felt that their marital satisfaction had improved, 12% felt that it had worsened, and 50% felt that it had stayed the same. Similarly, 46% felt that they had better relationships with their children, 3% felt that it had gotten worse, and 51% felt that it had stayed the same.

Arrests—Nine percent of the sample had been arrested during the six months prior to treatment, and two percent were arrested in the six-months following treatment ($x^2 = 7.6$; $p < .01$).

AA/NA and Abstinence

Patients who attended AA/NA on a regular and consistent basis did better than those patients who did not, and there appears to be a dose-response relationship between the frequency of attendance and six-month total abstinence rates, as seen in Table 2.

The categorizations of low, medium, and high are defined as follows: High is eight or more meetings per months for every month. Medium is four to seven meetings per month for every month. Low are those with less frequency and consistency than medium. Note that allowances were made for sickness or other brief departures from attendance.

The total abstinence rate varies from 50% for those with low attendance, to 58% for those with medium attendance, to 71% for those with high attendance. This dose-response relationship is statistically significant ($z = 2.34$; $p < .05$). Hence, those who attended at least once weekly for all weeks of the follow-up period had significantly better outcomes than those who did not. Further, the more meetings, the better the outcome.

DISCUSSION

The pessimistic position about alcoholism treatment is that very few people benefit from treatment, that treatment is not very robust, and that entirely new methods and paradigms must be sought since present treatment methods are ineffective. The optimistic position is that everybody can benefit from treatment. The truth is probably somewhere in between these extremes.

Our results indicate clearly that the answer to the question of alcoholism treatment effectiveness cannot be found in generalities, but must be addressed in terms of specifics. What treatment? In whose hands? For what patient populations? Effectiveness in terms of what outcomes?

In the present study, we chose to focus on a population of alcoholics that is largely neglected and understudied in research on treatment, that is, socially stable alcoholics with intact marriages, adequate resources, and the means to pay for treatment services. While understudied, this population of alcoholics comprises the majority of alcoholics in America.

Our follow-up rate in this study was 94% of the initial sample. This is clearly a high follow-up rate and the probability of bias on outcome due to sample attrition is essentially zero.

For this population of socially stable alcoholics, treatment had considerable impact and was effective. Sixty-one percent of these patients had been continuously sober since leaving treatment and 72% were currently abstinent at follow-up. We believe that these results indicate that alcoholism treatment in a specialized freestanding, private facility can be effective with populations of socially stable alcoholics.

These results do not agree with data on socially stable alcoholics reported by Edwards et al. (1977) and Orford et al. (1976). In these studies on British alcoholics, neither brief advice nor treatment were effective, since only 10% of the sample of married, socially stable, male alcoholics showed sustained abstention by four months after intake. Moreover, not a single man in either the advice or treatment group showed sustained abstention over the entire two years. Hence, despite the fact that these studies on advice versus treatment are frequently cited as showing equal effectiveness of alcoholism treatment and brief advice, the very high four-month relapse rate and universal two-year relapse rate indicate the need for alternative interpretation of these data by Edwards and his colleagues. Our results, showing a six-month continuous abstention rate of 66% for socially stable alcoholics not involved with other psychoactive drugs, contrast sharply with the four-month continuous abstention rate of only 10% reported by Edwards et al. (1977).

On the other hand, our findings are consistent with other studies of socially stable alcoholics. Patton (1979) reported a similar sustained abstention rate of 62% over an 18-month follow-up period. Hoffman and Harrison (1986) reported a one-year abstention rate of 62%. However, these results by Hoffman and Harrison were achieved with a considerably lower follow-up rate (50%).

While our findings suggest effectiveness of treatment, these sustained abstention rates can be expected to drop as the follow-up period is extended. Pettinati et al. (1982) reported considerably lower sustained abstention rates four years after treatment. As one might expect, treatment effects will probably decay over time as extra-treatment factors gain in strength and intensity.

In subsequent papers, we will examine the stability of these results for one-year, 18-month, and two-year outcome windows. Moreover, we will report other findings on this cohort.

REFERENCES

Baekeland, F. (1977). Evaluation of treatment methods in chronic alcoholism. In B. Kissin & H. Begleiter (Eds.), *The biology of alcoholism: Vol. 5. Treatment and rehabilitation of the chronic alcoholic* (pp. 385–440). New York: Plenum.

Billings, A.G., & Moos, R.H. (1983). Psychosocial processes of recovery among alcoholics and their families: Implications for clinicians and program evaluators. *Addictive Behaviors, 8,* 205–218.

Edwards, G., Orford, J., Egert, S., Guthrie, S., Hawker, A., Hensman, C., Mitcheson, M., Oppenheimer, E., & Taylor, C. (1977). Alcoholism: A controlled trial of "treatment" and "advice." *Journal of Studies on Alcohol, 38,* 1004–1031.

Hoffman, N.G., & Harrison, P.A. (1986). The CATOR 1986 Report. St. Paul: Ramsey Clinic Pub.

Longabaugh, R. (1986). *The matching hypothesis: Theoretical and empirical status.* Paper presented at the American Psychological Association, Symposium on the Matching Hypothesis in Alcoholism Treatment: "Current Status, Future Directions."

MacDonald, J.G. (1987). Predictors of treatment outcome for alcoholic women. *International Journal of Addiction, 32,* 235–248.

Nathan, P.E., & Skinstad, A.H. (1987). Outcomes of treatment for alcohol problems: Current methods, problems, and results. *Journal of Consulting and Clinical Psychology, 55,* 332–340.

Orford, J., Oppenheimer, E., & Edwards, G. (1976). Abstinence or control: The outcome for excessive drinkers two years after consultation. *Behavior Research Therapy,* *14,* 409–418.

Patton, M. (1979). Validity and reliability of Hazelden treatment followup data. Center City, MN: Hazelden Educational Services.

Pettinati, H.M., Sugerman, A.A., DiDonato, N., & Maurer, H.S. (1982). The natural history of alcoholism over four years after treatment. *Journal of Studies on Alcohol,* *43,* 201–215.

Schuckit, M.A. (1985). The clinical implications of primary diagnostic groups among alcoholics. *Archives of General Psychiatry, 42,* 1043–1049.

Wallace, J. (1986). The Wallace/Edgehill Inventory. (Unpublished Scale) Edgehill, Newport.

The Importance of Aftercare
in Alcoholism Treatment

Virtually all treatment professionals in the field of alcoholism agree that aftercare services are a critically important ingredient in providing for continuity of care and in decreasing relapse. Baekeland (1977), for example, in a review of the English language literature from 1957–1977, concluded that "aftercare confers additional benefit on the alcoholic patient," and "it has repeatedly been reported that patients who got group therapy after discharge do better" (Baekeland, 1977, pp 394–395).

Wallace (1983) has described two motives that are active in alcoholics in the period of early recovery: motive to drink and motive *not* to drink. He states, "In effect, the best that can be expected from various crises and interventions with an alcoholic, and even perhaps of early treatment, is *motivational conflict*—the alcoholic at these points wants both to drink and not to drink" (Wallace, 1983, p. 250). In order to resolve this motivational conflict, treatment must necessarily be long term with aftercare treatment comprising the major portion of care.

In addition to motivational conflict during the early months of recovery from alcoholism, this period is also characterized by various stresses and problems of adjustment to sober life. Many alcoholics in the first two years of recovery have been observed to be subject to problems associated with mood swings, anxiety and fearfulness, continued neuropsychological impairment, and physical health problems. Moos, Finney, and Chan (1981) reported that during the first 18 months after treatment, recovered alcoholics "did not function as well as community controls with respect to their mood and other health-related factors. They showed higher levels of anxiety and were more likely to use medications and to visit doctors. These differences may be due to some of the recovered alcoholics having physical and psychological dysfunction for which they need continuing treatment" (1981, p. 397).

Moos and his colleagues based their conclusions on a sample of 124 patients and their families who were compared to a matched control sample of 87 non-alcoholic persons and their families from the community. While the recovered alcoholics showed problems of adjustment during the first 18 months after treatment, alcoholics who relapsed had shown even more serious difficulties. As Moos et al. reported, "relapsed alcoholics showed poorer mood and health-related functioning and less social competence and self-confidence, and used less effective coping responses to handle current life stressors— they were more likely to use denial and avoidance responses, which like excessive drinking, alter emotional responses to external situations but do not effectively alter the situation itself" (Moos, et al. 1981, p. 398).

Recovering alcoholics also show problems with neuropsychological functioning since alcohol is a neurotoxin and is capable of causing brain damage in varying degrees. Neuropsychological impairments can persist for months and even years, and impact on important cognitive processes such as judgment, abstracting ability, concept formation, cognitive flexibility, problem-solving, and short-term memory. Goldman (1986) has pointed out that studies indicate that those neuropsychological impairments may require "a longer time span, as much as a few years, for recovery" (1986, pp. 137–138).

Obviously, the treatment needs of alcoholic persons do not end upon discharge from an inpatient treatment program. Because of motivational conflict over drinking or not drinking, dysphoric mood states, difficulties in coping and problem-solving, and neuropsychological impairments, active aftercare treatment must be provided for the vast majority of alcoholics who are discharged from inpatient care. As the following discussion will show, without aftercare services, the probability of relapse is increased greatly.

TEMPORAL NATURE OF RELAPSE

It is generally agreed that treated alcoholics are at great risk for relapse for at least nine months following treatment and at substantial risk from nine months to one year with risk for relapse decreasing thereafter. Milkman, Weiner and Sunderwirth (1984) discuss data showing that there is a rapid rise in alcoholism relapse rates between one and three months after treatment. While 66% of patients were sober at one month, 42% were still sober at three months after treatment. By one year, 39% were still sober. Hence, the bulk of relapses occurred between discharge and three months.

Pickens and his colleagues (1985) report data that agree closely with Milkman et al.'s conclusion. Pickens, et al. collected followup information on 432 male and female patients with a mean age of 44.2 years (range, 17–70). Approximately 64% were married, 86% full-time employed, and 51% were college graduates. For these patients, there was a sharp rise in relapse rates between time of discharge from treatment and three months later. Relapse rates remained at the three month level through six months and then decreased from nine months to one year.

In general, then, available data indicate that alcoholics require immediate aftercare services upon being discharged from inpatient care since relapse rates rise sharply from date of discharge to nine months following treatment. Patients continue to be at risk for relapse through the remaining months of the first year and stay at some risk thereafter. Studies generally show continued risk of relapse into the second year of recovery. For example, a two-year followup by Fink et al. (in press) of 115 patients treated in an inpatient or partial hospitalization setting showed declines in abstention rates from 43% showing continuous sobriety at 6 months, to 27.9% at 1 year, to 22.8% staying sober over the entire two year followup.

EFFECTS OF AFTERCARE ON RELAPSE RATES

Striking data showing impressive results in favor of aftercare services were reported by Walker and his colleagues (1983). Walker et al. studied 245 male patients who had been grouped according to neuropsychological functioning. The most salient findings in the study concerned the role of aftercare. Patients who attended weekly aftercare groups for 9 months following hospitalization were three times more likely to remain abstinent than were patients who dropped out of aftercare. The differences were large: 70.2% of those who completed aftercare were sober while only 23.4% of those who did not complete aftercare were sober. (These data are shown in Table 1.)

Milkman, et al. reported a study based on the New York State Parole Drug Experiment. 45% of the men who were abstinent at the end of treatment were able to maintain abstinence provided that continuing supervision was given. On the other hand, only 27% of the sample were able to remain abstinent when supervision terminated. In effect, addicted people continue to need supervision or therapeutic attention to avoid relapse.

TABLE 1 Abstinence and Drinking-Outcome Rates (in Percentages) as a Function of Aftercare Completion

Outcome variable	Aftercare status		
	Completed	Dropped out	Total
Abstinence			
Abstinent	70.2	23.4	44.0
Nonabstinent	29.8	76.6	56.0
Drinking outcome			
Successful	77.3	19.9	40.6
Drinking problem	22.7	63.5	48.8
Insufficient data	0	16.7	10.7
Total	35.9	64.1	

From: Walker, et al. Length of Stay, Neuropsychological Performance and Aftercare: Influence on Alcohol Treatment Outcome. *J. of Consulting and Clinical Psychology.* Vol. 51, No. 6, 900–911.

Studies conducted at Raleigh Hills Hospital in Portland, Oregon by Weins and Menustik (1983) clearly show the benefits of aftercare even for a highly specialized form of treatment called aversive therapy. In aversive therapy, efforts are made to develop a conditioned nausea response to alcohol by pairing chemically induced nausea with the sights, smells, and tastes of alcoholic beverages. As Weins and Menustik point out, aftercare reinforcements of this procedure (recaps) are of critical importance. Of those patients who had completed no aftercare recaps, only 6 were able to maintain abstinence for 12 months, but of 144 patients who completed all six aftercare recaps, 99% remained abstinent (these data are presented in Table 2).

Siegel and her colleagues (1984) showed that patients who did not receive aftercare services beyond six months in the community were likely to relapse and be readmitted to alcoholism treatment services. Patients receiving aftercare services ranging from at least 7 months through two years were less likely to relapse and seek readmission.

Cronkite and Moos (1984) followed 332 patients who had been treated for alcoholism at one of five residential programs. With regard to aftercare, they concluded that aftercare was an important service. Of the married men who did not relapse, 54% had received aftercare services while only 28% of the men who had relapsed had received aftercare services. For unmarried men who did not relapse, 49% had received aftercare services while only 31% who relapsed did.

Costello (1975) collated findings from 58 studies reporting 1-year follow-up results of evaluations of alcoholism treatment programs. Seven characteristics distinguished successful treatment programs

TABLE 2 Number of aftercare recaps and abstinence in Raleigh Hills Hospital patients (1978 patients).

Aftercare Recaps	Patients		Abstinent 12 months	
	Number	%	Number	%
0	25	7	6	24
1	44	11	9	21
2	50	13	20	40
3	44	11	12	27
4	39	10	25	64
5	39	10	28	79
6	144	38	143	99
Total	385	100%	243	—

Data from Weins, A.N. and Menustik, C.E. Treatment outcome and patient characteristics in an aversion therapy program for alcoholism. *American Psychologist*, October 1983, 1089–1096.

from unsuccessful programs in terms of treatment outcome results. One of these characteristics was an "aggressive outpatient followup or aftercare."

LIFETIME AFTERCARE SERVICES

At present, there is no cure for alcoholism. The disease can be arrested in the sense that its progression can be stopped. Abstinence from alcohol and all unauthorized psychoactive substances is necessary for the progression of the disease to be stopped.

In the absence of a total biological cure for the disease, the risk of relapse continues throughout the lives of alcoholics. Risk of relapse may increase greatly in recovering alcoholics if certain life events occur. Generally, negative life events increase the chances of a relapse. Some of these negative life events are as follows: divorce; death of a spouse; loss of a child; demotion or job termination; severe financial reversal; other serious physical illnesses; traumatic injuries; loss of social position and self esteem; psychological traumas such as rape, assaults, and other crimes against persons.

While negative life events are readily appreciated as possible factors in relapse, "positive" life factors are often overlooked. The following positive life happenings in the lives of alcoholics may also produce increased responsibility and/or stress: job promotion; marriage; sudden financial success; moves to a better home in a better neighborhood; professional recognition and success; extensive travel; return to higher education; career change.

Regardless of the source of increased life stress—positive or negative life factors—recovering alcoholics will need access to aftercare services throughout their lives. Such services should be readily available to recovering alcoholics so that relapse can be *prevented* through timely and appropriate therapeutic interventions. In effect, recovering alcoholics should not have to return to drinking in order to gain access once again to therapeutic services.

SUMMARY

Alcoholics who complete inpatient programs continue to need treatment services upon discharge. Motivational conflict over drinking or staying sober, dysphoric mood states, problems in adjusting to life sober, and neuropsychological impairments complicate continued recovery and require continuing treatment in the form of aftercare services.

Relapse back into active alcoholism following treatment increases sharply from discharge to nine months. Risk of relapse decreases from nine months but remains substantial through the second year following treatment.

Studies have shown that the risk of relapse in alcoholics can be reduced very substantially by provision of aftercare services for a lengthy period of time following inpatient treatment. Lifetime aftercare services should be available on an individual basis as the need for such services arises.

REFERENCES

Baekeland, F. Evaluation of treatment methods in chronic alcoholism. In Kissin, B. and Begleiter, H. (Eds.) *The Biology of Alcoholism Vol. 6 Treatment and Rehabilitation of the Chronic Alcoholic.* New York: Plenum Press, 1977, 385–440.

Costello, R.M. Alcoholism treatment and evaluation: In search of methods. 11. Collation of two-year follow-up studies. *The International Journal of the Addictions,* 10(5): 857–867, 1975.

Cronkite, R.C. and Moos, R.H. Sex and marital status in relation to the treatment and outcome of alcoholic patients. *Sex Roles,* 11(1/2):93–112, 1984.

Fink, E.B., Longabaugh, R., McCrady, B.M., Stout, R.L., Beattie, M., Authelet, A.R., and McNeil, D. Effectiveness of alcoholism treatment in partial versus inpatient settings: Twenty-four month outcomes. (in press).

Goldman, M.S. Neuropsychological Recovery in alcoholics: Endogenous and exogenous processes. *Alcoholism Clinical and Experimental Research* 10(2):136–144, 1986.

Milkman, H., Weiner, S.E., and Sunderwirth, S. Addiction relapse. In Shaffer, H.S. and Stimmel, B. (Eds.) *The Addictive Behaviors,* Haworth Press: New York, 1984, pp. 119–134.

Moos, R.H., Finney, J.W., and Chan, D.A. The process of recovery from alcoholism. *Journal of Studies on Alcohol,* 42(5):383–402, 1981.

Pickens, R.W., Hatsukami, D.K., Spicer, J.W., and Svikis, D.S. Relapse by alcohol abusers. *Alcoholism: Clinical and Experimental Research,* 9(3): 244–247, May/June 1985.

Siegel, C., Alenander, M.J., and Lin, S. Severe alcoholism in the mental health sector: II. Effects of service utilization on readmission. *Journal of Studies on Alcohol,* 45(6): 510–516, 1984.

Walker, R.D., Donovan, D.M., Kivlahan, D.R., and O'Leary, M.R. Length of stay, neuropsychological performance, and aftercare: Influences on alcohol treatment outcome. *Journal of Consulting and Clinical Psychology,* 51(6):900–911, 1983.

Wallace, J. After hospitalization: Treatment support of alcoholics. *Bulletin of the New York Academy of Medicine,* 59:250–254, 1983.

Weins, A.N. and Menustik, C.E. Treatment outcomes and patient characteristics in an aversion therapy program for alcoholism. *American Psychologist,* 38(10):1089–1096, October 1983.

Children of Alcoholics:
A Population at Risk

Among those persons who are close to alcoholics and affected seriously by the disease in myriad ways are the children of alcoholics. We have come to appreciate the fact that these children constitute the most readily identifiable high risk group for the development of alcoholism and alcohol-related problems. We have also come to realize that if the enormous personal, social, and financial costs of alcoholism are to be reduced in the future, then attention must be focused on the children of today. In order that the tragic and costly cycle of parental alcoholism followed by alcoholism in the offspring and other adverse outcomes is to be broken, a great deal more must be learned about etiology, consequences, interventions, and prevention approaches. This article commissioned by the Children of Alcoholics Foundation, explores some of the more promising leads that have emerged from recent research with regard to these important matters.

BACKGROUND

Much of the information reported here was drawn from series of conferences reports and publications by the Children of Alcoholics Foundation including: *Children of Alcoholics: A Review of the Literature* (Russell, Henderson & Blume, 1984); *Report of the Conference on Research Needs and Opportunities for Children of Alcoholics* (Children of Alcoholics Foundation, 1984); *Report of the Conference on Prevention Research* (Blume, 1985). In addition, an earlier report to the Governor of New York by Woodside (1982), *Children of Alcoholics,* has been useful in preparing this article.

Prevalence

Precise estimates of the number of children of alcoholics are not available. Unresolved problems in the definition of alcoholism, measurement, and survey research methodology complicate attempts to estimate the numbers of offspring of such persons. If, however, alcoholism and problem drinking are defined in terms of drinking problems, then recent national survey data (Clark & Midanik, 1982) on such problems can be used along with census data (US Department of Commerce, 1980) to arrive at approximations. This approach leads to an estimate of 6,600,000 children of alcoholics or problem drinkers under the age of 18.

Using other data from the National Drinking Practices Survey (Midanik, 1983), it is possible to estimate the numbers of persons 18 years of age or older who had an alcoholic or problem drinking parent. These data suggest that as many as 22,000,000 persons age 18 or over are children of alcoholics or problem drinkers.

In all, then, 28,600,000 Americans have been estimated to be offspring of parents who are alcoholics or problem drinkers. In effect, one out of every eight Americans has been estimated to have a parent who experienced some degree of difficulty with alcohol.

Concerning these prevalences estimates, however, several caveats are in order. The estimates are based upon self and other perceptions in response to survey questionnaires about alcohol-related problems. Data derived from such methods cannot be used to estimate the number of clinically diagnosed alcoholics in a population and hence cannot serve to estimate the number of children of clinically diagnosed alcoholics. Survey data simply provide an estimate of the numbers of people who report drinking problems of some kind or another in response to specific questions. Survey instruments do not diagnose alcoholism. Moreover, estimates of alcoholics or problem drinkers derived from national survey data can be expected to vary considerably depending upon the specific criteria used for categorizing such persons.

Psychological Consequences: Some Methodological Considerations

Due to events that take place in many alcoholic families, children of alcoholics are at increased risk for a host of psychological and social adverse consequences of parental alcoholism. However, beyond this general statement, little can be stated with much certainty. Alcoholics are not a homogeneous group and differences in such variables as severity of alcoholism, duration of drinking history, binge versus daily drinking, location of drinking, and so forth may be expected to have varying impact upon families and children. Moreover, alcoholism in mothers may affect children differently than alcoholism in fathers (Cork, 1969) as may one parent versus two parent alcoholism (Hesselbrock et al., 1982; Ackerman, 1987).

Aside from differences in drinking variables, one must also consider differences in psychological characteristics of alcoholic parents as well as differences in psychiatric histories. Obviously, a manic-depressive or schizophrenic alcoholic parent is likely to have a different impact on both the family system and the child than an alcoholic parent without such serious mental health problems.

Differences in family structure are also critical in determining the impact of parental alcoholism on children. Alcoholism in a single parent family is likely to have different consequences for children than alcoholism in a family where both parents are present. Other things being equal, child neglect is more likely when the only available caretaker is incapacitated by alcohol. Given the increasing number of single parent families in America today, alcoholism in this type of family should be of increasing concern to those involved with preventing or treating health, emotional, learning, and behavioral problems in children.

Alcoholism in a socially stable family (stable employment in head of household, some degree of marital satisfaction, stable residence pattern) may have different consequences than alcoholism in a socially unstable family. Unemployment, scarce finances, marital conflict, turmoil, and frequent residence changes are likely to interact with parental alcoholism to produce very severe effects upon children.

Characteristics of the non-alcoholic spouse are a further consideration in determining the effects of parental alcoholism on children. Wives and husbands of alcoholics may have serious physical and mental health problems of their own. These problems may (1) constitute a further stress on the alcoholic family, (2) react negatively with alcoholism in the spouse, and (3) render the non-alcoholic spouse ineffective in providing a buffer between the alcoholic parent and children.

In some instances, non-alcoholic spouses of alcoholics may be as dysfunctional as their alcoholic mates, even, perhaps more dysfunctional. In either case, the effects of such dysfunction can be expected to have serious impact on children.

The failure of most clinicians and clinical researchers to recognize and account for variability among drinking patterns and histories, characteristics of alcoholics and spouses, and family structural variables probably account for the many inconsistent and contradictory findings.

An excellent study by Ackerman (1987) illustrates the importance of avoiding stereotypes while examining the differences among adult children of alcoholics (ACOAs). Ackerman studied eight variables and showed that differences in these variables resulted in different consequences for ACOAs. The eight variables were as follows: (1) the degree of alcoholism and its effects on parenting; (2) types of parental behaviors; (3) personality characteristics and typical behaviors of children independent of parental alcoholism; (4) perception of the alcoholic parent and home; (5) gender of alcoholic parent; (6) number of alcoholic parents; (7) age of child when parental alcoholism developed; and (8) various "offsetting factors." Variation in each of these eight variables was associated with variations in the personalities and behaviors of ACOAs. Ackerman's study supports the growing conviction that children of alcoholics must not be stereotyped but must be viewed individually, assessed individually, and treated with individualized treatment plans and goals.

A final caveat is that many of the clinical observations and studies involve alcoholic families and children in treatment. Whether such findings can be generalized to the majority of children of alcoholics who are not in treatment is, of course, unknown.

STUDIES OF ALCOHOLIC FAMILIES

Most observers of alcoholic families agree that unpredictability and inconsistency are common characteristics of alcoholic homes. Because of fluctuations in parental drunkenness and sobriety and associated changes in behavior, attitudes, and moods, children are confused, frightened, frustrated, and angered by broken promises, unfulfilled expectations and parental inconsistency (Moorehouse, 1979). Intoxicated parents may behave in threatening, hostile, and confusing ways and these may contribute further to anxiety, fear, and insecurity in their children. Alcoholic homes are characterized by extreme tension and argumentativeness (Wilson & Orford, 1978). Shame, social stigma, isolation, and withdrawal are also commonly found (Sloboda, 1974; Woodside, 1982).

Parental role factors may also serve to confuse children. Some alcoholics have been reported by Park (1962) to be unable to structure their roles in accord with cultural expectations. Chafetz (1979) has commented upon the lack of an appropriate parental role model in the alcoholic home. Hence, children during critical developmental periods may experience difficulties in mastery and identity formation.

Because of the role reversals in which children are forced to act the part of parent when alcoholic mothers and fathers are incapacitated by drunkenness, hangovers, withdrawal symptoms, or hospitalizations, children of alcoholics may not have normal developmental experiences. Some are reported to become "super copers," often prematurely taking on adult characteristics and responsibilities that result in later difficulties (Black, 1979). Wegscheider (1978) sees children in alcoholic families adjusting to parental alcoholism by playing one or more temporarily adaptive but ultimately maladaptive roles.

As a rule, the few studies that have looked at the effects of parental alcoholism on behavioral and psychological characteristics do show adverse effects. Children of alcoholics in the age range 8–12 years old have been reported to be less able to maintain attention, less responsive to environmental stimulation, more prone to emotional upset, more anxious, and fearful, more emotionally detached, less able to regulate mood and less able to restrain aggression. Adolescent children of alcoholics showed more unethical behavior, paranoid thinking, hyperactivity, schizoid withdrawal, and poorer emotional controls than children of non-alcoholics (Fine et al., 1976).

Children of alcoholics have been found to have poorer self-concepts (Baraga, 1978), lowered self-esteem (O'Gorman, 1975), and to be oriented externally with regard to their locus of control (Kern et al., 1981). The external locus of control may be associated with feelings of powerlessness, lack of initiative, low school achievement, and troubled interpersonal relationships.

Adolescent children of alcoholics have been reported to show more antisocial behavior, trouble at home, deviant behavior, alcohol and drug use, and twice as many psychiatric diagnoses as a control group (Herjanic et al., 1977).

Adolescent suicide attempters have been found to be more likely to have alcoholic fathers and heavier drinking mothers (Tishler & McHenry, 1982). A study of 505 admissions of children and adolescents to pediatric emergency rooms revealed parental and sibling alcohol abuse to be a significant factor (Garfinkel et al., 1982).

The stress of living in an alcoholic home often reaches intolerable levels. This increased stress is probably related to findings of psychosomatic disorders in children of alcoholics. Roberts and Brent (1982) reported stress-related diagnoses involving gastrointestinal, nutritional, endocrine, and genito-urinary problems. Nylander (1960) found abdominal pains and sleep problems in girls and hyperactivity and attention in boys with alcoholic fathers. Insomnia and depression were noted on a health opinions survey administered by Rouse et al. (1973) to a random sample of adolescents.

There is little question that intoxication, problem-drinking, and alcoholism are related to family violence. However, the precise relationships of these to child abuse is far from clear. While intoxication and alcohol abuse are often involved in child abuse, researchers and writers in this area have not taken care to distinguish these from alcoholism per se. For example, in one study, it was apparent that individuals who were consistently drunk (daily drinking alcoholics) were among the least violent persons in a large sample of 2143 families (Coleman & Straus, 1979). Persons who were frequently drunk, however, did show increased spouse and child abuse. This latter category may confuse alcohol abusers with episodic or binge drinking alcoholics.

Child abuse and spouse abuse may be more pervasive in lower social economic classes, and mothers are reported to be more abusive toward their children across all social classes and at each level of alcohol abuse (Steinglass & Robertson, 1980). Mothers may be more likely to report child abuse since in their roles as primary caretakers of children, they are more responsible for discipline, spend more time with children, and are more likely to be drawn into conflict with them. Fathers, on the other hand, may simply avoid spouses and children during drinking periods in order not to be drawn into conflict with them that might result in abusive behavior (Mayer & Black, 1977).

In addition to failing to differentiate intoxication, alcohol abuse, and alcoholism, some studies in this area also fail to differentiate child neglect from child abuse. While many alcoholics do neglect either the physical or emotional needs of their children during drinking periods, neglect cannot be considered the same thing as family violence or child abuse. Black and Mayer (1978), for example, found that 27% of a sample of alcoholic parents either abused or neglected their children. Mothers were once again reported to be more frequent abusers than fathers. However, since abuse and neglect were summarized together in this study, and since mothers are the primary caretakers of children, they were more likely to be seen as "abusing" their children than fathers whose social roles involve behaviors other than child care.

In general, then, family violence and intoxication are clearly related. Studies that differentiate intoxication and alcohol abuse from alcoholism are needed. With regard to alcoholism, studies of family violence should attempt to take into account the heterogeneity of alcoholic populations with regard to drinking patterns and personal/social characteristics. The majority of alcoholic parents do not appear to be child abusers. Hence, neither alcoholism nor intoxication as such are sufficient to predict child abuse. What is needed are studies that clarify the factors that may interact with drinking and intoxication to produce family violence and child abuse in *both* alcoholic and non-alcoholic families. Moreover, since alcoholics are often the victims of violence, research into family violence should examine the possibility of violent behaviors by all members of alcoholic families. Alcoholic wives, for example, have been known to be abused by non-alcoholic husbands. Older children and relatives have abused alcoholic fathers. As a rule, violence in families tends to breed more violence. Hence, adults who batter wives or abuse children were possibly themselves battered and abused as children. And children who are abused by parents are more likely to abuse other children and their own parents as well when they become older, larger, and stronger.

INCREASED RISK FOR ALCOHOLISM

It has been known for some time that alcoholism tends to run in families. Cotton (1979) summarized a number of studies involving over 6,000 alcoholics and 4,000 non-alcoholics. Approximately half of the alcoholics were reported to have alcoholic near relatives. However, the evident increased risk for alcoholism in children of alcoholics could be attributable to genetic factors, psychological and social learning factors in the alcoholic home, or a combination of the two. Studies attempting to separate genetic and environmental factors have been conducted.

Goodwin and his associates (1973, 1974) conducted a series of studies on adopted children in Denmark. The basic design of these studies was simple: the rates of alcoholism among adopted children of parents who had been hospitalized for alcoholism were compared to the rates for adopted children whose biological parents had not been hospitalized for alcoholism. Also, the rates for adopted children were compared to the rates for children raised by their own biological parents. The results indicated a four times greater risk of developing alcoholism for the sons of alcoholics whether they had been raised by foster parents or by their biological alcoholic parents. Goodwin's study did not demonstrate any effect at all of home environment on subsequent alcoholism rates. More frequently, Cloninger et al. (1981) in Sweden, reported on female as well as male adoptees. Subtypes of alcoholics were examined as well. Cloninger reported two types of alcoholism, one that appeared to be independent of environment, while the other seemed to be dependent upon both genetic and environmental factors. The first type, "male limited" alcoholism, was a severe form of the disease characterized by adolescent onset of alcohol abuse, extensive treatment for alcohol abuse and criminality in the biological fathers. For this type of male alcoholism, there was a ninefold increase in risk of alcoholism in the sons whose biological fathers were alcoholics.

On the other hand, the second type, "milieu limited" alcoholism, was, for the most part, characterized by a lesser number of alcoholic problems with environmental factors determining the frequency and severity of expression. For men, there was a twofold increased risk for milieu-limited alcoholism when postnatal environmental provocation was present.

The Cloninger et al. study is perhaps the first to show that female offspring of alcoholic fathers and mothers are also at increased risk for the development of the disease. For women, a threefold increase in risk for alcoholism was apparent when the biological parents were alcoholic.

While available evidence from adoption studies does point to a genetic predisposition in alcoholism, the precise nature of this risk is still unknown.

Some evidence from twin studies does suggest a degree of genetic control over alcohol metabolism rates (Vesell, 1971), Schuckit and his colleagues (1979) found that acetaldehyde differences may differentiate high risk from low risk persons, but others (e.g., Behar et al., 1983) have not found such differences. In general, research on differences in metabolism rates has been inconclusive.

It is possible that the enzymes that enter into the metabolism of alcohol and acetaldehyde may play a role in differential alcohol sensitivity since these enzymes are thought to be genetically determined (Harada et al., 1980). Enzymes that serve to degrade or convert brain neurotransmitters are also under genetic control and deficiencies in these may result in altered transmitter supply or functions which, in turn, could be related to alcoholism.

Recent attention has focused upon the electrical activity of the brain. EEG studies of alpha rhythm have suggested the following relationships to the genetic factor in alcoholism: characteristics related to alpha rhythm are inherited; alcohol can serve to have a synchronizing effect on alpha rhythm, and alcoholics tend to have poorly synchronized alpha patterns on the EEG. Hence, children of alcoholics may be genetically predisposed to poorly synchronized alpha rhythm. They may "learn" that alcohol produces synchronization of alpha rhythm, and may be motivated to drink frequently due to the reward value of increased alpha synchronization.

An important lead has been provided by Elmasian et al. (1982) who found that a particular component (P3) of the evoked potential to an auditory stimulus was reduced in high risk children after drinking. Begleiter and colleagues (Begleiter, Porjesz, Bihari et al., 1984) have found decreased P3 components in male 6–13 year old children of alcoholics in relation to visual evoked potentials. Perhaps a decreased P3 component of the evoked potential is a biological marker for alcoholism.

In general, then, a genetic predisposing factor (or factors) for alcoholism does exist. Genetic vulnerability is most apparent in severe forms of the disease, most often found in males (although mother to daughter transmission has been reported as well), and may operate independent of environment depending upon type of alcoholism. While differences in sensitivity to alcohol do appear to be under genetic control to some extent or another, research that has attempted to clarify the nature of the genetic risk factor is far from conclusive.

While genetic influence in alcoholism has been reported, it is important to note that not all alcoholics have positive family histories for alcoholism. Studies, however, report earlier onset, more severe symptoms and greater adverse consequences in alcoholics with positive family histories versus those without such histories.

Given genetic predispositions to alcoholism, it has become apparent that children of alcoholics are the most readily identified high risk group for the development of the disease themselves. Obviously, there is an urgent need for sensitive, effective, and readily accessible education and prevention efforts targeted toward these children.

ALCOHOL TOXICITY AND THE FETUS

Scientific interest in the toxic effects of alcohol on the developing fetus increased after Lemoine and her colleagues (1968) in France reported abnormalities in infants born to alcoholic parents. Jones and his colleagues (1973) in the United States reported independently on a common set of birth defects in children born to alcoholic mothers and coined the phrase, "Fetal Alcohol Syndrome," or FAS to describe these defects.

In the absence of a full blown Fetal Alcohol Syndrome, maternal alcohol use has been associated with a broader spectrum of negative pregnancy outcomes. Termed Fetal Alcohol Effects or FAE, these negative outcomes may include spontaneous abortion, stillbirth, growth retardation, and some of the anomalies found in the full syndrome.

Heredity and maternal excessive drinking are also associated with hyperactivity, irritable and fussy behavior in infants, and behavior problems in children. It is possible, of course, that these problems are a result of genetic transmission, but it is equally possible that they are due to some insult in early pregnancy that mimics genetic transmission (Rapoport & Quinn, 1975). Maternal excessive alcohol consumption could be the insult in early pregnancy that mimics genetic transmission. For example, Streissguth et al. (1980) reported that irritability, jitteriness, and reported hyperactivity in childhood are characteristic of the majority of FAS cases. Iosub et al. found that 80% of a sample of FAS patients showed speech and language problems, half were mentally retarded, and three-quarters were hyperactive. Shaywitz et al. (1980) reported that a clinical sample of children of heavy drinking mothers had IQs ranging from 82 to 113 but all had experienced early school failure, 88% had been referred to special education by first grade, 99% were described in school records as hyperactive, and all had at least two of the physical anomalies characteristic of FAS.

While mental retardation has been associated with FAS, reported IQ scores have ranged widely. In one study (Streissguth et al., 1978), an IQ range of 16 to 105 was reported. Moreover, given the possibility that only the most serious cases of FAS were diagnosed and reported, it is probable that the mental retardation associated with the syndrome has been overestimated.

Bearing in mind these caveats, it is important to note that a review of the world literature (Clarren & Smith, 1978) on FAS found that of 126 of 245 reported cases, 85% scored two standard deviations below the mean on IQ tests. Also, studies in three countries revealed an average IQ of 68 in FAS children (Little & Streissguth, 1981).

In general, the extent to which genetic factors, parental alcoholism and postnatal environment contribute to IQ in FAS children is presently unknown.

GENETIC FACTORS IN ETIOLOGY OF FAS

Genetic factors may operate to produce differential susceptibility to Fetal Alcohol Syndrome. Reviews of the literature suggest that both interspecies and intraspecies differences in susceptibility to FAS exists. Moreover, these differences in susceptibility may be related to genetic influences upon tissue or neural sensitivity. Human twin studies have provided data consistent with a genetic factor in FAS but such studies are far from equivocal.

In general, then, Fetal Alcohol Syndrome effects pose serious risks for the children of alcoholic mothers. Not only is there a direct adverse effect of alcohol upon the developing fetus, an interaction with genetic factors may operate to increase risks in particular individuals. Hence, it is not possible to state in any general sense how much drinking is too much drinking for a pregnant woman. Given the many unknowns, women who are aware of being pregnant should abstain entirely from alcoholic beverages, and especially so during the first trimester of pregnancy. Women who are planning pregnancy and attempting conception should definitely abstain entirely from alcoholic beverages.

Even though the role that heavy drinking in the father may play in producing birth defects in offspring is presently unclear, fathers should also stop drinking during periods when couples are planning or attempting conception. By abstaining during critical periods, fathers are encouraging an alcohol-free environment in the home and, in this fashion, supporting the mother's decision to abstain.

TREATMENT CONSIDERATIONS

Given the variability among alcoholics and the heterogeneity among alcoholic families, it is exceedingly doubtful that a single stereotype will adequately describe the children of alcoholics. Moreover, it is equally unlikely that a single therapeutic modality or process will prove sufficient for dealing with the treatment needs of this highly diverse group. As with any clinical population, treatment must be based upon sensitive and careful individualized assessments rather than upon apriori lists of assumed characteristics. Therefore, any therapeutic effort with children of alcoholics or adult children of alcoholics must of necessity begin with a thoughtful and detailed examination of the presenting problems and a careful family history. As Cermack has pointed out, "children of alcoholics" is not a *diagnosis;* it is a *label.*

Clinicians treating children or adult children from alcoholic families must not assume that the presenting problems are of necessity attributable to parental alcoholism. Given the high rates of behavior problems among children in general in American society, particular problems may or may not be associated with parental alcoholism. And adjustment problems of adulthood can either be independent of or related to having been raised in a home with an alcoholic parent. In addition, particular problems of some children of alcoholics may be related more to the dysfunctional behavior of the non-alcoholic (co-dependent) parent than to the behaviors of the alcoholic parent. In some instances, problems may be associated with behaviors stemming from mental illness in an alcoholic family member and not alcoholic behaviors as such.

In short, treatment of children of alcoholics must avoid stereotypes, follow from careful individualized assessments of families, and involve multimodal processes and varied strategies.

SUMMARY AND IMPLICATIONS

The children of alcoholic parents are a population at risk for a host of adverse consequences. Having at least one alcoholic parent is associated with increased risk for birth defects, mental retardation, hyperactivity, school adjustment and learning problems, emotional and physical health problems, and a range of maladaptive behaviors. Moreover, these children are at substantially increased risk for the development of alcoholism as well. In fact, children of alcoholics comprise the most readily identified group of persons at risk for alcoholism.

Given the enormous personal, social, and financial costs of alcoholism, considerable attention must be paid to this high risk group, not only to alleviate present suffering, but to find ways to prevent adverse consequences in the future.

Further theory, research, and applications with regard to children of alcoholics will need to take into account the evident heterogeneity in both alcoholics and alcoholic families. Differences in a host of drinking styles, drinking behaviors, typical responses to alcohol, and characteristics of alcoholic parents and non-alcoholic spouses are likely to have varying impacts upon children with regard to both type and severity of adverse consequences.

Progress in this area will depend greatly upon the development of a detailed *typology of alcoholic families*. Differences in family compositions, structures, atmospheres, states, and processes are more likely to affect these children in different ways. Hence, research that continues to look at alcoholic families as though they are all alike will probably lead to a growing body of inconsistent, contradictory, and perhaps misleading findings. In short, while alcoholics and their spouses do not conform to stereotypes, neither do their families. Theory, research, and public policy with regard to children of alcoholics need to spring from awareness of differences as well as similarities.

Given the $100 billion total economic costs of alcoholism to American society, intervention and prevention programs with children of alcoholics should be of considerable interest to those seeking to contain health care costs. Since 30% of the total economic costs of alcoholism are health care costs, prevention and treatment programs with high risk groups such as children of alcoholics may prove to be very effective health care cost containment measures.

Costs aside, however, programs directed toward helping this very large population of the "other victims of alcoholism" would do much to prevent the needless suffering and tragic consequences that lie waiting for these future generations of adults. Given sufficient support for research with children of alcoholics, advances in scientific understanding of the genetic factors in the illness as well as of critical environmental factors could possibly lead to effective prevention programs for both alcoholism and adverse psychological consequences.

REFERENCES

Ackerman, R. J. (1987). *Same House, Different Homes: Why Adult Children of Alcoholics Are Not All The Same.* Monograph, Indiana State University, Indiana, PA.

Baraga, D. J. (1978). Self-concept in children of alcoholics. *Dissertations Abstracts International* 39:368-B.

Begleiter, H.; Porjesz, B.; Bihari, B. et al. (1984). Event-related brain potential in boys at risk for alcoholism. *Science* 225:1493–1496.

Behar, D.; Berg, C.J.; Rapport, J. L.; Nelson, W.; Linnoila, M.; Cohen, M.; Bozevich, C. & Marshall, T. (1983). Behavioral and physiological effects of ethanol in high-risk and control children: A pilot study. Alcoholism: Clinical and Experimental Research 7(4):404–410.

Black, C. (1979). Children of alcoholics. *Alcohol Health and Research World* 4(1):23–27.

Black, R. & Mayer, J. (1978). An investigation of the relationship between substance abuse and child abuse and neglect. Final report submitted to the National Center on Child Abuse and Neglect, ACYF, DHEW.

Blume, S. (1985). *Report of the Conference on Prevention Research.* New York: Children of Alcoholics Foundation.

Chafetz, M. (1979). Children of alcoholics. *New York University Education Quarterly* 10(3): 23–29.

Children of Alcoholics Foundation (1983). *Report of the Conference on Research Needs and Opportunities for Children of Alcoholics,* New York.

Clarren, S.K. & Smith, D.W. (1978). The fetal alcohol syndrome. *New England Journal of Medicine* 298:1063–1067.

Cloninger, R.; Bohman, M. & Sigvardsson, S. (1981). Inheritance of alcohol abuse. *Archives of General Psychiatry* 38:9654–969.

Coleman, D. H. & Straus, M. A. (1979). Alcohol abuse and family violence. Paper presented at the Annual Meeting of the American Sociological Association, February.

Cork, M. (1969). *The Forgotten Children.* Toronto: Paperbacks, in association with Addiction Research Foundation.

Cotton, N. S. (1979). The familial incidence of alcoholism. *Journal of Studies on Alcoholism* 40(1):89–116.

Elmasian, R.; Neville, H.; Woods, D.; Schuckit, M. & Bloom, F. (1982). Event-related brain potential are different in individuals at high and low risk for developing alcoholism. *Medical Sciences* 79:7900–7903.

Fine, E. W.; Yudin, L. W.; Holmes, J. & Heinemann, S. (1976). Behavioral disorders in children with parental alcoholism. *Annals of the New York Academy of Sciences* 273: 507–517.

Garfinkel, B. D.; Froese, A. & Hood, J. (1982). Suicide attempts in children and adolescents. *American Journal of Psychiatry* 139(10):1257–1261.

Goodwin, D. (1971). Is alcoholism hereditary? A review and critique. *Archives of General Psychiatry* 25:545–549.

Goodwin, D. & Guze, S. (1974). Heredity and alcoholism. In: B. Kissin & H. Begleiter, (eds.), *The Biology of Alcoholism Vol. III: Clinical Pathology.* New York: Plenum Press, pp. 37–52.

Harada, S.; Agarwal, D. P. & Goedde, H. W. (1980). Isozymes of alcohol dehydrogenase and aldehyde dehydrogenase in Japanese and their role in alcohol sensitivity. *Advances in Experimental Medicine and Biology* 132:31–39.

Herjanic, B. M.; Herjanic, M.; Penick, E. C.; Tomelleri, C. & Armbruster, R. B. S. (1977). Children of alcoholics. In: F. Seixas (ed.), *Currents in Alcoholism* Vol. II. New York: Grune and Stratton, pp. 445–455.

Hesselbrock, V. M.; Stabenau, J. R.; Hesselbrock, M. N.; Meyer, R. E. & Babor, T. F. (1982). The nature of alcoholism in patients with different family histories for alcoholism. *Progress in Neuro-psychopharmacology and Biological Psychiatry* 6:607–614.

Jones, K. L.; Smith, D. W.; Ulleland, C. N. & Streissguth, A. P. (1973). Patterns of malformations in offspring of chronic alcoholic mothers. *Lancet i:*1267–1271.

Kern, J. C.; Hassett, C. A. & Collipp, P. J. (1981). Children of alcoholics: Locus of control, mental age and zinc level. *Journal of Clinical Psychiatric Treatment and Evaluation* 3:169–173.

Lemoine, P.; Harousseau, H.; Borteyru, J. P. & Manuet, J. C. (1986). Les enfants de parents alcoholiques. Anomalies observees. A propos de 127 cas. *Quest Medical* 21:476–482, 1986. English translation of Lemoine et al. from the National Clearinghouse for Alcohol Information—STIAR (Selected Translations of International Alcoholism Research).

Little, R. E. & Streissguth, A. P. (1981). Effects of alcohol on the fetus: Impact and prevention. *Canadian Medical Association Journal* 125:159–164.

Mayer, J. & Black, R. (1977). The relationship between alcoholism and child abuse and neglect. In F. Sexias (ed.), *Currents in Alcoholism* Vol. II. New York: Grune and Stratton, pp. 429–445.

Midanik, L. (1983). Familial alcoholism and problem drinking in a national drinking practices survey. *Addictive Behaviors* 8:133–41.

Morehouse, E. (1979). Working in the schools with children of alcoholic parents. *Health and Social Work* 4(4):144–162.

O'Gorman, P. (1975). Self-concept, locus of control, and perception of father in adolescents from homes with and without severe drinking problems. PhD Dissertation, Fordham University.

Park, P. (1962). Problem drinking and role deviation: A study in incipient alcoholism: In: D. J. Pittman & C. R. Snyder (eds.), *Society, Culture and Drinking Patterns.* New York: John Wiley and Sons, Inc., pp. 431–454.

Rapoport, J. L. & Quinn, P. O. (1975). Minor physical anomalies (stigmata) and early developmental deviation: A major biologic subgroup of hyperactive children. *International Journal of Mental Health* 4:29–44.

Roberts, K. S. & Brent, E. E. (1982). Physician utilization and illness patterns in families of alcoholics. *Journal of Studies on Alcohol* 43(1):119–128.

Russell, M. (1982). The epidemiology of alcohol-related birth defects. In: E. L. Abel (ed.), *Fetal Alcohol Syndrome Vol. II: Human Studies*, Boca Raton, FL: CRC Press, Inc., pp. 89–126.

Schuckit, M. A. & Rayses, V. (1979). Ethanol ingestion: Differences in blood acetaldehyde concentrations in relatives of alcoholics and controls. *Science* 203:54–55.

Shaywitz, S. E.; Cohen, D. J. & Shaywitz, B. A. (1980). Behavior and learning deficits in children of normal intelligence born to alcoholic mothers. *Journal of Pediatrics* 96:978–982.

Sloboda, S. B. (1974). The children of alcoholics: A neglected problem. *Hospital and Community Psychiatry* 25:605–606.

Steinglass, P. & Robertson, A. (1983). The alcoholic family. In: B. Kissin & H. Begleiter (eds.), *The Biology of Alcoholism Vol. 6: The Pathogenesis of Alcoholism, Psychosocial Factors*. New York: Plenum Press, pp. 243–307.

Streissguth, A. P.; Herman, C. S. & Smith, D. W. (1978). Intelligence, behavior and morphogenesis in the fetal alcohol syndrome: A report on 20 patients. *Journal of Pediatrics* 92:363–367.

Streissguth, A. P.; Landesman-Dwyer, S.; Martin, J. C. & Smith, D. W. (1980). Teratogentic effects of alcohol in humans and laboratory animals. *Science* 209:353–361.

Tishler, C. L. & McHenry, P. C. (1982). Parent negative self and adolescent suicide attempts. *Journal of the American Academy of Child Psychiatry* 21(4):404–408.

U.S. Department of Commerce (1983). 1980 Census of Population: General Population Characteristics, U.S. Summary, PC80-1-B1. Washington, DC: U.S. Government Printing Office.

Vesell, E. S.; Page, J. G. & Passananti, G. T. (1971). Genetic and environmental factors affecting ethanol metabolism in man. *Clinical Pharmacology and Therapeutics* 2:192–201.

Waldrop, M. F.; Pederson, F. A. & Bell, R. Q. (1968). Minor physical anomalies and behavior in preschool children. *Child Development* 39:391–400.

Wegscheider, D. & Wegscheider, S. (1978). *Family Illness: Chemical Dependency, Nurturing Networks*. Crystal, MN.

Wilson, C. & Orford, J. (1978). Children of Alcoholics: Report of a preliminary study and comments on the literature. *Journal of Studies on Alcohol* 39(1):121–142.

Woodside, M. (1982). *Children of Alcoholics:* A report to Hugh L. Carey, Governor, State of New York. New York: Division of Alcoholism and Alcohol Abuse.

Part III

The Disease Model of Alcoholism

Frontiers of Biopsychosocial Research: Filling in the Biological Dimension

Despite the objections of moralists, mentalistic psychiatrists, and some traditional behavioristic psychologists, it is now widely believed that alcoholism is a biopsychosocial disease (Wallace, 1978; Tartar, 1983; Ewing, 1980). From this contemporary point of view, it is simply not useful to continue to think of the illness in terms of simplistic dichotomies, e.g., "Is alcoholism a learned or unlearned phenomenon?"

A biopsychosocial model is multidimensional and requires that attention be paid to a person's biology, psychology, and social surrounds if the origins and maintenance of the disease are to be understood. In this sense, alcoholism is not very much different from many diseases in which biology, behavior, and society or culture combine to produce illness. Diabetes, for example is one such illness in which biological pre-dispositions, individual food preferences, and cultural dietary patterns interact and eventuate in disease.

As with other biopsychosocial diseases, theoretical ideology tied to turf issues has served as a significant obstacle to the development of multidimensional thinking. Thinking in more than one dimension is thinking that requires flexibility and subtlety rather than the rigidity of a single theoretical persuasion and narrow professional identification. Some traditional behavioristic psychologists, for example, have overlooked the importance of psychogenetics and psychobiology in the origins of alcoholism, not because of a lack of scientific evidence for these, but because genetics and psychobiology do not fit neatly into a simplistic behavioristic worldview. If one assumes that everything is learned, then it is not surprising to find some traditional behavioristic psychologists arguing that alcoholism is a learned habit or response. And of course, if alcoholism is merely a learned habit or response, then it can be unlearned, i.e., alcoholics ought to be able to unlearn alcoholism and relearn social, normal, controlled, attenuated, or non-problem drinking. Despite the fact that the evidence from a large mixed bag of papers purporting to "document" the success of controlled drinking for alcoholics remains unimpressive when held up to rigorous scientific scrutiny, some traditional behavioristic psychologists continue to attempt to defend controlled drinking as a treatment goal and to attack abstention (See, for example, the October, 1983 issue of *American Psychologist* edited by Drs. Peter Nathan and Arthur Weins for a recent defense of the Sobell and Sobell controversial Patton State Hospital experiment on controlled drinking and a polemic against abstention. In particular, see A. Marlatt's piece, "The Controlled-Drinking Controversy" in this issue of the *American Psychologist*).

Despite traditionalists' opposition, however, progress towards a modern, biopsychosocial model continues at a rapid rate with much of the recent work centering on the brain.

Recent research clearly implicates biological factors in the etiology and maintenance of alcoholism. Numerous studies in animals on alcohol preference and consumption show hereditary influence (McClearn, 1981). Selective breeding in mice and rats has been achieved and strain differences have been shown.

Human genetic studies (Goodwin, Schulsinger, Moller, Hermansen, Winokur, and Cuze, 1974) (Kaij, 1981) (Schuckitt, 1981) indicate that the sons of alcoholics have at least a three times greater risk of becoming alcoholics than the sons of non-alcoholics. For some types of alcoholics, risk is nine times greater. This increased risk was found in studies where social learning effects were *absent* and was not further increased in studies where both genetic and social learning effects were jointly present. In addition, the rate of concordance for alcoholism in identical twins is 60 per cent and 30 per cent in fraternal twins. Moreover, young men with alcoholism in first degree family members metabolize alcohol differently than men without such family histories. Higher associated levels of acetaldehyde and less behavioral impairment after three drinks have been noted in young men with alcoholism in first degree family members (Schuckitt, 1981).

A recent study of patients with and without familial histories of alcoholism revealed numerous differences (Frances, Timm and Bucky, 1980). Patients with familial histories showed more severe symptomatology of alcoholism, more antisocial behavior, worse academic and social performance in school, unstable employment histories and more severe physical symptoms related to alcohol.

In a recent study by Gabrielli et al., young sons of alcoholic fathers showed a high frequency EEG activity (about 18Hz). Hence, fast EEG activity which is a heritable characteristic and is frequently found in adult alcoholics has been found in EEG records of the 11–13 year old sons of alcoholics. Since alcohol is known to slow brain activity, alcoholics may be persons who learn to reduce genetically determined fast brain wave activity by self-medication with alcoholic beverages. Recent work by Bohman (1981) and his colleagues indicates that female alcoholism is also partially genetically determined. In a study of female adoptees in Sweden, a 3-fold increase in subsequent alcoholism was found in adopted females whose biological mothers were alcoholic. For males, a cross-fostering analysis revealed a 9-fold increase in male adoptees whose biological fathers were alcoholic (Cloninger, 1981).

Numerous studies have centered on the effects of alcohol on brain neurotransmitters and the possible effects of neurotransmitter systems on drinking behavior. Serotonin (5-HT) metabolism is apparently altered by alcohol and lesions of neuron systems containing 5-HT result in increased preference for alcohol in rats (Myers and Melchoir, 1977). On the other hand, alcohol intake in rats can be suppressed by administration of a 5-HT precursor, 5-Hydroxytryptophan (5-HTP).

Alcohol preference may be related to norepinephrine levels (NE). When neuron systems of the rat containing NE are lesioned by a neurotoxin infused directly into the cerebral ventricle, suppression of preference for alcohol is observed (Myers, 1978).

In short, these studies on neurotransmitter systems suggest that alcoholism may be related to particular biochemical events in the brain.

In the past decade, considerable interest has developed in the possible role of aldehyde-biogenic amine combinations. Acetaldehyde, the first metabolic intermediary of alcohol, along with other aldehydes, in combination with various neurotransmitters yields a family of substances called tetrahydroisoquinolines (TIQs). For example, dopamine plus acetaldehyde yields salsolinol. Dopamine plus dopaldehyde yields tetrahydropapaveroline (THP), an alkaloid that is a morphine precursor.

Administration of TIQs to animals has been shown to increase preferences for ethanol solutions. Myers and his colleagues (Myers, 1978; Myers, et al., 1982) for example, have shown that in rats and monkeys when THP is infused into the cerebral ventricles, preferences for astonishingly high concentrations of ethanol (40 per cent) can be established. Moreover, it appears that such preferences are irreversible. These results are remarkable since monkeys do not naturally prefer alcohol to water. Also, the concentrations of ethanol are very high (equivalent to 80 proof alcohol).

Blum and his associates (1978) have hypothesized that alcohol and opiate addiction may be linked by morphine precursors formed by alcohol-biogenic amine condensation products. In effect, alcoholism may be related to the brain's production of various TIQs. The following findings support an alkaloid isoquinoline role in alcoholism.

1. Elevated tetrahydropapaveroline (THP) levels in patients entering alcoholism treatment have been noted.
2. THP and salsolinol interact with opiate receptor sites, i.e.; these isoquinolines appear to be similar to opiates.
3. Apparently irreversible preferences for *very high* concentrations of ethanol can be induced in animals by infusions of THP into the cerebral ventricles.

These findings clearly implicate biological factors in the origin of alcoholism. Moreover, research such as this on biological factors has reached a level of sophistication that renders the question of whether or not alcoholism is a disease non-productive, if not absurd.

While some pharmacologists and neurobiologists regard the work on TIQs as uncertain (see, for example, Dr. Adron Harris's critique in the November, 1983 issue of the *U.S. Journal*), further evidence indicates that the basic experimentation on TIQs in animals have been replicated by research groups in Colorado, Finland, and London. Moreover, the link to opiates is further established by the recent finding that naloxone, an opioid receptor antagonist, reduces alcohol intake by 50 per cent in rats previously treated by intracerebral injections of TIQ. The same effect is noted with the opiate receptor antagonist, naltrexone in monkeys. These findings with opiate receptor antagonists clearly point to a possible link between the neurochemistries of alcohol dependence and opiate dependence.

Finally, there is now overwhelming evidence that a host of TIQ metabolites are indeed synthesized in the brain by means of a condensation reaction between an aldehyde and a neurotransmitter. Not only has an increase in particular TIQs been found in rat brains following intake of alcohol, Swedish studies reveal significant levels of TIQs in the cerebrospinal fluid of intoxicated alcoholics. Postmortem studies of alcoholic individuals reveal elevated TIQs in the dopamine-rich areas of the brain (precisely where we would expect to find the TIQ, salsolinol, since it is formed by the reaction of an aldehyde with dopamine).

In general, then, biological research in alcoholism has made enormous strides forward, much of it occurring within the last five years.

It has certainly filled in the biological dimension of a biopsychosocial model of alcoholism with remarkable theory and data in psychogenetics and neurochemistry now available.

For the traditionalists in psychology, social sciences, and medicine, it is time to give up the old, poorly informed, and more-heat-than-light arguments that center around the same tired, old dichotomies. Alcoholism is a biopsychosocial disease. The scientific evidence for a potent biological factor is rapidly accumulating and is impressive. Let's move on.

REFERENCES

Blum, K., Hamilton, M., Hirst, M., and Wallace, J. "Putative role of Isoquinoline alkaloids in alcoholism: a link to opiates", *Alcoholism: Clinical and Experimental Research*, 1978, Vol. 2, pp. 113–120.

Bohman, M., Sigvardsson, S., Cloninger, C.R., Maternal inheritance of alcohol abuse: Cross-fostering analysis of adopted women. *Archives of General Psychiatry*, 38:965–969, 1981.

Cloninger, C.R., Bohman, M., Sigvardsson, S., Inheritance of alcohol abuse: Cross-fostering analysis of adopted men. *Archives of General Psychiatry*, 38:861–868, 1981.

Ewing, J.A., "Alcoholism—another biopsychosocial disease", *Psychosomatics*, 1980, Vol. 21, 371–372.

Frances, R., Timm, S., and Bucky, S., "Studies of familial and nonfamilial alcoholism", *Archives of General Psychiatry*, 1980, Vol. 37, pp. 564–566.

Gabrielli, W., Mednick, S.A., Volavka, J., Pollock, V.E., Schulsinger, F., and Itil, T., Electroencephalograms in children of alcoholic fathers", *Psychophysiology*, 1982, Vol. 19, pp. 404–407.

Goodwin, D., Schulsinger, F., Moller, N., Hermansen, L., Winokur, G., and Cuze, S., "Drinking problems in adopted and nonadopted sons of alcoholics", *Archives of General Psychiatry*, 1974, Vol. 31, pp. 164–169.

Kaij, L., *Alcoholism in Twins*, Almquist and Wiksell, Stockholm, 1960.

McClearn, G., "Genetic studies in animals", *Alcoholism: Clinical and Experimental Research*, Vol. 5, pp. 447–448.

Myers, R.D., and Melchoir, C.L., "Alcohol and alcoholism: Role of Serotonin", in, *Serotonin in Health and Disease*, Essman, W.B., Editor, New York, Spectrum, 1977, pp. 373–430.

Myers, R.D., Psychopharmacology of Alcohol, *Annual Review of Pharmacology and Toxicology*, 1978, Vol. 18, pp. 125–144.

Myers, R.D., "Tetrahydroisoquinolines in the brain: the basis of an animal model of alcoholism", *Alcoholism: Clinical and Experimental Research*, 1978, Vol. 2, pp. 145–154.

Myers, R.D., McCaleb, M.L., and Ruwe, W.D., "Alcohol drinking induced into the cerebral ventricle", *Pharmacology, Biochemistry, and Behavior*, 1982, Vol. 16, pp. 995–1000.

Schuckitt, M.A., "The Genetics of alcoholism", *Alcoholism: Clinical and Experimental Research*, 1981, Vol. 5, pp. 439–440.

Tarter, R.E., The Causes of Alcoholism: A Biopsychosocial Analysis. In Gottheil, E., Druley, K., Skoloda, T., and Waxman, H., (Eds.), *Etiological Aspects of Alcohol and Drug Abuse,* Springfield, Charles C. Thomas, 1983.

Wallace, J., "Compulsive drinking: a biopsychosocial model", unpublished manuscript, 1978, Edgehill Newport, Newport, Rhode Island 02840.

Alcoholism and Other Chemical Dependencies are Diseases

Many people today have come to believe that alcoholism and other drug dependencies are diseases. Polls of Americans continue to show increases in the numbers of persons who regard chemically dependent people as ill rather than morally deficient or psychiatrically abnormal. Others, including certain academicians (drawn largely from the behavioral sciences), have doubts about the biological bases of the chemical dependencies.

But despite the objections of moralists, psychoanalytically-oriented psychiatrists, and traditional behavioristic psychologists, the evidence for significant biological factors in addictions of all kinds continues to pile up. Behavior is surely involved in chemical dependencies, but behavior alone doesn't tell the whole story. Society and culture are also involved but these also lead to partial and insufficient explanations. Drugs and alcohol operate *within bodies* and these bodies must be considered if we are to make sense of the sets of behaviors we refer to as addictions or chemical dependencies.

In trying to understand the complex patterns of the drinking behavior we call alcoholism, it is important to fix firmly in mind the fact that alcoholism is not a symptom of something else but is a primary disease in its own right. Alcoholism is not a symptom of "underlying neurosis" or "latent schizophrenia" or "depression." Alcoholics are indeed often anxious, frightened, insecure and depressed people. Their behavior when they are drinking can be odd and unpredictable. In withdrawal (when their drinking is suddenly stopped), they may experience frightening hallucinations, become very restless, agitated and hostile. However, these emotional problems are more often than not the *result* of alcoholism and not its cause. In order to understand what alcoholism is and where it comes from we have to dig deeper than the surface behavioral picture and focus instead on genetics and events taking place in the brain.

The strongest evidence that we have for classifying alcoholism as a disease comes from studies of genetics. If it can be shown that alcoholism has a genetic predisposition or set of predispositions, then we know that biological factors are operating from one generation to the next to influence susceptibility to the disease. Indeed, this is precisely what research has shown. In animal genetic research, it is possible to breed mice that show many of the alcohol-related behaviors we associate with human alcoholism. Strains of animals have been bred through genetic manipulations alone to 1) seek out alcohol, 2) prefer alcohol to water, 3) engage in efforts to get alcohol, 4) show reduced sensitivity to the drug, 5) develop tolerance to alcohol, and 6) show withdrawal symptoms when the drinking is interrupted. Study of the brains of these "alcoholic" mice reveals differences in a number of brain chemicals when comparisons are made with the brains of mice who show no preference for alcohol over water and, in fact, avoid alcohol.

Human genetic studies have followed a different strategy. In these, the offspring of alcoholic parents are followed over long periods of time and drinking problems in these children as they reach adulthood are carefully documented. Typically, the studies have involved children who have been adopted at an early age. In this way, the social and psychological effects of being raised in an alcoholic home can be ruled out and increases in risk can be attributed more readily to genetic factors. One important study involving adopted children and biological alcoholic parents was conducted in Denmark. This study revealed a four times greater risk for alcoholism in the children of alcoholics when the children were adopted out at an early age. A later adoptive study in Sweden showed that, for certain types of alcoholism, the risk for developing alcoholism rose to nine times increased risk when alcoholism was present in the biological parents.

While there is striking evidence for a genetic predisposition (or a set of predispositions) to some forms of alcoholism, not all alcoholism seems to have a genetic basis. Some alcoholism appears to be *acquired* with a host of behavioral, social and cultural factors operating to produce the disease. But even in the case of acquired alcoholism or chemical dependency, powerful biological factors operate to insure maintenance of the diseases. Take dependence on cocaine, for example. How can repeated exposure to cocaine result in an irresistible compulsion to use the drug? The answer to this question appears to lie in the chemistry of the brain.

Cocaine operates on many brain chemical systems but its most potent addictive effects are upon nerve cells that involve the neurochemical called dopamine. This neurochemical is one of a number of chemicals produced in the brain that involve information transfer from one brain cell to another. We call these neurochemicals, neurotransmitters. Dopamine is a neurotransmitter that can be involved with diseases as different as Parkinson disease and schizophrenia. With too little dopamine, the person has Parkinson disease; too much—or more precisely, too sensitive a dopamine system—and the person shows schizophrenia. What cocaine does to the dopamine neurons of the addict is now fairly well understood. In the beginning, cocaine causes a dopamine excess in the brain's synapses (or region between nerve cells). This dopamine excess is experienced by the person as highly pleasurable. At this stage, cocaine makes the person feel in control, masterful and "high." In time, however, with repeated use of cocaine, dopamine levels in the brain fall and the dopamine system becomes super sensitized. Now, instead of euphoria, the cocaine dependent person is caught in a vicious circle of a brief high followed almost immediately by intense renewed craving for the drug, depression, agitation, paranoia and other unhappy states. The only relief seems to be in taking more drug. But this, of course, won't solve anything because the more the person uses the drug, the more she or he will change the chemistry of the brain, and the more the person will crave the drug, seek it out at all costs, and compulsively use it.

These vicious cycles of use, initial euphoria, and subsequent neurochemical entrapment are characteristic of most forms of chemical dependence. The more the person turns to any drug, the more he or she will set up bodily demands for the drug in order to feel just normal. Unfortunately, most addicted people will recall only the euphoria or "high" that they got out of the alcohol or some other drug initially. They deny or forget the negative and even tragic things that are happening to them in a desperate effort to recapture the long gone euphoria they once had with their chemical. It is not uncommon for an alcoholic to go through 10 or even 20 years of increasingly destructive drinking in this futile search for "yesterday's high." Tragically, many will die in the search without ever finding it.

Alcohol and drugs of many kinds set up seemingly paradoxical "rebound effects" in the brain. Once understood, however, these "rebound effects" are not paradoxical but predictable. Alcohol in large quantities will sedate the person initially but will result in rebound anxiety and tension that will set up a demand for more alcohol. Tranquilizers of various kinds, such as Valium and Librium, will do the same. These opposite rebound effects result from changes in brain cells. Heroin use, for example, can lead the addict to experience euphoria and a complete absence of body tension. But when the dose wears off, a small brain structure called the locus ceruleus will become hyperactive and flood the brain with a highly stimulating neurotransmitter called noradrenaline. The results of this high level of rebound neurochemical stimulation are most unpleasant and set up intense craving in the addict for another fix. And so it goes: Use. Temporary euphoria. Rebound unpleasant stimulation. More use. In time, the destructive bodily cycle of change, of action and reaction turns to addiction. At this point, it matters little whether the alcohol addict or heroin addict or cocaine addict has a predetermined or acquired disease. The bodily needs for the chemicals have been established and the awesome power of addictive diseases to distort thinking, belief, emotion, personality and behavior has begun. Nothing short of massive interventions and thorough changes in the addict's typical ways of construing himself, his world and his actions will suffice. Addicted people will not recover from these diseases by "just saying no." Asking an addicted person to "just say no" to alcohol or drugs is like asking the severely depressed person to "just smile and be happy!"

Modern thinking about alcoholism and other addictive diseases no longer sees these conditions as merely "behavioral problems." Alcoholics are not morally depraved persons of weak character. Nor are they "sociopaths" or "sinners." Some alcoholics may indeed have problems with moral behavior, but one must be careful not to stigmatize the lot for the behavior of a few. Alcoholics are not "bad people" trying to be "good people." They are ill people trying to get well.

Addicted people, in general, are not "crazy" people. Nor are they "stupid." Often, they are quite gifted, sensitive and talented. Of our seven American Nobel prize winners in literature, five were clearly alcoholic! Alcoholics and chemically dependent people of all types come from every walk of life. They are surgeons, airline pilots, school teachers, professional athletes, musicians, writers, train engineers, social workers, psychologists, psychiatrists, housewives, poets, movie actors, priests, ministers, rabbis and so on and so forth. All seem to have one thing in common. They all suffer from these addictive diseases on which we are just beginning to get a handle. These diseases involve the whole person—body, mind, behavior, social surroundings and spirit—not just a part. Like people who suffer from other diseases, chemically dependent people deserve our understanding, respect, compassion and care.

Alcoholism and Enzymes:

More New Light on the Disease

Given several recent impressive demonstrations of a genetic predisposition to some but not all forms of alcoholism, researchers have begun the arduous task of trying to discover the factors that determine genetic susceptibility. As yet, nobody has identified an alcogene, i.e., a single gene that transmits alcoholism from one generation to the next. Rather, it appears that there are multiple genes linked to multiple risk factors.

Recently, researchers have centered their attention on two important enzymes. These enzymes are monoamine oxidase and adenylate cyclase. One recent study on these enzymes by Dr. Boris Tabakoff and his colleagues was reported in the *New England Journal of Medicine* on January 21, 1988 (Volume 318, Number 3, p. 134). An editorial by Dr. Theodore Reich commenting on the significance of this study also appeared in the same issue of the *New England Journal of Medicine*. Media coverage was considerable. Television, newspapers, and magazines immediately picked up on the possibility that alcoholism is caused by enzyme "abnormalities" in alcoholics not found in nonalcoholics. What precisely did Dr. Tabakoff report?

First of all, the study involved the membranes of certain blood cells. As readers may recall, blood consists of three types of cells: red, white, and platelets. The researchers decided to study platelets because they are readily accessible through blood samples and reflect the activity of many of the enzymes found in the human brain. In effect, one can make reasonable guesses as to what is going on with brain cell enzymatic activity by studying blood cells rather than invading the human brain itself.

The first enzyme studied was monoamine oxidase. This enzyme is an important brain enzyme since it is involved in the oxidation of the neurotransmitters dopamine, noradrenaline, and serotonin. The subjects were alcoholic men from a VA inpatient program with at least five days of abstinence. A smaller group of recovering alcoholics with 12 to 48 months of sobriety were also studied along with a nonalcoholic control group.

The results showed that while there were no initial differences between alcoholics and nonalcoholics in their platelet monoamine oxidase activity, significant differences appeared when these blood cells were treated with alcohol. Platelets from alcoholics showed decreased monoamine oxidase activity after alcohol treatment. These results are of interest since lowered monoamine oxidase activity has important implications for the turnover (synthesis and release) of the neurotransmitters dopamine, noradrenaline, and serotonin.

The second enzyme studied was adenylate cyclase. This enzyme is involved in the so-called second messenger system in which the extracellular message is changed to an intracellular message. In effect, one can think of the neurotransmitters as "first messengers" carrying information from one neuron across the synapse (gap between neurons) to the receptor on an adjacent neuron (extracellular message). Adenylate cyclase is involved in the formation of cyclic adenosine monophosphate or "second messenger" found *inside* the cell (intracellular message). Any change in the activity of adenylate cyclase is important since this change will disrupt events in the interior of the cell.

When the platelets of alcoholics and nonalcoholics were assayed for adenylate cyclase activity, significant differences emerged between alcoholics and nonalcoholics after stimulation of adenylate cyclase activity by cesium fluoride, guanylylimidodiphosphate or prostaglandin E1. Enzyme activity following such stimulation was lower in the platelets of alcoholics compared to controls.

These results show that the cells of alcoholics do differ from nonalcoholic controls in the activity of two important enzymes. In the case of monoamine oxidase, the lowered enzyme activity was apparent after treatment of the cells with alcohol. And for adenylate cyclase, differences appeared after stimulation with natural substances known to affect this enzyme's activity.

But what do these results mean? First of all, they are consistent with other studies showing lower levels of monoamine oxidase in alcoholics and also altered adenylate cyclase activity in alcoholics compared to controls. Since monoamine oxidase levels have been shown in other research to be under strong genetic control, it is possible that the inhibitory effect of alcohol on monoamine oxidase activity in alcoholics may also be under genetic control.

Alternatively, the results may show nothing more than the effects of heavy drinking on enzymatic activity in the platelets of alcoholics. As the researchers are quick to point out, it would be premature to conclude that these differences in enzyme activity are the *cause* of alcoholism. But it would be equally premature to conclude that the results reflect only the influence of heavy drinking on enzyme activity in the human brain. More research is obviously needed. An interesting approach here might be to study these enzymes in the children of alcoholics. Since these children have not yet started to drink, any deficiencies found could not be attributable to heavy drinking but may indicate a pre-existing etiological factor in alcoholism.

Dr. Tabakoff and his colleagues (as well as other researchers) have opened still another pathway in our attempts to unravel the biological origins of alcoholism. Their work deserves our highest praise, closest attention, and greatest support.

REFERENCES

Reich, Theodore. Biologic-marker studies in alcoholism. *The New England Journal of Medicine*, 318(3):180–182. Jan. 20, 1988.

Tabakoff, B., Hoffman, P.L., Lee, J.M., Saito, T., Willard, B., and De Leon-Jones F. Differences in platelet enzyme activity between alcoholics and nonalcoholics. *The New England Journal of Medicine*, 318(3):134–139. Jan. 20, 1988.

The Relevance to Clinical Care of Recent Research in Neurobiology

Within the last decade, considerable progress toward a comprehensive neurobiological conceptualization of alcoholism and other chemical dependencies has been made. Studies in animal behavior genetics and human adoption research have pointed to a genetic predisposing factor or set of factors in alcoholism. While the exact nature of these genetically transmitted biologic risk factors is still not known with certainty, investigators are reporting abnormalities in several neurotransmitter systems as well as important enzymes involved in the oxidation of neurotransmitters and in the formation of cyclic adenosine monophosphate (cAMP). While such enzymatic abnormalities may be the result of heavy drinking, it is possible that these are genetically transmitted. Other research in both alcohol and drugs has involved alcohol induced changes in cell membranes, condensation products formed by aldehyde-neurotransmitter reactions, and other neurochemical events.

In effect, the field of alcoholism and other chemical dependencies has come a long way since Dr. William Silkworth's (1955) early speculation about a biopsychological etiology of alcoholism in terms of allergy to alcohol (biological) and obsession with alcohol (psychological). Today's clinicians have a wealth of information to draw upon in their efforts to explain alcoholism and other chemical dependencies to patients and their families and to motivate patients toward recovery. But while there is much new information with possible clinical relevance, many issues remain. In this paper, these issues bearing upon clinical applications of recent neurobiological research will be considered.

COGNITIVE APPLICATIONS

At present, the most important applications of recent research in neurobiology are cognitive. Hypotheses concerning the role of neurotransmitters, condensation products, enzyme abnormalities, and genetics are useful in clinical settings in providing patients with alternative theoretical models for understanding their behavior. Most patients entering alcoholism/chemical dependence treatment are baffled by their compulsive and self-destructive drinking and drug-taking. Their own attempts at explanation, that is, rationalizations, alibi systems, and blame assignment tactics, are not satisfactory. At some level or another, many patients seem dimly aware that their problems with alcohol and/or drugs are not attributable to their spouses, lovers, parents, bosses, jobs, and so forth. As the alibis, rationalizations, blaming, and denial begin to fall away, the patients are left with *interpretive vacuums*. They may have no idea why they are behaving in such irrational and self-defeating ways vis-à-vis alcohol and drugs. Patients may also entertain notions that they have serious personality disorders or are going "crazy." Alternatively, they may perceive themselves as "sinners," bad people, and immoral. These self-perceptions usually give rise to intense feelings of guilt, remorse, shame, fear, anxiety, anger at self and others, hopelessness, and depression. And, of course, these negative emotional states and thoughts have been conditioned to the initiation of drinking in the past and hence will increase the probability of continued relapse unless altered.

A modern, sophisticated disease model of alcoholism gives patients a way to construe their drinking and drug-taking behavior that facilitates recovery. Teaching patients some of the findings from genetic and neurobiological research is an effective way to break through denial, reduce negative emotional states that are associated with continued relapse, and encourage a positive view of self and the likelihood of recovery. Moreover, consideration of modern neurobiological theory provides many patients with information useful in increasing motivation toward abstinence. For example, consideration of changes in brain chemistry with chronic use of cocaine, alcohol, and other drugs is useful in helping patients to accept the need for complete abstention and to reject controlled or nonproblem drug use as realistic, attainable recovery goals.

Uncertainty of the Neurobiological Scientific Information Base: Dealing with Complexity

Given the uncertain and, in fact, controversial nature of many of the findings in recent neurobiological research, clinicians face a real dilemma in choosing what to tell patients. Today's patients quite rightly want to know why their counselors urge them to accept the "disease model" of alcoholism. Some patients are themselves scientifically trained and are not satisfied by simple metaphors or analogies, for example, "It's like you have an allergy to alcohol," or "It's like diabetes."

Unfortunately, it is difficult to communicate neurobiological theory and data to patients since recent findings are complicated by many issues. These issues are:

1. Failure or lack of replication of particular results;
2. Biphasic nature of response to alcohol and drugs (impact of acute vs. chronic administration);
3. Response differences across animals (e.g., mice vs. rat vs. primates);
4. Response differences across different brain locations (e.g., one brain location may show increases in particular neurotransmitter or opioid peptide levels in response to alcohol while other locations may show decreases);
5. Difficulties in using peripheral measures to infer changes in brain chemistry (e.g., estimating noradrenaline levels in brain by measuring the neurotransmitter's metabolite, MOPEG, in urine, or trying to infer brain endorphin levels from cerebrospinal (CSF) endorphin measurements).
6. Dose dependent differences (e.g., curvilinear relationship of some tetrahydroisoquinolines (TIQs) to alcohol drinking in animals).
7. Dose-species interactions (e.g., low-dose alcohol increases locomotor activity in rats but not in mice).
8. Response differences due to differing experimental procedures or measurements.

In short, recent neurobiological research is most complex and generalizations are hazardous. It is difficult to communicate this body of information to patients in a simple, comprehensible manner. Moreover, patients and others may attribute much more certainty to particular findings than warranted by the data. On the other hand, sharing hypotheses, theoretical ideas, and even frank speculation with patients has value if only in alerting patients to alternative models for construing their problems with alcohol and drugs. Since counseling alcoholics and other chemically dependent people involves altering behavior through inducing changes in belief systems, alternative models drawn from recent neurobiological research that challenge old, maladaptive beliefs are of considerable value.

This conflict between treating neurobiological findings too simplistically or too complexly with patient populations requires continuing study and attempts at resolution in particular clinical settings. However, it can be partially resolved simply by reminding patients that much of this information is still tentative and in need of further study.

GENETIC PREDISPOSITION: WHAT DO WE TELL OUR PATIENTS?

Recent research clearly implicates genetics in many but certainly not all cases of alcoholism. Work by Goodwin et al. (1973), Cloninger (1983), Bohman et al. (1981) as well as others has demonstrated a three to four times increased risk for alcoholism in offspring of alcoholic parents. This increased risk is apparent when children of alcoholics are adopted out at an early age and raised in adoptive homes rather than by their alcoholic biological parents. For one subtype of alcoholism ("male-limited"), the risk rises to nine times increased risk (Cloninger, 1983).

In addition to human studies, many animal studies from numerous labs in the United States and elsewhere have shown that mice and rats showing different alcohol-related behaviors can be selectively bred. Selective breeding experiments have shown that all of the following traits can be influenced genetically: preference for alcohol over water, variations in withdrawal symptoms, and differences in tolerance to alcohol.

Considering both animal and human studies, then, it is certainly appropriate to instruct patients in the genetic basis of many cases of alcoholism. In general, the following statements can be made:

1. Findings from genetic studies constitute the strongest evidence we have for a biological etiology of alcoholism;
2. Alcoholism per se is *not* inherited. What is inherited are a number of biologic risk factors that predispose the person to alcoholism once sufficient exposure to the drug has taken place;
3. A single "alcogene" has not been demonstrated. Alcoholism appears to be polygenic, and even a behavior as simple as the righting reflex after an alcohol load seems to involve as many as ten genes.
4. Environment clearly plays a role as well, since not all cases of alcoholism show a positive family history.

GENETIC/NEUROCHEMICAL DIFFERENCES

As yet, the biological risk factors to alcoholism are not completely understood. A role for preexisting neurochemical differences has been suggested by animal studies. T.K. Li and his colleagues at the Indiana University School of Medicine have reported important pre-existing differences in regional serotonergic neurotransmission in alcohol-preferring rat strains derived from a foundation stock of Wistar rats (Li et al., 1987). These rats, when compared to alcohol non-preferring rats, consistently show lower levels of serotonin in the cerebral cortex, corpus striatum, thalamus, hypothalamus, and hippocampus. Lower levels of 5-HIAA (5-hydroxyindole acetic-acid) are found in cerebral cortex and hippocampus. Less consistently demonstrated deficiencies in noradrenaline in cerebral cortex and pons medulla and dopamine in cortex have also been found. Deficiencies in serotonin and its principle metabolite 5-HIAA have been noted in the so-called brain reward system structures of the nucleus accumbens and the frontal cortex, while lower levels of dopamine and its metabolite have been found in the nucleus accumbens.

While T.K. Li and his colleagues have concentrated on serotonergic neurotransmission, Blum and his associates have centered their efforts on the possible etiologic significance of differences in brain opioid peptide levels. In a 14-day preference test, Blum's laboratory found a correlation of −0.90 between mouse whole brain met-enkephalin levels in the alcohol preferring (C57BL/6J) mouse strain and the alcohol avoiding (DBA/2J) mouse strain (1987). This lab also reported a significant difference in met-enkephalin levels between a substrain of the C57BL strain and the major strain. The C57BL/6N mouse reverts to an alcohol-avoidant pattern, while the C57BL/6J continues to show alcohol preference. The C57BL/6N mouse strain shows a normal met-enkephalin level after it reverts to alcohol avoidance (Blum et al., 1981, 1983).

Other genetic/neurochemical links have been suggested for lowered monamine oxidase activity as well as lowered adenylate cyclase activity (Tabakoff et al., 1988).

NEUROTRANSMITTERS

It is difficult to summarize research on neurotransmitters, since findings in this area are complicated by biphasic effects of low versus high dose, acute versus chronic administration, and either nonreplicated or conflicting results. Bearing in mind these caveats, it is possible to discern what appear to be consistent trends.

In rats, chronic treatment with alcohol results in increased turnover of noradrenaline in whole brain (Hunt et al., 1974; Pohorecky, 1974). Amit and Brown (1981) argue for a central role of noradrenaline versus dopamine in the actions of alcohol and opiates on brain reward systems. Increases in noradrenaline with heavy drinking persist into withdrawal. Borg and his colleagues (1983a; 1983b) found increased levels of the norepinephrine metabolite MOPEG in CSF in intoxicated alcoholics and in alcoholics undergoing withdrawal. MOPEG in abstinent alcoholics declined over time. With long-term abstinence (3 to 6 months) an association between craving for alcohol and low levels of CFS MOPEG was found (Liljeberg, Mossberg, and Borg, 1987). These investigators speculate on the possible role of low levels of noradrenaline on relapse in alcoholics sober for 3 to 6 months and also on the etiologic significance of lower levels of noradrenaline in alcoholics.

Daoust and his colleagues (1987) in France report data supporting an interaction between noradrenergic pathways and GABAergic pathways. GABA, or gamma amino butyric acid, is the brain's most abundant inhibitory transmitter. The GABA system is potentiated by alcohol and benzodiazepines like Valium and Librium. When ethanol preferring rats were treated with metapramine, which enhances noradrenaline release, ethanol consumption decreased very significantly. Similar results were obtained with Ca AOTA a new GABAergic agent. On the other hand, bicuculline, a GABA receptor blocker, appeared to block the effects of metapramine and Ca AOTA. That is, blocking GABA receptors seemed also to block the effects of two drugs hypothesized to increase both adrenergic and GABAergic transmission and hence also blocked the decrease in alcohol consumption in alcohol preferring rats.

With regard to dopamine, perhaps the most striking results have been obtained in studies of cocaine dependence. Dackis and Gold (1985) have hypothesized that cocaine dependence is linked to alterations in dopaminergic neurotransmission. While the acute administration of cocaine results in dopamine reuptake blockade, dopamine excess at the synapse, and euphoria, chronic use is associated with compensatory increases in dopamine postsynaptic binding sites, reduced dopamine availability at the synapse, and dysphoria. Changes in dopaminergic transmission may occur rapidly, with one study reporting receptor supersensitivity after a single dose. Memo and his colleagues (1981) observed a 37% increase in the number of striatal dopamine receptor sites following a single administration of cocaine.

Given the large numbers of young alcoholics who abuse cocaine, it is reasonable to speculate about alcohol-cocaine interactions in terms of the effects of alcohol on dopaminergic activity. Many patients report that alcohol increases their desire to use cocaine and vice versa. As Hoffman and Tabakoff (1985) state, the general conclusion that can be drawn from studies of mice and rats is that low dose alcohol depresses dopaminergic neuronal activity while high doses stimulate such activity. It is possible that cocaine craving is related to changes in mood associated with dopaminergic changes related to alcohol consumption. Cocaine-dependent patients seeking to remain abstinent from cocaine should therefore be counseled to avoid alcohol. And alcoholics seeking to stay sober should avoid cocaine because of the dysphoria associated with dopamine depletion attendant upon chronic use.

Considerable attention has centered on the role of serotonin in the maintenance of alcoholic drinking and perhaps in the etiology of the disease. As mentioned previously, alcohol motivated rats appear to have deficiencies in serotonergic neurotransmission. Moreover, Zhukov, Varkov, and Burov (1987) have shown that destruction (administration of 5,6-DHT or electrocoagulation of the dorsal or medial raphe nuclei) of the brain serotonergic system increased alcohol drinking in rats who previously were not motivated toward alcohol consumption. Such destruction did not lead to increases in consumption in rats who were previously motivated to drink. Moreover, Burov et al. (1986) reported a *decrease* in serotonin content in the hypothalamus of alcohol-motivated rats after a single alcohol dose. This decrease was maintained under chronic alcohol administration. On the other hand, rats not motivated to consume alcohol showed an *increase* in serotonin level in hypothalamus after a single alcohol dose.

Several studies have shown that increasing the availability of serotonin in brain reduces consumption of alcohol in both animals and humans. Amit et al. (1984) and Naranjo et al. (1984) showed that administration of serotonin reuptake blockers, which increase serotonin levels at the synapse does result in reductions in drinking in alcoholics as well as animals. Both zimelidine and fluvoxamine have resulted in attenuation of drinking, but zimelidine has been withdrawn because of a rare but serious hypersensitivity reaction characterized by polyradiculopathy and hepatitis. Although both drugs are relatively specific serotonin reuptake blockers, fluvoxamine has a very different chemical stucture from zimelidine.

The mechanisms by which serotonin reuptake blockers influence alcohol consumption remain unclear. As Linnoila et al. (1987) point out, these drugs may have no specific effect on alcohol craving but may operate by producing increased taste aversion, a generalized anorectic effect that extends to all consummatory behavior, or by a change in ethanol's psychoactive properties.

Other evidence pointing to serotonergic involvement in alcoholism involves serotonin uptake studies in platelets. These studies on animals and humans generally show increased serotonin uptake in platelets (Boismare et al., 1987), although Ahtee et al. (1974) provided only partial agreement.

Moss (1987) in a review of serotonergic activity and disinhibitory psychopathy in alcoholism speculates about links between low levels of serotonin and some form of disinhibitory behavioral disturbance (e.g., impulsivity, low frustration tolerance, attention-span deficits, impersistence, hyperactivity, and stimulus-seeking behavior). Moss points to studies linking low CSF 5-HIAA and other measures of low serotonergic activity to aggression and borderline personality. Roy et al. (1987) speculate that there is a sizable subgroup of alcoholics with reduced central serotonin turnover and these may be helped by serotonin reuptake blockers.

Studies of serotonin, then, do reveal linkages between this transmitter and drinking behavior in animals and humans. However, the underlying mechanism for this association remains unclear and may involve a nonspecific general affect on consummatory behaviors in addition to ethanol consumption.

Studies of other neurotransmitters and neuromodulators suggest associations between alcohol and brain biochemistry. Investigators have explored relationships between opioid peptides and drinking. Genazzani and his colleagues (1982) reported that beta-endorphin levels in the CSF of 29 "chronic alcoholic addicts" were threefold lower than those of controls. Borg et al. (1982) also reported lower levels of beta-endorphin in human CSF during intoxication and withdrawal. Chronic administration of alcohol to rats is associated with a marked decrease in met-enkephalin (Schulz et al., 1980), and this decrease is thought to be due to activation of enkephalinase A (Bruosov et al., 1982). Numerous animal studies have reported decreases in endorphins, enkephalins, and other opioid peptides in particular brain locations after chronic alcohol administration (e.g., Blum et al., 1982; Schulz et al., 1980; Seizinger, 1984b; Seizinger et al., 1984a; Seizinger et al., 1983).

Also, these studies suggested a decreased rate of the processing of the precursor beta-lipotropin to beta-endorphin in the anterior pituitary. However, Gianoulakis et al. (1981) reported that chronic treatment of animals with alcohol was associated with an increase in the synthesis and release of beta-endorphin like peptides from the neurointermediate lobe of the pituitary. Naloxone, an opiate receptor antagonist, has been reported to reverse alcohol coma. Contradictory reports, however, are evident in this area, with other investigators reporting no effect of naloxone on alcohol-induced coma (e.g., Hemmingsen and Sorensen, 1980) or effects on only 10% of a sample of cases (Jeffreys et al., 1980). While the many behavioral and biochemical actions of endorphins and enkephalins as neuromodulators do suggest that they are important endogenous substances in considering the chronic effects of alcohol on brain chemistry, the conflicting findings and methodological problems in this area suggest that a degree of caution is most appropriate.

With regard to opioids, Gold and Rea (1983) have reviewed a considerable body of evidence linking endorphins to the mechanisms of opiate addiction.

CONDENSATION PRODUCTS

With the publication of Davis' and Walsh's (1970) intriguing speculative paper on alcohol-amine condensation products, this topic has received much attention as well as criticism. Numerous studies by Myers and his colleagues (e.g., Myers, McCaleb, and Ruwe, 1982; Myers and Melchior, 1977; Myers, 1985) have demonstrated convincingly that aldehyde-neurotransmitter condensation products infused into rat and monkey ventricles result in large increases in voluntary ethanol intake. Three products have been studied: (a) salsolinol (a dopamine-aldehyde product); (b) tetrahydropapaveroline or THP (a dopaldehyde-dopamine product); and (c) tetrahydro-beta-carboline or THBC (a serotonin-aldehyde product). One of these products, THP, is a precursor to an opiate alkaloid found in the opium poppy.

As pointed out by Myers (1985), two important questions concerning these condensation products have arisen. These are as follows: (1) Are TIQs and THBCs actually formed endogenously in brain tissue as a result of excessive drinking?; and (2) Do amine-aldehyde products produce a "pathological action" on the nervous system leading to an addictive liability on alcohol?

With regard to in vivo formation of TIQs, abundant evidence for the formation of endogenous salsolinol has been reported. Sjoquist et al. (1982a) reported elevations of salsolinol in the corpus striatum and other limbic forebrain areas of the rat after chronic treatment with alcohol. The same laboratory (Sjoquist et al., 1982b) reported high levels of salsolinol in dopamine-rich areas of the brain of the alcoholic person postmortem in comparison to a nonalcoholic person. Also, Borg et al. (1981) and Sjoquist et al. (1981) reported increased levels of salsolinol in the CSF of alcoholic patients during intoxication and withdrawal. Matsubara et al. (1987) found significant increases in salsolinol in rat hypothalamus and striatum after chronic ethanol drinking.

While considerable evidence for in vivo formation of salsolinol has been available, the evidence for THBC has been mixed. Airaksinen et al. (1981a, 1981b) did demonstrate the formation of particular beta-carbolines in rat brain after alcohol challenge. On the other hand, Matsubara and his colleagues (1986) could *not* demonstrate the formation of any of the types of Beta-carbolines in human urine or rat brain that are normally formed by a direct condensation between serotonin and acetaldehyde. Evidence was found for a type of beta-carboline that is not formed by serotonin-aldehyde condensation by Rommelspacher et al. (1980). It is possible that a serotonin-aldehyde condensation product could be formed and then quickly converted to the type of beta-carboline that was detected by Rommelspacher et al.

Evidence for in vivo formation of THP, has been absent. This represented a serious and possibly fatal blow to TIQ theory, since without evidence for in vivo formation of THP, the theory was not defensible. Because of the similarity of THP to a precursor to an alkaloid found in the opium poppy, this condensation product is of greatest interest. The theoretical link between the opioid system of the brain, condensation products, and alcohol drinking depended upon in vivo formation of THP.

Recent evidence reported by Cashaw, Geraghty, McLaughlin, and Davis (1987) convincingly demonstrates in vivo formation of THP in rats treated with L-dopa. Using a newly developed multiple-stage separation technique that is highly specific for THP (high performance liquid chromatography with electrochemical detection), these investigators demonstrated a maximum increase in THP of 1048% after alcohol administration along with L-dopa treatment.

Two different underlying theoretical mechanisms have been postulated to mediate TIQ- and beta-carboline-induced drinking. In the case of TIQs, these products could "sequester in brain tissue and occupy opiate receptor sites or other receptor protein, which in turn would mediate alcohol drinking in an addictive-like manner" (Myers, 1985, pp. 205–206).

As for beta-carbolines, these are thought to arouse anxiety through the antagonism of elements of the benzodiazepine receptor complex. Hence, beta-carboline-induced drinking would, in effect, constitute a biological theory of cycles of anxiety arousal and reduction attendant upon alcohol intake. Ethanol consumption might lead to initial anxiety reduction followed by increases in anxiety as tetrahydro-beta-carbolines are formed by serotonin-aldehyde condensations.

Criticisms of this body of theory by Deitrich (1987) involve the following: (a) Salsolinol has been shown to bind only weakly to opiate receptor sites in brain; (b) levels of salsolinol found in brain are not high enough to bring about significant occupation of opiate receptors; (c) most investigators have failed to demonstrate in vivo formation of THP in brain; (d) the type of beta-carboline formed by a condensation between serotonin and an aldehyde is not the type of beta-carboline that interacts strongly with the benzodiazepine receptor site; and (e) the work of Myers et al. has not been replicated.

Some of Deitrich's criticisms are to the point, while others can be argued. It does appear that salsolinol binds weakly to opiate receptor sites. However, the bulk of the theoretical argument concerning TIQs and opiate receptor interaction seems to rest more with THP rather than salsolinol. The very recent findings of Cashaw et al. (1987) on the in vivo formation of THP in large quantities after alcohol loads indicates that an important interaction between an amine-aldehyde condensation product and brain opiate receptors is entirely possible. On the other hand, the theoretical mechanism hypothesized to mediate anxiety arousal by an interaction between tetrahydro-beta-carbolines and benzodiazepine receptor sites is not supported by presently available data.

With regard to the issue of failure of replication of basic experiments on TIQs, the results actually point to considerable success with replication. Of 16 experiments involving THP, salsolinol, and THBC, 15 provided either strong replication or partial replication of the original findings of Myers and Melchoir (1977) on increases in ethanol drinking following infusions of condensation products. Only the *attempt* at replication by Brown et al. (1980) failed to demonstrate an increase in alcohol intake after salsolinol infusion over that obtained with controls infused with Ringer's solution. However, important differences involving dose of compound infused, strain of animal tested, and control over basal gm/kg/day intake of alcohol may explain the results obtained by Brown et al. In short, numerous replications of the basic findings of TIQ research are evident in consideration of the larger body of work. Some of these replications have involved investigators other than Myers and his colleagues. Smith and Amit (1987) have also provided extensive criticisms of both the data upon which TIQ theory is based and the mechanisms that are proposed for TIQ-mediated drinking.

In summary, TIQ or "multiple metabolite" theory is a controversial but still intriguing body of work with possible bearing upon the etiology of alcoholism. It does, of course, require continuing revision in light of new evidence. Moreover, it cannot be taught as fact to patients with regard to the origins of their alcoholism. However, careful and appropriately cautious teaching of the theory along with other models that have been proposed can be most effective in providing patients with alternative cognitive schema for viewing the disease.

MEMBRANE HYPOTHESIS

A large body of research on cell membranes can be used to provide patients with interesting models of intoxication, tolerance, and dependence. Goldstein's (1983) work on the membrane disordering effect of various alcohols in relationship to their lipid solubility suggests that ethanol may produce intoxication by fluidizing membranes. It is of interest to note that alcohol-sensitive long-sleep mice have membranes that are more easily disordered by alcohol than are the membranes of the alcohol-resistant short-sleep strain. In general, there is widespread acceptance of the membrane model of intoxication. Tolerance in this model refers to an adaptation of the membrane to alcohol's disordering, fluidizing effect. How the membrane does this is not known with certainty—perhaps by an increased proportion of cholesterol in the lipid bilayer. However, in some experiments, no change in membrane cholesterol was found despite the fact that the animals studied were clearly alcohol tolerant and physically dependent. In the membrane model, physical dependence refers to the stiffening of the membrane to such an extent that it becomes hyperexcitable.

As attractive as the lipid disordering hypothesis is and as extensive the data in support are, there are serious questions about the model's adequacy in explaining intoxication, tolerance, and dependence. As Hunt (1985) has indicated, one of the "nagging problems" with the hypothesis is that other events can disorder membranes to the same degree without producing intoxication. For example, raising body temperature by only 1°C or less can mimic changes in the lipid bilayer that are produced by clinical levels of general anesthetics and an almost lethal dose of ethanol. But these temperature induced changes in the lipid bilayer do not produce intoxication. Moreover, Franks and Lieb (1987) have raised interesting questions about the alcohol lipid hypothesis from the perspective of research into general anesthetics. Halothane at anesthetic levels considerably in excess of those used surgically does not perturb the lipid bilayer measurably. Also, a point is reached as one ascends a homologous series of anesthetic agents at which anesthetic potency disappears. This "cut-off" effect remains a puzzle for the lipid hypothesis. Even though these higher order agents continue to partition into lipid bilayers, their anesthetic potency is nil.

In effect, Franks and Lieb and others are considering the possibility of a direct effect of ethanol on membrane-bound proteins. Rather than a lipid-disordering indirect effect on proteins, it is possible that phenomena such as intoxication, tolerance, and dependence are a result of direct effects of ethanol on proteins. Franks and Lieb discuss preliminary data on the luciferase enzyme system of the firefly that suggest a direct effect of even very low levels of ethanol on protein sites. The possibility that the primary site of action of ethanol is not on the lipid bilayer but on proteins is consistent with recent studies of enzymatic activity in animals and humans. In nonalcoholic, healthy volunteers, ethanol was shown to increase platelet adenylate cyclase activity (Saito et al., 1987a). However, in animals fed ethanol, diminished responsiveness of adenylate cyclase to various forms of stimulation was demonstrated (Saito et al., 1987b). In alcoholics, platelet adenylate cyclase activity in response to cesium fluoride and guanine nucleotide stimulation was lowered (Tabakoff et al., 1988). Moreover, monoamine oxidase activity in human platelets from alcoholic patients was significantly lower after treatment with alcohol in comparison to nonalcoholic controls.

Of great significance in the recent report of Tabakoff et al. (1988) on adenylate cyclase activity was the finding that activity of this enzyme was still depressed in alcoholics sober for 12 to 48 months. These findings suggest changes in membranes of alcoholics that can persist for very long periods of time with important implications for the functioning of the cell. Since adenylate cyclase is involved in the formation of cyclic adenosine monophosphate (cAMP), any change in the activity of adenylate cyclase is important since this change will disrupt further events in the interior of the cell.

In responding to patients' questions about how soon they will "return to normal" after stopping drinking, these studies on adenylate cyclase activity in alcoholics sober for many months, even years, can be helpful. Moreover, this information communicates to patients the serious impact of ethanol on neurobiological functioning and the wisdom of choosing abstinence as a personal recovery goal.

PHARMACOLOGICAL APPLICATIONS

As mentioned previously, the most important applications are cognitive, that is, useful in presenting patients with alternative models for explaining their behavior and in increasing their motivations to sobriety. At the present time, few pharmacological applications have appeared. However, there are notable exceptions and these will be discussed.

CLONIDINE

Gold et al. (1982), working from a norepinephrine hyperactivity hypothesis for opiate withdrawal, reported successful detoxification of opiate addicts through use of the alpha 2-adrenoceptor agonist, clonidine. Clonidine presumably works to lower noradrenergic activity in opiate withdrawal by reducing locus coeruleus hyperactivity. Other reports (e.g., Pickworth et al., 1982) showed that clonidine has many pharmacological characteristics of morphine. Tolerance to its analgesic action can develop (Paalzow, 1978), and withdrawal reactions with chronic administration have been noted in animals (Thoolen et al., 1981).

Since alcohol withdrawal has also been associated with increased norepinephrine turnover in brain (Borg et al. 1981), interest in the possible usefulness of clonidine in alcohol withdrawal has developed. Wilkins et al. (1983) reported that oral clonidine hydrochloride in a dose of 5 mg/kg suppressed some alcohol withdrawal symptoms and signs. Clonidine in this study significantly suppressed heart rate, arterial blood pressure, and an accumulated score of withdrawal symptoms and signs.

Baumgartner and Rowen (1987) have reported results comparing clonidine to chlordiazepoxide in the management of alcohol withdrawal in a double-blind trial involving 16 men. Clonidine (0.2 mg) was reported to be more effective than chlordiazepoxide (50 mg) at reducing alcohol withdrawal scale scores, systolic blood pressures, and heart rates over the entire study period. The authors point out that clonidine was as effective as chlordiazepoxide in relieving subjective complaints of withdrawal. It should be noted, however, that subjects with known seizure disorders were excluded from the research and also that the study involved acute, mild to moderate withdrawal states. Management of severe withdrawal or detoxifying alcoholics with known seizure disorders does, however, raise serious questions as to the appropriateness of clonidine alone. Stock (1988), in a discussion of Baumgartner and Rowen's study, raised questions about the prevention of seizures and delirium tremens through the use of clonidine alone in alcohol detoxification.

PHARMACOLOGICAL TREATMENTS FOR COCAINE WITHDRAWAL

The dopamine depletion hypothesis of cocaine dependence discussed earlier has led to interest in drugs that interact with dopaminergic pathways. Bromocriptine (Parlodel), amantadine (Symmetrel), methylphenidate (Ritalin), and carbidopa (Sinenet) have received attention.

Dackis and Gold (1985) have reported on the use of daily doses of bromocriptine (a dopamine agonist) in the range of 0.625 to 1.25 mg t.i.d. orally to reduce craving for cocaine. However, Gawin (1988) has pointed out that this study had no placebo control, nor were prebromocriptine levels of craving quantified. Potential disadvantages of bromocriptine use involve possible side effects, including nausea and headache. Perhaps the most serious problem in this area is the noticeable paucity of controlled research. Giannini and Billett (1987) did report decreases is Brief Psychiatric Rating Scale scores in a double-blind placebo controlled study, but did not report effects of bromocriptine on cocaine craving, use, and abuse. Tennant et al. (1987) compared bromocriptine to amantadine in a double-blind study with very small numbers of subjects ($N = 7$). More than 70% of the bromocriptine subjects dropped out. In short, the research evidence upon which bromocriptine treatment is based is clearly inadequate.

Turning to amantadine, the situation is not much improved. Amantadine increases dopaminergic neurotransmission and has been shown to be effective in Parkinson's disease. The mechanism through which amantadine increases dopaminergic neurotransmission is unclear and may involve reuptake decrease, dopamine release, or acute receptor effects. It is thought to be preferable to bromocriptine because of fewer side effects, and neither does it appear to have abuse potential.

Tennant (unpublished data) gave amantadine to more than 50 subjects and reported immediate reductions in cocaine craving. However, as Gawin (1988) has pointed out, comparison groups were not used, and there were no pre and post measures of levels of craving. Two studies (Handelman et al., in press; Morgan et al., in press) used amantadine with cocaine users in a methadone maintenance program. While amantadine did decrease craving, the decrease was not immediate but occurred after a lag of two weeks. Moreover, almost all subjects had dropped out of the research by the fourth week. Once again, comparison groups were not used.

As mentioned previously, Tennant et al. studied small numbers of patients treated with either amantadine or bromocriptine. While results favored amantadine, the study is difficult to interpret because of the high drop-out rate with bromocriptine. Amantadine needs to be evaluated in a random assignment, double-blind placebo controlled trial.

Methylphenidate (Ritalin) is a stimulant and as such will show tolerance and abuse potential. Khatzian (1983) did report improvement in an extreme case of cocaine dependence with methylphenidate. However, Gawin et al. (1985), while reporting a rapid transient decrease in craving and use, also reported an increase in tolerance, renewed craving, and subjective reports of mild stimulation that evoked a stronger desire for cocaine. Increases in cocaine use were noted by the second week of the study.

A single study of carbidopa (Rosen et al., 1986) with a small number of patients and no comparison groups did not show decreased craving until week 2.

With regard to tricyclic antidepressants and cocaine dependence, Gawin (1988) has reviewed the evidence from published reports. Three double-blind studies (Gawin et al., 1986; Giannini et al., 1986; O'Brien et al., 1988) have reported that desipramine improves outcome. While one study with low-dose desipramine noted no differences in comparison with a control group (Tennant & Tarver, 1984), Gawin cautioned that two of these positive studies are still in process and that caution is in order in clinical application of these findings.

In summary, considerably more research is needed to establish the safety and/or efficacy of all the drugs that are thought to interact with the dopamine system. Desipramine appears promising, but further research is needed on tricyclics as well.

ENKEPHALINASE INHIBITORS

Based on the work of Blum and his colleagues (1987) and others on endogenous opioids, efforts have been made to find ways to reduce alcohol craving by increasing brain levels of enkephalins. Since endogenous opiates are rapidly destroyed by enzymes that cleave amino acids such as the enkephalins, a strategy for raising brain enkephalin levels involves administration of enkephalinase inhibitors. Since D-phenylalanine has been reported by Ehrenpreis (1982) to inhibit enkephalinase and to cross blood-brain barrier readily, attention has centered on this amino acid as a possible way to alter brain enkephalin levels in alcoholics. Blum et al. (1987) have reported a statistically significant drop in alcohol consumption in alcohol-preferring mice following administration of D-phenylalanine. Also, anecdotal studies with select groups of volunteers (Blum & Topel, 1986) suggest promise for this approach. A compound called SAAVE has been developed and consists of the following: D-phenylalanine (enkephalinase inhibitor), L-phenylalanine (precursor to dopamine and norepinephrine), L-glutamine (contributes to the maintenance of GABA), L-tryptophan (precursor to serotonin), and Vitamin B6 (for facilitation of absorption of amino acids).

Research is currently under way to test the efficacy of SAAVE at several treatment centers throughout the United States. In one double-blind, placebo controlled study (Blum et al., in press), SAAVE-treated alcoholics and drug abusers had a significantly lower AMA drop-out rate from treatment, reduced stress responses, and improved social-emotional functioning while in treatment. Obviously, considerably more research employing random assignment, double blinds, and placebo controls is necessary before this product can be used routinely with alcoholics.

ANXIOLYTIC AGENTS AND ANTIDEPRESSANTS

Other than a role in detoxification, anxiolytic agents such as the benzodiazepines have shown little value in the longer-term management of alcoholism and other drug dependencies. Benzodiazepines and barbiturates potentiate GABA by binding to sites within the GABA, benzodiazepine, barbiturate complex and indirectly regulating conductance in sedating chloride ion channels. It now appears that ethanol may also stimulate chloride uptake through the GABA-receptor coupled chloride ion channel (Suzdak & Paul, 1987). Work on the novel compound Ro-15-4513 suggests that alcohol interacts with the GABA receptor and that Ro-15-4513 is a potent antagonist (inverse agonist) of the action of ethanol at this receptor site. Studies of Ro-15-4513 indicate that this compound can attenuate and reverse ethanol intoxication. At present, there are no clinical applications of Ro-15-4513 since it is a convulsant. It is possible, however, that further understanding of the benzodiazepine-GABA-barbiturate-ethanol complex may lead to novel compounds without dangerous side effects.

Recently, buspirone, an anxiolytic without benzodiazepine properties, has been reported to reduce alcohol consumption by monkeys (Collins & Myers, 1987). Advantages of buspirone over benzodiazepine anxiolytic agents have been reviewed by Meyer (1986). While buspirone is considered to be a nonbenzodiazepine with low abuse potential, the history of the use of other anxiolytic agents in alcoholism should discourage premature and incautious clinical application of new tranquilizers with alcoholic patients.

Possible uses of antidepressants to attenuate alcohol drinking by alcoholics has been reviewed by Sinclair (1987). Since, as has already been discussed, both noradrenergic and serotonergic systems have been reported to be involved in alcoholism, drugs that interact with these systems have been suggested. Murphy et al. (1985) reported that the serotonin reuptake blockers fluoxetine and fluvoxamine suppressed alcohol drinking in rats. Similar results were obtained with the norepinephrine reuptake inhibitor, desipramine, but Rockman et al. (1982) found effects on drinking for serotonin reuptake blockers but not norepinephrine reuptake inhibitors.

Because of potential serious side effects with antidepressants and the paucity of data, possible applications of these medications to alcoholism per se must await further research. Antidepressants may, of course, continue to be used to treat co-existing affective disorders in alcoholic patients, as may lithium for the treatment of co-existing manic-depressive illness.

Summary

Neurobiological study of alcohol and other drug dependencies has advanced considerably in recent years. At present, application of this material is largely cognitive in the sense that its usefulness lies in providing patients with alternative conceptual models for viewing their disease, increasing motivation for change, and deciding to remain abstinent from alcohol and other psychoactive chemicals.

Some new pharmacologic interventions appear to be promising for early treatment of withdrawal states, but none have been demonstrated to be appropriate for long-term maintenance of abstinence.

References

Ahtee, L., Pentikainen, L., Pentikainen, J.W., & Paasonen, M.K. (1974). 5-Hydroxytryptamine in the blood platelets of cirrhotic and hypertensive patients. *Experientia, 30, 1328–1329.*

Airaksinen, M.M., & Kari, I. (1981a). β-carbolines, psychoactive compounds in the mammalian body. *Medical Biology,* 59, 190–211.

Airaksinen, M.M., Peura, P., & Tuomisto, L. (1981b). Tetrahydro-β-carboline and 1-methyl-tetrahydro-β-carboline in the rat: Concentrations in plasma and brain after alcoholism and effect on alcohol preference. Bar Conference, Stockholm.

Amit, Z., & Brown, Z.W. (1982). Actions of drugs of abuse on brain reward systems: A reconsideration with specific attention to alcohol. *Pharmacology Biochemistry & Behavior,* 17, 233–238.

Amit, Z., et al. (1984). A review of its effects on ethanol consumption. *Neuroscience Biobehavioral Review,* 8, 35–54.

Baumgartner, G.R., & Rowen, R.C. (1987, July). Clonidine vs. chlordiazepoxide in the management of acute alcohol withdrawal syndrome. *Archives Internal Medicine,* 147, 1223–1226.

Blum, K., Briggs, A.H., Elston, S.F., DeLallo, L., Sheridan, P., & Star, M. (1982). Reduced leucine-enkephalin-like immunoreactive substance in hamster basal ganglion after long-term exposure. *Science,* 215, 1425–1427.

Blum, K., Elliott, C.E., Sexton, R.L., Trachtenberg, M.C., Dingler, M.L., Samuels, A.I., & Cataldie, L. (in press). Enkephalinase inhibition and precursor amino acid loading improves inpatient treatment of alcohol and polydrug abusers: Double-blind placebo controlled study of the nutritional adjunct SAAVE. *Alcohol: An International Biomedical Journal.*

Blum, K., Elston, S.F.A., DeLallo, L., Briggs, A.H., & Wallace, J.E. (1983). Ethanol acceptance as a function of genotype amounts of brain [met]-enkephalin. *Proceedings National Academy of Science, USA,* 80, 6510–6512.

Blum, K., & Topel, H. (1986). Opioid peptides and alcoholism: Genetic deficiency and chemical management. *Functional Neurology,* 1, 71–83.

Blum,K., Briggs, A.H., Trachtenberg, M.C., DeLallo, L., & Wallace, J.E. (1987). Enkephalinase inhibition: Regulation of ethanol intake in genetically predisposed mice. *Alcohol,* 4, 449–456.

Bohman, M., Sigvardsson, J., & Cloninger, C.R. (1973). Maternal inheritance of alcohol abuse: Cross-fostering analysis of adopted women. *Archives of General Psychiatry,* 28, 238–243.

Boismare, F., Lhuintre, J.P., Daoust, M., Moore, N., & Saligaut, C. (1987). Platelet affinity for serotonin is increased in alcoholics and former alcoholics: A biological marker for dependence? *Alcohol & Alcoholism,* 22, 155–159.

Borg, S., Czarnecka, A., Kvande, H., Mossberg, D., & Sedvall, G. (1983a). Clinical conditions and concentrations of MOPEG in cerebrospinal fluid and urine of alcoholic patients during withdrawal. *Science,* 213, 1135–1137.

Borg, S., Kvande, H., Mossberg, D., Valverius, P., & Sedvall, G. (1983b). Central nervous system noradrenaline metabolism and alcohol consumption in man. *Pharmacology Biochemistry & Behavior,* 8, (Suppl. 1), 375–378.

Borg, S., Kvande, H., Rydberg, U., Terenins, L., & Wahlstrom, A. (1982). Endorphin levels in human cerebrospinal fluid during alcohol intoxication and withdrawal. *Psychopharmacology,* 78, 101–103.

Borg, S., Kvande, H., & Sedvall, G. (1981). Central norepinephrine metabolism during alcohol intoxication in addicts and healthy volunteers. *Science,* 213, 1136–1137.

Brown, Z.W., Amit, Z., & Smith, B. (1980). Examination of the role of tetrahydroisoquinoline alkaloids in the mediation of ethanol consumption in rats. *Advances in Experimental Medicine and Biology,* 126, 103–120.

Brusov, O.S., Belygev, N.A., & Panchenko, L.F. (1983). Effect of acute and chronic alcohol intoxication on enkephalinase A activity in rat brain. Translated from *Byulletin' E'ksperimental 'noi Biologii i meditsiny,* 95, 205–209.

Burov, Yu.V., Zhukov, V.N., & Khodorova, N.A. (1986). Serotonin content in different brain areas and in the periphery: Effect of ethanol in rats predisposed and nonpredisposed to alcohol intake. *Biogenic Amines,* 4, 205–209.

Cashaw, J.L., Geraghty, C.A., McLaughlin, B.R., & Davis, V.E. (1987). Effects of acute ethanol administration on brain levels of tetrahydropapaveroline in L-dopa-treated rats. *Journal of Neuroscience Research,* 18, 497–503.

Cloninger, C.R. (1983). Genetic and environmental factors in the development of alcoholism. *Journal of Psychiatric Treatment & Evaluation,* 5, 487–496.

Collins, D.M., & Myers, R.D. (1987). Buspirone attenuates volitional alcohol intake in chronically drinking monkeys. *Alcohol,* 4, 49–56.

Dackis, C.A., & Gold, M.S. (1985). Bromocriptine as a treatment of cocaine abuse. *Lancet*, 1, 1151–1152.

Daoust, M., Lhuintre, J.P., Saligaut, C., Moore, N., Flipo, J.L., & Boismare, F. (1987). Noradrenaline and Gaba brain receptors are co-involved in the voluntary intake of ethanol by rats. *Alcohol & Alcoholism* (Suppl. 1), 319–322.

Davis, V.E., & Walsh, M.D. (1970). Alcohol, amines and alkaloids: A possible basis for alcohol addiction. *Science*, 167, 1005–1007.

Deitrich, R.A. (1987). Specificity of the action of ethanol in the central nervous system: Behavioral effects. *Alcohol & Alcoholism* (Suppl. 1), 133–138.

Ehrenpreis, S. (1982). D-phenylalanine and other enkephalinase inhibitors as pharmacological agents: Implications for some important therapeutic application. *Subst. Alcohol Actions Misuse*, 3, 231–239.

Franks, N.P., & Lieb, W.R. (1987). Are the biological effects of ethanol due to primary interactions with lipids or with proteins. *Alcohol & Alcoholism*, (Suppl. 1), 139–145.

Gawin, F.H., Riordan, C., & Kleber, H.D. (1985). Methylphenidate use in non-ADD cocaine abusers: A negative study. *American Journal of Drug & Alcohol Abuse*, 11, 193–197.

Gawin, F.H., Byck, R., & Kleber, H.D. (1986). Desipramine augmentation of cocaine abstinence: Initial results. Presented at the 15th Collegium Internationale Neuropharmacologicum. San Juan, Puerto Rico, December 15, 1986. (Proceedings in *Clinical Neuropharmacological*, 9 (Suppl. 4), 202–204.

Gawin, F.H. (1988). Chronic neuropharmacology of cocaine: Progress in pharmacotherapy. *Journal of Clinical Psychiatry*, 49 (Suppl. 2), 11–16.

Genazzani, A.R., Nappi, G., Facchinetti, F., Mazzella, G.L., Parrini, D., Sinforiani, E., Petraglia, F., & Savoldi, F. (1982). Central deficiency of β-endorphin in alcohol addicts. *Journal of Clinical Endocrinology & Metabolism*, 55, 583–586.

Giannini, A.J., & Billett, W. (1987). Bromocriptine-desipramine protocol in treatment of cocaine addiction. *Journal of Clinical Pharmacology*, 27, 549–554.

Giannini, A.J., Malone, D.A., Giannini, M.C., Price, W.A., & Loiselle, R. (1986). Treatment of depression in chronic cocaine and phencyclidine abuse with desipramine. *Journal of Clinical Pharmacology*, 26, 211–224.

Gianoulakis, C., Wood, N., Drovin, J.N., et al. (1981). Biosynthesis of beta-endorphin by the neurointermediate lobe from rats treated with morphine on alcohol. *Life Sciences*, 29, 1973–1982.

Gold, M.S., Pottash, A.L.C., & Extein, I.R.L. (1982). Clonidine: Inpatient studies from 1978–1981. *Journal of Clinical Psychiatry*, 43, 35–38.

Gold, M.S., & Rea, W.S. (1983). The role of endorphins in opiate addiction, opiate withdrawal and recovery. *Psychiatric Clinics of North America*, 6, 489–520.

Goldstein, D.B. (1983). *Pharmacology of Alcohol*. Oxford University Press.

Goodwin, D.W., Schulsinger, F., Hermansen, L., Guze, S.B., & Winokur, G. (1973). Alcohol problems in adoptees raised apart from alcoholic biological parents. *Archives of General Psychiatry*, 38, 238–243.

Handelsman, L., Bickel, W., Quesada, T., Chordia, P., Marion, I., Escovar, I., & Lowinson, J. (1987). Amantadine treatment of cocaine abuse. In: The Committee on Problems of Drug Dependence, Inc., *Proceedings of the 49th Annual Scientific Meeting*, p. 316. NIDA Research Monograph Series 81. (DHHS Publication No. (ADM) 88-1564). Rockville, MD: National Institute on Drug Abuse.

Hemmingsen, R., & Sorensen, S.C. (1980). Absence of an effect of naloxone on ethanol intoxication and withdrawal reaction. *Acta Pharmacology & Toxicology*, 46, 62–65.

Hoffman, P.L., & Tabakoff, B. (1985). Ethanol's action on brain chemistry. In R.E.

Tarter & D.H. VanThiel (Eds.), *Alcohol and the Brain: Chronic Effects.* pp. 19–68. New York: Plenum Publishing Company.

Hunt, W.A. (1985). *Alcohol & biological membranes.* New York: The Guilford Press.

Hunt, W.A., & Majchrowicz, E. (1974). Alterations in neurotransmitter function after acute and dopamine in alcohol-dependent rats. *Journal of Neurochemistry,* 23, 549–552.

Jeffreys, D.B., Flanagan, R.F., & Volans, G.N. (1980). Reversal of ethanol-induced coma by naloxone. *Lancet,* 1, 308–309.

Khatzian, E.J. (1983). Cocaine dependence: An extreme case and marked improvement with methylphenidate treatment. *American Journal of Psychiatry,* 140, 784–785.

Li, T.K., Lumeng, L., McBride, W.J., & Murphy, J.M. Rodent lines selected for factors affecting alcohol consumption. *Alcohol & Alcoholism,* (Suppl. 1), 91–96.

Liljeberg, P., Mossberg, D., & Borg, S. (1987). Clinical conditions and central noradrenergic activity in long-term abstinent alcoholic patients. *Alcohol & Alcoholism,* (Suppl. 1), 615–618.

Linnoila, M., Eckhardt, M., Durcan, M., Lister, R., & Martin, P. (1987). Interactions of serotonin with ethanol: Clinical and animal studies. *Psychopharmacology Bulletin,* 23, 452–457.

Matsubara, K., Fukushima, S., Akane, A., Hama, K., & Fukui, Y. (1986). Tetrahydro-β-Carbolines in human urine and rat brain—No evidence of formation by alcohol drinking. *Alcohol & Alcoholism,* 21, 339–345.

Matsubara, K., Fukushima, S., & Fukui, Y. (1987). A systematic regional study of brain salsolinol levels during and immediately following chronic ethanol ingestion in rats. *Brain Research,* 413, 336, 343.

Memo, M., Spano, P., & Trabucchi, M. (1981). Brain benzodiazepine receptor changes during aging. *Journal of Pharmacy and Pharmacology,* 33, 64.

Meyer, R.E. (1986). Anxiolytics and the alcoholic patient. *Journal of Studies on Alcohol,* 47, 269–273.

Morgan, C.J., Kosten, T.R., Gawin, F.H., & Kleber, H. (1987). A pilot trial of amantadine for ambulatory withdrawal for cocaine dependence. In: The Committee on Problems of Drug Dependence, Inc., *Proceedings of the 49th Annual Scientific Meeting,* (pp. 81–85). NIDA Research Monograph Series 81 (DHHS Publication No. (ADM) 88-1564). Rockville, MD: National Institute on Drug Abuse.

Moss, H.B. (1987). Serotonergic activity and disinhibitory psychopathy in alcoholism. *Medical Hypotheses,* 23, 353–361.

Murphy, J.M., Waller, M.B., Gatto, G.J., McBride, W.J., Lumeng, L., & Li, T.K. (1985). Monoamine uptake inhibitors attenuate ethanol intake in alcohol preferring (P) rats. *Alcohol,* 2, 349–352.

Myers, R.D., & Melchior, C.L. (1977). Alcohol drinking: Abnormal intake caused by tetrahydropapaveroline in brain. *Science,* 196, 554–556.

Myers, R.D., McCaleb, M.L., & Ruwe, W.D. (1982). Alcohol drinking induced in the monkey by tetrahydropapaveroline (THP) infused into the cerebral ventricle. *Pharmacology, Biochemistry and Behavior,* 16, 119–1000.

Myers, R.D. (1985). Multiple metabolite theory, alcohol drinking and the alcogene. *Aldehyde Adducts in Alcoholism,* pp. 201–220. New York: Allen R. Liss, Inc.

Naranjo, C.A., Sellers, C.M., Roach, C.A., Woodley, D.V., Sanchez-Craig, M., & Sykora, K. (1984). Zimelidine-induced variations in alcohol intake by nondepressed heavy drinkers. *Clinical Pharmacological Therapy,* 35, 374–381.

O'Brien, C.P., Childress, A.R., Arndt, I.O., McLellan, A.T., Woody, G.E., & Maany, I.

(1988). Pharmacological and behavioral treatments of cocaine dependence: Controlled studies. *Journal of Clinical Psychiatry*, 49 (Suppl. 2), 17–22.

Paalzow, G. (1978). Development of tolerance to analgesic effect of clonidine in rat's cross-tolerance to morphine. Naunyn-Schmiedeb. *Archives of Pharmacology*, 304, 1.

Pickworth, W.B., Sharpe, L.G., & Gupta, V.N. (1982). Morphine-like effects of clonidine on the EEG, slow wave sleep and behavior in the dog. *European Journal of Pharmacology*, 81, 551–557.

Pohorecky, L.A. (1974). Effects of ethanol on central and peripheral noradrenergic neurons. *Journal of Pharmacological Experimental Therapy*, 189, 380–391.

Rockman, G.E., Amit, Z., Brown, Z.W., Bourque, C., & Ogren, S.O. (1982). An investigation of the mechanisms of action of 5-hydroxytryptamine in the suppression of ethanol intake. *Neuropharmacology*, 21, 341–347.

Rosen, H., Flemenbaum, A., & Slater, V.L. (1986). Clinical trial of carbidopa-L-dopa combination for cocaine abuse. *American Journal of Psychiatry*, 143, 1493.

Rommelspacher, H., Strauss, S., & Lindemann, J. (1980). Excretion of tetrahydroharmane and harmane into the urine of man and rat after a load with ethanol. *FEBS Letters*, 109, 209–212.

Roy, A., Virkkunen, M., & Linnoila, M. (1987). Reduced central serotonin turnover in a subgroup of alcoholics. *Progress in Neuro-psychopharmacology & Biological Psychiatry*, 11, 173–177.

Saito, T., Ozawa, H., Tsuchiva, F., Ishizawa, H., & Tabakoff, B. (1987a). Effects of ethanol on adenylate cyclase system in the human platelet. *Alcohol & Alcoholism*, (Suppl. 1), 761–765.

Saito, T., Lee, J.M., Hoffman, P.L., & Tabakoff, B. (1987b). Effects of chronic ethanol treatment on the B-adrenergic receptor-coupled adenylate cyclase system of mouse cerebral cortex. *Journal of Neurochemistry*, 48, 1817–1822.

Schulz, R., Wuster, M., Duka, T., & Herz, A. (1980). Acute and chronic ethanol treatment changes endorphin levels in brain and pituitary. *Psychopharmacology*, 68, 221–227.

Seizinger, B.R., Bovermann, K., Maysinger, D., Hollt, V., & Herz, A. (1983). Differential effects of acute and chronic ethanol treatment on particular opioid peptide systems in discrete regions of rat brain and pituitary. *Pharmacology Biochemistry and Behavior*, (Suppl. 1), 361–369,

Seizinger, B.R., Hollt, V., & Herz, A. (1984a). Effects of chronic ethanol treatment in the in vitro biosynthesis of pro-opiomelanocortin and its post-translational processing to beta-endorphin in the intermediate lobe of the rat pituitary. *Journal of Neurochemistry*, 43, 607–613.

Seizinger, B.R., Bovermann, K., Hollt, V., & Herz, A. (1984b). Enhanced activity of the B-endorphinergic system in the anterior and neurointermediate lobe of the rat pituitary after chronic treatment with ethanol liquid diet. *Journal of Pharmacological Experimental Therapy*, 230, 455–461.

Silkworth, W.D. (1955). The doctor's opinion. In: *Alcoholics Anonymous*, pp. xxiii–xxx. New York: Alcoholics Anonymous World Services, Inc.

Sinclair, J.D. (1987). The feasibility of effective psychopharmacological treatments for alcoholism. *British Journal of Addictions*, 82, 1213–1223.

Sjoquist, B.S., Borg, S., & Kvande, H. (1981). Catecholamine derived compounds in urine and cerebrospinal fluid from alcoholics during and after long-standing intoxication. *Substance and Alcohol Act/Misuse*, 2, 63–72.

Sjoquist, B.S., Eriksson, A., & Winblad, B. (1982b). Salsolinol and catecholamines in human brain and their relationship to alcohol. *Progress in Clinical Biological Research*, 90, 57–68.

Sjoquist, B.S., Liljequist, S., & Engel, J. (1982a). Increased salsolinol levels in rat striatum and limbic forebrain following chronic ethanol treatment. *Journal of Neurochemistry*, 39, 259–262.

Smith, B.R., & Amit, Z. (1987). False neurotransmitters and the effects of ethanol on the brain. *Annals of the New York Academy of Science*, 384–389.

Stock, C. (1988). Impact of clonidine on alcohol withdrawal states. *Archives of Internal Medicine*, 148, 241–245.

Suzdak, P.D., & Paul, S.M. (1987). Ethanol, membranes, and neurotransmitters: Novel approaches to modifying the behavioral actions of alcohol. *Psychopharmacological Bulletin*, 23, 445–451.

Tabakoff, B., Hoffman, P.L., Lee, J.M., Saito, T., Willard, B., & DeLeon-Jones, F. (1988). Differences in platelet enzyme activity between alcoholics and nonalcoholics. *The New England Journal of Medicine*, 313, 134–139.

Tennant, F.S., & Tarver, A.L. (1984). Double-blind comparison of desipramine and placebo in withdrawal from cocaine dependence. *National Institute of Drug Abuse Research Monographs Series*, 55, 159–163.

Tennant, F.S., & Sagherian, A.A. (1987). Double-blind comparison of amantadine and bromocriptine for ambulatory withdrawal from cocaine dependence. *Archives of Internal Medicine*, 147, 109–112.

Thoolen, M.J.M.C., Timmermans, P.B.M.U.M., & VanZweiten, P.A. (1981). The clonidine withdrawal syndrome: Its reproduction and evaluation in laboratory animal models. *General Pharmacology*, 12, 303.

Wilkins, A.J., Jenkins, W.J., & Steiner, J.A. (1983). Efficacy of clonidine in treatment of alcohol withdrawal state. *Psychopharmacology*, 81, 78–80.

Zhukov, V.N., Varkov, A.I., & Burov, Yu.V. (1987). Effect of destruction of the brain serotoninergic system on alcohol intake by rats at early stages of experimental alcoholism. *Biogenic Amines*, 4, 201–204.

Predicting the Onset
of Compulsive Drinking
in Alcoholics:
A Biopsychosocial Model

Mark Keller [9] in a recent revisitation of the disease concept of alcoholism noted that criticism of it is once again on the rise. In addition to providing an historical perspective, Keller gave a logical defense of the concept. He concluded that the concept is still viable but not in simplistic form.

In this essay, an attempt is made to show that continued viability depends upon revisions in light of accumulating evidence. While *some* disease concept of alcoholism may still be viable, a naive disease concept is problematic. It is now clear that models that ignore biological, psychological, or social variables are partial and cannot account for the observations. Accordingly, an attempt will be made to develop a model for predicting the onset of compulsive drinking that incorporates these as well.

The following discussion begins with an examination of the evidence that some critics of any disease concept regard as sufficient for discarding it in any form.

NORMAL AND CONTROLLED DRINKING
AMONG ALCOHOLICS

The observation that some alcoholics appear to be capable of normal or controlled drinking over periods of varying duration has been reported frequently in the literature. Lemere [13], Davies [6], Moore and Ramaseur [20], Kendall [10], Selzer and Holloway [32], Bailey and Stewart [2], Pfeffer and Berger [23], Sobell and Sobell [27], and Armor, Polich, and Stambul [1] have provided reports of either normal drinking or controlled drinking following treatment.

Perhaps the most controversial of these reports is the recent one by Armor, Polich, and Stambul in which substantial percentages of alcoholics were reported to be drinking normally over appreciable periods of time [1]. Criticisms of these findings are not exclusively ideological as Roizen [25] has asserted. Emrick and Stilson [7] have criticized the report on methodological grounds and Blume [3] has raised objections from the perspective of clinical work with alcoholics. Wallace [31] reanalyzed the data and found both significant sample bias as well as internal contradictions in the data that could be explained most readily by invalid measurement of quantity and frequency of drinking.

Further work by Polich, Armor and Braiker [24], revealed that these nonproblem drinking rates fell dramatically as the followup period was extended. Polich, Armor, and Braiker's sustained nonproblem drinking rate of 4% agreed closely with Pettinati et al.'s [22] four year followup nonproblem drinking rate of 3%.

This is not to say that none of the patient's represented in treatment outcome data show patterns of nonproblem drinking at some time or another during the periods examined. Nor is it in order to argue that all of the studies cited at the beginning of this section are without value. The question is not one of controlled drinking per se among alcoholics. Rather, the critical questions that remain unanswered by these studies concern the generality of findings. These questions are as follows: How many can do this? Under what conditions does the behavior occur? Over what temporal intervals can the behavior be maintained? And perhaps most importantly, what are the general implications of these findings?

NORMAL DRINKING, CONTROLLED DRINKING AND SPONTANEOUS REMISSION

That alcoholics show evidence of moderating their intake of alcohol under particular conditions at various points in their drinking histories has long been appreciated in clinical, community, and research contexts. Clinicians are aware of the resistances that stem directly from the inconsistent drinking history itself. Alcoholics in treatment often point to numerous occasions on which they drank without compulsion and without negative consequences. This author has written elsewhere about the epistemological quandaries that confront patients as they review their inconsistent drinking histories and attempt to arrive at self-diagnoses [32].

The stories of individual members of Alcoholics Anonymous reveal varied patterns of drinking, many of which do not include drunkenness and compulsive drinking on every drinking occasion. In many cases the decision to become an A.A. member was not based on the inevitability of loss of control on each drinking occasion but on the unpredictability of persons' actions across various drinking occasions. Some A.A. members report periods of deliberate control over alcohol intake before lapsing once again into patterns of uncontrolled consumption. Still others report some ability to control intake along with an unwillingness to pay high emotional and psychic energy costs associated with continued preoccupation with alcohol and the necessity for constant decision-making.

Studies in laboratory and hospital research contexts (to be reviewed shortly) have yielded findings consistent with these observations derived from clinical and community contexts.

Of course, most of these observations of moderate alcohol intake among alcoholics concern short term behavior under atypical conditions. However, Davies [6] has reported long term moderate consumption among a small number of apparent alcoholic persons. And Cahalan, Cisin, and Crossley [4] have noted developmental changes in a substantial number of persons with regard to quantity of ethanol consumption.

In order to grasp the implications of these observations, it is important that careful distinctions among different concepts be maintained.

Normal drinking is, in effect, "norm-referenced" drinking. The term has meaning only with regard to some reference group. Obviously, there can be as many meanings of normal drinking as there are particular, identifiable reference groups. Moreover, separate norms for quantity of consumption, frequency of consumption, reasons for drinking, and behavior while drinking can exist in the same reference group. In a sense, normal drinking is unselfconscious drinking, a type of behavior sustained and legitimated by societal and cultural rules and meanings.

Controlled drinking is drinking accomplished deliberately in accord with consciously specified rules and goals. As with normal drinking, there are no fixed, absolute goals associated with controlled drinking. A particular controlled drinking goal concerning quantity of consumption could be either above or below acceptable limits for a given reference group but still be appropriate for a given individual. In this sense, controlled drinking can involve many drinking behaviors and drinking styles. The term does not signify a single value for either magnitude or frequency of ethanol consumption.

Spontaneous Remission refers to the absence of disease in a previously diseased person when that absence cannot be attributed to particular treatments. Obviously, spontaneous remission cannot be planned, predicted, or controlled. At present, its incidence has not been established with regard to either frequency or duration in the disease of alcoholism.

Bearing these distinctions in mind, let's review the implications of the studies and observations cited above. Firstly, it is apparent that the majority of the studies have to do with spontaneous remissions.

Secondly, spontaneous remission *per se* in some alcoholics has no bearing whatsoever on treatment goals. It does not constitute grounds for abandoning abstinence as a treatment goal. The fact of spontaneous remission in some alcoholics certainly does not call for lecturing treatment persons about their "abstinence fixation" as Roizen has done [25]. Nor does it lend support to the charges of Armor, Polich, and Stambul that the belief in abstinence is derived only from an "ideological paradigm" [1]. To argue that controlled drinking may constitute an appropriate treatment goal on the basis of adequate studies of controlled drinking is at least logical. But to imply that spontaneous remission justifies either normal or controlled drinking as *treatment goals* is, of course, neither logically nor empirically defensible. Since spontaneous remission cannot be planned, predicted, nor controlled, it serves neither as a basis for, nor a goal of treatment.

The frequent observations of intermittent or periodic normal drinking among alcoholics do raise serious problems for the naive disease concept, but do not eliminate biological variables as factors in a complex disease process. Nor do these observations argue for the abandonment of abstinence as a treatment goal. As already indicated, intermittent or periodic normal drinking of varying duration under certain conditions at various points in the drinking history is common in alcoholism and not indicative of its absence. Moreover, despite the stereotypes about them, alcoholism treatment people do not advocate abstinence because they fear that their patients will immediately "lose control" and drink to intoxication if they take one or several drinks. They counsel abstinence because of the *unpredictable* nature of both drinking and social behaviors in the alcoholic on any given drinking occasion. In addition, abstinence is advocated since an eventual return to alcoholic drinking is the rule not the exception in those alcoholics in treatment who continue to try to meet normative cultural standards for drinking behaviors. The clinician's judgement in this matter of treatment goals is neither "intuitive" nor "ideological." It is empirical. To be sure, clinical samples may be *biased,* but it is difficult to see how they are any more biased than the samples that have been used in more formal treatment outcome studies.

While spontaneous remissions do not rule out biological factors nor argue for the abandonment of abstinence as a treatment goal, neither does the scant and methodologically inadequate literature on controlled drinking. Isolated case studies are uninterpretable since changes in a single patient's drinking behavior may reflect spontaneous remission, intermittent normal drinking, or inaccurate diagnosis rather than achieved controlled drinking.

The study by Sobell and Sobell [27] seemed the most impressive claim for controlled drinking among alcoholics during follow-up in their natural environment. Unfortunately, as Chalmers [5] has shown, this study contains serious definitional, design and measurement flaws. Moreover, Chalmers has reinterpreted the Sobells' data as reflecting substantial abstinence as the means to being categorized as a "controlled drinker" at follow-up. More seriously, independent interviews of these patients by Pendery, Maltzman and West revealed virtually no *sustained* controlled drinking in this sample [21].

Available studies of spontaneous remission, normal drinking, and controlled drinking, then, do not justify abandonment of abstinence as a treatment goal. However, observations of intermittent or periodic normal drinking among certain alcoholics under certain conditions do suggest necessary revisions in a naive disease concept. In the next section studies in laboratory and hospital contexts will be examined for clues as to what these necessary revisions might be.

STUDIES IN LABORATORY AND HOSPITAL CONTEXTS

Alcoholics given small to moderate amounts of alcohol in laboratory and hospital settings do not show subsequent self-reports of craving nor loss of control over drinking. Mello [15], Mello and Mendelson [16], Mendelson and Mello [18], Thio [29], McNamee, Mello and Mendelson [14], Merry [19], Engle and Williams [8], and Sobell, Sobell and Christelman [28], have all reported such findings.

For some, these particular results in invalidate *all* disease notions about alcoholism. But this conclusion is unwarranted by these data. They do, of course, invalidate a simplistic and naive disease concept.

Sobell, Sobell and Christelman [28] seem especially to set up a "straw man" and then proceed to demolish it. Referring to their paper as showing the "myth of the first drink," they refute the claim that alcohlics will immediately lose control once drinking starts. But who had believed this myth of "first drink—then drunk" anyway? Is it true that A.A. members, treatment professionals and paraprofessionals believe this *literal* interpretation of a metaphor?

Readily accessible data reveal a "myth of the myth of the first drink." Five alcoholism counselors (they were A.A. members as well) and 10 patients were asked the following question: "If a recovered alcoholic should take a drink, he will (a) choose to continue drinking until drunk; (b) promptly lose control of his drinking and be unable to stop; (c) be placing himself in a vulnerable position in that he may be drawn eventually back into uncontrolled drinking."

Of the five recovered counselors, all five chose alternative (c). Of 10 patients, two said the alcoholic would choose to continue drinking until intoxicated because that's what they themselves usually did. The remaining eight patients chose alternative (c) above.

In short, none of the alcoholism counselors showed evidence of believing the literal meaning of the "myth of the first drink" and 80% of the patients didn't either.

Apparently, then, a more sober interpretation of Sobell, Sobell and Christelman's study is simply that A.A. argot should not be taken literally but viewed for what it is—figure of speech, metaphor and organizational codes for extended, complex meanings.

As Thune [30] has recently shown through phenomenological analysis, A.A. talk cannot be understood on the level of ordinary talk, but must be approached as a complex symbolic system that at times defies conventional and literal interpretations.

But aside from myths about first drinks and myths about myths about that, what do these various observations concerning "craving" and loss of control in laboratory and hospital settings actually tell us? They suggest several interesting alternate models to the naive disease concept of alcoholism. I intend to examine these one at a time and then select the one that seems most fruitful.

A BIOLOGICAL THRESHOLD MODEL

This model postulates a fixed, absolute, biological threshold. Below threshold, at low levels of consumption, compulsive drinking will not appear. At and above threshold compulsive drinking will become evident.

The evidence for the existence of such a threshold is provided by Mendelson's experiment [17]. When consumption reached thirty ounces of 86-proof whiskey after two weeks of daily drinking, compulsive drinking became apparent. Self-reported craving became evident when consumption reached forty ounces at three weeks of daily drinking. With consumption below thirty ounces and less than two weeks in duration, neither reports of craving nor compulsive drinking were observed.

Sobell, Sobell and Christelman [28] studied hospitalized alcoholics who consumed between one and six ounces of 86-proof liquor. Compulsive drinking was not observed in the sense that only two of 101 patients left the hospital for more alcohol. In further experiments, Sobel *et al.* permitted patients to drink up to 16 ounces of 86-proof liquor. Only five of 113 patients subsequently left the hospital for more alcohol.

It is clear then that in hospital and laboratory contexts, when consumption is high and sustained over long periods of time, compulsive drinking occurs. However, at low and moderate levels in these contexts, compulsive drinking does not occur.

At first blush, a biological threshold model appears to account for these observations. However, this model ignores the particular conditions under which the observations were made. Under some other set of psychological and social conditions, a very different threshold value is probable. For example, the free ranging alcoholic in his natural habitat is likely to show compulsive drinking at lower levels of consumption over shorter temporal intervals. In essence, the threshold model is a slightly more complicated version of the naive disease concept. It assumes a single absolute threshold for compulsive drinking with the threshold determined completely by two variables—quantity and duration of consumption.

A Psychosocial Model: Set and Setting

That "set" and "setting" are operative in alcohol research is not surprising since these variables have been shown to be present in drug research generally.

Set refers to the expectations a subject brings to a particular social context as well as the expectations developed there. These expectations are multiple and concern the expected effect of the drug upon the person's physical functioning, feelings, mood, thinking and behavior.

Setting refers to the particular physical and social stimuli that comprise the context in which the drug is taken. As can be imagined, the term "setting" refers to a highly complex collection of both recognized and unrecognized variables. An objective and complete description of the physical and social variables that comprise the multidimensional contexts in which alcoholism research takes place is a herculean task. Given present methodological and conceptual limitations, it is probably impossible.

Nonetheless, salient features of these contexts can be selected out as variables of some potency. Both formal and informal rules systems are important. Staff expectations, beliefs, attitudes, personalities, bases of power and behaviours are further factors of importance. Various rewards and punishments, explicit and implicit, are still other considerations. The physical environment of the lab or hospital setting is obviously a critical consideration.

The fact that small and even moderate amounts of alcohol did not result in reports of craving or loss of control in laboratory and hospital contexts indicates that compulsive drinking can be constrained by variables concerned with set and setting. However, these psychosocial variables alone are not sufficient to account for the observations. It will be recalled that when daily consumption reached 30 ounces of 86-proof whiskey after two weeks of drinking, compulsive drinking became more apparent even under the ecologically irrelevant conditions of the laboratory. Hence, psychosocial factors may partially constrain compulsive drinking at certain levels of consumption over limited temporal periods, but are eventually overcome by biological factors. It should be noted that laboratory conditions are inhibitory ones and that under some alternative set of socially facilitating conditions, compulsive drinking is likely to appear much earlier and at lower levels of consumption.

Obviously, neither a naive disease concept nor a naive psychosocial one adequately account for the observations. What is needed is an interactive model, one that combines both sets of factors. I will consider this third alternative now.

A BIOPSYCHOSOCIAL DISEASE MODEL

Since neither of the two naive concepts—biological or psychosocial—explain the observations, it is in order to examine a third and possibly more useful one. This model is appropriately termed a *biopsychosocial* one. It is an interactive model, one in which biological, psychological and social factors all enter into the prediction of compulsive drinking.

In this model, a biological, or *primary*, threshold for compulsive drinking is postulated. However, this threshold is far more complex than previously conceptualized. First of all, it is partially represented by but not isomorphic to either quantity or duration of consumption either singly or in combination. Because of recognized differences in both alcoholics and non-alcoholics in physical response to alcohol, objective measures such as quantity and duration of consumption imperfectly represent a primary threshold. For example, differences *between* alcoholics and non-alcoholics in peak blood ethanol concentrations, ethanol disappearance rates, and plateau acetaldehyde concentrations were apparent in the data reported by Korsten, Matsuzaki, Feinman and Lieber [11]. However *within* sample differences were apparent as well.

But even if it were possible to measure primary threshold indirectly by quantity and duration of consumption or by direct biological measures, it would soon become apparent that these measurements alone would not predict compulsive drinking *under all imaginable conditions*. We would soon discover that there is not a single biological threshold value for compulsive drinking, but many, each of which is related in some complex way to varying psychosocial conditions. In this sense, it is clear then that primary threshold is best thought of as a *range of values* rather than an absolute, fixed point.

Since the concept of a primary threshold is inadequate to account for the observations, we obviously need a second threshold concept to build an interactive disease model. I have termed this additional concept the *effective threshold.*

Effective threshold is defined as that value in a range of primary threshold values that elicits compulsive drinking under specific psychosocial conditions. Hence, effective threshold is neither exclusively biological nor exclusively psychosocial. It is biopsychosocial.

PHENOMENOLOGICAL REPRESENTATION OF PRIMARY THRESHOLD

Another way to grasp the meaning of the concept of primary threshold is to consider it in terms of the phenomenal experience of the compulsive drinker. For the alcoholic drinker, ethanol consumption is both positively reinforcing and punishing. The immediate effects are for the most part pleasant while the delayed effects are unpleasant. Most alcoholics speak of the initial effects of ethanol ingestion in positive terms—a pleasurable sensation of warmth spreading throughout the body, a heightened sense of well-being, euphoria, increased self-confidence, grandiosity, decreased tensions and improved self-image. These are represented by phrases such as the following: "I was feeling good"; "I was feeling no pain"; "I felt I could do anything"; "I was feeling that glow"; "I took a drink and it fixed me right up"; "I felt relaxed and warm all over."

Delayed punishments vary across individuals and time periods. They involve three classes of negative outcomes of ethanol ingestion. These are: (1) *Physical* (hangover symptoms; physical diseases; general feelings of ill health and malaise; ethanol withdrawal symptoms); (2) *Psychological* (shame; guilt; depression; free-floating anxiety; fear of specific consequences of behavior while drinking; decreased self-confidence; decreased self-esteem; remorse; agitation; identity confusion); and (3) *Social* (legal, financial, marital and employment difficulties).

While I have drawn these conceptual distinctions among classes of delayed punishments, I suspect that the interrelationships between and among them are many. For example, psychological negative consequences such as depression and anxiety are surely magnified by both transient and chronic physical abnormalities associated with alcoholsim. In turn, psychological factors can contribute to intensification of physical withdrawal symptoms.

Delayed punishments do not occur all at once but show temporal distributions. It is inaccurate to speak of a single temporal distribution of delayed punishments since there are, in fact, several conceptually and operationally distinct distributions. Some effects must be viewed in light of duration of the drinking history *per se* while others need to be considered in relation to the duration of a given drinking bout. Some delayed punishments appear early in the drinking history and shortly after the onset of a particular drinking bout, (e.g., hangover; fear of particular consequences of behavior while drinking; shame). Others may make their appearance later, (e.g., free floating anxiety; identity confusion; problems of relationship; guilt; remorse; depression). And still others may have even longer periods of delay (e.g., physical diseases of liver, pancreas and heart; frank expression of ethanol withdrawal symptoms).

The precise nature of the relationship between these two important temporal gradients—duration of drinking history and duration of drinking bout—with regard to delayed punishments is still far from clear. Moreover, the relationship is probably complicated by large individual differences.

But whatever the relationship between or among various temporal gradients, it is apparent that punishments do occur and summate over time for alcoholic drinkers. At any point in time, the alcoholic represents this cumulative set of delayed punishments in subjective terms. *Perceived level of discomfort* is defined as the alcoholic's phenomenological representation to self of the particular set of delayed punishments present in his life at a given point in time.

The alcoholics perceived level of discomfort, then, is a complex variable that subjectively represents the cumulative stress associated with interacting delayed physical, psychological and social aversive consequences of drinking. From a phenomenological perspective, perceived level of discomfort serves as an estimator of a *complex primary threshold*. It incorporates not only physical factors, but psychological and social ones as well.

This complex primary threshold is described by a range of values, no one of which predicts compulsive drinking under all imaginable social conditions. Under certain conditions, the alcoholic will initiate and sustain compulsive drinking at a relatively low level of perceived discomfort. On other occasions, even with perceived discomfort at very high levels, he will refrain from drinking altogether or avoid compulsive drinking patterns. In other words, perceived level of discomfort alone is not sufficient for the prediction of compulsive drinking. Other variables must be considered as well.

PHENOMENOLOGICAL REPRESENTATION OF EFFECTIVE THRESHOLD

While the alcoholic has a perceived level of discomfort, he also has expectations of positive reinforcements associated with ethanol ingestion. Not only are the initial effects of drinking primarily positively reinforcing in their own right, they are secondarily reinforcing since they temporarily relieve the delayed punishments of prior ethanol consumption. In technical terms, ethanol ingestion is positively reinforcing, punishing and negatively reinforcing (the latter being defined as the withdrawal or cessation of aversive stimuli).

In addition to perceived level of discomfort and expectations of positive reinforcement, *subjective estimates of immediate punishments* are held and recognized by the alcoholic at various points in his drinking history and in a given drinking bout. On the other hand, *subjective estimates of future punishments* are virtually zero or low immediately prior to the onset of a drinking bout or during it.

The common observation that alcoholics very often hide their supplies, conceal their drinking from significant others, deny intake, and minimize reported consumption while continuing to drink excessively in the face of worsening physical and social circumstances is congruent with this analysis of estimates of immediate future punishments.

Further variables are necessary to complete a phenomenological analysis. *Perceived situational appropriateness and inappropriateness* are defined as the alcoholic's perception of the situation in terms of its appropriateness/inappropriateness for excessive drinking, or, for that matter, any drinking at all. That alcoholics are capable of attenuating their drinking in accord with self-definitions of situational appropriateness should come as no surprise to those who have observed them directly in natural contexts. Nor should it be surprising to note that as the drinking history unfolds, more and more situations are defined as appropriate for drinking!

Perceived situational appropriateness partially overlaps with a variable already discussed—subjective estimates of immediate punishment. While the possibility of immediate punishment certainly enters into the subjective definition of appropriateness, it does not determine it completely. In a sense, self-definition of a situation is the phenomenological equivalent of more objectivist concern with such things as "learned cues" or "stimuli" previously "conditioned to" or "associated with" drinking situations. In the language of everyday life, we are concerned here with such things as bars, cocktail lounges, hotel rooms, restaurants, street corners, private homes and doorways as opposed to such places as churches, schools, hospitals, scientific laboratories, alcoholism treatment centers and so forth.

These six variables represent a phenomenological approach to the meanings of the concepts of primary and effective threshold. In the phenomenological approach, perceived level of discomfort serves as an estimator of primary threshold. The expectation variables are largely individual psychological variables that enter into the determination of effective threshold. Subjective estimates of immediate and future punishment are both psychological and social-psychological in nature and comprise additional determinants of effective threshold. Finally, perceived situational appropriateness/inappropriateness contributes to effective threshold.

CONSTRUCTING A BIOPSYCHOSOCIAL MODEL FROM PHENOMENOLOGICAL CONCEPTS

A model is more than a list of definitions of hypothesized variables. One must, of course, first devise operational definitions of these variables. And one must try to specify the relationships between and among the variables however measured. With regard to the former, operational definitions of these particular variables are yet to be constructed. As to the latter, guesses can be made, not so much in the spirit of pure speculation, but rather to provide a systematic basis for empirical testing of hypothesized relationships.

It will be recalled that effective threshold (ET) is defined as that value in a range of primary threshold (PT) values that elicits compulsive drinking under specific psychosocial conditions. And in the present model, perceived level of discomfort (PLD) is assumed to partially represent primary threshold (PT).

It follows then that ET is determined by PLD in combination with the following variables: Expectation of positive reinforcement (EPR); Subjective estimates of immediate punishment (SIP); Subjective estimates of future punishments (SFP); Perceived Situational Appropriateness (PSA); Perceived Situational Inappropriateness (PSI). Hypothesizing certain functional relationships, the following obtains: ET = PLD × EPR × PSA − (PSI × (SIP + SFP)).

The biopsychosocial model asserts that while perceived level of discomfort (or primary threshold) is indeed a powerful determinant of compulsive drinking, this variable alone cannot predict such drinking under all psychological and social conditions. A given perceived level of discomfort under one set of psychosocial conditions will eventuate in compulsive drinking. Under some other set of psychosocial conditions, the *same* perceived level of discomfort will not.

In essence, the biopsychosocial model is a conflict model involving both facilitating and inhibiting factors in the prediction of compulsive drinking. PLD, EPR and PSA are facilitating factors, PSI, SIP and SFP are inhibitory factors.

Assume perfectly reliable measurement on each of these six variables. Further assume that each has been scaled to provide psychologically and statistically meaningful intervals or values ranging from 1 to 10. Bearing in mind these assumptions, let's consider several hypothetical cases.

(1) A low level of perceived discomfort coupled with moderate expectations of positive reinforcement in a situation of low perceived appropriateness and high perceived inappropriateness where estimates of immediate punishment are moderate and estimates of future punishments are low. The model would predict the following:

$$ET = 2 \times 5 \times 1 - (9 \times (5 + 1))$$
$$= 10 - (54)$$
$$= -44$$

In this instance, inhibitory factors predominate and a substantial negative value for ET does not predict compulsive drinking.

(2) A moderate level of perceived discomfort coupled with moderate expectations of positive reinforcement in a situation of moderate perceived situational appropriateness and high perceived inappropri-

ateness where estimates of immediate punishment are high and estimates of future punishments are moderate:

$$ET = 5 \times 5 \times 5 - (9 \times (9 + 5))$$
$$= 125 - (126)$$
$$= -1$$

In this instance, a substantial positive value for ET is not obtained and compulsive drinking is not predicted.

(3) A moderately high level of perceived discomfort coupled with moderately high levels of expectations for positive reinforcement in a situation of moderate perceived appropriateness and moderate perceived inappropriateness where estimates of both immediate and future punishments are low:

$$ET = 7 \times 7 \times 5 - (5 \times (1 + 1))$$
$$= 245 - (10)$$
$$= +235$$

In this case, a substantial positive value for ET is obtained and compulsive drinking would be predicted. Case number one above resembles the situations studied and observations made by Merry [19] and Engle and Williams [8] in which one ounce of vodka was given to hospitalized alcoholics surreptitiously.

Case number two resembles the situation studied and observations made by Sobell, Sobell and Christelman [28] in which up to 16 ounces of 86-proof liquor was given to hospitalized alcoholics under conditions of threat of both immediate and future punishments (i.e., patients could leave the hospital for more alcohol but were threatened with immediate transfer to a locked unit and eventual discharge if they were to do so).

Case number three resembles Mendleson's [17] experiment in which between 30 and 40 ounces of 86-proof whiskey over a two to three week period of daily drinking resulted in compulsive drinking among 12 skid row (gamma) hospitalized alcoholics.

Let's examine one last possible case. Consider a hypothetical alcoholic drinker in a situation characterized by moderately low PLD, moderately high expectations of positive reinforcement, high perceived appropriateness, and low perceived inappropriateness where subjective estimates of both immediate and future punishments are low:

$$ET = 2 \times 7 \times 9 - (1 \times (1 + 1))$$
$$= 126 - 2$$
$$= +124$$

In this case, despite a lowered value for perceived level of discomfort, the obtained substantial positive value for ET predicts compulsive drinking. This is precisely one of the situations reported by many alcoholics at the beginning of a compulsive drinking bout; they did not feel particularly troubled, upset, or uncomfortable but did expect a drink or two to be pleasant and found themselves in social and physical surrounds highly supportive and encouraging of drinking.

The biopsychosocial model presented here is, of course, purely theoretical. It is also simplistic and crude. (PLD, for example, may stand in a curvilinear relationship to ET in the same sense that at very high levels of PLD, compulsive drinking may cease. All hypothesized functional relationships in this model as it stands may very well be partially or completely inaccurate. The variables may, for example, all summate in a simpler, linear, additive manner. Precise information concerning functional relationships between and among the hypothesized variables obviously requires systematic empirical testing. Moreover, the model as presented is static rather than dynamic. With the addition of time dimension to the model, changes in the relationships of all variables to ET can be expected. In other words, as drinking behavior progresses through time, the contribution of each variable to ET is likely to change.) It's assumptions are many and the numbers used in the hypothetical cases entirely arbitrary. It does, however, contain more than a hint as to the steps toward a new necessary interactive disease concept of alcoholism.

RECONCILING DIFFERENCES

An interactive, biopsychosocial disease concept of alcoholism permits reconciliation of the differences obtained when alcoholics are studied in laboratores, hospitals, and simulated conditions versus their natural habitats. It also permits reconciliation of the differences among those who approach the disease from the varying perspectives of different disciplines, ideologies and paradigms [30].

As Mark Keller [9] has made clear, it is not that the very notion of disease must be abandoned but that our concept of it must be enlarged, enriched and extended. That diseases of all kinds require redefinition in terms of psychological, social, cultural and even political factors seems to me to be one of the more exciting paradigm changes slowly taking place in enlightened quarters of modern medicine.

In closing, several further caveats are in order. While this paper has attempted to construct a single biopsychosocial model to describe and predict the behavior of an assumed homogenous group of alcoholics, the heterogeneity of this clinical population suggests that different biopsychosocial models may be required for different alcoholic subgroups. For certain alcoholics, biological factors may be primary. For others, psychological factors may carry the weight of prediction in a biopsychosocial model. And for still other alcoholics, social cultural factors may require greater emphasis than do biological or psychological factors. These extensions of the model presented here require further development.

REFERENCES

1. Armor, D. J., J. M. Polich and H. B. Stambul. *Alcoholism and Treatment*. Santa Monica: Rand Corp., 1976.
2. Bailey, M. and J. Stewart. Normal drinking by persons reporting previous problem drinking. *Q J Stud Alcohol* **28**: 305–315, 1967.
3. Blume, S. The "Rand Report." Some comments and a response. *J Stud Alcohol* **38**: 163–168, 1977.
4. Cahalan, D., I. H. Cisin and H. M. Crossley. American drinking practices: A national survey of behavior and attitudes. Monograph No. 6, New Brunswick, NJ: Rutgers Center for Alcohol Studies, 1969.
5. Chalmers, D. Controlled drinking as an alcoholism treatment goal: A methodological criticism. Paper presented at the North American Congress on Alcohol and Drug Problems, San Francisco, December, 1974. (Cassette Series on Alcoholism, Faces West Productions, 1975.)
6. Davies, D. L. Normal drinking in recovered alcohol addicts. *Q J Stud Alcohol* **23**: 94–104, 1962.
7. Emrick, C. D. and D. W. Stilson. The "Rand Report." Some comments and a response. *J Stud Alcohol* **38**: 152–163, 1977.
8. Engle, J. B. and T. K. Williams. Effects of an ounce of vodka on alcoholics' desire for alcohol. *Q J Stud Alcohol* **33**: 1099–1105. 1972.
9. Keller, M. The disease concept of alcoholism revisited. *J Stud Alcohol* **37**: 1694–1717, 1976.
10. Kendell, R. E. Normal drinking by former alcohol addicts. *Q J Stud Alcohol* **26**: 247–257, 1965.
11. Korsten, M. A., S. Matsuzaki, L. Feinman and C. S. Lieber. High blood acetaldehyde levels after ethanol administration. *N Engl J Med* **292**: 386–389, 1975.
12. Kuhn, T. S. *The Structure of Scientific Revolutions, vol 2, International Encyclopedia of Unified Science*. Chicago: University of Chicago, 1970.
13. Lemere, F. What happens to alcoholics? *Am J Psychiatry* **109**: 674–676, 1953.
14. McNamee, H. B., N. K. Mello and J. H. Mendelson. Experimental analysis of drinking patterns of alcoholics, concurrent psychiatric observations. *Am J Psychiatry* **124**: 1063–1069, 1968.
15. Mello, N. K. Behavioral studies on alcoholism. In: The Biology of Alcoholism, vol

2, Physiology and Behavior, edited by B. Kissen and H. Bergleiter. New York: Plenum, 1972, pp. 219–291.

16. Mello, N. K. and J. H. Mendelson. Operant analysis of drinking patterns of chornic alcoholics. *Nature* **206:** 43–46, 1965.

17. Mendelson, J. H. (Ed.) Experimentally induced chronic intoxication and withdrawal in alcoholics. *Q J Stud Alcohol* Suppl 2, 1964.

18. Mendelson, J. H. and N. K. Mello. Experimental analysis of drinking behavior of chronic alcoholics. *Ann NY Acad Sci* **133:** 828–845, 1966.

19. Merry, J. The loss of control myth. *Lancet* **1:** 1257–1258, 1966.

20. Moore, R. A. and F. Ramaseur. Effects of psychotherapy in open-ward hospital on patients with alcoholism. *Q J Stud Alcohol* **21:** 233–252, 1960.

21. Pendery, M., I. Maltzman and L. J. West. Controlled drinking by alcoholics? New findings and a re-evaluation of a major affirmative study. *Science* **217:** 169–175, 1982.

22. Pettinati, H., A. Sugerman, N. DiDonato and H. Maurer. The natural history of alcoholism over four years after treatment. *J Stud Alcohol* **43:** 201–215, 1982.

23. Pfeffer, A. and S. Berger. A follow-up study of treatment on alcoholics. *Q J Stud Alcohol* **4:** 49–72, 1957.

24. Polich, J. M., D. J. Armor and H. B. Braiker. *The Course of Alcoholism: Four Years After Treatment.* Santa Monica: Rand Corporation, 1980.

25. Roizen, R. The "Rand Report." Some comments and a response. *J Stud Alcohol* **38:** 170–178, 1977.

26. Selzer, M. L. and W. Holloway. A follow-up of alcoholics committed to a state hospital. *Q J Stud Alcohol* **18:** 98–120, 1957.

27. Sobell, L. C. and M. B. Sobell. Individualized behavior therapy for alcoholics. *Behav Res Ther* **4:** 49–72, 1973.

28. Sobell, L. C., M. B. Sobell and W. C. Christelman. The myth of "one drink." *Behav Res Ther* **10:** 119–123, 1972.

29. Thio, K. T. Loss of control in alcoholism. Unpublished Doctoral Dissertation, 1969, Queen's University, Kingston, Ontario.

30. Thune, C. E. Alcoholism and archetypal past: A phenomenological perspective on Alcoholics Anonymous. *J Stud Alcohol* **38:** 75–88, 1977.

31. Wallace, J. Ideology, belief and behavior: Alcoholics Anonymous as a social movement. In: *Etiologic Aspects of Alcohol and Drug Abuse,* edited by E. Gottheil, K. Druley, T. E. Skoloda and H. M. Waxman. Springfield: Charles C. Thomas, 1983.

32. Wallace, J. Alcoholism from the inside out: A phenomenological analysis. In: *Alcoholism: Development, Consequences and Interventions,* edited by N. J. Estes and M. Heinemann. St. Louis: C. V. Mosby, 1977, pp. 3–14.

Part IV

The Politics of Alcoholism

The Attack of the "Anti-Traditionalist" Lobby

Once upon a time, alcoholism was a sleepy little disease to which only a few professionals paid much attention. Physicians didn't recognize it in their practices, even though it occupied as many as half the beds in the medical/surgical units of some of our big-city hospitals. Psychiatrists and social workers apparently were more interested in treating the "neuroses" they thought alcoholism was "caused by" rather than confronting the disease itself. Psychologists didn't bother much with alcoholism at all and seemed to prefer life in and around the academic dichotomy, e.g., behaviorism vs. psychodynamic theory; heredity vs. environment; learned vs. unlearned behavior, and so forth.

Since most professionals seemed to be looking elsewhere, early alcoholism workers and recovered persons were able to work unencumbered. They linked arms against a disease that causes great suffering and enormous personal, social, and national costs. Unity, common welfare, common cause—these became the passwords of generations of alcoholism workers faced with prejudice, hostility, stigma, ignorance, or indifference.

Somewhere along the line, however, things began to change. As money for prevention, treatment, and research became increasingly available, professional indifference turned to definite interest. Alcohol research centers appeared on university campuses. Physicians began to recognize that alcoholism was present in their practices and in the medical/surgical units of hospitals. Psychiatrists and social workers, while still determined to treat the "underlying neuroses," became more concerned with such things as intervention, family treatment, and adult children of alcoholics. Psychologists took aim at the "traditional disease concept of alcoholism" and wondered why the field had gotten so hung up on abstinence; surely there could be other goals of treatment.

Sadly, while interest in alcoholism was definitely on the rise, prejudice, hostility, and ignorance did not disappear. Consider the thoughts of G. Alan Marlatt, a psychologist, university professor, and researcher into relapse among alcoholics (while Dr. Marlatt begins by talking about what "some observers" think, it becomes clear that he is talking about what he thinks):

> "To some observers, the diagnosis of alcoholism carries the moral stigma of a new scarlet letter. Such critics argue that the contemporary disease model of alcoholism is little more than the old "moral model" (drinking as a sinful behavior) dressed up in sheep's clothing (or at least in a white coat). Despite the fact that the basic tenets of the disease model have yet to be verified scientifically (e.g., the physiological basis of the disease and its primary symptom, loss of control), and even though there is a lack of empirical support for the effectiveness of any particular form of alcoholism treatment (including inpatient programs geared toward abstinence), advocates of the disease model continue to insist that alcoholism is a unitary disorder, a progressive disease that can only be temporarily arrested by total abstention. From this viewpoint, alcohol for the abstinent alcoholic symbolizes the forbidden fruit (a fermented apple?), and a lapse from abstinence is tantamount to a fall from grace in the eyes of God. Clearly, one bite of the forbidden fruit is sufficient to be expelled from paradise. Anyone who suggests controlled drinking is branded as an agent of the devil, tempting the naive alcoholic back into the sin of drinking. If drinking is a sin, the only solution is salvation, a surrendering of personal control to a higher power." (Marlatt, 1983, p. 1107)

Marlatt's astonishing misconceptions did not appear in some obscure journal. Quite the contrary. They appeared in a recent special edition of the *American Psychologist,* the official journal of the American Psychological Association. Moreover, these idiosyncratic views on the "moral nature" of the disease concept, the lack of evidence for biological factors in alcoholism, the religious basis for abstinence as a treatment goal, and surrender as "salvation" did not appear in this influential journal by accident. Their publication apparently was recommended by Dr. Peter Nathan, the director of the Rutgers Center for Studies on Alcohol, who served as editor for this special edition of the *American Psychologist.*

Editorial sympathies aside, however, it is odd that some contemporary psychologists still haven't grasped the essence of the disease concept, seem unaware of the voluminous literature on the biology of alcoholism, persist in confusing the spirituality of the alcoholism movement with the religiosity of organized religions, refuse to accept the fact that alcoholism can be arrested but not cured, disbelieve that the disease is indeed progressive for many victims, and think that controlled drinking as a treatment goal is rejected by recovering alcoholics because drinking is sinful. But while these concepts and points of view may appear odd to experienced alcoholism workers, they do form the belief system of an aggressive emergent group, the "Anti-Traditionalists." Basically, this lobby is opposed to the disease concept of alcoholism and would like to see most alcoholics trying to drink rather than trying to stay sober.

Abstinence, it seems, is not a desirable thing to some of these contemporary thinkers. Dr. Stanton Peele, the author of *Love and Addiction,* for example, has this to say about abstinence from alcohol and drugs:

> "Cigarettes aside, abstinence is often a poor way to change a habit. The reason is that abstinence makes the heart grow fonder of the thing it no longer has—and a rebound often results. Because the relapse rate for abstinence methods is so high, psychologists have now developed several moderate-drinking programs for problem drinkers." (Peele, 1985, p. 38)

As for AA's position, Dr. Peele states the following:

> "A.A. preaches a doctrine of total redemption, teetotaling forever. And many a former alcoholic believes that a single drink will send him on the short, slippery slope to alcoholic hell. It's true that for some alcoholics who have been uncontrolled drinkers for many years and whose health has deteriorated, the option of moderation is no longer workable. However, the resolution never to have a drink again is not always a cure-all. The vast majority of alcoholics who try to abstain eventually return to the bottle or to another addiction." (1985, p. 39)

One wonders how an empirical scientist like Dr. Peele has managed to get his observations of AA so dreadfully confused by religious metaphor. Having attended several thousand AA meetings, I have never heard anybody stand up and preach a doctrine of redemption (salvation from sin through the atonement of Christ). Moreover, considering the day-at-a-time program that AA actually is, Dr. Peele's assertion that AA people preach "teetotaling forever" has a strange, almost resentful ring.

Drs. Peele and Marlatt are not alone in their skepticism about ideas of the so-called "traditionalists." Dr. Nick Heather of Scotland's University of Dundee has argued that controlled drinking may be a preferred drinking goal for all types of alcoholics, regardless of level of dependence. According to Dr. Heather, there is no "theoretical limit" to the application of controlled drinking treatment to alcoholics. Heather comments:

"I notice a regrettable tendency to conclude that controlled drinking is only suitable for certain people and is not suitable for another whole class of individuals called addicted alcoholics, gamma alcoholics, or whatever you like. I think for one thing that this kind of conclusion plays into the hands of the 'abstinence lobby' and can be used by them to say, 'well, we were right all along, real alcoholics can only succeed through abstinence. Controlled drinking is only suitable for people who are not real alcoholics . . . ' Alcoholics Anonymous has believed that all along. They're quite ready for that kind of message . . . There's a premature closure . . . Why do I think this? Well, actually I think there are six reasons. One, there's Sobell's work, which is relevant to this, which has not been discredited and shows that gamma alcoholics treated by controlled drinking methods do better at followup than control groups given abstinence-goal treatment." (Heather, 1985, pp. 129–130)

Apparently, Dr. Linda Sobell is in agreement with Dr. Heather about the merits of her controversial research with husband Dr. Mark Sobell on controlled drinking treatment of alcoholics. In an article in *The Journal* of the Addiction Research Foundation of Toronto, Dr. Sobell is quoted as follows:

"We are fighting about which set of ideas will guide future research and treatment. We're engaged in the struggle because we're committed to this field and because the empirical body of knowledge which has evolved suggests different directions and conceptualizations for treatment and research from that firmly espoused by traditionalists." (Linda Sobell, 1984)

Apparently, Dr. Linda Sobell's enthusiasm for controlled drinking treatment goals is undaunted by the recent failure of an independent team of researchers (Pendery, Maltzman, and West, 1981) to find evidence for sustained controlled drinking among the patients she and husband, Mark Sobell, treated with controlled drinking methods at Patton State Hospital (San Bernardino, California) in the early 1970s.

But then, why should Dr. Sobell have doubts about her early research into controlled drinking? The work has received much professional praise and continues to be defended by other "Anti-Traditionalists." Consider what Dr. Marlatt wrote about the Sobell research in his recent *American Psychologist* article:

"Several years ago, in a review of a book by the Sobells describing their controlled-drinking study (Sobell and Sobell, 1978), I concluded that despite shortcomings in the research, 'the work of the Sobells will stand as an early landmark on the empirical road ahead' (Marlatt, 1979b, p. 21). Despite the attack on their findings by Pendery, Maltzman, and

West, my earlier opinion of their work remains unchanged. The land-mark still stands. Let's move on." (Marlatt, 1983, p. 1109)

The question here, of course, is, "move on to what?" Where would this group of "Anti-Traditionalists" like to take alcoholism services and research? The answers to this question are quite obvious and are apparent in numerous journal articles, editorials, commentaries, conference reports, and pieces in popular magazines. The "Anti-Traditionalist' lobby would like to see:

1. Widespread acceptance of controlled or "nonproblem" drinking goals,
2. Elimination of not only the disease concept of alcoholism, but of the very concept of alcoholism itself,
3. Radical cuts in the funding of biological research concerning such things as the genetics of alcoholism, neurochemistry of addiction, and search for biological interventions,
4. Increases in psychosocial research spending,
5. Enormous cuts in inpatient alcoholism treatment,
6. Rapid development of outpatient services at the expense of inpatient services,
7. Cuts in both public and private third-party payment for inpatient alcoholism treatment, and
8. Substitution of *brief* treatment (preferably in an outpatient setting) for intensive, longer term treatment in any setting.

Consider the recommendations of Dr. William Miller and Dr. Reid K. Hester. In an attack upon inpatient and residential models of care that appeared in a recent issue of the *American Psychologist*, these authors concluded:

"Given that the only clear, significant overall differences between residential and nonresidential programs is in the cost of treatment, it would seem prudent for public and private third-party payers to enact policy that de-emphasizes the hospitalization model of care where it is nonessential and encourages the use of less expensive but equally effective alternatives. A '3 R's' model of treatment (remove *from society,* repair *the problem, and* replace *in society) is outmoded and inadequate as a means for addressing alcohol problems." (American Psychologist, 1986, p. 803)*

The "Anti-Traditionalist" Lobby likes to think of itself as concerned above all else with "evidence," with science, data, and dispassionate search for the truth. Everybody else, i.e., "The Traditionalists," trades in uninformed opinion, dogma, myth, and ideology. Hence, Miller and Hester believe sufficient empirical, scientific "evidence" exists to support their radical public policy recommendations that would ensure the tearing down of the inpatient and residential alcoholism treatment systems of this country. Dr. Linda Sobell believes that the "evidence" is all in on controlled drinking and all that remains to be done is to change the service delivery system. Here is how she is quoted in *The Journal* of the Addiction Research Foundation of Toronto:

> "The scientific level of the debate is all but over. Alternative beneficial outcomes" [controlled drinking] "do occur and are being reported with ever-increasing frequency in the literature, even in the abstinence-oriented programs. What we're fighting for now is acceptance at the service delivery level and the opportunity to do the research to further advance this field." (Linda Sobell, 1984, p. 10)

Dr. Martha Sanchez Craig of the Addiction Research Foundation of Toronto believes that sufficient "evidence" exists to justify radical alterations of "traditional" methods of intervention. Presumably concerned with less severely alcohol-impaired persons, Dr. Sanchez Craig recommends the following in a recent editorial in the *British Journal of Addiction:*

> "A radical alternative to development of surreptitious methods of early identification is to provide treatment services that would appeal to persons with less severe problems and to rely upon them to *identify themselves.* If those presenting for treatment were willing volunteers rather than apprehended deniers, there might be better outcomes." (Sanchez Craig, 1986, p. 598)

Dr. Sanchez Craig goes on to describe treatment programs for these less-impaired troubled drinkers. Her programs would offer brief, outpatient counseling and choice of self-management training in either abstinence or reduced (non-problem) drinking. It is important to note that since Dr. Sanchez Craig believes that the "majority of persons with problems are at the lower end of the severity continuum," it is clear that her recommendations are aimed at the majority of *alcoholics.* I doubt, however, that she would agree, since she apparently does not accept the concept of alcoholism as such and, moreover, would direct her programs at "persons who have an alcohol problem but do not consider themselves 'alcoholic.'" (1986, p. 599)

Dr. Sanchez Craig's contempt for "traditionalist" views are readily apparent in her choice of language. Intervention is described as employing "surreptitious methods." Recognized alcoholics are referred to sarcastically as "apprehended deniers." The metaphors reek of deceit and criminality. One can only speculate as to how she really feels about alcoholics and those people who treat them.

But aside from Dr. Sanchez Craig's sarcasm, one has other objections. Implicit in her conceptions is the position that controlled drinking is preferred for the less severely impaired person, while abstinence is suitable for the severely impaired.

Dr. Peter Nathan (1985) is very clear that he now believes that abstinence is the treatment goal of choice for "chronic" alcoholics, despite his belief that "the two Rand Reports, then, lent strong support to the idea, the legitimacy, of controlled drinking treatment . . ." (p. 171). To Dr. Nathan, craving, loss of control, and, in fact, the disease concept are simply metaphors. In effect, according to him, alcoholics crave alcohol and lose control of their drinking because they:

" . . . believe that craving and loss of control are inevitable components of alcoholism, rather than simply the pharmacologic impact of alcohol. So, again, the realization grows that what we think and what we believe in and what we are convinced of is much more important in determining our own behavior than a narrow pharmacologic response. The *metaphorical sense* in which we now view the whole concept of craving and loss of control, in fact, the disease model of alcoholism, is justified by this history." (p. 171–172)

In effect, to Dr. Nathan, alcoholism is all in the mind and not in any "narrow pharmacologic response." The psychological ideology is quite clear in this biased and limited view of neuropsychopharmacology.

In my opinion, these positions that would reserve abstinence treatment goals only for the severely impaired or "chronic" alcoholic miss the point of over 50 years of progress in alcoholism studies. Must we wait until alcoholics have severe liver disease, cardiomyopathy, pancreatitis, severe brain damage, destroyed careers, and failed marriages before we urge them to stop drinking alcohol? Must we ignore an impressive body of animal and human research on genetic predispositions to alcoholism and support drinking among high-risk individuals? Must we stand by and wait for earlier-stage *alcoholics* to *choose* abstinence for themselves as they make messes of their own and other people's lives? Must we ignore the tragically high death and traumatic injury rates among *young alcoholics* in order to support and legitimate their decisions to keep drinking rather than to choose abstinence as a goal for themselves? Do the "Anti-Traditionalist" forces intend to stop with controlled alcohol intoxication, or do they wish to move on to other forms of psychoactive substance use? What of controlled marijuana or LSD use? Controlled PCP use? Controlled heroin use? Nonproblem crack use? Dr. Stanton Peele gives us more than a hint:

"What about drugs? Although prohibition of liquor failed in the U.S., we persist in Prohibition-style thinking about substances from heroin and cocaine to marijuana and barbiturates." (Peele, 1985, p. 39)

Is it possible that Dr. Peele would not mind a moderately "stoned" American population at all? Furthermore, is it possible that Dr. Peele finds something inherently wrong and unappealing about sober consciousness? Once again, consider his words:

"In my research on addiction (to a wide variety of substances and experiences), I find that the vast majority of people employ moderation most of the time . . ." "It almost doesn't matter what the substance or experience is. Alcohol. Cocaine. Heroin. Jogging. Sex. Tranquilizers. Food. In each case, moderate users keep the activity within bounds. Believe it or not, this is true even for heroin users . . ." (Peele, 1985, p. 36)

Notice how Dr. Peele's list lulls us into easy accpetance. Alcohol, cocaine, heroin, jogging, sex, tranquilizers, food. How harmless heroin appears in a list containing a wholesome activity such as jogging. Tranquilizers are neatly sandwiched between sex and food. Snorting cocaine or tossing down a couple of "quick ones" is somehow equated with running three miles a day. How wholesome the moderate daily use of Valium begins to appear.

Underlying all of this is an implicit message . . . why not join this "vast majority of people who employ moderation most of the time?" What harm could there possibly be in moderately snorting cocaine, smoking marijuana, taking tranquilizers, shooting heroin, downing barbiturates, and so forth, since the "vast majority" of people who are already doing these things are managing to "keep the activity within bounds." What a devastating message for impressionable adolescents and young adults, whose standards and behavior concerning drugs and alcohol are dervied largely from conformity, imitation, and other forms of social learning.

There are many ironies apparent in this continuing skirmish between the "Anti-Traditionalist" lobby and the alcoholism movement in America. Perhaps the most striking irony is that the thought of the "Anti-Traditionalist" lobby is sadly outmoded and not nearly as radical or innovative as it would like us to believe. For example, given the remarkable advances in the past decade alone in neurobiology, psychopharmacology, neurochemistry, and the behavioral genetics of the addictions, it staggers the scientific imagination that anybody would continue to insist that there is a lack of evidence for biological factors in addiction to alcohol and drugs of all kinds.

A second irony concerns the apparent willingness of the "Anti-Traditionalist" lobby to champion particular pieces of research that happen to fit their ideology regardless of scientific rigor, adequacy, or ambiguity. Witness how long it took for many of this camp to concede that there were problems with the 1976 Rand Corporation study of treatment outcome. In fact, many "Anti-Traditionalists" continue to cite this methodologically shoddy study as an illustration of how "science" ran smack up against the entrenched ideology of "traditionalists" in the alcoholism field. Other studies that would not pass muster in an undergraduate course on experimental design are heralded as "landmarks" and as methodologically sophisticated. Even the most casual reading of the literature of this group readily informs one that, despite their "scientific" huffing and puffing, the "Anti-Traditionalists" are neither short on ideology nor long on scientific rigor.

Finally, the "Anti-Traditionalist" lobby, in my opinion, seems determined to recreate the past in the sense that many of their proposals would return alcoholism services to where they were 40 or 50 years ago. It seems to me that if this group had its way, we would have the following undesirable outcomes:

1. We would go back to advising most alcoholics to try to cut down on their drinking and drug use rather than urging them to stay sober and clean,
2. Psychological views of etiology and treatment would prevail,
3. Patients would not be informed as to the biological basis of their disease. In fact, patients wouldn't be told they had a disease at all,
4. Inpatient and residential services would largely disappear,
5. Early intervention with alcholics would grind to a halt and, instead, we would wait for alcoholics to identify themselves,
6. Insurance coverage (private and public) for anything but brief outpatient treatment and minimal detoxification stays in hospitals would dry up,
7. Alcoholism services would again resemble revolving door detoxes,
8. The moral concept of alcoholism would return with a vengeance, as would centuries of stigma, and
9. Many more alcoholics would destroy themselves and their families.

Obviously, it is in the interests of alcoholism counselors to pay greater attention to the politics of alcoholism and appreciate the inroads the "Anti-Traditionalist" lobby already has made into universities, research centers, academic journals, and large government agencies. Given their present positions in teaching institutions, on editorial boards of influential journals, and on peer review committees of agencies that fund research, many are in a position to determine who gets degrees in alcohol studies, who and what ideas get published, and who receives a research grant. In time, perhaps, they also could be in a position to determine who gets credentialed or licensed to treat alcoholics, and how alcoholics will be treated.

For the health of our patients and the viability of our emerging comprehensive system of alcoholism research, prevention, and treatment services, we must stand together in common cause and insure that this does not happen.

References

Craig, M.S. The Hitchhiker's Guide to Alcohol Treatment. *British Journal of Addiction,* 1986, 82, 597–600.

Heather, N. Abstinence and controlled drinking: Alternative goals for alcoholism and problem drinking? *Bulletin of the Society of Psychologists in Addictive Behavior,* 1985, 4, 123–150.

Marlatt, G.A. The controlled-drinking controversy: A commentary. *American Psychologist,* October 1983, 1098–1109.

Miller, W.R. and Hester, R.K. Inpatient alcoholism treatment: Who benefits? *American Psychologist,* July 1986, 794–805.

Nathan, P. Alcoholism: A cognitive social learning approach. *Journal of Substance Abuse Treatment,* Vol. 2, No. 3, 1985, 169–173.

Peele, S. Change without pain. *American Health,* January/February 1985, 36–39.

Pendery, M.L., Maltzman, I.M., and West, L.J. Controlled drinking by alcoholics? New findings and a re-evaluation of a major affirmative study. *Science,* 1982, 217, 169–174.

Sobell, L. *The Behaviorists.* As quoted in *The Journal* of the Addiction Research Foundation of Toronto. 1984, February 1, 13, No. 2.

The Attack Upon The Disease Model

In Part I of this series (January/February) I described an aggressive lobby and called attention to its agenda for alcoholism intervention, treatment, and research. Opposed to many important accepted ideas about alcoholism and chemical dependency, members of this group propagandize in favor of its "Anti-Traditionalist" perspective.

The basic elements of the ideology of this group are as follows: alcoholism is not a disease but merely a pattern of learned behavior; not only can alcoholism be arrested but often cured; total abstinence from alcohol and all illicit or unauthorized psychoactive substances is not necessary for recovery to be achieved and maintained.

In denouncing the disease model and the need for abstention, the "Anti-Traditionalist" Lobby prides itself on its insistence upon "scientific evidence." According to the lobby's leading figures, "solid scientific evidence" exists to buttress their case against the disease model of alcoholism and chemical dependency, and also against abstention. What is the nature of this "evidence," and does it really show what the "Anti-Traditionalist" Lobby claims it shows?

Consider the following quote from a recent article in the *American Psychologist* by Dr. Alan Marlatt:

> "Over two decades ago, (D.L.) Davies sent shock waves through the alcoholism field by publishing the results of a longterm follow-up of patients treated for alcoholism at the Maudsley Hospital in London. In his report, Davies (1962) challenged the traditional emphasis on total abstinence as the only viable 'cure' for alcoholism by showing that of 93 male alcoholics who were followed up for a period of from 7 to 11 years following treatment, seven reported a pattern of normal drinking." (Marlatt, 1983, p. 1097)

The study cited by Marlatt was the so-called classic in the alcoholism field conducted by British physician and researcher, Dr. D.L. Davies.

While the study did indeed generate a great deal of controversy, and while its putative "findings" did fit the ideological biases and prejudices of anti-traditionalists like Dr. Marlatt, can these numbers be trusted? Did D.L. Davies actually *show*, as Marlatt strongly implies, that seven of 93 nonrandomly selected alcoholics did indeed modulate out of their destructive drinking to stable patterns of "normal" drinking? Let's consider the "evidence" a bit more carefully.

In 1985, Dr. Griffith Edwards published an important footnote to Davies' "classic" study. Dr. Edwards conducted a further follow-up of the patients originally followed by Dr. Davies. Of the seven men whom Davies had categorized as "normal" drinkers, five were discovered by Edwards to have resumed destructive drinking patterns. Three of these five destructive drinkers apparently were drinking "non-normally" even during the original follow-up by Davies. One of the seven men eventually experienced Wernicke-Korsakoff syndrome (brain damage) as a result of continued heavy drinking, one was hospitalized with peptic ulcer, and another experienced liver enlargement as a result of heavy drinking. Three of the seven men also used large amounts of psychoactive drugs in addition to drinking heavily.

In effect, only two of the entire sample of 93 seemed to be drinking in a non-problematic fashion at both the initial and subsequent follow-ups. Of these two "nonproblem" drinkers, one had never been anything more than "slightly dependent" on alcohol. Hence, of 93 nonrandomly selected cases, only one appeared to meet criteria for a diagnosis of alcohol dependence prior to Davies' initial follow-up and then could be said to have engaged in "normal drinking" throughout the subsequent follow-up period reviewed by Edwards. These results are vastly different from the results as represented by Dr. Marlatt in his 1983 *American Psychologist* article. Marlatt may indeed *believe* that D.L. Davies showed that seven of 93 men with drinking problems were able to modulate these problems into stable patterns of "normal" drinking; but this is not what subsequent *data* have shown. Hence, the "evidence" here is on the side of the traditionalists and the traditional disease model of alcoholism.

While the Davies study set the stage for aggressive development of the controlled drinking issue by the "Anti-Traditionalist" Lobby, it remained for psychologists Drs. Mark and Linda Sobell to attempt to provide the "convincing" experimental proof that alcoholics could actually be taught controlled drinking skills and that these controlled drinking skills would work outside the hospital environment. Numerous arguments have been raised both pro and con the Sobell study, but the most important questions to be raised of the Sobells' data are as follows:

Did the Sobells show that hospitalized gamma alcoholics could sustain patterns of controlled drinking over time?

Can the Sobell data be used to legitimate and justify substitution of controlled drinking goals for the traditional abstinence goal in the treatment of hospitalized *gamma* alcoholics?

Do the Sobell data require us to question the traditional disease concept of alcoholism?

To any disinterested observer, the answers to these critical questions are quite obvious: no, no, and no. No, the Sobells did not show that sustained controlled drinking was possible for hospitalized *gamma* alcoholics taught controlled drinking skills. The vast majority of their patients apparently returned to problem drinking, many immediately upon release from the hospital (Pendery, Maltzman, and West, 1981). No, the Sobell data cannot be used to legitimate and justify the substitution of controlled drinking goals for the traditional disease model goal of complete abstention. Even Dr. Peter Nathan, the director of the Rutgers Center of Studies on Alcohol and a long-time supporter of controlled drinking researchers (the Sobells in particular), now concedes that there are problems with the controlled drinking data and with the Sobell data in particular. Referring to the Sobell study, Dr. Nathan recently stated:

> "That study, I think, was an anomaly. While there are a variety of reasons to question the data, none of them involves fraud. I know the Sobells. I know their data. They did not commit fraud, as has been claimed. However, these data are an anomaly. No one else has reported data of this kind and, therefore, I believe that the Sobells' data and those of others whose studies were marginally encouraging to this view were simply, for a variety of reasons, given far more credence than turns out to have been justified on any scientific basis." (Nathan, 1985, p. 172)

But why was the Sobell research given "far more credence than turns out to have been justified on any scientific basis?" And why are the Sobell data "an anomaly" with nobody else reporting "data of this kind?" What is it about their data that persuades Dr. Nathan that the Sobells did not commit fraud?

While I suppose we are to be grateful for Dr. Nathan's concession that the Sobell study wasn't so wonderful after all, one wonders why it took him so long to realize this. Six years ago, at the Fourth Annual Coatesvile V.A.-Jefferson University Conference on Addiction Research and Treatment, I told not only Dr. Nathan but the entire conference that serious problems with the Sobell research on controlled drinking had been uncovered. I further informed the conference participants that a California team headed by Dr. Mary Pendery and including Dr. Irving Maltzman and Dr. L.J. West had failed to find evidence of sustained controlled drinking among the patients treated by the Sobells. Dr. Nathan's response to this apparently unwelcome information was to get angry.

In short, Dr. Nathan's belated admission, in effect, that the "traditional disease concept theorists" were right all along when they began to question the scientific merits of the Sobell study more than a decade ago raises more questions than it answers. Perhaps what Dr. Nathan might have said is simply that the "Anti-Traditionalists" gave "far more credence than turns out to have been justified on any scientific basis" to the Sobell data *because they wanted these data to be true.* Hostile to Alcoholics Anonymous, contemptuous of any and all established beliefs about alcoholism, and eager to disprove the disease model, the "Anti-Traditionalists," in my opinion, grabbed at any data that would support their ideology, prejudices, and biases regardless of scientific adequacy. The widespread and seemingly uncritical acceptance of the Sobell data by the behavioral science community raises very serious question about the sociology of knowledge and the ability of the social and behavioral science research enterprise in alcoholism to self-correct. This entire affair will surely come to occupy the attention of scholars who labor at the interface between politics and reliable knowledge.

Obviously, the Sobell data cannot be used to legitimate and justify controlled or nonproblem drinking treatment goals for hospitalized *gamma* alcoholics. To argue that these data support the abandonment of abstinence as a treatment goal for alcoholics is equivalent to urging widespread adoption of laetrile in the treatment of cancer or psychic surgery in organ removal.

Finally, it should be obvious that the Sobell data in no way compromise the disease model of alcoholism. Aside from the fact that studies of treatment outcome are not proper tests of theoretical models of etiology, there is the further objection that the Sobells actually demonstrated very little in this study that Dr. Marlatt heralds as a "landmark" study.

As the data gathered by Pendery, Maltzman, and West (1981) strongly suggest, the Sobells in this particular study not only did not know how to produce sustained controlled drinking, but they apparently did not know how to produce sustained *abstinence* either. By any reasonable criteria, the vast majority of the Sobells' patients relapsed whether they had been given controlled drinking treatment or abstinence treatment. In short, these investigators were *equally ineffective* in their attempts to produce either sober alcoholics or alcoholics capable of sustained controlled drinking over time. The Sobell study, then, taught us very little about how to do alcoholism treatment. It did, however, teach us a great deal about the belief systems, ideology, and prejudices of the behavioral science community, and the manner in which these beliefs, ideological persuasions, and prejudices enter into "scientific" constructions of reality. Consider the constructions of reality of Dr. Stanton Peele:

> "It is this last issue—the question of absolute abstinence as a necessary step in eliminating alcoholism or addiction—that is a major threat to academic freedom, even freedom of speech, in the U.S. today. If I may backtrack briefly, a concern with alcoholism developed in America in the nineteenth century. Embodied by the temperance movement and eventually national prohibition, it achieved ferocious proportions. This folk movement was religious in its form and social roots; it emphasized the inherent evil of drinking and the requirement that people expunge the devil liquor entirely from their lives as a sign of salvation and spiritual redemption. This devil theory of alcohol was transposed in the twentieth century into the idea that it is only the alcoholic who need abstain, an idea that eventually became a medical and disease theory truism." (Peele, February 4, 1986, p. 2)

Dr. Peele's broadbush approach to historical events, sequences, and causal antecedents certainly does give pause. But would this sort of thing stand up to careful scrutiny by competent historians or serious students of the disease concept of alcoholism? Is Dr. Peele presenting us with defensible historical analysis, or are we being asked to take on faith what may be little more than ideologically inspired armchair ruminations on the origins of the modern scientific study of the biological basis of alcoholism? Who, for example, was responsible for "transposing" the "devil theory of alcohol" into the idea that it is only the alcoholic who need abstain? When did this happen, and how did it happen? Are there documents available that would lead competent historians to agree that Peele has given us a defensible analysis of the historical antecedents of the modern study of the chemistry of the brain and of behavioral genetics? I doubt it.

While ideological wishes of the "Anti-Traditionalists" may have led them to throw caution to the winds in uncritically accepting the Sobell research on controlled drinking, many seemed to have lost all scientific perspective in their eagerness to embrace the "findings" of the Rand Corporation's study of treatment outcome. The qualities we normally expect in scientific research appraisal—skepticism, tough-minded insistence upon methodological rigor, precise attention to detail—were absent in this curious affair. When the 1976 Rand Corporation study's "findings" that nearly a quarter of the alcoholics studied in NIAAA-funded treatment centers were drinking "normally" hit the front pages of the *New York Times*, a storm of protest followed. Critics of the Rand Corporation study were dismissed as "ideologically inspired traditionalists." Ron Roizen of Berkeley took the occasion to lecture alcoholism treatment professionals on their "abstinence fixation." Dr. Morris Chafetz, in an article under his own byline that appeared in the *Rochester Democrat and Chronicle* (August 15, 1976), had this to say about the Rand Report: "To the many devoted workers in the field of alcoholism who are themselves recovered alcoholics, it is upsetting to learn that the abstinence to which they adhere may not be necessary." Dr. Chafetz added the astonishing statements that "the Rand Report should make those interested in the plight of alcoholic people jump for joy" and that "opponents of the report have little respect for alcoholic people."

Dr. Peter Nathan of Rutgers University recently stated that "the two Rand Reports, then, lent strong support to the idea, the legitimacy, of controlled drinking treatment . . ." (1985, p. 171)

But how could the two Rand Reports lend strong support to the idea, the legitimacy, of controlled drinking when the first Rand Report (1976) was so methodologically inadequate that *nothing* could be concluded from it (Wallace, 1977), and the second Rand Report (1981) failed to provide much evidence at all for *sustained* "nonproblem" drinking. The 1976 Rand Report was seriously marred by an enormous "lost to follow-up" rate, sample bias on outcome, unreliable and invalid measurements of quantity and frequency of consumption, loss of entire treatment centers from the original sample of centers, shoddy data-gathering procedures by treatment staffs, and a follow-up window of such short duration (30 days of drinking behavior) that it was an embarrassment (Wallace, 1979). If anything, the first Rand Report lent "strong support to the idea" that poor research data and methods invariably lead to wrong conclusions.

The second Rand Report (1981) was methodologically superior to the 1976 report. However, when the results are examined for sustained nonproblem drinking over time and are corrected for invalid measurement of quantity/frequency, the best estimate of the sustained nonproblem drinking rate is around 3–4 percent. In short, at least 96 percent of the second Rand Report subjects failed to give evidence of *sustained* nonproblem drinking over the four-year follow-up period.

Considering the scientific inadequacies of the first Rand Report and the actual data from the second Rand Report, it is difficult to believe that anybody with even a modicum of training in research methodology and interpretation would describe these reports as providing "strong support to the idea, the legitimacy of controlled drinking treatment."

The only way that the "Anti-Traditionalists" can get support for their ideas about controlled drinking from the Rand Reports is to ignore a tangled web of scientific inadequacies, or to try to interpret the findings in a highly questionably manner. For example, Dr. Marlatt claims the following about the second Rand Report:

> "Approximately 18% of the patients were reported to be drinking without problems or symptoms of dependence, and less than 10% were able to maintain total abstinence during the four-year period following initial treatment." (Marlatt, 1983, p. 1101)

Marlatt's comparison here that claims a supposed superiority in favor of nonproblem drinking over abstinence is, in my opinion, so dangerously misleading as to raise questions about the care with which certain "Anti-Traditionalists" read research. What is wrong with Dr. Marlatt's comparison between success at nonproblem drinking versus staying sober? Plenty. First of all, he fails to inform the reader that the rates are for vastly differing time periods. The nonproblem drinking rate of 18 percent was based upon drinking behavior during a time interval that varied from one to six months (last drinking episode before the follow-up interview). On the other hand, Dr. Marlatt gives us the four-year sustained abstention rate of 10 percent! The comparison is obviously scientifically absurd.

Aside from failing to inform the reader of these vastly differing time frames being compared, Dr. Marlatt also fails to point out that the Rand authors found a 25 percent underreporting of consumption rate in their subjects. (Polich, Armor, and Braiker, 1981, p. 245)

As the Rand authors showed, a conservative correction of their data results in a reduction of the short-term nonproblem drinking rate from 18 percent to 14 percent. Applying the same corrections to the *sustained long-term* nonproblem drinking rate yields an estimate of only 3–4 percent. Hence, at least 96 percent of the Rand subjects did not achieve sustained nonproblem drinking over the four-year follow-up period. This is hardly an advertisement for the success of controlled drinking in alcoholics.

There are of course, other studies that have reported remissions of some type or another in alcoholics. Pattison, Sobell, and Sobell (1977), for example, have alluded to a substantial body of evidence comprising 74 "scientific studies." In a later book by Sobell and Sobell (1978), six additional studies were added to the original list of 74.

When this body of putative evidence in favor of controlled drinking is examined, one is impressed not only by the astonishingly wide variation in reported outcomes, but by the equally wide variation in scientific rigor, comprehensiveness, and methodological sophistication. Of these "scientific studies," several are anecdotal; two are case studies; one is a newspaper report from the *Los Angeles Times;* several refer to Japanese interest, now over a decade ago, in the chemical cyanamide; some are survey research studies of questionable methodological adequacy; a number are either unpublished dissertations or papers presented at conferences; many are outcome studies characterized by common methodological problems ubiquitous to outcome research in alcoholism; and five are papers that refer to work conducted by Pattison, Sobell, and Sobell themselves.

While there are studies in this collection that require serious attention, it would be misleading for anyone to advertise the entire collection as constituting "strong" scientific evidence in favor of controlled drinking as a viable treatment goal. Moreover, it is statistically meaningless to "average" the results of this uneven collection, and misleading to promulgate this average as a reliable estimate of a population value (1978).

Even Dr. Nathan concedes that this collection of studies bearing on controlled drinking is unimpressive:

> "When you look carefully at the series of studies on which the presumed efficacy of controlled drinking treatment was based, you quickly come to realize that only one study, the very well-known study by Mark and Linda Sobell (1973, 1976), yielded positive data. While there were other studies which, when viewed through the microscope of the statistician, yielded data encouraging to advocates of controlled drinking treatment, basically only the Sobell study yielded data that strongly encouraged the view that controlled drinking treatment could work." (Nathan, 1985, p. 172)

For advocates of controlled, nonproblem, reduced, social, or normal drinking goals for alcoholics, the belief that their position is based upon solid scientific evidence is, in my opinion, not only indefensible, but probably delusional as well. And especially so since recent research continues to pile up in defense of the traditional goal of abstention and the traditional disease concept of alcoholism. Helzer et al (1985), for example, followed 1,289 diagnosed alcoholics over a five- to seven-year period. Only 1.6 percent appeared able to meet criteria for "moderate drinking." More than 98 percent of the males in the Helzer study were unable to sustain moderate drinking patterns when moderate was defined most liberally as up to six drinks per day.

Foy et al (1984) studied 62 alcoholics who received broad spectrum behavioral treatment for alcoholism. The results were generally very disappointing, but even more so for those patients given training in controlled drinking skills. The subgroup of 30 who received training in controlled drinking skills had significantly fewer abstinent days and more abusive drinking days at six months' follow-up than the 32 patients not given such training.

Pettinati et al (1982) studied the functioning of 61 alcoholics before treatment and at four years after treatment. Psychological functioning (as pro-abstinence treatment professionals have always maintained) was most improved in those who were able to maintain consistent and complete abstinence. Moreover, only two patients were able to sustain nonproblem drinking over the entire follow-up period. Considering the likelihood of errors in diagnosis in this population, a 3 percent nonproblem drinking rate is of *no* theoretical or practical significance.

In general, then, the claims of the "Anti-Traditionalists" are not borne out by the data. In fact, the data indicate that the controlled drinking issue is not a controversy at all but a *pseudo* controversy. In the absence of data supporting the controlled drinking position, the issue is controversial only in the sense that cod liver oil would be "controversial" in the treatment of smallpox. Controlled drinking is controversial in the sense that Vitamin C would be "controversial" in the treatment of syphilis or copper bracelets in the treatment of arthritis. Obviously, competent medical authorites do not regard cod liver oil, Vitamin C, and copper bracelets as reasonable treatments for these diseases. For a physician to advocate these treatments openly would be to invite professional censure and, ultimately, revocation of rights to practice medicine.

With regard to the controlled drinking issue, I feel that the alcoholism field has too long suffered these outrageous attacks by certain members of the "Anti-Traditionalist" crowd. In the interests of our patients and their families, and in the interests of alcoholics who still suffer, we must begin to scrutinize more closely the activities of this group and to take steps to ensure they do no harm.

Academic freedom is a privilege that carries with it enormous responsibilities. Academic freedom is not license. Surely, free speech must be tempered by responsibility, fair representations of reality, scientific objectivity, and respect for current standards of knowledge and practice within disciplines. And when thousands of lives and so much human tragedy is at stake, as they are in alcoholism and chemical dependence, then we must demand that the right to freely express our opinions be tempered by reasonable caution, healthy skepticism, fairness, and attention to scientific method and data. We must not forget that it is the duty of members of the various professions to defend the public against quackery.

But while the "Anti-Traditionalists" are quick to regard the controlled drinking issue as a special case of academic freedom and free speech, it is ironic to note the efforts some members of this group have made to silence opposition to their views.

Consider the actions taken against Dr. Irving Maltzman, the former chairman of the Department of Psychology at UCLA. A distinguished scientist, Dr. Maltzman coauthored the classic paper with Dr. Mary Pendery and Dr. L.J. West that appeared in *Science* (1981) and refuted the Sobell research on controlled drinking. For more than a decade, Dr. Maltzman has pursued the truth about the Sobell research with remarkable tenacity. Along the way, he has been sued by the Sobells in California state court, has been brought before the "Ethics Committee" of the American Psychological Association because of his public statements that it is his belief that the Sobells committed scientific fraud, and has endured various efforts to discredit him in the profession of psychology, in his own department at UCLA, and in the alcoholism field.

None of these efforts by various "Anti-Traditionalists" succeeded. The lawsuit brought against Dr. Maltzman by the Sobells was designed to stop him from gaining the identities of the Sobells' former patients. As a result, he would not be able to locate and interview them. That lawsuit was dismissed. The charges of unethical conduct against Maltzman were not upheld by the American Psychological Association's Ethics Committee. The committee concluded from its hearing on the matter on June 17, 1983, that, with regard to his belief that the Sobells had committed scientific fraud, Maltzman had a "plausible basis" for his "personal conclusion that fraud was involved in the research in question." It should be noted that the committee did not say that they agreed that fraud had been committed. They decided that Dr. Maltzman had provided sufficient evidence from his perspective to provide a plausible basis for his personal conclusion.

But, while Dr. Maltzman's earlier censure by the Ethics Committee of the American Psychological Association was rescinded on June 17, 1983, attempts to discredit him have continued. Letters and other communications attempting to discredit Maltzman have been sent to his department chairman at UCLA and also to the American Psychological Association's Study of Threats to Academic Freedom by Stanton Peele (Peele, 1986). He has been criticized unfairly in a book having nothing to do with the subject of alcoholism (Kohn, 1986) and has endured other threats to his academic freedom, freedom of speech, and personal integrity.

In a letter to Dr. David H. Mills, the administrative officer for ethics of the American Psychological Association, Maltzman has revealed his motivations and tenacity of purpose:

> "I am most sensitive to community needs and the community trust in psychology. I try, by example, to demonstrate to the community that when one of our colleagues has allegedly engaged in scientific fraud, we will have the interest of the community at heart. Despite personal abuse,

lawsuits, and harassment by the Sobells, Caddy, and their supporters, I have persisted in promoting the truth and the well-being of the public at all times." (Maltzman, May 29, 1985)

But what was Dr. Irving Maltzman's "crime" that brought so much unpleasantness into his life? I believe it was simply that he had the courage to stand up and say that he disagreed with the current prejudices, biases, and scientifically unsupported ideology of the "Anti-Traditionalist" Lobby with regard to the controlled drinking issue.

But aside from these attacks on a single individual, what can we say about the success of the "Anti-Traditionalists'" larger war on the disease model of alcoholism and the traditional goal of abstinence from alcohol and all illicit and unauthorized psychoactive substances?

In my opinion, the "Anti-Traditionalists" have lost and lost big. Not only have they failed to refute abstinence from drugs and alcohol as a treatment goal, their attack upon the disease model is clearly faltering before an avalanche of studies on the biological bases of alcoholism and other chemical dependencies (Wallace, 1983, 1985). Even as Dr. Marlatt was protesting that there is no evidence on the biological basis of alcoholism, more than a thousand studies had already been conducted on such important topics as the genetics of alcoholism, the relationships of the chemistry of the brain to drug addictions of all kinds, membrane biochemistry, biologic risk factors, and so forth.

Unfortunately, however, as studies of such ideologically motivated groups as the "Anti-Traditionalists" show, these groups do not alter their rigid ideologies in the face of disconfirming scientific evidence. Typically, such groups demand even greater adherence by their members to rigid doctrines, attempt to protect their sacred cows, rationalize or otherwise distort contradictory observations, and try to discredit opposing voices.

I believe that a fair, impartial, and disinterested scientific/political analysis of the past two decades in the alcoholism field will reveal that the "Anti-Traditionalists" have done all these things. Moreover, I believe that such an analysis also will reveal that the "Anti-Traditionalists" are guilty of many of the ideologically motivated "sins" of which they have accused the alcoholism movement in America.

REFERENCES

Armor, D.J., Polich, J.M. and Stambul, H.B. *Alcoholism and Treatment.* Santa Monica. The Rand Corporation. R-1739-NIAAA, 1976.

Chafetz, M.E. "Alcoholism Report Draws Overreaction," *Rochester Democrat and Chronicle,* Sunday, August 15, 1976.

Davies, D.L. Normal drinking in recovered alcohol addicts. *Quarterly Journal of Studies on Alcohol,* 23, 1962, pp. 94–104.

Edwards, G. A later follow-up of a classic case series: D.L. Davies' 1962 report and its significance for the present. *Journal of Studies on Alcohol,* Vol. 46, No. 3, 1985, pp. 181–190.

Helzer, J.E., Robins. L.N. et al. The extent of long-term moderate drinking among alcoholics discharged from medical and psychiatric treatment facilities. *New England Journal of Medicine,* June 27, 1985, pp. 1678–1682.

Kohn A. *False Prophets,* Basil Blackwell, 1986, pp. 127–129.

Maltzman, I. Letter to David H. Mills, Ph.D., Administrative Officer for Ethics, American Psychological Association, May 29, 1985.

Marlatt, G.A. The controlled drinking controversy: A Commentary. *American Psychologist,* October 1983, pp. 1098–1110.

Mills, David H. Letter to Irving Maltzman, Ph.D., Professor, Department of Psychology, UCLA, June 17, 1983.

Nathan, P.E. Alcoholism: A cognitive social learning approach. *Journal of Substance Abuse Treatment,* Vol. 2, 1985, pp. 169–173.

Pattison, E.M., Sobell, M.B., and Sobell, L.C. *Emerging Concepts of Alcohol Dependence,* New York: Springer, 1977.

Peele, S. Letter to Seymour Feshbach, Ph.D., Professor and Chairman of the Department of Psychology, UCLA, February 4, 1986.

Peele, S. Letter to Michele Fine, Ph.D., SPSSI Study of Threats to Academic Freedom, Graduate School of Education, University of Pennsylvania, undated.

Pendery, M.L., Maltzman, I.M., and West, L.J. Controlled drinking by alcoholics? New findings and a reevaluation of a major affirmative study. *Science,* 1983, 217, 169–174.

Pettinati, H., Sugerman, A., et al. The natural history of alcoholism over four years after treatment. *Journal of Studies on Alcohol,* 1982, Vol. 43, 201–215.

Polich, J.M., Armor, D.J., and Braiker, H.B. *The Course of Alcoholism: Four Years After Treatment.* New York: John Wiley, 1981.

Sobell, M.D. and Sobell, L.C. *Behavioral Treatment of Alcohol Problems: Individual Therapy and Controlled Drinking.* New York: Plenum, 1978.

Sobell, M.B. and Sobell, L.C. Individual behavior therapy for alcoholics. *Behavioral Therapy,* 1973, 49–72.

Wallace, J. Alcoholism: Is a shift in paradigm necessary? *Journal of Psychiatric Treatment and Evaluation,* Vol. 5, No. 6, 1983, 479–485.

Wallace, J. Alcoholism and Treatment: A critical analysis. ALFAWAP Journal. Vol. 1, No. 2, 1978.

Wallace, J. Alcoholism and Treatment Revisited. *World Alcohol Project,* 1979, 3–18.

Wallace, J. *Alcoholism: New Light on the Disease.* Newport, RI: Edgehill Publications, 1985.

Wallace, J. The politicalization of alcoholism. I: The Attack of the "Anti-Traditionalist" Lobby. PROFESSIONAL COUNSELOR Magazine, January 1987.

The Forces Of Disunity

Among the qualities that have characterized the alcoholism movement in America and accounted for its spectacular achievements, none are as important as those bearing upon unity. Common welfare, common cause, common purpose—these are the wellsprings from which the dedication, commitment, and personal sacrifice of many have flowed. The greats of Alcoholics Anonymous, Bill W. and Dr. Bob, knew instinctively that the major threats to recovery would not come from the lure of the bottle alone, but also from the forces of disunity either within ourselves or without. As the first tradition of Alcoholics Anonymous makes clear: "Our common welfare should come first; personal recovery depends upon AA unity."

But it was not only in AA that the need for unity was recognized as the lifeblood of the alcoholism movement. Faced with prejudice, ignorance, indifference, and stigma in both lay and professional communities, dedicated alcoholism workers knew instinctively that they had to have solidarity if they were to get anywhere. Alcoholism services would not automatically come into being. They would have to fight for them at all levels of government—in local communities, counties and states. And they could not look to organized religion, psychology, medicine, or psychiatry for help since these forces were more often against them rather than sympathetic to their cause. After all, if drinking is a sin, why build hospitals to treat sinners? Or, if drinking is nothing more than learned behavior, why hold insurance companies responsible for providing benefits and third-party reimbursement? Or, if drinking is simply a symptom of an underlying psychiatric disorder, why worry about the need for specialized alcoholism facilities when there are plenty of mental health clinics and psychiatric hospitals already available?

Fortunately, there were men and women in the alcoholism movement with both vision and dedication who understood that adequate services for alcoholics would not come from churches or from the departments of psychology and psychiatry in our colleges and universities. Schools of Social Work would not build halfway houses. The American Psychiatric Association would not invest money in the construction of freestanding alcoholism facilities. And the American Psychological Association would not lobby on behalf of services for homeless alcoholics.

But people like Senator Harold Hughes, R. Brinkley Smithers, Chester H. Kirk, Marty Mann, Thomas Pike, and many others were willing to give of their time, energies, personal resources, and, indeed, their very lives to ensure that a comprehensive system of alcoholism services would be built to meet the needs of suffering alcoholics and their families. These men and women of great vision and dedication labored at all levels of government and within the private sector to build a halfway house here, a freestanding inpatient facility there, or an outpatient clinic where there was need. At the Federal level, Senator Harold Hughes provided the spiritual and political leadership necessary to ensure the development of a comprehensive system of alcoholism services. In many states, legislative battles followed. Where it had been a hopeless task to try to get an alcoholic into a hospital, or impossible to pay for his care if he were fortunate enough to be admitted, the passage of mandated insurance coverage laws in some states made it possible for many thousands of desperately ill people and their families to receive care.

But while the alcoholism movement in America has achieved much, we must realize that we cannot rest on our laurels. Sadly, all that has been achieved over the past decade alone could be destroyed rapidly, since forces are at work to undo much of what has been accomplished.

These forces of disunity tried first to divide the alcoholism field over the issue of controlled drinking, and then through various attacks upon sobriety, on the disease model of alcoholism, on recovered people, and on the concepts, principles, and activities of Alcoholics Anonymous. Now it appears that the target has become the still-emerging and fragile comprehensive system of alcoholism treatment services. Considering the enormous struggle that many dedicated alcoholism workers have recently gone through (and, in fact, are still going through) to achieve adequate insurance coverage for alcoholism treatment, it is very difficult to comprehend the motivations behind the recent attack by Dr. William Miller and Dr. Reid Hester upon inpatient alcoholism treatment services. Psychologists with obvious interests in both controlled drinking and outpatient treatment,

Miller and Hester have argued their case in the *American Psychologist* as follows:

> "Given that the only clear significant overall difference between residential and nonresidential alcoholism programs is in the cost of the treatment, it would seem prudent for public and private third-party payers to enact policy that deemphasizes the hospitalization model of care where it is nonessential and encourages the use of less expensive but equally effective alternatives. A '3 R's' model of treatment (*remove* from society, *repair* the problem, and *replace* in society) is outmoded and inadequate as a means for addressing alcohol problems." (Miller and Hester, 1986, p. 803)

I doubt that the staffs of Hazelden, the Betty Ford Center, St. Mary's Hospital, or the many other fine inpatient and residential programs that treat or otherwise provide for the desperately ill people that alcoholics actually are, would agree that their programs are "outmoded and inadequate as a means for addressing alcohol problems."

Moreover, I am certain that the many thousands of dedicated alcoholism treatment providers who work in such contexts will not be pleased to have their efforts on behalf of suffering alcoholics described in these negative, insensitive, and thoughtless terms.

Aside from the issue of the scientific merits of their case against inpatient and residential treatment of alcoholics, it does seem odd that Miller and Hester would appear so eager to take a position that suits the interests of the multi-billion-dollar insurance industry that historically has sought any justification for not paying for alcoholism services. One should think that two psychologists with both professional and financial interests in a string of outpatient clinics in New Mexico would be nervous about calling for an end to third-party reimbursement for *any* alcoholism treatment service lest the axe fall on their heads as well. Once again, it is important to remember that third-party reimbursement for alcoholism services was achieved through unity and not by one group of entrepreneurs seeking personal advantages at the expense of another.

But aside from the possibility that Miller and Hester's radical public policy recommendations seem both politically naive and alarming, is it also possible that their conclusions are scientifically premature? Can we argue with their evidence, or is their case against inpatient and residential care so airtight that nothing remains to be done at Hazelden and other centers except to send all the patients home and lock the doors? I believe there are very serious problems with Miller and Hester's evidence despite the fact that they believe that numerous studies support their case.

Typical of their "evidence" is the so-called "classic" study of "advice versus treatment." This study, conducted by British researchers Dr. Griffith Edwards and Dr. James Orford, has been accepted uncritically and widely cited by virtually every behaviorally oriented psychologist and social scientist writing about treatment. Drs. Edwards, Orford, and their colleagues (Edwards, et al. 1977; Orford, et al. 1976) took a group of employed, married, professional and managerial-level alcoholics and gave half of them intensive treatment while the other half received a single, brief session of advice. Presumably, brief advice was shown to be just as effective as intensive treatment, since no significant differences were found between the groups. Professor Miller and Dr. Hester believe this study and others like it support their case against inpatient treatment. What is wrong with their belief? In my opinion, a great deal.

First of all, this study by Edwards and Orford really has very little to say about inpatient treatment since it was largely a comparison of patients given advice only and patients given *outpatient* treatment, not inpatient treatment. (Patients who failed at outpatient treatment were then offered inpatient treatment.) For Miller and Hester to present this study in their article under a heading entitled "Inpatient versus Outpatient Care" and to display its results among those of other studies in a table entitled "Relapse Rates in controlled Comparisons of Inpatient Versus Outpatient Settings" is dangerously misleading.

Secondly, and perhaps more important, is the fact that questions can be raised about what the Edwards and Orford study actually did show, since not a single man of the nearly 100 men followed over two years was able to stay sober! As Orford, Oppenheimer, and Edwards (1976) pointed out on subsequent followup, the majority of men drank within a few weeks of their initial consultation. By the first year, all but 8 of 95 men had drunk. By the second year followup, only two remained whose wives reported no drinking since the initial consultation but these two men returned to drinking shortly thereafter. In short, every man in this study, whether he had received advice, inpatient care, or outpatient treatment got drunk.

Rather than showing that a single, brief outpatient session of advice was just as good as intensive long-term inpatient treatment, this "classic" study actually showed that in the early 1970's the British were giving very poor advice and very poor treatment. Since both advice and treatment were ineffective, it certainly is puzzling why this study, from which absolutely nothing can be learned about how to conduct either inpatient or outpatient alcoholism treatment, has been "one of the most widely cited studies in the alcoholism treatment field" (Miller and Hester, 1986, p. 796). Perhaps it says more about what behavioral scientists want to believe about treatment rather than treatment itself.

When all of the studies cited by Miller and Hester on this issue of inpatient versus outpatient care are examined closely, much the same picture emerges: very high relapse rates regardless of type of treatment received. In fact, these *particular programs* reported on by Miller and Hester had relapse rates for both inpatient and outpatient treatment ranging from 71% to 100% when relapse was defined as failure to maintain abstinence.

What can be concluded from studies of *particular programs* in which virtually everybody is relapsing? In my opinion, very little can be concluded with certainty. It is difficult, and in fact, impossible, to conclude as Miller and Hester attempt to do that outpatient treatment is more cost-effective than inpatient treatment when the particular programs being compared are both *equally ineffective*. What does it matter that a particular program is cheap if it gets nobody sober?

Given the fact that numerous other inpatient programs are reporting *far better* results than these particular programs reported on by Miller and Hester, one can draw sharply different conclusions from these studies comparing outpatient to inpatient treatment. These other conclusions are as follows:

1. The particular patient populations studied in these reports reviewed by Miller and Hester were difficult populations and not likely to respond to either outpatient or inpatient treatment at the levels of intensity at which treatment was provided;
2. If anything, much longer courses of inpatient treatment and residential care (longer than any of the programs mentioned by Miller and Hester) must be provided to avoid these high relapse rates for some patients entering the treatment system;
3. For some segments of the alcoholic population inpatient treatment alone is not enough, and we must struggle to get governments to provide the resources necessary to help recovering people get job training and retraining, meaningful vocational rehabilitation, decent places to live, food, access to the opportunity structure of America, escape from endless cycles of poverty, racism, and despair, and so forth. Why blame treatment when the problems may lie in lack of support systems for recovering people once they have achieved initial sobriety and are now struggling to survive in their communities?
4. Some alcoholics may never be able to function in society and it is both cruel and unthinking of Miller and Hester to recommend that these people be given cheap, ineffective treatment as a sub-

stitute for very long-term, controlled, supervised living arrangements.

Given these many alternative conclusions that can be drawn from the studies reported on by Miller and Hester, their call for an end to third-party reimbursement for inpatient treatment and residential care of alcoholics is, in my opinion, premature, irresponsible, unthinking, and inhumane. Imagine a world of alcoholism treatment and rehabilitation without freestanding facilities, without medical detoxification units, hospital programs, halfway houses, or long-term care facilities. Imagine further the suffering, sorrow, devastation, and despair of sick alcoholics and their families, locked once again into hopelessness and awaiting the inevitable tragedy. Is this the future of alcoholism treatment and rehabilitation we wish to bring about? Is this the world of alcoholism services that many who have come before us labored so long and so hard to bring about? Must we bow to these impoverished visions of our future? I think not, for there is much that we can do.

First, and perhaps most importantly, we must insist that researchers in the treatment field give us research that is every bit as adequate and unbiased as research in other areas of alcohol studies. We must reject ideology disguised as science, premature conclusions, poorly designed studies, faulty data-gathering procedures, and unwarranted social policy recommendations based upon data bases capable of yielding equally plausible, and even more plausible, alternative social policy recommendations.

Second, we must appreciate the fact that the politics of alcoholism treatment has given us, more often than not, pseudo controversies rather than meaningful, real, and potentially productive scientific disagreements. The controlled drinking issue, for example, is now properly construed as a pseudo controversy. I suspect that the inpatient versus outpatient issue is another pseudo controversy. In truth, the various components of our comprehensive alcoholism treatment system need not be construed as in competition with one another. It is not a question of inpatient *versus* outpatient, day care *versus* halfway houses, outpatient *versus* long-term residential care, and so on and so forth. In many cost-effective systems, these various services are in *complementary* relationship to one another and are neither intended nor capable of being *substitutes* for one another. Numerous studies of health care systems described by Freiberg (1977), for example, have shown that changing the mix of outpatient to inpatient services in health care generally has not typically resulted in overall system reductions in costs. At best, introduction of outpatient services in these studies of general health care systems resulted in costs remaining the same. More often, however, as Freiberg pointed out, the costs increased but so did quality of services. Therefore, it doesn't follow that costs of treatment will fall automatically as outpatient services are introduced into particular health care systems. Freiberg's observations could scarcely be biased in favor of treatment providers since he was at the time a Research Economist with the National Association of Blue Shield Plans.

Aside from issues of cost, however, there are other very good reasons for resisting these unwarranted attacks by various members of the "Anti-Traditionalist" lobby upon our comprehensive system of alcoholism services. As anybody who has worked in a variety of alcoholism treatment contexts knows, no single context is appropriate for the full range of problems and types of alcoholic persons who present themselves for treatment. One patient may need the full array of services including a family intervention, medical detoxification, inpatient rehabilitation, and eventual halfway house placement coupled with outpatient treatment. Another patient may do just fine with outpatient services alone coupled with AA, while still another alcoholic may go directly to AA and bypass the treatment system entirely. That alcoholics have been following all of these paths to recovery (and more too) has been well known to treatment professionals for decades. It therefore comes as no great news to hear of experts from this center or that one purporting to have "discovered" that some alcoholics do well without formal treatment, some respond to only minimal treatment, and others seem to need everything we have to offer and more. Given the variability among alcoholics, their diverse needs, and their many possible paths to recovery, it is obvious that we need integrated, cooperative, and comprehensive systems of treatment services—not fragmented, dissociated, competitive, and impoverished services. We had the latter for years. That did not work.

In closing this series on the politics of alcoholism, I would like to remind all of us regardless of whether we work in outpatient programs, halfway houses, day treatment, or inpatient facilities of the importance of unity if our field is to survive at all. We must recognize and resist the various tactics and strategies of the "Anti-Traditionalist" lobby to divide us. We must stand shoulder to shoulder in solidarity. Otherwise, alone and divided we will be weak and easy targets for those who do not want to pay for alcoholism services. The most costly outcome of the current debate over the cost-effectiveness of alcoholism treatment would be the blind and mindless destruction of the comprehensive system of treatment services that benefits so many desperately ill people and took so many years of struggle to build. We cannot, must not let that happen.

References

Edwards, G., Orford, J. et al. Alcoholism: A controlled trial of "treatment" and "advice." *Journal of Studies on Alcohol*, 38, 1977, 1004–1031.

Freiberg, L. Alternatives to inpatient care. Paper presented at the Conference on Health Care Financing, the Center for Public Law and Service of the University of Alabama, April 29–30, 1977.

Miller, W.R. and Hester, R.K. Inpatient alcoholism treatment: Who benefits? *American Psychologist*, July 1986, 794–805.

Orford, J. et al. Abstinence or control: The outcome for excessive drinkers two years after consultation. *Behavior Research and Therapy*, 14, 1976, 409–418.

Inpatient vs. Outpatient Alcoholism Treatment Revisited: A Response to Miller and Hester

Miller and Hester's article, "Inpatient Alcoholism Treatment: Who Benefits?" (American Psychologist 1986) is comprehensive but misleading with regard to important detail. While it is true that alcoholism treatment has become (and, in fact, has always been) a "major health care cost," these costs must be considered in light of the total economic costs of alcoholism and problem drinking to American Society. At $15 billion dollars, alcoholism treatment costs are a very small percentage of the total estimated economic costs of alcoholism of $116 billion (Research Triangle Institute 1980). Moreover, Miller and Hester do not make it sufficiently clear that the majority of this $15 billion dollar treatment price tag is for *medical treatment* of the *medical consequences* of alcoholism. Medical treatment of such things as alcoholic hepatitis, cirrhosis of the liver, pancreatitis, traumatic injuries, and so forth have always been with us and consume roughly $12.5 billion (J. Noble, Personal Communication). But psychological treatments directed at the *drinking behavior* cost only $2.5 billion. Ironically, as pointed out in a recent *New England Journal of Medicine* editorial, the costs for just the drugs used to treat hypertension in America amount to $2.5 billion. Moreover, a single diagnostic medical procedure, cardiac catheterization, costs the American people approximately $800 million a year. Considering these examples of medical care costs, a price tag of $2.5 billion for treating alcoholism through psychological methods (as compared to treating its very expensive medical consequences) does not appear excessive. Nor does this sum appear congruent with Miller and Hester's projection of costs of $10 billion by 1986 for the "specific treatment of alcohol abuse."

While it is true that inpatient alcoholism treatment does cost more than outpatient treatment (Knowles, 1983), it is misleading to describe such treatment as the "popular context for treating adolescent and adult alcohol abuse (Miller and Hester, 1986, p. 794)." In fact, available data (NIAAA 1984) have indicated that on September 28, 1984, the national alcoholism case load was as follows: outpatient treatment (82 percent), residential treatment (10 percent), and inpatient treatment (8 percent). By far, the vast majority of alcoholic patients are already being treated in outpatient or residential treatment settings rather than in inpatient settings.

With regard to cost-effectiveness studies, it is true that most studies have reported no differences on outcomes between patients treated in outpatient settings and patients treated in inpatient settings. However, these findings of no differences must be viewed in light of the rather high relapse rates in most of the studies cited by Miller and Hester. When relapse is defined in terms of the scientifically rigorous criterion of sustained abstention, one is tempted to conclude that a more compelling interpretation of these studies is as follows: *neither outpatient nor inpatient treatment were effective in the particular programs studied.*

For example, Miller and Hester cite the putative classic study in this area by Edwards et al. (1977) in which brief "advice" was presumably just as effective as intensive treatment. (The Edwards et al. study by the way was a comparison of "advice" to *outpatient* treatment, for the most part, and not to inpatient treatment in that patients who failed at outpatient were offered the chance at inpatient treatment.) What Miller and Hester fail to point out is that the relapse rates in the Edwards et al. classic "advice versus treatment" study were 100% for both advice and treatment groups. As Orford, Oppenheimer, and Edwards (1976) pointed out on subsequent followup, the majority of men drank within a few weeks of their initial consultation. By the first year, all but 8 of 95 men had drank. By the second year followup, only 2 remained whose wives reported no drinking since the initial consultation but these 2 men returned to drinking shortly thereafter. Hence, a more sober interpretation of this so-called classic experiment is not that brief "advice" is just as good as long term intensive treatment but that the British in this case were giving very poor advice and very poor treatment.

When we examine other studies that Miller and Hester believe support their case, a similar situation obtains—high relapse rates in the particular programs compared. With relapse defined as failure to sustain abstinence, Mosher et al. (1975) found relapse rates of 82% for outpatients and 77% for inpatients. Wilson et al. (1978) reported relapse rates of 74% for both outpatients and inpatients. Pittman and Tate (1972) observed relapse rates of 71% for outpatients and 78% for inpatients. Stein et al. (1975) found somewhat lower relapse rates of 64% for outpatients and 57% for inpatients, but these do not appear to be sustained abstention rates, but group rates at progressive followup intervals. Hence, a person sober at one followup "window" may be drinking pathologically at another "window," and vice-versa.

In general, given relapse rates in the programs studied that varied from 71% to 100%, Miller and Hester's rush to public policy statements concerning cost-effectiveness seems most incautious. When neither of the programs, inpatient or outpatient, is effective, statements about *cost-effectiveness* appear questionable despite the fact that one program may seem cheaper than another. Since considerably lower relapse rates have been reported for other inpatient programs (e.g. Laundergan 1982; Patton, 1979; Neuberger et al. 1982; Pickens et al. 1985; Weins and Menustik, 1983), one might draw alternative conclusions from the studies presented by Miller and Hester. These alternative conclusions are as follows: 1) the particular programs studied may not have had much expertise in treating alcoholics and, as a result, the majority relapsed regardless of the context in which they were treated; 2) the particular alcoholic populations studied were, for the most part, difficult and not likely to respond to either outpatient or inpatient treatment at the levels of intensity studied; 3) if anything, much longer courses of treatment—longer than any of the programs mentioned in Miller and Hester's review—must be provided for particular alcoholic populations to avoid the high relapse rates reported here; 4) some portion of the alcoholic population is not likely to be able to function in society no matter where or how long they are treated and it is both cruel and unthinking social policy to recommend that they get cheap, outpatient treatment as a substitute for long-term supervised, controlled living arrangements.

In effect, given data such as these reported by Miller and Hester, it is most incautious to draw a single unambiguous conclusion from the null hypothesis no matter how many studies or how consistent they appear to be. One not only "proves the null hypothesis" with considerable hazard of being very wrong, one interprets it with the same degree of hazard.

For many who have fought long and hard over the past several decades to make comprehensive alcoholism services systems a reality, Miller and Hester's public policy recommendations will have a naive and alarming ring. Given the past (and present) machinations of important private third-party payers in their attempts to avoid paying for alcoholism treatment services, Miller and Hester's urging of "private third-party payers to enact policy that de-emphasizes the hospital model of care (p. 803)," is both naive, alarming, and incautious.

First of all, it is naive to expect many important private third-party payers to act in a disinterested manner and in the best interests of alcoholics and their families when their histories and present behaviors suggest that they won't. Private third-party insurers have paid for alcoholism treatment services when they were ordered to do so by state government mandates, or were forced to do so by subscribers (particularly corporate subscribers). States that do not have mandated inpatient alcoholism treatment services typically have few insurance policies covering inpatient alcoholism treatment.

Miller and Hester's public policy recommendations are alarming since they seem to involve an apparent misunderstanding of private third-party payers and their relationship to the public. Private third-party payers do not "enact" policies that de-emphasize various forms of health care nor should they be urged to do so. Insurance companies are rightfully regulated by state governments who, in turn, are responsive to the will of the electorate. It is odd that the rights of the people to choose the health care services they wish are not mentioned by Miller and Hester, but they do consider the interests of private insurance companies. Miller and Hester do not seem to realize that up until relatively recently it was impossible to find an inpatient alcoholism treatment bed for an alcoholic. And in many states, it is still very difficult or impossible to do so. Approximately 18 years ago in Southern California, one could get an alcoholic into a hospital only with extreme difficulty, and often, not at all. In Rhode Island just 10 years ago, there were zero inpatient alcoholism treatment beds. With the passage of mandated insurance coverage for inpatient treatment, alcoholism treatment beds and clinics have increased in accordance with need. And as would be expected when a system goes from zero treatment capacity to several hundred beds, treatment as reimbursed by third-party payers has increased accordingly. Given facts such as these, it is exceedingly doubtful that most alcoholism treatment providers and consumers of alcoholism services will be pleased by Miller and Hester's willingness to hand back to third-party payers important gains made on behalf of alcoholic people and their families.

Finally, aside from the interpretive problems posed by the high relapse rates observed in these studies, Miller and Hester do not take into account the often paradoxical relationships that exist between micro and macro levels of complex systems such as health care systems. As health care systems analysts know, it is hazardous to leap from micro level analysis of one hospital program versus another to large scale system policy recommendations. As Freiberg (1977) has pointed out, numerous studies have shown that outpatient services do not stand in a substitutive relationship to inpatient care but are complementary. That is, changing the mix of outpatient to inpatient services in medicine in general has typically resulted in increases in *both* quality of care and cost of care in large health care systems over time. In the numerous studies reviewed by Freiberg, introduction of an outpatient service resulted *at best* in inpatient services' costs remaining constant. In most studies, inpatient costs actually increased as outpatient services were introduced.

As a growing number of people in the alcoholism treatment field believe, the issue is not one of inpatient versus outpatient treatment. We obviously need both. What is needed are reliable and valid criteria that will enable us to predict which patients will do best where. Miller and Hester might consider turning their considerable analytical and scholarly talents to this important task.

REFERENCES

Edwards, G., Orford, J., Egert, S., Guthrie, S., Hawker, A., Hensman, C., Mitcheson, M., Oppenheimer, E. & Taylor, C. (1977). Alcoholism: A controlled trial of "treatment and "advice." *Journal of Studies on Alcohol,* 38, 1004–1031.

Freiberg, L. "Alternatives to Inpatient Care." Paper presented at the Conference of Health Care Financing at the Center for Public Law and Service of the University of Alabama, April 29–30, 1977.

Laundergan, J.C. The outcome of treatment: A comparative study of patients 25 years old and younger and 26 years old and older admitted to Hazelden in 1979. Center City, MN: Hazelden Foundation, 1982.

Miller, W.R. and Hester, R.K. Inpatient alcoholism treatment: Who benefits? *American Psychologist,* July 1986, 794–805.

Mosher, V., Davis, J., Mulligan, D. & Iber F.L. (1976). Comparison of outcome in a 9-day and 30-day alcoholism treatment program. *Journal of Studies on Alcohol,* 36, 1277–1281.

Orford, J., Oppenheimer, E., & Edwards, G. (1976). Abstinence or control: The outcome for excessive drinkers two years after consultation. *Behaviour Research and Therapy,* 14, 409–418.

Patton, M. Validity and reliability of Hazelden treatment followup data. City Center, MN: Hazelden Educational Services, 1979.

Pittman, D.J. & Tate, R.L. (1972). A comparison of two treatment programs for alcoholics. *International Journal of the Addictions,* 19, 183–193.

Pickens, R.W., Hatsukami, D.K., Spicer, J.W., and Svikis, D.S. Relapse by alcohol abusers. *Alcoholism: Clinical and Experimental Research,* Vol. 9, No. 3, 1985, 244–247.

Stein, L.I., Newton, J.R., & Bowman, R.S. (1975). Duration of hospitilization for alcoholism. *Archives of General Psychiatry,* 32, 247–252.

Wiens, A.N., and Menustik, C.E. Treatment outcome and patient characteristics in an aversion therapy program for alcoholism. *American Psychologist* 38(10):1089–1096, 1983.

Part V

The Controlled Drinking Controversy

Alcoholism & Treatment:
A Critical Analysis

This paper is addressed to the recent report *Alcoholism and Treatment* published by the Rand Corporation (Armor, D., Polich, J.M. and Stambul, H.B., June, 1976). It is concerned primarily with certain serious methodological flaws apparent in the research design taken as a whole.

WHAT IS THE RAND REPORT?

The Rand Report has been publicized widely as a scientific study of certain critical issues in the field of alcoholism treatment.

In actuality, the Rand Report is little more than a collection of statistical analyses conducted upon data gathered from a *totally uncontrolled* "experiment" in alcoholism treatment. In all, three agencies or organizations were involved. Stanford Research Institute (SRI) designed and tested the monitoring system through which data were obtained. The National Institute on Alcohol Abuse and Alcoholism (NIAAA) was responsible for gathering the data from clients attending their Alcoholism Treatment Centres (ATC's). And Rand provided after the fact data analysis services.

The authors of the Rand Report are not unaware of the fatal deficiencies of the NIAAA-SRI data base. However, they assume that inadequate data are better than no data at all. As shall be pointed out shortly, such an assumption is dangerously misleading. Bad data lead quite naturally to erroneous conclusions whereas no data permit no conclusions. With regard to an issue of such far-reaching import as the possibility of "normal drinking" in recovering alcoholics, no conclusions are preferable to life threatening erroneous conclusions.

Let us now examine in greater detail the methodological problems in the NIAAA-SRI data base that render the Rand analyses and conclusions meaningless and unwarranted.

EXTREME SUBJECT MORTALITY

In the Rand Six Month study, the original sample at the time of intake was 11,500 clients. The Six Month Study was conducted upon only 2,371 subjects. An astonishing 9,129 subjects were lost during the course of treatment. It is interesting to note that the Rand authors persist in referring to these missing 9,129 subjects as "lost to follow-up". In actuality, since the measures were gathered *during treatment* and not six months following treatment, the missing subjects are treatment *drop-outs*.

An enormous potential for bias is apparent in this study at the very outset since it is common knowledge in any field of scientific research that those who withdraw from experimental treatments are likely to differ in both known and unknown ways from those who remain. In the case of the 9,129 subjects who dropped out of treatment, one suspects that a very great number were treatment failures. Both experience and research suggest that alcoholics who withdraw from treatment and those unavailable to follow-up have returned to dangerous drinking.

Rand, of course, recognizes the seriousness of such extreme subject mortality rates. They attempt to minimize the seriousness of this threat to the validity of the experiment by showing that the remaining 2,371 subjects do not differ from the full intake sample in terms of certain client characteristics.

Unfortunately, Rand's own regression analyses presented in a later section of the report call into question the wisdom of this after the fact "matching" procedure. The known client characteristics used by Rand to demonstrate no sample bias *do not predict* the variance in remission rates. According to Rand's own analyses, only 8.8% of the total variance in remission rates is accounted for by the measurements on client characteristics. Hence, the Rand researchers cannot assure us of lack of sample bias since the variables predicting remission are largely unknown to them. Lacking knowledge of the critical variables that predict remission, the Rand group is faced with unrecognized, and therefore uncontrolled, bias in the six month sample. As is generally recognized in experimental design, the attempt to equate samples after the fact is inferior to randomization prior to treatments. And when the critical variables are largely unknown as they are in the Rand research, such a procedure is mere window-dressing for shoddy prior data gathering procedures and experimental design.

Turning to the 18 Month Study, much the same situation is in evidence. Out of an initial sample of 2,161 clients at intake, the 18 Month Study was conducted upon 1,340 subjects. Once again, an unacceptable subject mortality rate obtains. A total of 821 subjects were lost to the analyses of results.

Combining both the 6 Month Study and the 18 Month Study, the initial sample at the time of intake was 13,661 subjects. The Rand analyses were conducted on 3,711 subjects. A grand total of 9,950 subjects were lost—a subject mortality rate of 73%. One cannot imagine a more serious departure from elementary principles of experimental design than to attempt to analyze and give meaning to results in which only 27% of the initial sample is represented in the final analyses.

SUBJECT MORTALITY AND PERCENT NORMAL DRINKERS

The Rand researchers claim to find "22%" normal drinkers in their 18 Month Study and "12%" in the 6 Month Study. The real question is, of course, 22 and 12 per cent of what? By glossing over the very real potential for bias in their reduced samples, the authors want us to believe that the results are generalizable to the full-intake samples. In actuality, they are not. The only acceptable way to provide full-sample estimates is to add back in 9,950 treatment drop-outs and other missing subjects. In other words, in the absence of any convincing evidence to the contrary, it is reasonable to assume that drop-outs and other missing subjects in alcoholism treatment research have returned to dangerous drinking.

When the 270 "normal drinkers" in the 6 Month Study are reconsidered in light of the original sample from which they were drawn, Rand's 12% estimate for "normal drinkers" drops to 2%. When the 131 subjects in the 18 Month Study who are said to be drinking normally are reconsidered in light of their original sample, the estimates drop markedly from 22% to 6%. Combining both samples and recomputing the percentages of "normal drinkers" as defined by Rand yields an overall percentage figure of 3%.

Given the high probability of errors of measurement, diagnostic error, and the likelihood of pressures upon both alcoholics and treatment staff to underestimate actual drinking, a 3% figure of "normal drinking" is of no consequence.

One might object that the 3% estimate has been arrived at far too conservatively. However, given the seriousness of the "normal drinking" issue, we must not only expect research to meet minimal standards of scientific quality, we must demand that it meet the highest standards of precision and rigor. Unfortunately, the NIAAA-SRI data reported by the Rand authors does neither. In challenging some forty years of extensive clinical and community experience with alcoholism, the Rand authors should not enter the ring with an apology for the shortcomings of their data. Nor should they expect sympathy for their lamentations over the difficulties involved in doing outcome research in alcoholism treatment. Rand should be offering the strongest, most convincing, and rigorous test of their hypothesis possible rather than conclusions based upon data generated from a clearly inadequate research design.

Who, for example would abandon chemotherapy or radiation therapy in the treatment of cancer on the basis of results from a medical experiment in which 9,950 subjects or 73% of the original sample were dropped from the analysis?

Low Level of Sophistication of Measurement

One searches in vain throughout the pages of this report for evidence of multimethod approaches to measurement. Behavioral measures are entirely lacking. With the exception of data contributed by an independent researcher involving BACs, biochemical, physiological, and neurological measurements are unreported. Measurement consists almost entirely of self-reports gathered through the familiar method of the interview-questionnaire. Given the by now not so recent advances in behavioral, biochemical, physiological, and bioelectrical assessment procedures, one wonders why the designers of the NIAAA "Monitoring System" chose to rely upon a method of measurement popular among clinical researchers some twenty years ago.

The difficulties inherent in the questionnaire are now widely recognized as legion. It is exceedingly doubtful that the NIAAA-SRI data base has managed to escape even a fraction of these.

With regard to the critical self-report variable of amount of consumption among heavy drinking and alcoholic persons, the authors readily admit that underreporting is apparent in the "upper one-third or one-fourth of the consumption distribution, with underestimation being of the order of 50 to 60 percent of this group". They further state, "Therefore, persons in the general population who say they drink between 1 and 5 ounces of ethanol daily may in fact be drinking about twice that amount (p. 166)."

Curiously, the authors fail to apply this conclusion to the *NIAAA intake data* reported much earlier in the body of the report. At the time of admission to the ATC's, 25% of the 6 month study subjects and 25% of the 18 month study subjects are drinking more than zero but less than 3 ounces a day. Paradoxically, these limits of consumption are well within the authors' consumption criterion for "normal drinking." But if 25% of the clients have been drinking within "normal" limits at the time of admission to an alcoholism treatment centre, why in the world are they seeking treatment? The authors neglect the obvious possibility that at the time of admission 25% of each sample are grossly underestimating the quantity of their drinking over the past 30 days. Instead, they present several alternative arguments for which no data are presented, e.g. in long-term alcoholics, even small amounts of alcohol produce intoxicating effects; some clients entering the ATC's came from other institutions such as jails and hospitals where the researchers assume that alcohol use is restricted.

But to admit that 25% of the clients in each study were underreporting quantity of consumption at the time of admission to the ATC's would of course raise serious questions about the possibility of similar underreporting of consumption at follow-up. Given the authors' apparent commitment to the "normal drinking" hypothesis, the possibility of underreporting either prior to treatment or at follow-up must be thoroughly discredited either by alternative explanation or by appeal to data gathered by other researchers. Accordingly, the authors report data gathered by Linda Sobell of the Orange County (California) Alcoholism Service.

Sobell's data yielded comparisons of estimated BACs from self-reports of consumption to actual BACs measured immediately after self-report. In Sobell's study, the subjects were measured at intake and comprised persons who drank alcohol in the past 24 hours. It should be noted that the Sobell data are not comparable to the intake data nor the outcome data of the NIAAA ATC's. In the ATC intake data, the clients were asked to estimate *typical* quantity and frequency over the 30 days prior to admission. In the Sobell study, clients were asked to estimate quantity consumed during the 24 hours immediately prior to intake and measurement of BAC.

Moreover, the facility in which Sobell's data were gathered had a stated policy of refusal to admit if clients had been drinking within the past 12 hours. As a consequence, of the 593 clients studied at the Orange County facility, only 150 male clients who had positive BACs or self-reports of consumption entered into Rand's major analysis of estimated BACs and actual BACs.

Once again, extreme subject selection has taken place. Not only do the Sobell subjects differ from NIAAA subjects in the sense that they are being admitted to different treatment programs, they have each been exposed to *varying selection procedures*. One could argue that the approximately 470 subjects who in a sense selected themselves out of the Sobell study by obeying the rules of the center differed in important ways from those who either did not obey the rules or had consumed enough alcohol to show positive BACs 12 hours later.

If tendency to underreport quantity consumed is related to guilt and shame over drinking, then it is possible that the alcoholics most likely to underreport quantity of consumption in the Orange County study were those screened out because of relative *sobriety* on the day of intake. Clients who abide by the rules of an alcoholism service may be precisely those who have more highly developed superego functions. And it is these who may be most likely to experience guilt and shame *when drinking* and hence, most likely to underreport consumption.

In any case, the 150 male clients reported in the Sobell study of estimated and actual BACs can hardly be considered representative of alcoholics in general or of alcoholics admitted to NIAAA treatment centers. But even in this highly self-selected and hence, nonrandom group of clients considerable underreporting is apparent.

Combining the data somewhat differently from the authors, we note that 35% of those who estimated their BACs to be in the range from .0–.04 underreported. 62% who estimated their BACs in the range from .05–.09 underreported. 12% of those with BACs in the .10–.19 range underreported. Overall, 32% of the subjects in this highly self-selected study underreported the quantity of their consumption.

Three separate sources of information then have raised serious questions about the NIAAA-SRI self-report data on quantity of consumption. These are as follows: 1) "Normal Drinking" levels in 25% of each sample prior to admission to the ATC's caution us against placing much faith in these very same measures at outcome; 2) National surveys indicate that for those whose consumption falls in ranges characteristic of alcoholics, underreporting of quantity consumed approaches 50%; and 3) even in a highly self-selected and non-random group of alcoholics, underreporting occurred in 32%.

These data bearing on the validity of self-reported quantity consumed, raise serious questions about the Rand group's inferences concerning not only "normal drinking" but *relapse and spontaneous remission as well*.

One further comment concerning underreporting by alcoholics of quantity consumed is in order. We must remember that the NIAAA-SRI data were gathered in a definite context—ongoing treatment in agencies under the supervision and funding control of the Federal government. The possibility that alcoholic clients in therapy would perceive valid reporting of abnormal levels of quantity consumed as threatening in some manner to both themselves and clinic staff is not unlikely.

In short, the *demand characteristics* of these particular therapeutic contexts, either as perceived by clients or communicated by treatment personnel, cannot be glossed over in assessing the likelihood of serious underreporting of quantity consumed and behavioural impairment at later points in treatment.

FAILURE TO CONTROL EXPERIMENTER BIAS

Given the widespread awareness in the social and behavioral sciences of the serious effects of experimenter bias, it is remarkable that the designers of the NIAAA-SRI monitoring system produced a system highly vulnerable to such effects. In effect, the staffs of the NIAAA ATC's who gathered most of the intake and outcome data were in the position of experimenters in an uncontrolled experiment. Even in the 18 months study where "specially trained interviewers" were employed to gather follow-up data, the possibility of bias was still apparent since the training and supervision of these interviewers was conducted by treatment center staffs.

It is a commonly accepted requirement in treatment outcome research that the persons involved in delivering the treatments should not be involved in assessing the outcomes. One need not indict the NIAAA Center staffs on grounds of dishonesty and lack of integrity in raising the issue of experimenter bias. It is well known that such effects can occur non-deliberately and without awareness.

Given the obvious pressures on treatment staffs to "look good up top" and also the possibility of perceived competition among staffs of the varying ATC's used in the Rand report, the possibility of significant experimenter bias in outcome measures cannot be overlooked. And given the very low rates of abstinence, achieved at the majority of the ATC's, the pressures to minimize quantity of consumption and behavioral impairment in drinking alcoholics at follow-up must surely have been present.

In order to satisfy even the most elementary principles of experimental design in outcome research, we must insist that the persons involved in delivering treatments be *entirely independent* from those assessing the effects of such treatments. Since this elementary requirement was not met in the NIAAA-SRI Monitoring System, we can have virtually no faith in the Rand inferences concerning "normal drinking", relapse rates, or spontaneous remissions.

BIAS IN POLICY STATEMENTS CONCERNING TREATMENT

Since the Rand conclusions were drawn from data generated by a completely uncontrolled "experiment" in alcoholism treatment, any implications for policy and further research contained in this report must be treated with extreme caution or ignored entirely.

Since the NIAAA ATC's used in this study do not comprise a random sample of the population of alcoholism treatment programs throughout the country, the authors of the Rand report are in no position to make highly general remarks about "alcoholism treatment." In actuality, Rand is not even in the position to generalize the results of the 18 month study to the NIAAA ATC's taken as a whole since no information is provided as to how the 8 ATC's chosen for study were selected. We are told by the Rand authors that they are "representative." Unfortunately, a statement of that nature is no substitute for a truly random selection process.

In the final analysis, the Rand inferences are *sharply restricted in generality* because of the multiple methodological problems already discussed above. Rand is justified only in making statements about these particular NIAAA centers studied, these particular samples of clients, and these particular measures of treatment outcomes. Hence, the generality of the Rand conclusions and policy implications are sharply limited by a host of methodological problems: 1) Non-random selection of both treatment centers and clients, 2) a completely unacceptable and, in fact, rather astonishing subject mortality rate (treatment drop out rate), 3) lack of behavioural, biochemical, physiological, and bioelectrical measurement procedures, 4) use of self-report measures that, by a number of estimates, are known to result in underreporting of quantity of consumption of alcohol 5) uncontrolled demand characteristics in the research context, and 6) uncontrolled experimenter bias effects. The list reads like all the faults in an unacceptable student paper in a first course in experimental design.

To the above list of methodological shortcomings apparent in this report, still another bias is apparent. Throughout the report there is a subtle but pervasive bias in favor of the authors' belief in the possibility of "normal drinking" in recovering alcoholics. This bias is reflected first of all in the authors' persistent efforts to minimize glaringly obvious shortcomings in the NIAAA-SRI data. It is also apparent in the authors' ready acceptance of reports of the "controlled drinking" literature without any serious attempt to cite or discuss the methodological criticisms that have accompanied these reports.

The authors regard abstinence as a rare event among recovering alcoholics. Abstinence is not a rare event among committed members of Alcoholics Anonymous. It is, in fact, the rule in that organization. And in certain alcoholism treatment programs that work in close cooperation with Alcoholics Anonymous and other community organizations, abstinence is not a rare event but a highly probable outcome of a well designed and properly conducted treatment facility—community rehabilitation process (see for example the excellent outcome studies conceived and executed by Professor Douglas K. Chalmers of the Department of Psychology, University of California at Irvine).

The fact that sobriety is a rare event in the Rand outcome study is a reflection on the quality of service rendered by NIAAA ATC's under the direction of the former director of NIAAA, Dr Morris Chafetz. The failure of these ATC's to produce abstinent clients is neither an indictment of alcoholism treatment generally, nor of abstinence as the proper goal for recovering alcoholics.

Alcoholism and Treatment Revisited

My paper, "Alcoholism and Treatment: A Critical Analysis" (Wallace, 1978), was written over two years ago within several days of publication of the Rand report. It was prepared at the request of the National Council on Alcoholism and served as the basis for my remarks at a press conference called by the National Council and held in Washington, D.C. in July, 1976. My perhaps too hasty examination of the report at that time persuaded me that the research upon which it was based was suspect with regard to virtually every important element of scientific inquiry. The sampling was a shambles, data collection shoddy, data analysis arguable, and results incapable of generalization to *any* population—certainly not to alcoholics in general. Having arrived at these conclusions, I turned to more pressing matters and abandoned any intentions I might have had about pursuing a more searching analysis of the report and its implications. Fortunately, my decision to publish these earlier critical comments in ALFAWAP Journal (Wallace, 1978) and David Armor's reply to these have provided me with the opportunity to revisit the Rand report and to observe possible changes in my reaction to it.

At the outset, I do think it fair to warn the reader that I am not dispassionate with regard to the general hypothesis that alcoholics, or even a substantial minority of them, can drink without hazard. I do not, however, in principle oppose the consumption of beverage alcohol by people in general, and prefer instead to view rational decisions concerning use of this drug as necessarily involved with individual differences among people, variations in situations, social-cultural variations, and scientifically demonstrated properties of the drug itself.

One individual difference variable that has not failed to impress me with regard to identifying persons at risk for grave personal and social

278 JOHN WALLACE: WRITINGS

outcomes associated with alcohol consumption is the presence or absence of a prior history of alcoholism.

But while I am not yet convinced that the vast majority of alcoholics can drink beverage alcohol without substantial risk to self and others, I would welcome a scientific demonstration of any novel intervention that would enable such persons to do so.

If, for example, the Rand authors had shown that the majority of alcoholics could indeed drink without dire personal and social consequences, I would be delighted. A scientific demonstration of a hitherto unsuspected capability of this kind for the majority of alcoholic people would no doubt increase my effectiveness as a therapist and simplify my life as a program administrator immeasurably. It would also save many lives, spare national economies the loss of many billions of dollars, and rescue millions of people from the anguish and suffering that go with life in or around active alcoholism.

But, alas, the Rand report did not show that the majority of alcoholic persons could drink normally and, of course, its authors made no such claim. Moreover, it is doubtful, for reasons I shall explain shortly, that the report showed that even a sizeable minority of alcoholics could drink normally. In fact, other than raising the possibility that some persons with prior diagnoses of alcoholism might be able to drink particular quantities of alcohol in particular patterns of frequency over brief temporal spans, the Rand report shows nothing at all. When we realize that this statement of possibility under these particular constraints could have been made *prior to the research* reported by the Rand authors, we are made immediately aware of the considerable hyperbole on both sides of the normal drinking issue that accompanied its publication.

To assert that some (number of) persons with prior diagnoses of alcoholism may be capable of normal drinking given further particular constraints on the assertion, is to make a trivial statement. We realize precisely how trivial the assertion is when it is understood that all that is required for its empirical verification is the discovery of just *one* person of this class. The assertion becomes interesting if and only if the numbers become appreciable, are capable of estimation with an acceptable degree of accuracy, and the particular constraints surrounding the assertion are either removed entirely or considerably broadened.

In light of these considerations, it is apparent that any assertions concerning normal drinking among alcoholics inferable from *either* the data or the conclusions of the Rand authors are trivial since the numbers reported cannot be taken to represent population parameters, the likelihood of the phenomenon has not been established, and the particular constraints evident here require, at best, a magnificent leap of the scientific imagination and, at worst, an act of faith for generalization to be warranted. How many alcoholics can be expected to drink normally?

Two percent? Five percent? Twelve percent? Twenty-two percent? The answer to this question for me, for the Rand authors, and for anybody with any sense at all in these matters must be that the percentage is unknown. "The answer", as folk singer Bob Dylan put it with regard to the very different question of his generation, "is blowing in the wind."

At the outset, let me also state that I concur (and have always concurred with the Rand authors) that they have not advocated nor are in a position to advocate anything at all about normal drinking goals for alcoholics since "the data from this study, and other similar studies, are simply not adequate to establish beyond question, the long-term feasibility of normal or "controlled" drinking among alcoholics" (Armor, Polich, and Stambul, 1976, p. 140).

Since virtually every conclusion of any importance reported by Armor and his colleagues is necessarily couched in the language of possibility and bracketed neatly by caveat on the one hand and conjecture on the other, it is entirely possible to advocate nothing while implying a great deal. My concern with this report is not, and has not been, with advocacy since the authors and I are in agreement that they have not and, indeed, could not advocate normal drinking as a treatment goal for alcoholics since the data do not justify such advocacy.[1] My concern here is with bias.

Let me begin with Armor's rather petulant and gratuitous attack upon my credibility as a critic of work bearing on treatment goals for alcoholics. He accuses me of using the wealth of methodological detail contained in his report in a "highly selective and erroneous fashion to promote preconceived and unsubstantiated beliefs about treatment goals."

At a later point in my report, I intend to show that Armor is capable of bias with regard to his numbers. Here, I shall explore his bias with regard to his words.

---

[1]It is interesting to note that in his reply to me, Armor presents a rather different explanation of his failure to advocate normal drinking as a treatment goal. In the report, it is the data that do not justify advocacy. But here, in his reply to me, it is "precisely because of this clinical tradition (abstinence) that the Rand study avoided recommending any change from the commonly accepted policy of abstention." The implication, of course, is that while Armor privately believes that his data do justify such advocacy, he will ignore the data and bow to clinical tradition. If the implication drawn is correct, then the position taken by an avowed empiricist is indeed a curious one.

The fact that there are errors—some no doubt egregious—in my account of this complex and richly detailed report is regrettable and I do apologize to the authors and my readers for any that may have already been committed and also, for any that may occur here.

One of my more egregious errors was to leave the reader with the impression that Armor's major analyses in the 18-month study were conducted upon 1,340 subjects. Actually, the facts of "sampling" in this study are complex, incompletely described, and, in some critical particulars, elusive and controversial. A reasonably informed source (Hyde, 1976) has stated that from a group of 3,243 eligible clients at the ACT's involved in the 18-month study, 2,320 subjects were somehow assembled. The sampling was not random. While the Rand authors assert that the sampling was "representative", Hyde (1976) maintains that it was "convenience sampling" (italics my own) based largely upon the numbers each treatment center could contribute. Of these 2,320 clients, 1,340 were located and interviewed at follow-up. From these 1,340 interviewed clients, 600 clients were non-randomly assembled (all women and driving-while-intoxicated clients were systematically elimated) and served as the principal sample for the major analyses. Further non-random and systematic reductions resulted in analyses conducted upon still fewer clients. For example, the very important analyses conducted upon relapse rates comparing abstinent clients to normal drinking clients were conducted upon 220 clients in one analysis and 161 clients in another.

To complicate matters further, concern has been reported with regard to the unintentional loss of entire treatment centers. In a memorandum to the Director of NIAAA from a Deputy Director dated June 23, 1976, it is claimed that the sample of 8 treatment centers analyzed by Armor and his colleagues was originally 10 centers with two entire centers dropping out of the study as data collection began (Kissko, 1976).[2]

And, of course, as I pointed out in my original paper, from an original full-intake sample of 11,500 clients in the Rand six-month study, the analyses were conducted upon only 2,371 non-randomly assembled clients.

Earlier in this paper I referred to the sampling in this study as a

---

[2]Armor claims an interview rate of 21 percent for the six-month study and an interview rate of 62 percent for the 18-month study. Some confusion is evident here with both Hyde (1976) and Kissko (1976) contradicting this claim of 62 percent for the 18-month study and claiming instead an interview rate of 58 percent. Hyde attributes the discrepancy to still further reductions of clients due to death or screening by treatment center staffs. For my purposes here, I shall assume Armor's rate to be correct.

"shambles." Reviewing the observations reported here, I find it difficult to believe that any serious student of sampling theory and statistical inference would describe it as otherwise. But while it is possible, I suppose, to make a silk purse out of a sow's ear through the magic of sophisticated statistical analysis alone, we cannot pretend that the enormous epistemological dilemmas posed by unsystematic and systematic sample reductions will yield easily to after-the-fact data manipulations.

Armor and his colleagues arrange three "tests" of sample bias and, on the basis of these, conclude that their samples are unbiased. We shall be forced to examine these "tests" of sample bias in greater detail shortly for, given the rather exotic nature of the sampling problems evident here, it is unlikely that the purse is truly silk. Rayon perhaps, or more possibly whole cloth.

Returning again to Armor's charges against me, I am surprised to note the charge of "selectivity." I readily admit to the charge that my criticisms are "selective", but only in the sense that my concern is not with the myriad of detail that make up the study but with certain critical elements of data collection, sampling, data analysis, and inference. I believe such "selectivity" is the staple fare of scientific criticism, standard and mundane, in fact, rather than extraordinary.

As to Armor's charge that I have "preconceived beliefs" about the treatment of alcoholics, I readily concur—if, of course, that term is to be understood not in the pejorative, *ad hominem* sense, but in reference to the complex collection of many thousands of empirical observations, hypotheses held with varying degrees of certainty, hunches, notions, convictions, speculations, frankly exotic constructions, and downright trivia that invariably go with over a decade of intense involvement in the lives of alcoholic people and their families. All of these, I might suppose could at least be euphemistically labeled as the "cognitive contents and processes" of a seasoned alcoholism therapist.

To insist that I must approach the topic of alcoholism as a "tabula rasa" is not only unrealistic but actually a bit absurd. That would be rather like having asked Margaret Mead to have refrained from thinking, talking, and writing about those Balinese and Samoans until the lady and gentlemen at the Rand Corporation were able to clarify her experiences for her on the computer.

As to the charge that I seek to "promote" my own treatment goals for alcoholics through an attack on his research, Armor is more than a little presumptuous. He seems scarcely to have considered the possibility that his research is entirely capable of discrediting itself without any assistance from my personal beliefs. Armor in this instance is committing the classical error of the poorly trained clinician—the confusion of correlation with causality. The syllogism is as follows: "Wallace believes that alcoholics cannot drink normally. My research has shown that some alcoholics might be able to do so. Therefore, Wallace has attacked my research because of his beliefs". Obviously, this argument is specious, the logic contemptible, and the error not only egregious but mundane.

As a program administrator legally accountable for the lives of large numbers of alcoholics, I have no choice but to advocate abstinence since research to date, including the research under examination here, has failed to provide me with reliable answers to the following questions:

1. How many alcoholics can be expected to be able to drink normally?
2. Over what temporal intervals can the behavior be maintained?
3. What factors serve to differentiate those who cannot do this from those who can?
4. What levels of risk inhere in varying operational definitions of "normal drinking" for various alcoholic populations given particular individual, situational, and societal constraints?
5. Does a valid technology exist for producing normal drinkers out of alcoholics?

To pretend, either in open advocacy or by implication, that reliable knowledge exists with regard to these questions would be to invite censor and disgrace (and deservedly so) from any scientific or professional body concerned with, and knowledgeable about alcoholism since research to date has not yet produced such reliable knowledge.

If the reader will permit me a moment's digression here, I should like to reproduce a few observations made by myself on particular alcoholics. Such anecdotal evidence, is of course, notoriously unreliable with regard to establishing particular population values, but it does serve to acquaint those whose observations are made distally rather than proximally with the awesome considerations in the issue at hand. While I cannot attest to the frequency of outcomes such as the following among alcoholics who continue to drink, I can assure the reader that these are but a handful of the many that I could report space permitting.

Consider the following:

1. A 35 year old Hispanic, stably employed, married, middle income postal worker who, despite three hospital detoxifications and progressive diagnoses of "fatty liver," "alcoholic hepatitis," and "cirrhosis of the liver" continues to come to group therapy obviously intoxicated. In group, he insists that he is "controlling" his drinking, that he is drink-

ing only "two or three" beers after work each day, and things are going fine in his marriage and at work. Six months later he is dead of cirrhosis of the liver, death attributable to massive hemmorage of the esophagus.

2. A 39 year old caucasian, married employed construction worker. He will not attend A.A. because he believes he can control his drinking and wishes to try. Three months later he is found dead in his car in his enclosed garage. Death is attributed to carbon monoxide poisoning and is associated with either suicide or accident. All available data indicate that he was severely intoxicated at the time of death.

3. A robust, physically powerful, 31 year old truck driver drops out of A.A. after eleven months of abstinence. He believes that he is now "cured" and can drink as others do. Within a week he is obviously intoxicated in a local bar. He picks a fight with a much smaller man. The latter, frightened for his safety pulls a gun. Within a week, of leaving A.A., the truck driver is dead of multiple gunshot wounds to the head.

4. A 38 year old male caucasian is released on parole from a maximum security prison after having served three years of a "zip to ten year" sentence for having stabbed a woman 28 times in a frenzied attack while intoxicated. One of the conditions of his parole is that he not drink alcoholic beverages. He dismisses the conditions of parole as "unfair", asserts that he is not an alcoholic, and that he can control his drinking. He further asserts that he will drink in the privacy of his home and avoid bars and taverns in which his troubles started. Three months after his release on parole, he is remanded to a maximum security prison for having threatened to kill the woman and her entire family. At the time he has made the threats, he has been observed intoxicated in a public bar, having returned there drunk after a physical altercation at the home of the woman's son.

5. A 42 year old black, unemployed ghetto alcoholic sits in my group therapy session. He must use a cane to walk since he reports having leaped several years before from a third floor window of an alcoholism treatment unit and shattered both legs and a hip. He admits in group that he made the leap because he "needed a drink so badly that he was going crazy." Despite a history of multiple hospitalizations for detoxification, he maintains in the group that although he has never been able to do so, he believes he can control his drinking. Six weeks later, he has dropped out of group therapy and is observed drunk on the streets by both patients and staff. After an absence of a couple of weeks, he returns to treatment, admits that he couldn't "handle it again this time" but still has reservations about the necessity to stay completely sober.

6. A 35 year old professional, caucasian female dependent upon both tranquilizers and alcohol decides that she needs psychiatry and not A.A. During intensive psychotherapy her drinking problem is not discussed and attention is addressed to her many "underlying emotional conflicts." Six months after entering therapy, she deliberately drives her car off a Southern California cliff and is found dead in the morning in the wreckage of her car among the jumble of rocks that crowd the shore. She had been observed drinking heavily at a friend's home

prior to the accident. Some time later, an acquaintance of the victim with an uncontrolled alcohol problem of her own, leaps from the very same cliff while intoxicated.

7. A 21 year old ghetto black who refuses to abstain from alcohol completely wanders onto a busy city street while intoxicated and steps in front of a truck. He sustains severe head injuries but survives. He returns to the alcoholism clinic with his head a swarm of bandages. He admits that drinking has caused him problems, but he will now control it. A month later he is intoxicated on the streets, steps in front of a bus, and is killed instantly.

8. A 29 year old female with a history of both drug and alcohol dependence has been ordered by a child protective agency to enter alcoholism treatment. She regards this as "unfair" since she can control her drinking. She insists that she does not have a problem with alcohol despite the fact that her history shows massive evidence to the contrary. Her infant is taken away from her when the child protective agency discovers that she has driven home from an all night drinking party with the infant in its car seat on the roof of the car. Miraculously, the baby is still on the roof of the car when the mother has arrived home.

9. A 58 year old alcoholic male, independently well-off, sits in a group therapy session with me. He has had multiple hospitalizations for alcoholism. He does not believe that he can control his drinking. He informs me that his father was an alcoholic who sobered up twelve years before his death. His family consisted of three brothers and one sister. The three brothers are dead of alcoholism and his sister is near to death because of alcoholism. Of his uncles on his father's side of the family, all four are dead of alcoholism. Among his nieces and nephews, several do not drink at all and the remainder appear to him as "on the way to alcoholism."

10. A 27 year old, caucasian, married, unemployed man with a history of heroin addiction and alcoholism attends two group therapy sessions and then decides to test his ability to control his drinking. He fails and while intoxicated consumes large quantities of other non-selective general depressant drugs. He suffers the effects of severe drug synergy, collapses, and is taken to the hospital where life support systems are necessary to maintain him in coma. He remains in coma for a month, regains consciousness but is found to be severely impaired neurologically. After two years of intensive rehabilitation, he has recovered speech and upper body motor functions. However, he cannot walk, is incontinent, and remains in a wheelchair.

"On the other hand, we have found no solid scientific evidence—only nonrigorous clinical or personal experience—for the belief that abstention is a more effective remedy than normal drinking. The conclusion, therefore, must be that existing scientific knowledge establishes neither an abstention theory nor a normal drinking theory of recovery from alcoholism" (Armor, Polich, and Stambul, 1976, p. 140).

Considering the very grave consequences that follow for some alcoholics who refuse to accept an abstinence theory for themselves, the above statement deserves closer examination. Let's take it apart.

1. "We have found no solid scientific evidence." This assertion is dangerously misleading since it implies that the Rand study constituted a rigorous test of the merits of abstinence relative to normal drinking. No solid scientific evidence was found for anything in this uncontrolled study since the study was not capable of generating such evidence. If anything, it constitutes still another failure of the social and behavioral science research community to develop ingenious and scientifically adequate research designs for generating reliable knowledge to guide clinical decision-making.

2. "Only nonrigorous clinical or personal experience was found for the belief that abstention is a more effective remedy than normal drinking." This assertion is particularly offensive since the Rand study was not a direct empirical study of the beliefs, opinions, and experiences of clinicians nor of the processes through which clinicians generate, process, and evaluate information concerning alcoholism and its treatment. In the very few instances where particular data might be construed as relevant to the cognitive contents and processes of clinicians, we must remember that the study involved a non-randomly selected group of such people (workers in particular NIAAA centers) in non-randomly selected contexts. Hence, the authors are in no position to generalize about the rigor of clinical evidence among other clinicians working in other contexts. For example, in some clinical contexts, very high (much higher, in fact, than those reported for the Rand study) client follow-ups over long temporal spans are possible. In other clinical contexts, the clinician has virtually no idea what has happened to his clients once they leave treatment.

3. "Existing scientific knowledge establishes neither an abstention theory nor a normal drinking theory of recovery from alcoholism." This assertion is particularly self-serving when it is realized that much the same statement could be made about virtually any theory drawn from the social and behavioral sciences concerning the vast majority of phenomena other than alcoholism of interest to the clinical psychiatrist or psychologist.

Finally, even if we were to accept the Rand author's statement about "solid scientific evidence" and treatment goals as justifiable from their data (which it is not), then it constitutes a strong case for continued reliance upon the most reliable clinical observations at hand. In the face of the continued failure of the social and behavioral science research community to provide competent scientific tests of competing, rival hypotheses (and the Rand research is no exception to this failure), we have no other choice but to rely upon the information at hand.

If clinical workers in alcoholism were forced to rely only upon "solid scientific evidence" from the social and behavioral sciences generally, they would, at present, simply have no way to proceed in the treatment of their clients, not only with regard to treatment goals, but with regard to virtually any issue we might care to examine. Such notable failures of the research community are scarcely to be laid at the doorstep of clinicians. Clinicians should not only demand more research, but far more competent research than they have been given at the expense of previous treatment, rehabilitation, and prevention dollars.

In short, if it indeed be true that "solid scientific evidence" of the kind alluded to by Armor and his colleagues cannot be marshalled in support of either side of the normal drinking issue, then the extant body of clinical and community observations concerning alcoholism and recovery from it must assume *greater* rather than lesser import in the attempt to arrive at rational decisions concerning treatment policy.

It is one thing to sit in one's office in Santa Monica shooting statements into the blue about what you think "science" does and does not show about alcoholics and their drinking. It is quite another thing to sit deep in the Harlem Ghetto, as I have done, surrounded on all sides by the awesome wreckage of the devastating interface of American racism, drug addiction, and alcoholism. There, in the Harlem Ghetto, face to face with the terrifying facts of alcoholism as evidenced in the lives of the people around you, the questions before you are not academic and abstract. You do not shoot words into the blue in Harlem. You survive. And if you are an alcoholic, on those violent streets, you cannot drink alcohol and survive for very long.

The final charge Armor makes against me is that my beliefs about treatment goals are "unsubstantiated." This, of course, is a damaging criticism and especially so when it comes from somebody who pretends to be on far more defensible empirical foundations than I.

I assume that Armor has studied computer printouts in his offices at Santa Monica. In contrast, I have studied very large numbers of alcoholics directly—in locations as widely varied as middle and upper middle class Southern California communities, in the Harlem Ghetto, on the streets of New York and in the rural Northeast. The fact that I have made many thousands of direct empirical observations on alcoholics of widely varying backgrounds in a multiplicity of contexts—clinics, hospitals, detoxification wards, on the streets, in private homes, bars, taverns, all night coffee shops, parking lots, street corners, rehabilitation programs, A.A. meeting rooms, drying out houses, and universities—is, of course, all to the good. However, I do not mention these many observations made over an eleven year period in an effort to persuade the reader that my observations are unbiased. As Armor correctly points out, all clinical observations are biased, some to a greater extent than others. But although that is most certainly true, it surely cannot be the issue here.

What is at issue here is Armor's belief that the printouts he has examined are somehow less biased than the massive body of direct, empirical observations that are subsumed under such rubrics as "tradition," "conventional wisdom," "folk science," and "clinical observations." While we cannot settle this issue here, we can objectively show that Armor's printouts are far more biased than he has maintained.

A Re-examination of Bias in Armor's 18-Month Follow-up Study

The population to which Armor wishes to generalize from his 18-month follow-up study is the 11,500 clients upon whom full-intake data exist in the NIAAA monitoring system data base. In order to do this, he attempts to show that his 18-month follow-up sample is not biased on both outcome and intake characteristics. While I intend to examine both types of bias, let's turn first to bias on outcome since Armor feels this is the more important issue. I agree.

The issue of possible bias on outcome is particularly crucial in this study since large numbers of subjects were either systematically or nonsytematically eliminated from the analyses. High treatment drop out rates in particular are troublesome since both clinical experience and research indicate clearly that patients who drop out of treatment are likely to have returned to alcoholic drinking. Hence, percentage recovery rates computed on those who remain in treatment are likely to be spuriously elevated (Baekeland, et al., 1975; Hill and Blane, 1969). Equally important is the finding that as inaccessibility to follow-up increases, percent recovery rates rise dramatically. Bart and his colleagues (1973), for example, succeeded in locating 81% of a treatment follow-up sample. When they developed a second wave of follow-up in an effort to locate more subjects, they searched for and found an additional 10%. It is instructive to note that "virtually *none* of this previously unlocated group was doing well" (1976, p. 6). It is, of course, not entirely fair to compare Barr's 81% retrieval rate to Armor's claimed 62% retrieval rate for his 18-month follow-up sample.

Armor and his colleagues examined the issue of bias on outcome in the 18-month sample in several ways. One interesting and, in fact, ingenious test was to correlate percent remissions with interview non-completion rates across the eight treatment centers studied. In this, as in other analyses, percent remission is a *composite* score in which abstention and normal drinking rates were combined to yield a single value.

If the 18-month sample is unbiased, then the correlation computed between percent remission rates and noncompletion rates should be roughly zero. And this is precisely what Armor found. When the eight treatment centers are ranked on both variables, the correlation between the two sets of ranks is -.07. Armor concludes from this analysis that his remission rates are not spuriously high due to very low retrieval rates, i.e., the sample is not biased on outcome.

Before we accept this too ready conclusion, let's rearrange Armor's data and pose different questions of the rearrangement. Table I presents these rearranged data.

TABLE I. Percent abstinence separated from percent normal drinking for 8 ATCs

Treatment Center	% Abstinence	% Normal Drinking	% Composite
B	35	46	81
G	42 (41)	38	79*
F	60	14	74
D	51 (52)	20	72*
E	54 (55)	15	70*
C	46	19	65
H	47 (45)	18	63*
A	32	17	49

*These composite scores do not sum here or in Armor's Table because of minor errors of addition evident in Armor's Table No. 27 (p. 100). Corrected abstinence rates appear in parentheses under the assumption that composite rates and normal drinking rates were unaffected by these trivial computational errors.

The rearrangement of Armor's data permits us to see some rather curious facts that might otherwise go unnoticed. First of all, the -.07 rank order correlation between his composite remission rates and percent noncompletion rates is influenced by the extremely deviant normal drinking rates obtained by treatment centers B and G. Treatment Center B shows a 46% normal drinking rate while Center G shows a 38% rate.[3]

To illustrate just how deviant these rates are, instead of asking "what percentage of the clients in treatment Center B are drinking normally?", let's pose a different question:

"Of those alcoholics in treatment Center B who are drinking at all, what percentage of these are drinking normally?" The answer is roughly 70%.

In other words, almost three out of every four alcoholics in these

[3]The rank order correlation is, of course, not influenced by sample skewness since it is computed on pairs of ranks. My meaning here will become evident as the argument progresses.

two centers who resumed drinking were able, according to these data, to drink normally.

But why should such deviant normal drinking rates occur in these two treatment centers? Possible answers to this question might involve *treatment centers, sampling,* and *interviewers.*

Differences among treatment centers are an unlikely explanation of these deviant normal drinking rates since all were reported to be abstinence-oriented. Moreover, there is no reason to believe that treatment center staffs possessed special knowledge, skills, and techniques for producing normal drinkers. Moreover, treatment effects *per se* were not substantial in this research.

It is, of course, possible that these deviant rates are attributable to the fact that a small number of units (N = 8) were selected nonrandomly. These particular rates for Centers B and G are deviant with regard to other research (Pattison, et. al., 1977) as well as in relationship to other data gathered by the authors. For example, the normal drinking rate of 46% for Center B (N = 78) is nearly four times greater than the 12% rate found in the much larger six-month study sample (N = 2,250).

While the rates are deviant for both other research and the obtained rate found in the six-month study sample, are they deviant with regard to their own sample, i.e., the eight treatment centers who comprise the 18-month study sample? Let's clarify the data on raw percentages and ask a different question: Taking into account different achieved abstinence rates and percent non-remissions, what are the expected and actual values for each center in the sample as a whole?

Table II presents the data for this analysis.

TABLE II. Expected and observed normal drinking rates for the 8 ATCs

Treatment Center	% Non-Abstinence	Ratio of Normal Drinkers/ All Drinkers	% Expected Normal Drinking	% Observed Normal Drinking	Difference
B	65	.71	27	46	+19
G	59	.66	25	38	+13
F	40	.35	17	14	−3
D	48	.41	20	20	−0
E	45	.33	19	15	−4
C	54	.35	23	19	−4
H	55	.34	23	18	−5
A	68	.25	29	17	−12

$$\bar{X} = .42$$

An inspection of these values for expected and observed normal drinking rates is consistent with the hypothesis that Centers B and G seriously misrepresent population values for the 44 treatment centers from which they have been selected. Hence, the data for the 18-month study are consistent with the hypothesis of a spuriously high normal drinking rate with regard to 1) other research, 2) other data in the six-month study, and 3) these data themselves.

But while these data are consistent with the hypothesis of serious sampling error, they also raise questions about *interviewers*. In my earlier paper, I raised the possibility of uncontrolled "experimenter bias" effects with interviewers in the 18-month study viewed as "experimenters" in a totally uncontrolled "experiment." Since different interviewers were employed across treatment centers and were selected non-randomly, possible differences among centers attributable to *systematic* error (as opposed to random measurement error) of measurement cannot be dismissed out of hand, i.e., *differential invalid* measurement over treatment centers.[4]

But, of course, the data presented here, while consistent with the hypothesis of differential validity in normal drinking measures across treatment centers, do not prove either covert or overt collusion between interviewers and staffs in some centers and not in others. Sampling error and, possibly, sampling bias due to subject loss remain as plausible, rival explanations for these deviant rates.

But while we cannot choose among these three sources of uncontrolled variation among centers at this point, we can at least raise serious questions about the representativeness of these particular data for normal drinking rate for the 44 treatment centers and, of course, for the full-intake sample of 11,500 clients of the six-month study. We must also raise questions about the decision of the Rand authors to combine these rates with abstinence rates to yield a composite rate. If the normal drinking rate is suspect, then the composite rate must necessarily be suspect as well.

But if the composite score is abandoned, what measure can be used to test for sample bias? The answer, of course, is quite obvious— *abstinence rate.*

Given the two outcome measures, abstinence rate and normal

---

[4]Treatment centers B and G which have the highest deviations of observed rates from expected rates also show the 6th and 7th lowest achieved abstinence rates. Treatment Center A, however, which shows an opposite direction of deviation from expectations is the lowest of all in achieved abstinence rate. It is difficult to assess Center A's performance since it is generally poor on all counts. However, one cannot overlook the fact that Treatment Center A was the second largest of the eight subsamples (N = 113) and showed the lowest interview non-completion rate of all (16%).

drinking rate, there can scarcely be any question as to which of the two measures, even on an *a priori* basis, can be expected to yield measurements with desirable scientific properties. Both experience and research (Chalmers, 1978) indicate quite clearly that when an alcoholic is asked to state whether he is drinking or not, reliability and, more importantly, *validity* can be expected at quite high levels (reliability and validity coefficients in the .90's).

However, when an alcoholic is asked to recollect over periods of time, questions related to frequency, quantity, and daily patterns of consumption are complicated by a host of factors: 1) such judgments are more difficult even for non-alcoholic people; 2) it is easier for drinking alcoholics to misrepresent quantity, frequency, and daily patterns of consumption to others than it is to misrepresent drinking *per se*; 3) even if honest, alcoholics have difficulty remembering precise patterns of consumption once the drinking starts. The classic example is, of course, the alcoholic who goes into a blackout after several drinks and awakens to a room full of empty pints.*

But no matter, let's assume for the moment that abstinence rate is a more valid measurement than normal drinking rate and observe how the data behave. Using a measure of known reliability and validity, let's re-analyze the relationship between remission rate defined as abstinence and interview non-completion rate.

Table III presents data for this analysis.

TABLE III. Abstinence rates, interview non-completion rates, and ranks for the 8 ATCs in the 18-month Study

Treatment Center	% Abstinence	% Interview Non-Completions	Rank Order Abstinence	Rank Order Non-Completion
B	35	21	7	7
G	41	30	6	6
F	60	32	1	4
D	52	64	3	1
E	55	52	2	3
C	46	56	4	2
H	45	31	5	5
A	32	16	8	8
			Rank order correlation	= +.79*

*Significant below the .05 level of significance.
*The Rand authors readily admit that underreporting of amount of alcohol consumed is apparent in the upper one-third or one-fourth of the consumption distribution, with underestimation being of the order of 50 to 60 percent of this group. For a more complete discussion of why the Rand authors' normal drinking rates can be expected to be spuriously elevated, see my original paper (WALLACE, 1978).

As the analysis in Table III indicates, the correlation between abstinence rates and interview non-completion rates is +.79 and indicates that the 18-month sample is, contrary to Armor's claim, biased on outcome. This obtained rank order correlation of +.79 contrasts sharply with Armor's correlation of -.07 between composite remission rates and interview non-completion rates.

But what about the correlation between normal drinking rates and interview non-completion rates? While there may be no compelling *a priori* reason to suppose that the 18-month sample is *differentially* biased with regard to abstinence and normal drinking rates, it may be so empirically.

The rank order correlation between normal drinking rates and interview non-completion rates is -.14 and this value is consistent with the hypothesis of differential bias for abstinence and normal drinking rates. But when we recall that this correlation is confounded by either possible sampling error and/or differential *invalid* measurement of normal drinking across treatment centers, then the correlation is ambiguous.

Although not entirely legitimate, let's observe how the rank order correlation between normal drinking rates and interview non-completion rates behaves when the two deviant treatment centers B and G are removed from the analysis.

Table IV presents the data for this analysis.

TABLE IV. Normal drinking rates, interview non-completion rates, and ranks for 6 ATCs

Treatment Centers	% Normal Drinking	% Non-Completion	Normal Drinking Rank	Non-Completion Rank
F	14	32	6	4
D	20	64	1	1
E	15	52	5	3
C	19	56	2	2
H	18	31	3	5
A	17	16	4	6
			Rank order correlation =	+.54*

*Given an N of only 6, a correlation of .89 is required for significance at the .05 level. The trend, however, is clearly evident even with small numbers.

The obtained rank order correlation of +.54 is not consistent with the hypothesis of differential bias on outcome for abstinence rates relative to normal drinking rates. True, the data do show that Centers B and G have the highest normal drinking rates as well as the 7th and 6th lowest interview non-completion rates. But is it possible for Armor to argue either on an *a priori* basis or on an empirical basis that the 18-month sample may be biased on outcome for abstinence rates but not for 2 of 8 treatment centers for normal drinking rates? And is it possible for him to do so when the reported normal drinking rates themselves may be spuriously high due to either sampling error or differentially invalid measurement across treatment centers?

With these analyses and discussion in mind, let's turn to Armor's second effort to demonstrate that his 18-month sample is unbiased on outcome. He argues that if his 18-month sample is unbiased, then the composite remission rate in the 18-month study should be at least equal to or even greater than the composite remission rate for the 6-month study. This is what one would expect under the assumption of little or no bias on outcome since the interview completion rate in the 18-month study was 62% and 21% in the 6-month study. As Armor contends, if the 18-month study sample were biased on outcome, then, as a result of its higher interview completion rate relative to the 6-month study, we would expect its composite remission rate to be *lower* than the rate found in the 6-month study.

Armor, in fact, found that the composite remission rate for the 6-month study and the 18-month study were virtually identical (68% and 67%). He concluded that these results were consistent with the assumption of no bias on outcome for his samples.

But, bearing in mind, our previous analysis of abstinence and bias on outcome, let's pose a different set of questions of Armor's data.

If the 18-month study is not only biased on outcome but characterized by spuriously high normal drinking rates for reasons already discussed, what should the data comparing remission rates in the 6-month study and the 18-month study look like? The answer is quite obvious:

a. abstinence rate should *decrease* in the 18-month study.
b. normal drinking rate should increase.
c. the composite score should show no change from study to study.

The data confirm all three expectations. Table V presents the results obtained by Armor for abstinence separated from normal drinking.

As the data in Table V indicate, in the absence of a compelling *a priori* reason to explain differential bias on outcome for abstinence versus normal drinking rates, the 18-month sample is not only biased on outcome but the measurement of normal drinking rates is probably spuriously high due to differentially invalid measurement of normal drinking rates across treatment centers.

Armor's final way to deal with the question of bias was to ask after possible bias in the 18-month sample with regard to *intake character-*

TABLE V. Remission rates for the 6-month and 18-month samples

Sample	% Abstinence	% Normal Drinking	% Composite Remission
6-Month	56	12	68
18-Month	45	22	67
Difference	−11	+10	−1

istics for the full intake sample of 11,500 clients in the 6-month study. Accordingly, he compared his 18-month sample to the full-intake sample on the intake characteristics available in the ATC monitoring system data base.

There is, of course, nothing wrong in principle with this way of proceeding. However, as I pointed out in my earlier paper, it can be a weak and unconvincing test of sample bias since the in-take characteristics that the samples are compared on do not predict remission rates. Armor's own regression analyses inform us that only 8.8% of the variance in remission rates can be accounted for by client characteristics at in-take.

One could, I suppose, show that the samples are unbiased with regard to eye color, hair color, and preferences for particular T.V. programs. But so what?

In short, Armor's analysis here informs us that his 18-month sample is, for the most part, not seriously biased *on this particular collection of in-take characteristics*. The analysis does not inform us that the 18-month sample is *unbiased* since the data necessary for a general conclusion of that nature are not available in this study.

THE EPISTEMOLOGICAL DILEMMA REVISITED

On the basis of my examination of the facts of sampling in the Rand study, I earlier stated that the epistemological dilemma posed by such extreme subject loss would not yield easily to resolution. My further analyses on the questions of bias on outcome and intake and the issue of the validity of the normal drinking measurement (and hence, the composite remission rate) not only underscore my earlier convictions as to the stubborness of this epistemological dilemma but expand its proportions.

A reanalysis of Armor's estimates of possible bias indicates that the 18-month sample is biased on outcome for two of Armor's "tests."

The third method of "testing" for bias was seen as providing weak but insufficient information as to the general question of likely bias attendant upon extreme subject loss. Moreover, serious questions have arisen with regard to the validity of measurement of the normal drinking rate, and particularly so in two treatment centers where the rate was deviant with regard to other research, with data from the 6-month study, and with appropriate expectations.

In effect, the data from the 8 ACT's cannot be generalized to the 44 ACT's. The data from the 18-month study sample cannot be generalized to the full-intake sample of 11,500 clients. The data from the 2,250 clients who comprise the decimated full-intake sample cannot be generalized to the full-intake sample. It is even the case that the data from the two deviant treatment centers that comprise one quarter of the 8 treatment centers for the 18-month study cannot be taken as representative of the sample of centers of which they are purported to be a part. And above all else, none of these data can be generalized to *alcoholics in general*.

In short, there is *no* population to which *any* of the findings (not only those concerning normal drinking) of the Rand authors can be generalized. What Armor chooses to dignify by calling scientific "samples" are more properly construed as raggedy aggregates in search of a population. Hence, it is not immediately evident that one solution rather than another as to what to do with Armor's numbers is, on scientific grounds alone, prudent rather than in "egregious error," conservative rather than "totally illegitimate," and informative rather than "misleading."

But the dilemma remains, doesn't it? What to do with Armor's numbers? Perhaps there are other alternatives.

How Shall We Construe Armor's Numbers?

On the basis of composite remission rates, Armor claims a 70% remission rate for the NIAAA Treatment Centers taken as a whole. However, this claimed rate is confounded by multiple sources of uncontrolled variation. Since both abstinence rate and normal drinking rate are biased on outcome due to extreme loss of subjects, *both* measures are spuriously high as reported by Armor. Furthermore, since the normal drinking measure employed can be expected, on the basis of other research, to be spuriously high in general, i.e., generally invalid measurement, the claimed normal drinking rate is not only spuriously elevated but differentially so in relation to the abstinence rate. Finally, the strong suggestion of differentially invalid measurement of normal drinking across treatment centers in the 18-month study suggests that the true score for normal drinking rate is lowered further.

What is the true remission rate in this study? Certainly not 70%. All indications point to markedly lower remission rates—for abstinence, normal drinking, and composite rates.

Is it possible that one set of Armor's numbers leads us inexorably to one body of conclusions while the other set points in the opposite direction? Let's review. One set of numbers—abstinence rates—possesses properties normally expected of scientific measurements. From this set of numbers, we are able to conclude that the samples were biased but, more importantly, that successful treatment in NIAAA centers, during the period under examination, was considerably less than anybody might have liked.

From the other set of numbers—composite remission—rates we could conclude that the samples were unbiased and that successful treatment in NIAAA centers was far more common than perhaps anybody had hoped for.

Hence, one set of numbers can be construed as empirical-scientific quantities to be entered into rational decision processes as to how treatment should or should not be conducted in Federal centers. That much is clear. As to the other set of numbers, I am frankly unwilling to advocate anything at all, and nothing said here should be interpreted as such advocacy.

But is it not possible that the other set of numbers might best be construed as quasi-empirical events whose meanings are to be sought not in the factual world of treatment outcome but rather as entries in a complex matrix of political values? Where would such an analysis lead us if we were to follow it through? Unfortunately, I am not a political scientist and therefore not competent to perform such an analysis nor to claim to have discovered fact if I were to conduct such an analysis. But, for those serious students of the politics of alcoholism, let me throw out a few probably unrelated and possibly irrelevant bits and pieces of observation suitable for little more than a beginning since the ultimate question to be answered in political analysis is— "who benefits?"

Alcoholics, either recovered or in treatment, clearly could not have benefited from these findings. Any study that comes to us, not only under the auspices of science and a prestigious research institute, but also with the apparent approval of a powerful Federal Agency,[5] cannot be taken lightly. For those dedicated recovered alcoholics who

---

[5] I hasten to point out that Dr. Ernest Noble, the Director of NIAAA who succeeded Dr. Morris Chafetz, neither commissioned the Rand study nor was responsible for its release to the press. Noble, in fact, publicly addressed himself to the many shortcomings of the research.

have worked unceasingly to have their concepts and observations treated with due consideration by professionals and the lay public alike, the Rand study, even if only by implication, misunderstanding, and inappropriate hyperbole on the part of others, cannot have helped but constitute an important set back.

For alcoholics in treatment, particularly those in NIAAA centers at the time of the research or who subsequently became candidates for such centers, the report was clearly not in their interests. If the true measure of success in these centers at the time was reflected in abstinence rates, then every effort should have been addressed to demanding more dollars from Congress for research, prevention, and rehabilitation rather than in convincing members of the House and Senate that all was well in the world of alcoholism treatment.

But if members of the recovered alcoholic community and alcoholics in treatment could not and indeed, did not benefit from the report, who did?

Unfortunately, here we are well beyond any available scientific data and simply cannot advocate nor conjecture. But there are a few observations that might ultimately prove of relevance.

It is curious to note that Dr. Morris Chafetz, former Director of NIAAA and the sponsor of the Rand research, had taken his case to the people shortly after the Rand Report had appeared. In an article, under his own byline, that appeared in the *Rochester Democrat and Chronicle* (August 15, 1976) Chafetz states, "The Rand Report should make those interested in the plight of alcoholic people jump for joy, for it scientifically reemphasizes an important fact: It is possible to treat alcoholic people." Chafetz added the astonishing statement that "opponents of the report have little respect for alcoholic people." And "to the many devoted workers in the field of alcoholism who are themselves recovered alcoholics, it is upsetting to learn that the abstinence to which they adhere may not be necessary."

In short, on the basis of a composite remission rate that, for reasons already discussed, overestimates *both* abstinence and normal drinking rates and shares in the invalid measurement of normal drinking, Chafetz is advising us all to "jump for joy." Alcoholism may indeed be capable of successful treatment but the stubborn fact remains that it wasn't treated very well in Federal treatment centers under Chafetz' reign as Director of NIAAA. And no amount of mud-slinging at "opponents of the report" or at recovered alcoholics themselves will alter this fact.

Dr. David Armor is distressed to observe some critics such as myself, using his research material "in a highly selective and erroneous fashion to promote preconceived and unsubstantiated beliefs about treatment goals." He is further distressed that "these critiques are in turn used by non-scientists to strengthen their goal for alcoholics, and to bolster anti-scientific sentiments . . ."

I leave it to the reader to judge whether the charges brought against the kettle more deeply color the pot.

References

Armor, D. J., Polich, J. M., and Stambul, H. B. *Alcoholism and Treatment.* Rand Corporation, Santa Monica, CA., June, 1976.

Baekeland, F., Lundwall, L. and Shanahan, T. Correlates of patient attrition in the outpatient treatment of alcoholism. *Journal of Nervous and Mental Disorders,* 1973, 157, pp. 99–107.

Barr, H. I., Rosen, A., Antes, D. E., and Ottenberg, D. J. Two year follow-up study of 724 drug and alcohol addicts treated together in an abstinence therapeutic community. Paper presented at the 81st Annual Convention of the American Psychological Association, Montreal, August, 1973.

Chafetz, M. E., "Alcoholism Report Draws Overreaction", Rochester Democrat and Chronicle, Sunday, August 15, 1976.

Chalmers, D. The Alcoholic's Controlled Drinking Time. *World Alcohol Project,* Vol. 2, No. 1, 1979.

Hill, M. I. and Blane, H. T., Evaluation of Psychotherapy with Alcoholics: A critical review. *Quarterly Journal of Studies on Alcohol.* 1976, 28, pp. 76–104.

Hyde, G. Unpublished paper. Supervisor of data collection for St. Luke's Hospital, one of the 8 centers in which data for the 18-month study was gathered.

Kissko, J. A. Memorandum, Department of Health, Education, and Welfare, NIAAA, June 23, 1976.

Pattison, E. M., Sobell, M. B. and Sobell, L. C., *Emerging Concepts of Alcohol Dependence,* New York: Springer Publishing Co., 1977.

Wallace, J. Alcoholism and Treatment: A Critical Analysis. ALFAWAP Journal. Vol. I, No. 2, 1978.

The Alcoholism Controversy

I am delighted that the *American Psychologist* has devoted a Psychology in the Public Forum section to alcoholism (October 1983). A biopsychosocial disease as devastating as this one deserves far more attention than it has received from psychologists. Several of the contributions are outstanding.

But although delighted, I am also eager that psychologists not familiar with developments in the field of alcoholism understand that the views represented in that special section (Emrick & Hansen, 1983; Goldman, 1983; Langenbucher & Nathan, 1983; Marlatt, 1983; Matsunaga, 1983; Mayer, 1983; Moos & Finney, 1983; Nathan & Wiens, 1983; Wanberg & Horn, 1983; Wiens & Menustik, 1983) constitute a rather narrow and certainly partial glimpse of a complex and rapidly evolving specialty.

Psychologists should first note that extraordinary developments are taking place in psychobiology and include enormous strides forward in behavioral genetics and in the relationship of neurochemistry to behavior. Other than Goldman's (1983) excellent contribution on cognitive impairment in chronic alcoholics, this Public Forum provided nary a hint that alcoholics have bodies and that these may be involved in their illness. Evidence continues to accumulate from both animal and human studies conducted internationally that genetic factors enter into the etiology of alcoholism (McClearn, 1981; Schuckitt, 1981). Moreover, work conducted by psychobiologists such as R. D. Myers at the University of North Carolina strongly implicates condensation products formed by aldehydes such as acetaldehyde interacting with neurotransmitters such as dopamine and serotonin (Blum, Hamilton, Hirst, & Wallace, 1978; Myers, McCaleb, & Ruwe, 1982). Studies also point to possible roles of single neurotransmitters such as norepinephrine (NE), serotonin (5-HT) and its precursors and also to altered metabolism of these (Myers, 1978; Myers & Melchoir, 1977).

If psychologists in the field of alcoholism do not want to be caught looking into the rearview mirror of a simplistic and naive behaviorism, they are well advised to eschew ideology and doctrine and to pay attention to rapid information change in associated sciences.

Aside from neglect of psychobiology, the Public Forum left the unmistakeable impression that aversion therapy is the only promising modality on the current treatment scene. Moreover, the authors in the section apparently believed that a lack of consensus exists among alcoholism workers as to how to design and operate effective treatment programs. Actually, aversion therapy is barely visible on the alcoholism treatment scene and is currently utilized in very few programs, most notably at Raleigh Hills Hospital.

In contrast to the rather dismal picture painted by Nathan and Wiens (1983) of the lack of "consensus among alcoholism workers" (p. 1035) as to how to treat alcoholism effectively, alcoholism treatment is characterized by quite the opposite—increasing convergence of philosophies, paradigms, and operations. Alcoholism treatment is (within limits of cost and cost effectiveness) multimodal, multidisciplinary, individualized, and supportive of Alcoholics Anonymous as a continuing recovery program. The program with which I am affiliated follows this rather commonly accepted model, treats approximately 2,000 alcoholics a year, and is currently showing the following short-term abstention rates on follow-up (3 months): alcoholism uncomplicated by either emotional illness or drug dependence (84%); alcoholism complicated by accompanying emotional illness (75%); alcoholism complicated by additional drug dependence (68%).

These results were obtained by conducting a questionnaire survey of all patients (follow-up rate of 78%) that involved independent evaluators (research personnel not involved in delivery of treatments). Results can be expected to degrade to some extent as the follow-up period lengthens. As the potency of treatment factors diminish over time, the influence of extra-treatment factors become more pronounced.

Nathan and Wiens (1983) editorialized about various "unhelpful views on alcoholism (p. 1035)." They included in the Public Forum only those psychologists who, in their opinion, were instrumental in altering these "unhelpful views" and in offering alternatives in conceptualization of both the disease and its treatment. In part, this translated to further editorializing by Marlatt (1983). Marlatt provided psychologists with a defense of the experiment on controlled drinking conducted by Sobell and Sobell (1973). This editorial also provided an indirect attack on the recent refutation of the controversial Sobell and Sobell experiment by Pendery, Maltzman, and West (1982).

Despite Marlatt's efforts to salvage a sinking ship, any empiricist with an eye for the real cannot help but be impressed with the fact that the Sobell results are not reliable. Sobell and Sobell found that 19 of 20 hospitalized alcoholics could be said to be functioning well on follow-up after experimental controlled drinking treatment. However, Pendery, Maltzman, and West (1982), on independent follow-up, found that the results for these same patients were just the opposite; 19 of 20 could *not* be classified as functioning well over time. To argue, as Marlatt attempted to do, that one must contrast the Sobell results for controlled drinking patients with results for those patients given abstention-oriented treatment misses a fundamental point of experimental design; when subjects are *not* randomly assigned to experimental and control conditions, comparisons between conditions are meaningless. In the Sobell research, assignment to conditions was not random.

Instead of taking an attitude of self-righteousness about former Sobell experiment patients who have banded together to monitor the further activities of psychologists committed to behavior modification procedures in alcoholism, Marlatt should have asked, "Why is this happening?" Why do these former patients fear behavioral modification procedures in the service of controlled drinking? Why do patients find it necessary to organize against perceived threat and against perceived ideology? Why are some psychologists so threatened by the consumers of their services?

Why should psychology cast its future in alcoholism with a treatment goal for which empirical support is unimpressive (controlled drinking), when psychology can make enormous contributions to helping alcoholics to achieve and maintain sobriety?

As I mentioned, our specialized facility treats approximately 2,000 alcoholics a year. These patients are socially stable adults who represent all stages of the disease from early to late alcoholism. During a recent lecture to 160 patients, I asked the following questions and got the following not atypical responses: (a) How many of you tried through a variety of means to control either your drinking or its negative consequences before coming into treatment? Response: 160; (b) How many of you succeeded in doing so? Response: 0; and (c) How many of you believe that you will be able to drink safely after treatment? Response: 0.

Despite the obvious demand characteristics of the situation, the results of such simple questioning lead to several reasonable conclusions: Alcoholics have tried to control their drinking and the negative consequences of drinking *before* coming to treatment, and they report what appears to be universal failure. Hence, perceptions of inability to control and expectations of future failure seem to be very much a result of alcoholics' experiences and are not entirely attributable to treatment staff belief systems.

At best, Marlatt's concluding statement that the Sobell's work "will stand as an early landmark on the empirical road ahead" (p. 1108) staggers the scientific imagination. At worst, the statement stands empiricism on its head.

References

Blum, K., Hamilton, M., Hirst, M., & Wallace, J. (1978). Putative role of isoquinoline alkaloids in alcoholism: A link to opiates. *Alcoholism: Clinical and Experimental Research, 2*, 113–120.

Emrick, C. D., & Hansen, J. (1983). Assertions regarding effectiveness of treatment for alcoholism: Fact or fantasy? *American Psychologist, 38*, 1078–1088.

Goldman, M. S. (1983). Cognitive impairment in chronic alcoholics: Some cause for optimism. *American Psychologist, 38*, 1045–1054.

Langenbucher, J. W., & Nathan, P. E. (1983). Psychology, public policy, and the evidence for alcohol intoxication. *American Psychologist, 38*, 1070–1077.

Marlatt, A. G. (1983). The controlled drinking controversy: A commentary. *American Psychologist, 38*, 1097–1110.

Matsunaga, S. (1983). The federal role in research, treatment, and prevention of alcoholism. *American Psychologist, 38*, 1111–1115.

Mayer, W. (1983). Alcohol abuse and alcoholism: The psychologist's role in prevention, research, and treatment. *American Psychologist, 38*, 1116–1121.

McClearn, G. (1981). Genetic studies in animals. *Alcoholism: Clinical and Experimental Research, 5*, 447–448.

Moos, R. H., & Finney, J. W. (1983). The expanding scope of alcoholism treatment evaluation. *American Psychologist, 38*, 1036–1044.

Myers, R. D. (1978). Psychopharmocology of alcohol. *Annual Review of Pharmacology and Toxicology, 18*, 125–144.

Myers, R. D., McCaleb, M. L., & Ruwe, W. D. (1982). Alcohol drinking induced in the monkey by tetrahydropapaveroline (THP) infused into the cerebral ventricle. *Pharmacology, Biochemistry, and Behavior, 16*, 995–1000.

Myers, R. D., & Melchoir, C. L. (1977). Alcohol and alcoholism: Role of serotonin. In W. B. Essman, (Ed.), *Serotonin in health and disease* (pp. 373–430). New York: Spectrum.

Nathan, P. E., & Wiens, A. N. (1983). Alcoholism: Introduction and overview. *American Psychologist, 38*, 1035.

Pendery, M., Maltzman, I. & West, L. J. (1982). Controlled drinking by alcoholics? New findings and a reevaluation of a major affirmative study. *Science, 217*, 169–175.

Schuckitt, M. A. (1981). The genetics of alcoholism. *Alcoholism: Clinical and Experimental Research, 5*, 439–440.

Sobell, M., & Sobell, L. (1973). Individualized behavior therapy for alcoholics. *Behavior Therapy, 4*, 49–72.

Wanberg, K. W., & Horn, J. L. (1983). Assessment of alcohol use with multidimensional concepts and measures. *American Psychologist, 38,* 1055–1069.

Wiens, A. N., & Menustik, C. E. (1983). Treatment outcome and patient characteristics in an aversion therapy program for alcoholism. *American Psychologist, 38,* 1089–1096.

Studies in Prestigious Journals Invalidate Controlled Drinking for Alcoholics

Two recent reports from prestigious scientific journals should finally put to rest the debate over whether or not alcoholics can learn to drink moderately. In the June *New England Journal of Medicine*, a distinguished group of alcohol researchers headed by Dr. John Helzer and Dr. Lee Robins, both of the Medical School of Washington University, report results from their seven year study.

Following the lives of 1,289 diagnosed alcoholics over a five to seven year period, Drs. Helzer and Robins found that less than 1% of the men were able to engage in nonproblem or moderate drinking. Even when extremely liberal criteria for moderate drinking were used (up to seven drinks a day), the vast majority of alcoholics showed no ability to do moderate drinking. The results for women were not much different: ninety-six percent of the women alcoholics were unsuccessful at moderating their alcohol intake.

At the same time that this study cast grave doubts upon the feasibility of teaching alcoholics to drink normally, it raised questions about the efficacy of providing care for alcoholics in general medical-surgical hospitals and treatment in psychiatric facilities. While fifteen percent of the patients who had received care of some kind or another in these types of facilities were abstinent from alcohol, the results are not as impressive as those achieved by free-standing, specialized alcoholism treatment centers. Free-standing treatment centers typically report abstention rates ranging from 50 to 70 percent depending upon length of the followup period after treatment is completed. Of course, in defense of the other types of facilities mentioned, not all of the patients followed in the Helzer and Robins research had actually received alcoholism treatment. Many had been diagnosed only, detoxified only, treated for short periods of time, or received medical-surgical treatments for the medical illnesses and traumatic injuries that frequently accompany alcoholism rather than treatment of their alcoholism.

The second study that destroys the credibility of the moderate drinking idea appeared in an equally prestigious journal: the Rutgers University *Journal of Studies on Alcohol.* In this study, Dr. Griffith Edwards of London's Institute of Psychiatry located the patients who had been reported upon in a classic study of D.L. Davies. The Davies study was reported in 1962 and claimed to find that 7 out of 93 patients discharged from Maudsley Hospital were able to drink normally. This early study quickly became a rallying point for people who didn't accept the fact that alcoholism is a disease; if 7 alcoholics could control their drinking, then others could be taught to do the same thing.

Unfortunately, on closer examination, Davies' study does not bear scientific scrutiny. Of the 7 patients, 5 were relapsing back into alcoholism shortly after being released from the hospital and none were able to control their drinking. Only 2 of the relocated patients actually seemed to be successful, controlled drinkers but one of these did not appear to be alcoholic to begin with. In effect, 1 of 92 alcoholics seemed to have succeeded where 91 clearly failed.

The moral here is obvious: claims that alcoholics can either spontaneously or formally be taught to control their drinking should be taken with a grain of salt until all the scientific evidence is in. None of the major studies—the Rand Corporation study and the research on controlled drinking by psychologists Mark and Linda Sobell—have held water when subjected to the kind of scientific scrutiny we demand in other areas of medical research.

In conclusion, alcoholism treatment works best when the goal is total abstinence. And it works best when it is treated as a primary disease in specialized free-standing alcoholism treatment centers staffed by people knowledgeable about the disease.

REFERENCES

Edwards, Griffith. "A Later Follow-up of a Classic Case Series: D.L. Davies's 1962 Report and Its Significance for the Present." *Journal of Studies on Alcohol,* Vol. 46, No. 3, 1985.

Helzer, John and Robins, Lee (and colleagues). "The Extent of Long-term Moderate Drinking Among Alcoholics Discharged From Medical and Psychiatric Treatment Facilities." *The New England Journal of Medicine,* June 27, 1985.

Part VI

Dual Diagnosis

The Other Problems of
Alcoholics

Recent research suggests that alcoholism may be thought of as a genetically influenced disease of the chemistry of the brain that is complicated by psychological and social factors (Wallace, 1983; 1985a). Hence, it is a biopsychosocial disease, one that involves biology, behavior, and sociocultural factors (Wallace, 1985b). The disease is characterized by inconsistent control over one's behavior while drinking and/or one's drinking behavior. A cardinal feature is continued compulsive use in the face of frequent negative psychological, biological, or social consequences of use. Alcoholism is, in effect, not a primary psychiatric disorder.

But to say that alcoholism is not a psychiatric disorder does not mean that alcoholics never develop psychiatric problems. Given the life time rates of psychiatric problems in American society for people in general, it is reasonable to expect some alcoholics to show these problems as well. Alcoholism does not make one immune to problems such as suicide, drug addiction, depression, brain disorders, eating disorders, personality disorders, sexual disorders, and so forth. The facts are actually to the contrary since these and many other medical, social and psychological problems are consistently associated with the primary disease of alcoholism. In fact, it is standard practice to point to many of these other problems as the negative consequences, outcomes, or complications of alcoholism in order to show just how serious the disease really is.

But if we are so willing to accept these other problems of alcoholics as consequences of the primary disease of alcoholism, why have we been so slow to design treatment programs that address these as well? The answers to this question are surely many and involve complex issues of ideology, interdisciplinary political turf issues, financial considerations, practical treatment concerns, and variants of denial among alcoholism treatment professionals.

From an historical perspective, it is easy to see why alcoholism treatment professionals were uncomfortable with mention of psychopathology among alcoholic populations. Struggling to establish adequate treatment programs in the face of either indifference to or open hostility from many professionals in medicine, psychiatry, psychology, (e.g., Marlatt, 1983) and social work, alcoholism workers had little choice but to forge a separate identity around a "naive" disease concept of alcoholism. On the positive side, this move toward separatism led to the development of bodies of theory, research, and practice specific to the disease of alcoholism. Theorists used imagination and empirical observations of clinical alcoholism populations to formulate theories of treament unique to alcoholics rather than to psychiatric populations in general (e.g. Zimberg, Wallace, & Blume, 1985). Instead of blindly accepting and mindlessly generalizing theories of treatment developed on neurotics, schizophrenics, laboratory rats, and male college sophomores, some workers in the alcoholism field have insisted that it is quite proper, indeed scientifically necessary, to conceive of theories of treatment derived from direct empirical observations of alcoholics (Wallace, 1985a; Brown, 1985).

A second positive outcome of separatism was the encouragement of research aimed directly at understanding the biological basis of alcoholism. It is exceedingly doubtful that many of our present exciting research advances in such fields as genetics, psychopharmacology, neurochemistry, membrane physiology, and neuroendocrinology, could have happened at all if alcoholism were to have become dominated by psychodynamic psychiatry, traditional behavioristic psychology, cognitive-social psychology, or sociology.

A third positive outcome of a separate identity built around a naive disease concept of alcoholism was the acceptance of practical treatment methods directed to the drinking behavior itself and to the direct negative consequences of such behavior. Instead of searching for the assumed underlying primary psychological and psychiatric antecedents, clinicians began to address the alcoholism directly. Treatment of primary alcoholism became a specialty in and of itself in which the drinking as such was assigned first priority and dealt with realistically, directly, firmly, and openly. Tough love became the standard rather than permissiveness, flexibility and inadvertent professional enabling. The here and now of active alcoholism and its consequences became the focus of clinical activity rather than the there and then of psychosexual development and analytic probing into the distant past. First things first, a slogan borrowed from AA, indicated that we had to deal with the alcoholism first if any progress could be expected. Alcoholism counseling became a specialty built around the critically important issues of the patient's recognition of the problem, identification of self as an alcoholic, acceptance of alcoholism, and how to live a comfortable, productive and fulfilling life without alcohol.

These great strides forward in theory, research, and treatment could not have happened so rapidly and perhaps not at all if alcoholism workers had not centered their activities around a naive disease concept.

On the other negative side of the ledger, however, separatism has had costs as well as benefits. A "naive" disease concept is, in effect, a "defensive" concept. It is defensive in the sense that it protects the field from inappropriate, ineffective, and incorrect views of the primary disease of alcoholism. Unfortunately, a "naive" disease concept may also block necessary and helpful input from knowledgeable and understanding professionals in allied fields of psychiatry, psychology, and social work. While providing order, security, and direction, a "naive" disease concept may have fostered another kind of denial—professional denial of the other problems of alcoholics. In a sense, it is all rather like the blindman and the elephant. Each of us has a piece of the whole animal and is in constant danger of confusing the part with the whole. It is important that we remain skeptical of all naive conceptions of alcoholism, biological, behavioral, psychiatric or sociocultural, and embrace a holistic conception of the disease. Alcoholism is, in my opinion, a biopsychosocial disease in which biology, behavior, and social cultural factors interact to maintain illness. Indeed, several biopsychosocial models may be necessary in the sense that in any given case, biological, psychological or sociocultural factors may predominate in the clinical picture (Wallace, 1985b).

But regardless of how we choose to construe alcoholism, the changing nature of today's alcoholism treatment populations indicates that far more attention must be paid to the other problems of alcoholics. What are these other problems? And what implications do they hold for alcoholism treatment?

OTHER DRUG DEPENDENCE

Today's treatment populations show considerable other drug use and dependence. In 1982 a fairly rigorous retrospective study of our records at Edgehill Newport revealed that approximately 25% of our patients showed dependence on some other drug in addition to alcohol (Wallace, 1982). By 1986, this figure of other drug dependence has risen sharply to 45% with much of the increase attributable to cocaine involvement. Schuckit (1985) in a study of 557 alcoholic consecutive admissions to the San Diego VA Medical Center for the three year period, 1982–1984, found an incidence of 11% with a diagnosis of primary drug abuse and secondary alcoholism. Of Schuckit's primary alcoholic group, 53% had used marijuana, 23% stimulants, 14% cocaine, and 11% depressants.

Of our current admissions to Edgehill Newport, 35% report some involvement with cocaine with 18% characterized as cocaine dependent. A fairly large number (22%) report current use of minor tranquilizers with 7% reporting dependence. It is curious to note that our current data show a marked drop in current use of marijuana with approximately 15 percent reporting serious involvement.

Sokolow and his colleagues (1981) in a study of 1,340 alcoholic patients in 17 New York State alcoholism rehabilitation centers found current substance use in 46% of the patients in the 30 days prior to treatment.

Freed, (1973) in a review of the literature from 1925 to 1972 concluded that 20% of alcohol-dependent individuals also use other addictive drugs. By 1977, Carroll's review (1977) suggested that between 60 and 80 percent of alcoholics use other drugs. Hesselbrock et al., (1985) found a lifetime incidence of other drug abuse in 45% of male primary alcoholics and 38% of female primary alcoholics.

Thus, most studies agree in reporting substantial drug abuse in alcoholic treatment populations. There are a number of important implications of this finding.

First, alcoholism treatment program staffs must be prepared to alter perceptions of, and expectations toward current treatment populations. As studies have shown, alcoholics who abuse other drugs tend to be significantly more impaired both physically and psychologically than are alcoholics who do not abuse drugs (Sokolow, Welte, Hyness, & Lyons, 1981). Schuckit (1985) reported many more childhood antisocial problems among primary substance abusers who abuse alcohol than among primary alcoholics. Primary substance abusers who abuse alcohol were considerably more likely to have played hookey, been suspended/expelled from school, run away from home, categorized as incorrigible, sent to reform school, been arrested before and after age 16, committed a felony after 16, hurt someone in a fight, and used a weapon. Moreover, primary substance abusers with secondary alcoholism showed more psychiatric hospitalizations, more depressions, suicide attempts, and visits to mental health workers. Khantzian and Treece (1985) found 93% of a sample of narcotics addicts met the criteria for one or more psychiatric disorder other than substance abuse.

During follow-up, primary substance abusers with secondary alcoholism showed more police problems as well as more substance abuse.

Alcoholics who abuse other drugs and primary drug abusers who abuse alcohol may be at greater risk for various types of disorders. Cocaine, for example, is believed to result in an initial surge of dopamine in brain, but chronic use is now believed to result in transmitter depletion (Gold, Pottash, & Extein, 1986). Not only is dopamine believed to be depleted by chronic use, but so are serotonin and noradrenaline. Therefore, we can expect the cocaine dependent alcoholic to show much more mood vacillation as well as more drug hunger during primary treatment than the pure alcoholic. Moreover, the mood vacillation in the recovering cocaine dependent alcoholic is likely to be longer lasting than in the recovering alcoholic who is not dependent on cocaine.

Since cocaine is associated with coronary artery spasm as well as cardiac arrhythmias, alcoholic patients who abuse cocaine must be advised as to the cardiac risks associated with the compulsive use of cocaine (Estroff & Gold, 1986). Those patients with underlying valvular diseases and other cardiac abnormalities, regardless of their ages, must be educated about the effects of cocaine on the heart and the associated risks of sudden cardiac death.

Schizophrenic alcoholics who abuse cocaine must be counseled to avoid doing so as schizophrenia has been associated with either a dopamine excess or sensitivity of the dopamine system. Cocaine may further augment dopaminergic sensitivity and exacerbate schizophrenic symptoms. For cocaine dependent alcoholics, care must be exercised in prescribing phenothiazine drugs or Haldol for cocaine induced hallucinations since these drugs may further reduce dopamine levels in the brain and actually give rise to intense craving for cocaine.

Alcoholics who abuse drugs must be counseled about the dangers of injecting cocaine, narcotics, and other drugs. Shared needles are a common source of AIDS with 50% of new cases in New York and New Jersey appearing among intravenous drug users. Hepatitis with potentially fatal outcome is a further risk of shared needles.

Still another educational need for alcoholics who abuse drugs is consideration of the risks involved with designer drugs. A designer drug is a drug that is produced to resemble some other drug but not replicate its exact molecular structure. In this fashion, unscrupulous manufacturers of such drugs can produce and sell drugs that mimic illicit drugs without fear of prosecution. A recent case involving sale of a designer "synthetic heroin" in Northern California resulted in tragic results for a number of persons. The drug, MPTP, in brain, resulted in an abnormal metabolite, MPP^+. MPP^+ resulted in damage to the Substantia Nigra, a dopamine rich area of the brain. As a result of this damage, addicts began to appear at treatment centers with symptoms of severe Parkinson's Disease within only several weeks of use (Nova, 1986; Smith, 1986).

Alcohol, of course, is a neurotoxin and as such is capable of causing death of brain cells, brain atrophy, and neuropsychological dysfunction. Mixed with other drugs that are also neurotoxic, the neurological impact is significantly increased. A drug like "ecstasy", for example, has been reported to destroy serotoninergic neurons at doses sufficient to produce psychological effects. Amphetamines have been reported to have sustained effects on purkinje neurons and also on the dopaminergic system. In one experiment, purkinje neurons treated with amphetamines were reported to be functioning abnormally 50 days later (Sorensen et al. 1982).

Due to the increased neurotoxicity of alcohol and drugs, clinicians working with alcoholics who abuse other drugs and primary drug abusers who abuse alcohol should realize that these patients are likely to show persistent information processing/cognitive deficits in primary treatment and beyond. These patients simply may have more difficulty in assimilating new information and grasping its implications as well as in information storage and retrieval. Such patients may show difficulties in impulse control, frustration tolerance, irritability, and stress-related symptoms.

Alcoholics who abuse other drugs must be made aware of drug half-lives, synergy, and cross-tolerance. The half-life of a drug is the amount of time necessary for one half of the initial dose to be metabolized. Some drugs like cocaine have very short half-lives. Others like benzodiazpines (Valium, Librium) and tetrahydrocannabinol (the active ingredient in marijuana) have very long half-lives. In general, the more fat soluable a drug, the more readily it enters into the fatty tissue and is stored. PCP, for example, an animal tranquilizer, is very fat soluable and can be stored in fatty tissue for long periods of time. PCP may be released from stores by exercise long after use is stopped. Physical dependence on benzodiazpines (Valium, Librium) has been shown to develop at therapeutic doses over sufficient periods of time. Alcoholic patients need to be counseled to stay away from benzodiazepines because of the long half-lives of these drugs and the clear danger of development of physical dependence even at therapeutic doses. Moreover, because of cross-tolerance associated with all drugs of the non-selective general depressant or sedative-hypnotic group, alcoholics are at even greater risk for the development of physical dependence on drugs such as Valium, Librium, barbiturates, quaaludes, sleeping pills, and so forth.

Today's alcoholic treatment populations also need to be cautioned about drug synergy, or the non-additive, multiplicative manner in which drugs of certain classes combine to produce dangerous and even lethal effects.

Finally, alcoholics who take many drugs may be risking sudden dangerous effects because of different half-lives. Alcoholics going up on stimulants and down on alcohol and other depressants can easily misjudge how much depressant chemical is in their bodies because of the offsetting effects of stimulants like cocaine. Unfortunately, the opposing effects of cocaine may rapidly decay because of the shorter half-life of the drug leaving the person vulnerable to the longer lasting effects of equally large doses of depressants. If such rapid changes should occur while a person is driving a car, the sudden onset of unopposed depressant effects could have tragic outcomes.

Case Illustration. The patient was a 23 year old male admitted for inpatient alcoholism treatment. During the course of treatment, the patient revealed that he was also taking significant amounts of cocaine and was smoking marijuana. Moreover, the medical history indicated that he suffered from a cardiac problem—serious mitral regurgitation as a result of prior rheumatic fever. The patient had been taking prescribed cardiac medications but the effects of these were offset by cocaine, marijuana, and alcohol. Moreover, immediately prior to admission to alcoholism treatment, he had been seen and treated for life threatening cardiac arrhythmias on several occasions at area hospital emergency rooms. Apparently, neither emergency medical personnel nor his cardiologist had investigated his extensive use of illicit drugs known to cause both coronary artery spasm and/or serious cardiac arrhythmias. The effects of cocaine and THC on coronary arteries and/or the heart's electrical activity were explained carefully to the patient. He was counseled that because of his underlying cardiac problem, drinking and drug taking (especially cocaine and THC) were setting him up for sudden cardiac death. The patient's reaction indicated that he had been unaware of the effects of cocaine on his heart. He was visibly shaken by this information, showed evidence of greatly increased commitment to treatment and to abstinence from alcohol and other drugs, and completed the program successfully.

PSYCHOLOGICAL AND PSYCHIATRIC PROBLEMS

A second major class of other problems that characterize today's treatment populations are psychological and psychiatric. In discussing these problems, it is important to stress once again that alcoholism is not a symptom of a psychiatric disorder, but a primary disease in and of itself. However, we must be alert to posssible other problems in our patients and be prepared to treat these accordingly. Our own data here at Edgehill Newport suggests that anxiety problems are common with 29% of patients reporting symptoms associated with such things as phobias, generalized anxiety, and panic states. Depression is a close second with 20% of our patients receiving an Axis I diagnosis on the MCMI (Million Clinical Multiaxial Inventory). Both of these statistics for anxiety disorders and depression are likely to be overestimates since these data were gathered shortly after detoxification. As is well recognized, many alcoholics often show transient depressions and anxiety symptoms early in treatment with these resolving fairly quickly in most cases as the effect of the depressant chemical is removed, and therapeutic support, care, and peer involvement are made available. This caveat aside however, anxiety disorders and affective disorders are potential problems in alcoholic and chemical dependence populations of which we must remain aware. The incidence of these in any particular clinical population is likely to vary greatly depending upon the facility. Higher incidence occurs in facilities that treat dual diagnosis patients and lower incidence occurs in free-standing facilities that do not. Moreover, we can expect the incidence of these problems to be low in programs directed to special populations, (e.g. physicians' programs).

Sheila Blume (1982) in a recent review of psychiatric problems in female alcoholics discussed the findings of Halikas et al. (1983) on psychiatric problems of female alcoholics. Of 71 alcoholic women interviewed in a systematic, structured interview, 50% fulfilled criteria for some psychiatric diagnosis other than alcoholism. The most common diagnosis was affective disorder with 24% showing unipolar disorder, and 4% showing bipolar affective disorder. An additional 10% had anxiety disorders of some kind or another while 6% had manifested psychotic symptoms at some point in the past.

Hasselbrock and her colleagues (1985) also found high levels of depression and anxiety disorders in hospitalized alcoholics. 18% of the men and 38% of the women were seen as depressed ($N = 231$, men; $N = 90$, women). The results for mania were as follows: 27% of the men and 1% of the women. Anxiety disorders included the following: 15% of the men and 29% of the women showed phobias; 4%

of the men and 7% of the women were obsessive-compulsive; 5% of the men and 9% of the women met diagnostic criteria for panic disorder. Only 25% of the women were free of additional psychopathology.

Bedi and Halikas (1985) found a lifetime rate of affective disorder of 43% in females and 29% in males. They point out, however, that reports of prevalence of depression in alcoholics vary from 3% to 90%!

Shuckit (1985) showed how follow-up results can vary as a result of primary diagnostic group. In a large group of 577 consecutive admissions to a VA hospital, Shuckit was able to differentiate four primary diagnostic groups: 1) Primary Alcoholics (78%); 2) Primary Substance Abuse (11%); 3) Primary Antisocial Personality (7%); and 4) Primary Affective Disorder (1%).

The best outcome results in terms of patterns of social functioning at follow-up were for primary alcoholics and the worst results were for primary antisocial personalities. Schuckit's results were consistent with the hypothesis that primary alcoholism and primary antisocial personality disorder are two independent disorders with some overlapping symptoms.

Primary antisocial personality disorder patients were younger, less well educated, and more likely to have reported secondary affective episodes, suicide attempts, and psychiatric hospitalizations. They also reported patterns of drug abuse almost as intense as primary drug abusers. At follow-up, primary antisocial personalities showed the worst outcome of any group with higher rates of police problems, drug-related problems, using a weapon while drunk, and living on the streets.

Of the primary alcoholics in Schuckit's research, 11% had had psychiatric hospitalizations, 6% had attempted suicide, and 23% had had depressions lasting longer than two weeks. Few of Schuckit's subjects met criteria for primary anxiety disorders, but many did show anxiety symptoms during drinking and withdrawal. Bowen et al. (1984) did report anxiety symptoms in 44% of a group of alcoholic patients with ten patients showing panic attacks and six with agoraphobia.

Nerviano and Gross (1983) have provided a review of research into personality characteristics of alcoholics. They report seven subtypes:

1. *A Chronic Severe Distress Group* of long term alcoholics who resemble borderline personalities and appear to drink to medicate feelings of tension;
2. *Passive-Aggressive Sociopaths* who are self-centered, emotionally unstable and resentful:

3. *Antisocial Sociopaths* are superficially friendly, exploitive and who treat others with hostility and arrogance at times;
4. *Acute Reactive Depressives* who deal with others in a passive-aggressive fashion and display reactive depression after antisocial episodes;
5. *Mixed Character Dysphoria Type* who seem to be tense, excitable persons who worry obsessively about their inadequacies, suppress feelings of anger, and are guarded and non-disclosing;
6. *Paranoid Alienated Type* are hostile, immature, suspicious individuals who tend toward polydrug abuse, have more pathological social histories, drink more than other types, and tend to be belligerent or violent when drunk;
7. *Severely Neurotic Psychophysiological Type* who are demanding, dysphoric, and dependent people who focus on physical illness and are resistant to psychological treatment.

A recent cluster analysis of Million Clinical Multiaxial Inventory (MCM) profiles by Bartsch and Hoffman (1985) appears to provide some support for the taxonomy hypothesized by Nerviano and Gross.

The fact that alcoholic treatment populations can be described in terms of factors, clusters, or types derived empirically from multivariate analysis is not surprising. Analyzing personality test scores of any clinical population (and non-clinical populations as well) will yield subtypes. Pattison (1982) and Bartsch and Hoffman (1985), however, believe that empirically derived subtype descriptions invalidate a "unitary disease model" of alcoholism. Such typologies, while of definite interest, do not invalidate a "unitary" model of alcoholism nor a "disease" model of alcoholism. *Alcoholism* is a pathological condition. *Alcoholics* are persons who suffer from this pathological condition. To infer that variation in the latter necessarily implies variation in the former is inappropriate. Moreover, to infer that the evident variation in psychological characteristics in alcoholics necessarily implies an absence of biological factors in *alcoholism* is equally inappropriate. By this type of reasoning one would be forced to conclude that *syphilis* is not a unitary, biologic disease because personality tests of *syphilitics* are capable of being grouped into subtypes on the basis of factor or cluster analysis. And while over one hundred types of cancer have been identified, no reasonable person would argue that cancer is not a disease.

It is important that we recognize psychological variability among alcoholics not for the ideological purpose of refuting biological factors in the disease, but for improving care given to alcoholics by addressing individual problems within the structure of a common, unified

TABLE 1. Items from Wallace/Edgehill Inventory

Items	$(N = 161)$	%
Frightened and anxious about my future		70%
Resent somebody deeply for what he did to me		49%
My emotions up & down like a roller coaster		44%
Loneliness even when there are lots of people		42%
I feel depressed a lot of the time		38%
Sometimes this feeling of panic comes over me		36%
Sleep is a real problem		28%
Irritable with people around me		27%
Guilt over what I've done in the past overwhelming		27%

approach to alcoholism treatment. Given variability among alcoholics, individual treatment planning is clearly essential.

In this spirit, I would like to mention data yielded by my scale, the Wallace/Edgehill Inventory (Wallace, 1986). These results were obtained from patients in their fourth week of inpatient treatment.

These results suggest that by the fourth week of treatment, issues concerned with anxiety, resentments, emotional lability, intimacy, depression, panic, insomnia, irritability, and guilt characterized fairly large numbers of patients late in primary treatment. The classic alcoholism issues of denial, rationalization, and minimization are not clearly at issue at this point in treatment with less than 7% of the patients showing evidence of these. In effect, we do a very good job of reaching our goals of primary inpatient alcoholism treatment. However, as alcoholism specific issues are resolved, we can expect psychological concerns centering around anxious thoughts, resentments, loneliness, insomnia, stress reactions, emotional lability, and so forth to become manifest. In effect, alcoholism treatment is a time-dependent process in which it is necessary to deal with primary recovery issues first and the more complex issues of secondary recovery in turn. However, for certain patients we must be prepared to treat both primary and secondary issues concurrently. For example, failing to treat panic disorder, agoraphobia, or a biological depression in primary alcoholism treatment while addressing alcoholism issues only practically ensures relapse shortly after the patient is released from treatment.

On the other hand, in certain psychiatric settings, the tendency to ignore alcoholism issues while the primary diagnosis of affective disorder or schizophrenia is attended to is also likely to result in alcoholism relapse.

In approaching these other problems of alcoholics, we must be cautious about confusing criteria for diagnosing primary psychiatric disorders and symptoms. As Schuckit (1985) has pointed out, depressive symptoms in alcoholics need not imply primary depressive disorders. Many alcoholics show depressive symptoms, some of which may be quite severe, but still do not meet diagnostic criteria for unipolar depression. Similarly, alcoholics may show many anxiety symptoms but do not qualify for a diagnosis of anxiety disorder. Many alcoholics tend to modulate out of depressive and anxiety symptoms as they gain distance from their drinking and drugging pasts and take up growth-oriented, supportive recovery programs like AA. Hence, we should not rush immediately to antidepressant medications on observing depressive symptoms; but neither should we refrain from treating a primary affective disorder with medication when it becomes clear that the disease is not transitory and not likely to lift with sobriety.

What is needed is further research directed toward finding out what factors are associated with persistent symptoms in alcoholics in treatment. Some recent research by Overall and colleagues (1985) illustrates the type of research needed. These investigators studied persistent depression in alcoholics in a four week inpatient hospital program. In this sample of alcoholics, persistence of depression was associated with disruption of close personal relationships. Recovering alcoholics who lost people close to them because of their drinking remained depressed for a longer period of time after entering treatment.

Attempts to identify depressions likely to persist have utilized the Dexamethasone Suppression Test (DST) and TRH/TSH test of thyroid functioning (Carroll et al., 1981; Gold et al., 1981). While initial enthusiasm for both of these tests was high, subsequent research on these two biological tests suggests caution (Dackis et al., 1984). DST results are not reliable in early recovery and of only moderate discriminate validity later on. The early promise of TRH/TSH testing is now complicated by the direct effect of alcohol on the thyroid gland. A blunted TRH/TSH response in an alcoholic may not reflect an underlying biological depression, but may be an outcome of excessive drinking.

Case Illustration. A 21 year old female alcoholic began drinking frequently after her marriage to a career naval officer. The stresses of military life contributed to rapid development of her underlying alcoholism. She began drinking very heavily while in postpartum depression after the birth of her first child. Referral to a physician resulted in prescriptions for benzodiazepines. On minor tranquilizers, the patient's condition worsened. She became more depressed and drank even more heavily. After some years of suffering both uncontrolled alcoholism and depression, she experienced a second postpartum depression during which she could not function at all. On this occasion, she was referred to a psychiatrist knowledgeable about alcoholism and was treated with antidepressant medications. She responded extremely well, interrupted her drinking, and eventually found her way to Alcoholics Anonymous. Periodically, she must resume short courses of antidepressant treatment as well as brief psychotherapy because of recurrent bouts of depression. She has, however, maintained her sobriety over eight years and is a highly motivated member of Alcoholics Anonymous.

Neuropsychological Deficits A third type of other problems concerns the possibility of persistent neurological effects due to drinking and drug taking. As mentioned previously, alcohol and some drugs are neurotoxins. As a consequence, patients in treatment may show variable neuropsychological symptoms of brain damage.

Numerous studies have demonstrated that alcoholics are deficient on neuropsychological tests of short term memory, paired associate learning, and digit symbol substitution (Ryan et al., 1980). With regard to recoverability, the data showed alcoholics sober for one year performed as poorly as alcoholics sober for only one month. Butters and Cermak (1980) pointed to the possibility that long term alcoholics do not spontaneously generate "effective learning and memory strategies." Sparedo (1981) suggests that long term alcoholics have a "subtle information processing deficit that impairs their ability to learn and remember efficiently . . ." (P. 11). Studies of social drinkers suggests a continuum of impairment linked directly to the amount of alcohol consumed (Parker & Noble, 1977, McVane, 1980). In effect, these information processing deficits are not restricted to long term alcoholics and Korsakoff patients but can appear in early to middle stage alcoholics as well.

Studies of abstraction (concept formation) show similar deficits (e.g., Tarter & Parsons, 1971). Compared to non-alcoholics, alcoholics make more errors, require more time to reach criteria, and show particular deficits on tests such as the Wisconsin Card Sorting Test. The underlying deficit may be a disability in shifting set from one concept to another.

These subtle deficits in short term memory, learning, concept formation, and information processing have important implications for how information is presented to patients in lectures, films, group therapy, and individual counseling settings. These can all be seen as situations in which new learning is required, new concepts must be assimilated, and information processing and learning strategies are developed. The neuropsychological condition of many alcoholics suggests that information presentations in primary treatment need to be simple, direct, structured, redundant, and focussed on only one or two concepts at a time. McCrady and Smith (1988) have discussed the relevance of neuropsychological impairment for treatment of alcoholics.

IMPLICATIONS

These other problems of today's treatment populations have important implications for treatment. Increasing heterogeneity of patient populations indicates that treatment programs will necessarily have to become more differentiated and multimodal in order to meet the varied therapeutic needs of patients. Multimodal therapies do not require the abandonment of a biopsychosocial disease model of alcoholism. Nor do they require dropping the 12-step oriented philosophies, core programs, and standard approaches to treatment that characterize today's programs. These programs can only be enhanced by alertness to individual problems and treatment needs, and appropriate individualized treatment planning.

Multimodal treatments, however, will require major shifts in treatment and administrative staff attitudes toward new ideas, innovations, and research. We will have to accept the fact that while many of our patients will do fine in programs as they exist today, many will not.

Multimodal treatments in response to increasing heterogeneity of patient populations will encounter resistance associated with increasing per patient costs. At a time when cost-containment issues loom large in health care generally, third-party payers are not likely to welcome increased costs and neither are program administrators who must operate programs within tighter budgetary constraints.

The heterogeneity of today's treatment populations suggests that a single, overall outcome statistic cannot possibly describe the effectiveness of alcoholism treatment programs. Instead of asking if treatment is effective, we need to be asking, "effective for whom?" Outcome statistics need to be developed and reported for different clinical alcoholic groups. Such statistics can be expected to vary considerably for different groups.

Attitudes toward medication in the alcoholism treatment field will necessarily have to become more flexible as more complex patients are encountered and as more is learned about the underlying chemistry of the brain in alcoholism, drug dependence, and in psychiatric problems. It does not make sense to deny a biologically depressed alcoholic patient effective antidepressant medications. And we must understand that many dual diagnosis patients will simply have to be given phenothiazines, Lithium, or Haldol if they are to function at all.

In depressed drug dependent alcoholics, openness to experimentation with amino acid precursors like L-Tryptophan, L-Tyrosine, L-Glutamine, and also to enzyme inhibitors that affect opioid transmitter levels in brain seems in order (Blum & Trachtenberg, in press).

Some patients who suffer from panic disorder may respond to treatment with low dose imipramine since antidepressants may serve to reduce Locus Ceruleus hyperactivity and associated excess noradrenaline (Sweeney, Pottash, Gold & Martin, 1981). In some cases of panic disorder, symptomatic mitral valve prolapse of the heart may be involved. Treatment with a beta blocker like *Inderal* or a calcium channel blocker like Verapamil may have important anxiolytic benefits as well as cardiovascular effects. These examples involving individualized medical treatments of what have often been construed as purely "psychological" problems suggest a need for openness in the alcoholism treatment field to developments in basic neurobiological science and to possible novel treatments flowing from basic research (Wallace, 1985a).

Given the fact that numerous chemicals (some formed in the body itself) can provoke intense anxiety, the possibility that some drug dependent and alcoholic people may have inherited or acquired defective biological anxiety arousal and reduction systems must be considered seriously (Redmond & Huang, 1979; Skolnick & Paul, 1983). Treatment of such patients might of necessity require corrective treatment similar to the manner in which diabetics require dietary control and/or insulin. Obviously, we don't know that such patients actually exist, nor do we have safe medications to treat them. The point is, however, that we must remain open to emerging possibilities.

In summary, the increasing heterogenity of alcoholism treatment populations with regard to problems other than alcoholism require us to be open to innovation, research, and experimentation on novel treatment methods. In order to meet these new challenges, alcoholism treatment professionals will need to be open to change. They will need to explore more comprehensive bodies of clinical and scientific information than that contained in the alcoholism literature. Training of alcoholism professionals including alcoholism counselors will of necessity require a broader scope and will involve scientific information drawn from genetics, neurobiolgoy, drug dependence, psychology, sociology, medicine, and psychiatry. Alcoholism professionals will need to put aside old perceptions, and attempt to establish cooperative relationships with health care professionals from many disciplines.

The changing nature of today's alcoholism treatment populations requires us to be alert to differences as well as commonalities, to differentiate among patients in a more systematic manner, and to engage in thorough individualized treatment planning with regard to both biomedical and psychosocial matters.

REFERENCES

Bartsch, T.W., & Hoffman, J.J. (1985). A cluster analysis of Million Clinical Multiaxial Inventory (MCMI) profiles: More about a taxonomy of alcoholic subtypes. *J. of Clinical Psychology* 41(5), 707–713.

Bedi, A., & Halikas, J.A. (1985). Alcoholism and Affective Disorder. *Alcoholism: Clinical and Experimental Research*, 9(2).

Blum, K., & Trachtenberg, M.C. (in press). Alcoholism: Scientific basis and chemical management. *International Journal of the Addictions*.

Blume, S.B. (1982). Psychiatric problems of alcoholic women. In J. Soloman (Ed.) *Alcoholism and Clinical Psychiatry*, New York: Plenum Publishing Corporation.

Bowen, R.C., Cipywnyk, D., D'Arcy, C., & Keegan, D. (1984). Alcoholism, anxiety disorders, and agoraphobia. *Alcohol Clin. Exp. Res.*, 8, 48–50.

Brown, S. (1985). *Treating the Alcoholic: A Developmental Model of Recovery.* New York: John Wiley & Sons, Inc.

Butters, N. & Cermak, L.S. (1980). *Alcoholic Korsakoff's Syndrome: An Information-Processing Approach to An Amnesia.* New York: Academic Press.

Carroll, J.F., Malloy, F.E., & Kenrick, F.M. (1977). Drug abuse by alcoholics and problem drinkers: A literature review and evaluation. *American Journal of Drug and Alcohol Abuse*, 4, 317–341.

Carroll, B.J., Feinberg, M., Greden, J.F., et al. (1981). A specific laboratory test for the diagnosis of melancholia. *Arch. Gen. Psychiatry* 38, 15–22.

Dakis, C.A., Baily, J., Pottash, A.C.L., Stuckey, R.F., Extein, I.L., & Gold, M.S. (1984). Specificity of the DST and the TRH Test for major depression in alcoholics. *American Journal of Drug and Alcohol Abuse*, 4, 317–341.

Estroff, T.W., & Gold, M.S. (1985–1986). Medical and psychiatric complications of cocaine abuse with possible points of pharmacological treatment. *Advances in Alcohol and Substance Abuse*, 5, (1/2), 61–76.

Freed, E.X. (1973). Drug use by alcoholics: A review. *The International Journal of Addictions*, 8:451–473.

Gold, M.S., Pottash, A.L.C., & Extein, I. (1981). Hypothyroidism and depression: Evidence from complete thyroid function evaluation. *JAMA*, 245(19), 1919–1922.

Gold, M.S., Pottash, A.L.C., Extein, I., & Waston, A. (1985–1986). Cocaine update: From bench to bedside. *Advances in Alcohol and Substance Abuse*, 5(1/2), 30–60.

Halikas, J.A., Herzog, M.A., Mirassou, M.M., Lyttle, M.D. (1983). Psychiatric diagnosis among female alcoholics. In M. Galanter (Ed.), *Currents of Alcoholism*, (Vol. 8): New York: Grune & Stratton.

Hesselbrock, M.N., Meyer, R.E., & Keener, J.J. (1985) Psychopathology in hospitalized alcoholics. *Arch. Gen. Psychiatry*, 42, 1050–1055.

Khantzian, E.J., & Treece, C. (1985). DMS-III psychiatric diagnosis of narcotic addicts. *Arch. Gen. Psychiatry*, 42, 1067–1071.

MacVane, J.B. (1980). A study of cognitive functioning of social drinkers. Unpublished doctoral dissertation, University of Rhode Island.

Marlatt, A.G. (1983). The controlled drinking controversy: A commentary. *American Psychologist*, 38, 1097–1110.

McCrady, B.S., & Smith, D.E. (1986). Implications of cognitive impairment for the treatment of alcoholism. *Alcoholism: Clinical and Experimental Research*, 10(2), 145–149.

Nerviano, V., & Gross, W., (1983). Personality types of alcoholics in objective inventories. *Journal of Studies on Alcohol*, 44, 837–851.

Nova, No. 1305. (1986, February 18) *The Case of the Frozen Addict*, broadcast on PBS. WGBH Educational Foundation.

Overall, J.E., Reilly, E.L., Kelley, J.T., & Hollister, L.E. (1985). Persistence of depression in detoxified alcoholics, *Alcoholism: Clinical and Experimental Research*, 9(4), 331–333.

Parker, E.S., & Noble, E.P. (1977). Alcohol consumption and cognitive functioning in social drinkers. *Journal of Studies on Alcohol*, 38, 1224–1232.

Pattison, E.M. (1982). The concept of alcoholism as a syndrome. In E.M. Pattison (Ed.), *Selection of Treatment for Alcoholics*. New Brunswick, NJ: Rutgers Center of Alcohol Studies.

Redmond, D.E., & Huang, D.X. (1979). New evidence for a locus coeruleus norepinephrine connection with anxiety. *Life Science*, 25, 2149–2162.

Ryan, C., Butters, N., Montgomery, K., Adinolfi, A., & Didario, B. (1980). Memory deficits in chronic alcoholics: Continuities between the intact alcoholic and the alcoholic Korsakoff patient. In H. Begleiter and B. Kissin (Eds.), *Alcohol Intoxication and Withdrawal*. New York: Plenum Press.

Schuckit, M.S. (1985). The clinical implications of primary diagnostic groups among alcoholics. *Arch. Gen. Psychiatry*, 42, 1043 + .

Skolnick, P., & Paul, S. (1983). New concepts in the neurobiology of anxiety. *Journal of Clinical Psychiatry*, 44, 12–20.

Smith, D. (1986). Opiate Narcotics. Speech delivered at Northeast Conference on Addictions, Newport, RI.

Sokolow, L., Welte, J., Hynes, G., & Lyons, J. (1981). Multiple substance used by alcoholics. *British Journal of Addiction*, 76, 147–158.

Sorensen, S.M. et al., (1982). Persistent effects of amphetamine on cerebellar purkinje neurons following chronic administration. *Brain Research*, 247, 365–371.

Sparedo, F. (1981). Alcohol-related cognitive deficits: A review. Unpublished manuscript.

Sweeney, D.R., Pottash, A.L.C., Gold, M.S., & Martin, D. (1981). Panic anxiety: Tricyclic antidepressant levels and clinical response. *Proceedings of 134th Annual Meeting of the American Psychiatric Association* (pp. 200–201, abstract). New Orleans.

Tarter, R.E., & Parsons, O.A. (1971). Conceptual shifting in chronic alcoholics. *Journal of Abnormal Psychology*, 77, 71–75.

Wallace, J. (1982). Unpublished data, Edgehill Newport.

Wallace, J. (1983). Alcoholism is a shift in paradigm necessary? *Journal of Psychiatric Treatment and Evaluation*, 5, 479–485.

Wallace, J. (1985a). *Alcoholism: New Light on the Disease*. Rhode Island: Edgehill Newport.

Wallace, J. (1985b) Predicting the onset of compulsive drinking in alcoholics: A biopsychosocial model. *Alcohol*, 2, 289–295.

Wallace, J. (1986). The Wallace/Edgehill Inventory. Edgehill Newport.

Zimberg, S., Wallace, J., & Blume, S.B. (1985). *Practical Approaches to Alcoholism Psychotherapy*. New York: Plenum Press.

Part VII

Alcoholics Anonymous

Myths and Misconceptions About Alcoholics Anonymous*

It has been nearly fifty years since the Fellowship of Alcoholics Anonymous had its quiet beginnings in Akron, Ohio. But, despite its presence on the alcoholism scene for nearly a half century, A.A. is still often misunderstood by many. Without careful and thorough reading of A.A. literature or direct experience in the Fellowship for lengthy periods, it is not easy to grasp the purposes, processes, concepts, and activities of this critically important social movement.

Myths about A.A. and misconceptions of its concepts and approaches abound. It is imperative that we identify these myths and misconceptions so that open, knowledgeable, and sensitive communication can take place.

First, despite opinion to the contrary, A.A. is not a prohibitionistic organization. A.A. does not condemn the social use of alcoholic beverages by all persons. The Fellowship emphasizes abstention for its members since alcoholics have proven time and time again that they cannot consistently manage either their drinking and/or their behavior while drinking.

While abstention from alcoholic beverages is a critical first step for the newcomer to the Fellowship, A.A.'s program of growth does not stop with the end of drinking. A.A. members distinguish between being merely "dry" and being "sober." To be dry and dry alone is not a very satisfactory condition. For the alcoholic, it is misery. At best, dryness is a traditional step, a "bridge" to the more complex state of sobriety. Whereas dryness refers only to not drinking alcohol, sobriety refers to major changes in the recovering person's approach to physical health, emotional well-being, mental clarity, social relations, fam-

---

*This article appeared in About AA: A Newsletter for Professional Men and Women, Spring, 1984. Reprinted courtesy of Alcoholics Anonymous.

ily life, work, love, and spirituality. Only the First Step of A.A.'s Twelve Step program of recovery deals with alcohol: *We admitted we were powerless over alcohol—that our lives had become unmanageable.* The remaining eleven Steps deal with learning how to live comfortably (and with fulfillment) with oneself, with others, and with one's Higher Power.

Because of the central role of spiritual development in A.A., many people confuse the Fellowship with organized religions. A.A. is not a religious organization, but it is a spiritually-centered organization. The Fellowship is not an organized religion since it does not require members to accept a single conception of a deity, has no religious ritual, and enforces no single body of religious beliefs. The Steps to recovery do suggest that belief in a higher power, as each member understands that concept, is of great value in the restoration of sanity and in finding a life of personal satisfaction and fulfillment without alcohol. But it is important to note that the A.A. higher power concept is an entirely open and free concept. The member may believe exactly what he or she chooses to believe and nobody in A.A. can tell them to believe otherwise.

A further misconception of Alcoholics Anonymous is that it endorses a simple and naive disease concept of alcoholism. This is a difficult misconception to understand since A.A., from its very beginning, embraced a subtle, complex, and multi-dimensional concept of the disease. By attending to the physical, mental, emotional, and spiritual aspects of alcoholism, A.A. anticipated very recent developments in modern medicine, psychiatry, and psychology—not only for the disease of alcoholism but for many other diseases as well. The emerging discipline of behavioral medicine is one notable recent attempt to wed psychology and medicine in efforts to deal with many diseases; A.A., in 1935, was already embracing a psychosomatic view in which body (allergy to alcohol) and mind (obsession with alcohol) were joined to explain the origins and maintenance of the disease. Over the years, several disciplines have brought to bear many of the magnificent achievements of modern 20th-century biological sciences on the problem of alcoholism. These scientific advances in neurochemistry, neuropharmacology, neuroanatomy, and behavior are welcomed since they are entirely consistent with A.A.'s early emphasis upon psychosomatic relationships. Moreover, these scientific achievements promise to shed new light on alcoholism as they have on many other diseases from which humankind suffers.

The belief that A.A. is hostile to psychological and psychiatric knowledge is unfortunate. Some A.A. members may have received inadequate treatment in the hands of poorly trained and inadequately educated professionals in the past. However, this unhappy situation is changing rapidly as the curricula of professional and graduate schools reflect the realities of the disease of alcoholism and more and more professionals are achieving accurate and sensitive understanding. A.A., despite strong opinion to the contrary, is a psychologically very sophisticated Fellowship. Many of its concepts and procedures are psychology in action at its very best.

In A.A., members recognize the importance of psychological matters such as resentments, self-pity, egotism, unrealistically high expectations, frustration, stress, sexual and love relationships, self-esteem, fear, anxiety, guilt, grandiosity, self-will, melancholy, depression, security needs, envy, power over others, control and domination of others, and fear of financial failure. For an organization that presumably does not feel that psychological factors are important, the list is long indeed! Not only does A.A. involve itself with psychological matters, its activities are clearly and intelligently planned psychological processes. The A.A. group meeting, for example, could be a textbook example of the social psychological processes that characterize healthy, strong, and positive human relationships: open, honest, and trusting communication; caring, respect, and consideration for others; commitment to the growth and well-being of self and others; and empathy for and identification with others. Many of A.A.'s other processes and Steps either implicitly or explicitly recognize the importance of both individual and interpersonal psychological processes in the recovery from alcoholism.

Some people hold the misconception that A.A. forces people to admit that they are alcoholics and public confession of one's alcoholism must be made. Aside from the fact that A.A. does not require anybody to do anything, this misconception is off the mark because A.A. does not diagnose anything. Professionals diagnose diseases. A.A. members help each other to stay sober. The A.A. Preamble states: "The only requirement for membership is a desire to stop drinking." Many A.A. members, perhaps most, eventually choose to call themselves alcoholics, but this is not a condition for belonging. The very First Step of the A.A. program of recovery is to admit to being powerless over alcohol. Even here, however, this is a suggested step to recovery and not an order. Moreover, the Step does not say that one must diagnose oneself as an alcoholic, nor does it require one to accept such a diagnosis from somebody else.

Finally, it is sometimes believed by certain people that A.A.'s position on the necessity for abstention if alcoholics are to recover from alcoholism is purely an ideological position with no empirical basis. Moreover, these persons believe that modern science has proved A.A.

wrong on this point and that alcoholics can be taught normal, controlled, or nonproblem drinking. Of all myths and misconceptions, this one is potentially the most dangerous since sufferers from the disease of alcoholism will place themselves at risk for grave and even tragic consequences if they embrace this myth.

The A.A. belief in abstention for alcoholics did not just appear out of the blue in a burst of ideological inspiration. It grew out of empirical observation in the real world. It grew out of direct observation of suffering too painful to bear, of tragedy and shattered dreams, of broken bodies, alcohol-related diseases, ended careers, and destroyed families. A.A. recognized early that a relationship existed between the continued ingestion of alcohol by alcoholics and the eventual but inevitable negative consequences of an active alcoholic life. In effect, A.A.'s beliefs have come from literally hundreds of thousands of direct observations of men and women in the real worlds of small towns, cities, the suburbs, ghettos, and megalopolises. A.A.'s have had plenty of direct experience with drinking alcoholics and with sober alcoholics. They don't report seeing much controlled or nonproblem drinking at all. What they do report is that life for countless alcoholics and their families improves beyond imagination when they get the message, stop drinking, and begin to work a Twelve Step program of recovery.

The scientific evidence against abstention, when viewed objectively, is unimpressive. The numbers are simply too small for any responsible and ethical professional to announce to the world that a cure for alcoholism has been achieved.

It is time for the many myths and misconceptions of A.A. to be exposed and discarded. A.A. needs open, trusting, and distortion-free channels to the professional communities that are, in some way or another, involved with the alcoholic. Moreover, these professional communities need the same kind of communication channels to Alcoholics Anonymous. Even though opening such channels may be painful to some, our mission is too critically important to fail to do so. In the final analysis, it is the suffering alcoholic and his or her family who will be helped ultimately from clear, sensitive, and accurate communication between A.A. and the professional communities.

It is important for members of the professional communities to try to understand A.A. more accurately, but it is equally important for members of A.A. to try to communicate concepts, approaches, and activities clearly and effectively. A professional who has very limited experience with A.A. doesn't know what "turn it over" means. Nor could such a professional possibly understand "First Things First" or concepts such as the "dry drunk." A.A.'s spend a lot of time talking to other A.A.'s and rarely have to explain what they mean by the slogans and Steps. In talking to nonmembers, A.A.'s need to keep in mind that it takes a lot of meetings before the ideas in the Fellowship really make sense.

In a nutshell, communication is everybody's business in reaching out to the still-suffering alcoholic. If we all strive to understand each other better, we will see each other more clearly and realistically. This cannot help but benefit alcoholics everywhere.

Ideology, Belief, and Behavior:

Alcoholics Anonymous as a Social Movement

It is important to begin this discussion with several caveats. First, my remarks should not be construed as official AA policy. I am not a spokesman for Alcoholics Anonymous and make no claims to such a position. My comments are most appropriately considered to be one person's perceptions of AA. Second, of all issues dealt with by AA, etiology is the least developed. Alcoholics Anonymous literature is strongest on the nature of alcoholism, its manner of expression, consequences, and on practical approaches as to how sobriety can be achieved and maintained. Aside from the general notion of "alcoholism as a disease," AA's position on the origins of alcoholism is not rich in detail.

While the AA concept of etiology is not well developed, it is possible to discern an AA point of view. It is perhaps most appropriate to discuss this point of view in terms of a number of common misconceptions about this important social movement.

SOME COMMON MISCONCEPTIONS OF ALCOHOLICS ANONYMOUS

The first AA group in the United States developed out of events taking place in Akron, Ohio in the summer and fall of 1935. In the forty-five years since that time, AA has grown into a worldwide social movement of considerable influence and has established itself as a primary resource in the continuing struggle against alcoholism. But despite its ubiquitous presence on the alcoholism scene, Alcoholics

335

Anonymous is not well understood by the general public nor by the professional communities that either are directly or indirectly involved in the delivery of services. Much of what has been written about AA has concerned assumptions about AA "ideology." Outside of AA circles, little is known about the actual beliefs of AA members. Most important, virtually nothing is known about the *behavior* of AA members vis-à-vis one another. Behavioral transactions among AA members either in the formal setting of the AA meeting or in the multifarious informal inteventions that take place in the external community have received scant attention.

Because of this apparent concentration upon assumed AA ideology to the neglect of actual beliefs and behaviors of the AA membership, distorted and inaccurate views of the movement are not uncommon. Some of the more common misconceptions are as follows:

1. AA promulgates a simplistic, naive disease concept of alcoholism. In actuality, the AA concept of alcoholism is multidimensional, subtle, and complex. In AA circles, alcoholism is commonly described as a "four-fold disease," one that involves physical, mental, emotional, and spiritual factors. As early as 1939, both biological and psychological factors were evident in the speculations of AA members as to the origins of their disease. One particular biological concept, allergy, was advanced by a physician with great interest in and admiration for AA—Dr. William Silkworth. In the foreword to the 1939 first edition of the book, *Alcoholics Anonymous*, an invited statement from Silkworth entitled "The Doctor's Opinion" set forth the physician's beliefs that alcoholism was an allergic disorder. Silkworth wrote: "We believe, and so suggested a few years ago, that the action of alcohol on these chronic alcoholics is a manifestation of an allergy: that the phenomenon of craving is limited to this class and never occurs in the average temperate drinker. These allergic types can never safely use alcohol in any form at all; and once having formed the habit and found they cannot break it, once having lost their self-confidence, their reliance upon things human, their problems pile up on them and become astonishingly difficult to solve" (p. xxvi).

Silkworth, of course, has never been shown to have been correct in his beliefs about alcoholism and allergy. In historical perspective, however, it is quite clear how he could have been led to this position. The notion of alcoholism as an allergy had been available since 1896, and given the then extant body of scientific information, allergy was probably as attractive an hypothesis as any other. In any case, the founders of AA and early members, in keeping with what appeared to be respectable medical opinion of the time, concluded that alcoholism was an allergy of the *body* coupled with a *mental* obsession to drink alcohol.

Currently, a variety of positions can be identified among AA members with regard to the allergy concept. There are those members who accept the hypothesis as fact and consider alcoholism, in part, an allergy to alcohol. Others make metaphorical use of the concept and think of it as a useful analog. Still others reject the hypothesis entirely and consider some other biological concept more plausible *or* reject biological etiological factors entirely. And, of course, other members simply do not have an opinion either way.

2. *AA ignores psychological etiological factors.* AA's emphasis upon the disease concept has led some to believe that the social movement ignores psychological factors entirely. In actuality, psychological factors are given considerable importance in the AA program of recovery. Moveover, a careful reading of AA literature suggests that these psychological factors carry some etiological weight as well. Step four of the program's twelve-step recovery program is very much a "psychological step." In step four, members are invited to engage in a "searching and fearless moral inventory of ourselves." For most members, this step involves an extensive examination of past behaviors. It calls for a fairly classic psychological activity—intense self-examination with the purpose of developing awareness of self-destructive and self-defeating patterns of behavior. Depending upon the thoroughness of the inventory, the step can include an extensive examination of values, beliefs, feelings, attitudes, and motives as well.

That psychological factors are involved in the AA etiological view is evident from the following passages in the book, *Twelve Steps and Twelve Traditions:* "Alcoholics especially should be able to see that instinct run wild in themselves is the underlying cause of their destructive drinking. We have drunk to drown feelings of fear, frustration, and depression. We have drunk to escape the guilt of passions, and then have drunk again to make more passions possible. We have drunk for vainglory—that we might the more enjoy foolish dreams of pomp and power" (p. 44).

The role of depression is remarked upon in the following passage from the same book: "If temperamentally we are on the depressive side, we are apt to be swamped with guilt and self-loathing. We wallow in this messy bog, often getting a misshapen and painful pleasure out of it. As we morbidly pursue this melancholy activity, we may sink to such a point of despair that nothing but oblivion looks possible as a solution. Here, of course, we have lost all perspective, and therefore all genuine humility. For this is pride in reverse. This is not a moral

338 JOHN WALLACE: WRITINGS

inventory at all; it is the very process by which the depressive has so often been led to the bottle and extinction" (p. 45).

Other psychological factors considered of great importance in AA are as follows: resentments towards others, self-pity, fear, self-esteem, security needs, envy, sexual needs, and social-recognition needs.

While AA does not describe itself as a program of behavior modification, it is apparent that a number of its processes and activities are entirely consistent with basic principles of behavioral psychology. Even the most casual observer of AA in action would come to the conclusion that the program is a source of rather massive and consistent positive reinforcement. Alcoholics Anonymous values are quite clear, and reinforcements at both interpersonal and group levels are readily dispensed for behavior in accord with these values—positive reinforcement for staying sober and nonreinforcement or withdrawal of positive reinforcement for continued drinking and intoxication. Members who sustain abstentation achieve recognition, status, and numerous positive verbal rewards. In some AA groups, tangible physical rewards are administered (e.g. colored tokens denoting differing lengths of continuous abstention achieved, lapel pins that signify years of sobriety, parties complete with cake and presents on the anniversary of each progressive year of sobriety, and so forth).

In addition to positive reinforcement, AA in action is consistent with other behavioral-modification procedures. Recent trends in *social learning theory* approaches to behavioral change are evident in AA. Models who display patterns of behavior useful in imitative learning and who dispense social reinforcers directly are abundant. Moreover, these models possess attributes that encourage identificatory learning. They are successfully recovered alcoholics themselves and, hence, are regarded as possessing knowledge, expertise, and practical skills useful to newcomers to the program.

The perception of members that they share a common disease and a likely common fate contributes to the development of AA as a *primary reference group.* Members identify with each other and with AA as a whole. As a result, they are open to social influence processes and mechanisms that are common to reference groups generally.

Something quite similar to *systematic desensitization therapy* takes place routinely in AA. While members do not systematically pair a relaxation response with carefully devised stimulus hierarchies, they are encouraged (by example) to publicly disclose personal experiences previously associated with much pain, anxiety, guilt, embarrassment, and negative self-regarding attitudes. These self-disclosures are typically made to highly accepting audiences in social atmospheres characterized by informality, relaxation, trust, and, often, laughter and merriment.

Changes in affect and behavior that result from this AA analog to "desensitization therapy" may be explained in terms of extinction or cognitive-social concepts. Obviously, the social response contradicts, or is incompatible with, the previous personal cognitive-emotional response. In time, the private personal response to one's own experience yields to the public group response. In a sense, the public group response invalidates the private, personal construction of one's experience and forces both cognitive and affective restructuring.

In general, then, more thoughtful analysis of AA literature and of the behavior of AA members vis-à-vis one another reveals that psychological concepts and processes are central to AA perceptions of etiology as well as to AA methods of influencing drinking behavior.

3. *AA addresses the drinking behavior only.* Critics of AA frequently confuse AA *priorities* with recovery *goals.* The ideal recovery in AA is not one of "dryness" alone but a complex set of outcomes involving major changes in behavior, attitude, belief, emotions, and general psychosocial functioning. The first priority of AA is the achievement of abstention from alcohol, but abstention alone is not considered sufficient. The familiar AA slogan, "First things first," is, in fact, a simple reminder of the order in which things must be carried out. In the beginning, the newcomer to AA is urged to deal with his drinking first to the exclusion of other problems that might involve family, financial, or employment matters. This concentration upon the drinking problem to the exclusion of other problems early on in recovery stems from the conviction that nothing else will get better if the drinking continues. As abstention proceeds, the member becomes capable of seeking solutions to additional problems. Alcoholics Anonymous is not only a program that concerns drinking; it is commonly referred to by members as a "program for living" as well. Of the twelve steps to recovery that form the heart of the program, only the first step (i.e. we admitted we were powerless over alcohol; that our lives had become unmanageable) deals explicitly with alcohol or, for that matter, even mentions alcohol. The remaining eleven steps of the program comprise a program for dealing with the broader issues and problems that confront all human beings, alcoholic or not.

In AA, members distinguish between being dry and being sober. To be dry and dry alone is perceived by members as, at best, a transitional state on the way to sobriety and, at worst, a miserable, uncomfortable, and undesirable condition. "Dry but not sober" is a commonly heard description in AA that refers to a person who is not drinking but who has failed to come to grips with important aspects of self that involve values, attitudes, feelings, typical patterns of behavior, and personality factors.

Among AA members, *sobriety* refers to a complex, subtle, and multidimensional state in which aspects of the drinking personality, lifestyle, and world view are no longer evident. Sobriety is, in effect, a change of consciousness, an altered state or, if you will, an heightened spiritual awareness in which elements of serenity, acceptance, contentment, gratitude, and joyfulness are evident. Words like "balance," "wholeness," "fulfillment," and "spiritual transformation" are necessary if the AA concept of sobriety is to be grasped and distinguished from mere dryness or abstention alone.

A further quote from *Twelve Steps and Twelve Traditions* illustrates the AA link between psychological etiological factors and the arduous road to sobriety: "By now the newcomer has probably arrived at the following conclusions: That his character defects, representing instincts gone astray, have been the primary cause of his drinking and his failure at life; that unless he is now willing to work hard at the elimination of the worst of these defects, both sobriety and peace of mind will still elude him; that all the faulty foundation of his life will have to be torn out and built anew on bedrock" (p. 50).

4. *AA forces members to admit to being alcoholic.* The origin of this particular misconception of AA is difficult to understand. On this point, AA literature is most clear: *The only requirement for membership is a desire to stop drinking.* In actuality, AA does not diagnose anybody in a formal sense. An interesting passage from the book *Alcoholics Anonymous* makes this point clear: "We do not like to pronounce any individual as alcoholic but you can quickly diagnose yourself. Step over to the nearest barroom and try some controlled drinking. Try to drink and stop abruptly. Try it more than once. It will not take long for you to decide, if you are honest with yourself about it. It may be worth a bad case of jitters if you get a full knowledge of your condition" (pp. 31–32). As this passage makes clear, inability to consistently control one's drinking is central to the AA definition of alcoholism.

With regard to this issue of self or other diagnosis, the first step of the AA program is pertinent: It does not require the person to admit to being an alcoholic. Rather, it asks for the admission that one is powerless over alcohol and that one's life has become unmanageable.

5. *AA's rejection of controlled drinking is purely ideological, and empirical research has proven AA wrong on this point.* Of all misconceptions of AA, this one is probably the most dangerous. First, the AA position on controlled drinking did not just appear out of the blue in a burst of ideological inspiration. The AA position grew out of hundreds of thousands of *empirical observations* of the drinking behavior of countless individuals in their natural social ecologies. It is cor-

rect to say in this instance that AA ideology grew naturally out of AA empirical observation of hundreds of thousands of individuals.

Second, a careful reading of the more influential pieces of controlled drinking research reveals that formal research on this matter has not been characterized by the care, thoroughness, and precision that one expects of scientific research. In fact, the more widely publicized pieces of formal research concerning controlled drinking have shown numerous serious methodological shortcomings.

For example, despite a high level of loss of subjects at follow-up, a brief thirty-day window on drinking behavior, and serious questions concerning the validity of drinking-behavior measurements, the so-called Rand study by Armor, Polich, and Stambul received front-page coverage in the *New York Times* and extensive reportage throughout the nation. While the authors of this report clearly did not intend that persons draw the implication that their research had proven that alcoholics could drink normally, many persons—professional and lay—did draw precisely that conclusion. Armor, Polich, and Stambul did not advocate controlled drinking as a treatment goal for alcoholics, but did suggest that the possibility for some alcoholics should be explored further.

At issue in the research by Armor, Polich, and Stambul is not the assertion that some alcoholics might be able to drink normally, since such an assertion is trivial. The assertion is trivial since it can be proved correct with the discovery of just *one* alcoholic capable of doing so. Moreover, the assertion is trivial since it leaves out the important dimension of time. Brief periods of moderate or controlled drinking are a commonplace observation in the natural history of alcoholism. However, sustained moderate or controlled drinking among alcoholics without serious physical, emotional, or social consequences has not been characteristic of the natural history of the disease.

What is at issue in the research by Armor, Polich, and Stambul is the very high rate of normal drinking of 22 percent that these authors reported. Moreover, a number of persons mistakenly concluded that this high rate referred to sustained moderate drinking over an eighteen-month period when, in fact, it referred to self-reported drinking behavior for only a thirty-day period immediately prior to follow-up interview.

That the 22 percent normal-drinking rate reported by Armor, Polich, and Stambul was spuriously high is suggested by my own reanalyses of their data. First, the differences among treatment centers in reported normal-drinking rates were quite large and not easily explained. For example, in one of the eight treatment centers studied

TABLE I. Sample Bias Estimates for Various Outcome Measures in the Data Reported by Armor, Policy, and Stambul (1976)*

	Composite Remission		Normal Drinking
	Rates	Abstention Rates	Rates
Interview noncompletion rates	−0.07	+0.79	−0.14

Source: Wallace, J. Alcoholism and treatment revisited. *World Alcohol Project*, February 1979, pp. 3–18.
* Rank-order corrections.

in Armor, Polich, and Stambul's eighteen-month follow-up study of those alcoholics who were drinking at follow-up, nearly 70 percent reported themselves to be drinking normally. This rate is obviously grossly discrepant with prior research, clinical and community observation, and even in comparison with rates from other treatment centers in the same study.

Second, internal contradictions in the data exist with regard to correlations between various remission measures and measures of sample bias. It is important to note that Armor, Polich, and Stambul's estimates of sample bias were based upon a composite remission-outcome measure. This composite remission measure was obtained by summing abstention rates and normal-drinking rates for each treatment center. Armor et al. computed a rank-order correlation between composite-remission rates and interview-noncompletion rates across treatment centers. This correlation was essentially zero and suggested an absence of sample bias despite a rather large subject-dropout rate.

What the Rand authors either failed to compute or failed to report, however, was a set of sample bias estimates involving the correlation between abstention rates and interview-noncompletion rates and, also, the correlation between normal-drinking rates and interview-noncompletion rates. Table I shows these correlations.

The large and positive correlation between abstention rates and interview-noncompletion rates indicates a very high degree of sample bias as one would expect given the large subject-dropout rates in the studies reported by Armor, Polich, and Stambul. More important, however, are the contradictions apparent in the discrepancies among these correlations and the implications these discrepancies hold for the validity of the normal-drinking measure. In the absence of any compelling a priori reason that would explain why abstention rates would be greatly affected by sample bias while normal-drinking rates would not be affected at all, one can only conclude that the measurement of normal drinking in this study was invalid. In effect, these methodological correlations concerning sample bias comprise an indirect way to answer the question of the validity of the normal-drinking measure. Abstention—a measure of high reliability and validity—reveals substantial sample bias. On the other hand, self-reported normal drinking, and the composite-remission measure of which it is a part, reveals little or no sample bias. While some novel explanation may be found to resolve this contradiction, parsimony demands a far simpler one: *invalid measurement of normal drinking.* Moreover, given the large and not easily explained differences among treatment centers in normal-drinking rates, one must further conclude that not only was the normal-drinking measure invalid but differentially so across treatment centers.

This conclusion concerning the invalid nature of the Rand authors' normal-drinking measure receives further support from a comparison of remission rates from their six-month follow-up study and their eighteen-month follow-up study. In the six-month study, the subject-loss rate was rather astonishing (9,129 subjects out of 11,500, or 80%, were lost to follow-up). In the eighteen-month study, the subject-loss rate was considerably less (980 subjects out of 2,320, or 38%, were lost to follow-up). Given this difference in subject-loss rates between the two studies, it is possible to examine the questions of possible sample bias and invalid measurement further. If subject loss were biasing the results, then remission rates would be lower in the eighteen-month study than in the six-month study. And given such sample bias, there is no compelling reason to expect it to operate differently on the abstention measure versus the normal-drinking measure.

If, however, the studies are not only biased on outcome but characterized by invalidly measured normal drinking in the eighteen-month study, then the following results would obtain:

1. Abstention rate should decrease in the eighteen-month study.
2. Normal-drinking rate would increase in the eighteen-month study.
3. The composite-remission rate would remain the same between the two studies.

Table II presents the data bearing on these questions of sample bias and invalid measurement of normal drinking.

An examination of Table II reveals that, as with the sample bias estimates discussed previously, a similar set of internal contradictions emerges. While the abstention rates show a *decrease* of eleven percentage points from the six-month study to the eighteen-month study, the normal-drinking rates reveal a ten-percentage point *increase*. And, of course, as an obvious result of these contradictions, the composite-

TABLE II. Remission Rates for the 6-Month and 18-Month Studies Reported by Armor, Polich, and Stambul (1976)

Sample	Percentage of Abstention	Percentage of Normal Drinking	Percentage of Composite Remission
6-month	56	12	68
18-month	45	22	67
Difference	−11	+ 10	− 1

Source: Wallace, J. Alcoholism and treatment revisited. *World Alcohol Project*, February, 1979, p. 15.

remission rate shows very little change. Once again, parsimony requires us to accept the most economical explanation for these internal contradictions: invalid measurement of normal drinking.

Taken together, these reanalyses of the 1976 study by Armor, Polich, and Stambul indicate that the 22 percent normal-drinking rate reported by these authors was seriously in error due to sample bias and invalid measurement of normal drinking. This 22 percent rate is spuriously high and cannot be generalized to any population, nor can it be considered a likelihood estimate of either brief or sustained moderate drinking among alcoholics in NIAAA-funded treatment centers, and certainly not among alcoholics in general.

These conclusions concerning the spuriously high normal-drinking rate in the 1976 Rand study gain further support from consideration of the further work of Polich, Armor, and Braiker on the same cohort of subjects at four-year follow-up. In the context of a greatly improved methodology and more rigorous definitions, these authors reported a brief (30-day window on drinking behavior) nonproblem drinking rate among treated alcoholics of 14 percent (the rate corrected by the authors for invalid measurement). The sustained normal-drinking rate, uncorrected for invalid measurement and some degree of error in initial diagnosis, was 7 percent. If the reported sustained rate of nonproblem drinking of 7 percent were corrected for invalid measurement and some degree of error in initial diagnosis, the true sustained nonproblem drinking rate would very likely be 3 percent to 4 percent.

These most recent results suggest rather strongly that while a minority of alcoholics following treatment appear capable of brief nonproblem drinking, *sustained nonproblem drinking is not likely*. The very low rates of sustained nonproblem drinking reported by Polich, Armor, and Braiker raise serious problems in differentiating persons at the time of admission to treatment for purposes of assignment of differential treatment goals prior to treatment. The nature of these problems in prediction involve the complexities involved generally in accurately predicting phenomena with low base rates in a population.

Assuming that 4 percent of persons admitted to alcoholism treatment may be capable of sustained nonproblem drinking, one must devise instruments or prediction formulas that would yield predictions at least as accurate as one could make simply by assuming that no person admitted to treatment could do so. If the true rate of sustained nonproblem drinking among those admitted to treatment is 4 percent, the assumption that none can do so would lead to correct decisions about treatment goals 96 percent of the time. On the other hand, even with an instrument of moderately high predictive validity (say, 0.60), one would be failing to account for 64 percent of the variance in treatment outcome, and prediction would be highly inaccurate. Needless to say, validity coefficients of 0.60 in alcoholism-treatment-outcome research have not even been approached. Even the most complex of multiple-regression equations fail to account for more than 10 percent to 20 percent of the variance in outcome. In short, the most recent research by Polich, Armor, and Braiker does not contradict the AA position on controlled drinking but rather appears to provide strong support for it.

In addition to the Rand studies, the work of Sobell and Sobell is cited by a number of persons as evidence that AA's position on controlled drinking for alcoholics has been disproved scientifically. Working with state hospital inpatients in California, the Sobells reported data that suggested that alcoholics could be trained to control their drinking. In contrast to the survey methods employed by Armor et al. and Polich et al., the work by the Sobells was frankly experimental with deliberate efforts to train hospitalized patients to control their drinking. Most important, the Sobells reported follow-up data that indicated that experimentally trained controlled drinking in the hospital could be generalized to nonhospital contexts and sustained over time. While the Sobells' follow-up procedures raised serious questions about the possibility of experimenter-bias effects on follow-up data gathering (the person administering the treatment was involved in the follow-up assessment of the treatment), independent, later follow-up by Caddy reported confirmation of the results of the initial follow-up effort.

Chalmers, however, has provided extensive methodological criticism of the research by Sobell and Sobell. Among other criticisms, Chalmers raised the intriguing criticism that controlled drinking as *training* was confused with controlled drinking as *behavior* in the Sobell

346 JOHN WALLACE: WRITINGS

outcome data. According to Chalmers, the reported "well functioning" of the Sobells' controlled drinkers was due primarily to their *abstinence time* and not their *controlled-drinking time* during follow-up. As Chalmers remarked: "The data show that controlled-drinking time declines over the two-year period, while abstinence time dramatically increases. Hence, by the second year, the functioning-well time of the clients taught to control their drinking is primarily accounted for by abstinence, not controlled drinking. We must not confuse controlled drinking as training with controlled drinking as behavior. In the Sobell research, controlled-drinking training produces a systematic increase in abstinence, not in controlled-drinking behavior" (p. 23).

In addition to methodological criticism, the Sobell and Sobell research on controlled drinking has been faulted for failure of independent replication. An ongoing follow-up of the patients treated by Sobell and Sobell conducted by Maltzman and Pendery has failed to replicate the Sobells' claim of successful controlled drinking among the majority of these alcoholic patients who had been trained to control their drinking.[1] The follow-up by Matlzman and Pendery also failed to replicate Caddy's previous independent follow-up of the Sobells' patients.

In short, closer scrutiny of two of the more widely publicized and cited studies that have provided reports suggesting the existence of controlled or moderate drinking among alcoholics reveals serious, even perhaps grave, methodological shortcomings. Formal scientific research on this critical question has not been characterized by the rigor, precision, and thoroughness one normally expects of research bearing upon high-risk intervention procedures and concepts. In fact, one is tempted to conclude that formal research in this instance has been a contributor to the ideological skirmish rather than as a source of much-needed empirical enlightenment.

6. *AA is a religious organization.* This myth about AA is surprisingly common. Although AA is a spiritually based program, it is not allied with nor wishes to be confused with any sect, denomination, organization, or institution, and it clearly states this position in its traditions. Members of AA are not required to accept, practice, or promote any religious belief or concept. Members are *encouraged* to find a "power greater than self," but this external power can be construed in any manner that each individual member chooses. For many

---

[1] Irving Matlzman, Ph.D.: personal communication.

AA members, the AA group itself serves as a power greater than self. For others, abstract concepts such as love or truth may serve as higher powers around which a life can be oriented and through which direction can be sought. For still other AA members, a higher power may be construed in terms of historical or legendary figures (e.g. Christ, Buddha, God, Yahweh, and so forth).

The AA emphasis upon spirituality in the form of a power greater than self serves the important psychological function of encouraging the member to seek out alternative bases for belief, attitude, and behavior. Turning one's will and one's life over to a power greater than self encourages the member to reexamine his or her own way of doing things and to seek out and practice alternative beliefs and behavioral patterns. Many members come to realize something like the following: "I insisted upon doing things my way, and it got me nowhere but deeper into trouble. It's time I tried it some way other than my own." In effect, such a statement is the beginning of AA spirituality and constitutes acceptance of the third step of the program: "we made a decision to turn our will and our lives over to the care of God *as we understood Him.*"

While spirituality is a critical ingredient of the AA approach to recovery, it is not clear what role AA assigns to spiritual factors in etiolgoy. It is implied at various places in AA literature that "self-will run riot" lies at the very core of alcoholism. Certainly self-will is viewed as problematic in general and a major contributor to the *maintenance* of active alcoholism: "Our whole trouble has been the misuse of willpower. We had tried to bombard our problems with it instead of attempting to bring it into agreement with God's intention for us" (p. 40).

Given the AA view of the "typical alcoholic personality," it is not difficult to understand AA's emphasis upon acceptance of a power greater than self and reliance upon an external source for guidance and direction. According to much AA literature and discussion, active alcoholism is characteized by a grandiose ego, fierce efforts after self-determination in the presence of a serious dependence-independence conflict, extreme self-centeredness, and a characteristic blindness to the expectations, needs, and sensitivites of others. Whether these personality factors or, in AA argot, "character defects," operate as etiological factors or as factors that maintain the disease in its active form is treated inconsistently in both AA literature and members' accounts. However, change in character defects is considered essential, and a reorganization of the personality along spiritual lines through reliance upon an intelligence or power greater than self is construed as the major force in bringing about such necessary change.

SOURCES OF MISCONCEPTIONS OF
ALCOHOLICS ANONYMOUS

Misconceptions, both lay and professional, about Alcoholics Anonymous are attributable to numerous factors. The following discussion concerns some of the more important reasons underlying these misconceptions.

1. *Lack of direct empirical observation.* Many people, lay and professional, form and promulgate opinions and beliefs about AA in the absence of direct empirical observation of members' behaviors. It is not possible to understand the AA approach to changing alcoholic behavior without careful, direct empirical observation *over a lengthy period of time.* Alcoholics Anonymous is a complex social organization and as such cannot be understood through "armchair" analysis, superficial consideration of assumed AA ideolgoy, rumor, or media exposure of the experiences and perceptions of small numbers of celebrities.

2. *Failure to adopt an anthropological perspective.* In many respects, AA constitutes a separate and distinct American subculture. While it necessarily shares some things in common with the dominant national culture, it is in many respects a culture of its own. The language of AA cannot be comprehended if taken literally and in isolation from the common core of AA experience from which meanings derive. In effect, meaning does not lie in bits and pieces but inheres in systems as a whole. Metaphor is the salt and pepper of AA argot, and the unwary translator may find himself banging away at the concrete rather than flowing with the analogy. Also, AA slogans are particularly vulnerable to miscomprehension. Short, seemingly simple declarative statements of the obvious, such slogans are member codes for complex, subtle, extended meanings. The AA aphorism that "It's the first drink that gets you drunk" is illustrative. This aphorism can be taken to mean one or any of the following:

a. If an alcoholic takes one drink, he or she will immediately lose control and drink until he or she becomes intoxicated.
b. It is not the last drink that gets an alcoholic drunk, but the first, since this is the way all drunks commence—with a first drink.
c. An alcoholic is "drunk" when he or she picks up the first drink and becomes intoxicated later. For that matter, an alcoholic is probably drunk *before* he or she ever picks up the first drink.
d. If you don't drink alcohol, you can't get intoxicated.
e. If an alcoholic knowingly and deliberately consumes alcohol, he or she is back on the path that will eventually lead to destructive drinking.

f. Deliberately and knowingly taking a first drink is a symbolic rejection of a sober life-style and signifies a return to a state of consciousness (i.e. a drunk mode of being in the world). This drunk mode of being in the world is a reinstatement of attitudes, perceptions, feelings, beliefs, and actions that make up the drinking personality and life-style and may or may not be accompanied by intoxification and/or loss of control over the amount of alcohol consumed on any given drinking occasion.

The first interpretation in the list above is a literal interpretation, while the remaining five are possible extended meanings that different AA members may attach to the aphorism, or different meanings that the same member may attach to it, depending upon varying contexts, circumstances, or purposes of communication.

Naive observers of AA fail to grasp the meaning structure of AA communications while latching onto the literal. In some instances, this mistaken focus on the literal has led researchers to devise experiments that attack an assumed AA position that in actuality does not exist. The research, for example, by Sobell, Sobell, and Christelman entitled "The Myth of One Drink" demonstrated the obvious: Alcoholics do not inevitably get intoxicated immediately after drinking particular quantities of alcohol. To imply, however, that this research disproved a central AA tenet is wide of the mark. From an AA perspective, this study by Sobell, Sobell, and Christelman would be better titled "The Myth of the Myth of One Drink."

The extended meanings that characterize the AA language system will continue to elude external observers who remain at literal, concrete levels of analysis and fail to consider the nature of symbolic communication and the purposes it serves in complex social contexts and transactions. The meanings that AA members attach to seemingly straightforward words such as "disease," "drunk," "Spiritual," "Allergy," and so forth must never be assumed by investigators seeking to understand AA but must be analyzed empirically with regard to instrumentality, contextual and experiential influence, extended meaning, and symbolic content. It is quite likely, for example, that the concept of *disease* as used by AA members is characterized by heterogeneity, ambiguity, and contextual variations rather than homogeneity, precision, and contextual invariance. Hence, the meaning any member wishes to imply by use of the term disease cannot be inferred from ordinary or dictionary definition.

3. *Tactics, audience, and crisis orientation.* Alcoholics Anonymous is a social movement developed, maintained, and operated by and for lay persons. The vast majority of its activity can be seen as various

tactical influence attempts directed toward still-drinking or recently drinking persons, the majority of whom are experiencing serious life crises. According to AA mores, the "newcomer to the program" is the most important person in the meeting room, and it is to this person that the bulk of the communications are directly or indirectly addressed. Much of AA literature is written with the newcomer in mind and is also "pitched" at a level that drinking alcoholics and their family members may find useful. As a consequence, AA communications, written and oral, are structured by a need for simplicity, economy, repetition, directness, and a certainty that seems to ignore complexity. Obviously one does not engage intoxicated alcoholics, or alcoholics caught up in the misery of physical withdrawal, in a searching theoretical discussion of the etiology of their affliction. Nor does one debate the epistemological quandaries inherent in categorical thinking generally with newcomers to AA whose principal reason for having come at all may be to get back a spouse who has just thrown the alcoholic out of the house, or to be rehired to a job from which he or she has just been fired, or because a judge told the newcomer to come, or because he doesn't have a place to stay the night, and so on and so forth. Nor does one present one's comments in terms of testable hypotheses or operational definitions when confronted with a desperate alcoholic whose overriding concern is whether he can make it through the night without "shaking apart," "going crazy," or "taking a drink."

Communications of AA, written or oral, rarely, if ever, are cast in terms acceptable to the scholar or research scientist. When one appreciates the purposes of these communciations, the contexts out of which they have developed, the audience to whom they are addressed, and their historical development by and for lay people, it is not difficult to see why these communciations have not been understood readily by professionals whose languages, assumptions, and paradigms require different conceptual filters. "Folk talk" and "science talk" obey radically different rule systems, proceed from differing assumptions, and serve different purposes.

4. *Membership rules and members as informants.* A further source of confusion about AA stems from the membership of AA itself. Persons are members of AA if they say they are. No other rules or "tests" of membership are necessary. Hence, a person who has been abstinent for one week, attends AA, desires to stop drinking, and says that he is a member *is* a member. As a result of such liberal membership rules, AA members as informants can and do vary greatly in terms of knowledge of AA, experience in the program, sophistication with regard to observation of individual and social be-

havior, personal interpretations of AA concepts, length of sobriety, and so forth. Obviously, the reliability and quality of material gathered from members as informants can and do vary considerably. Such variations in members' reports are a further source of confusion about the movement.

AA members, in general, are not always cognizant of the necessity to translate program concepts into terms accessible to nonalcoholic outsiders. Often, members fail to articulate the extended meanings inherent in AA concepts and do not appear to realize that many external observers have neither the experiential base nor the repertoire of symbolic associations to AA talk that permit effortless and meaningful intra-fellowship communication.

SUMMARY

The concepts of AA concerning etiology are less well developed than are other program concepts. However, an AA point of view involving both biological and psychological factors can be discerned. This chapter has attempted to present the AA point of view in the context of a number of commonly encountered misconceptions of this important social movement. An examination of several of the more important sources of these misconceptions about AA was presented. In general, observers of AA are encouraged to study members' beliefs and behaviors directly rather than to rely upon often erroneous assumptions about ideology.

REFERENCES

Alcoholics Anonymous. New York: Alcoholics Anonymous Sorld Services. 1976.

Alcoholics Anonymous: *Twelve Steps and Twelve Traditions.* New York: Alcoholics Anonymous World Services, 1953.

Armor, D. J., Polich, J. M., and Stambul, H. B.: *Alcohol and Treatment.* Santa Monica: Rand Corporation, 1976.

Caddy, R., Addington, H. J., and Perkins, D.: Individualized behavior therapy for alcoholics: A third-year independent double-blind follow-up. *Behavior Research and Therapy, 16:*345–362, 1978.

Chalmers, D. K.: The alcoholic's controlled drinking time. *World Alcohol Project, I:* 18–27, 1979.

Jellinek, E. M.: *The Disease Concept of Alcoholism.* New Haven: College and University Press, 1960.

Polich, J. M., Armor, D. J., and Braiker, H. B.: *The course of Alcoholism: Four Years After Treatment.* Santa Monica: Rand Corporation, 1980.

Sobell, L. C., Sobell, M. B., and Christelman, W. C.: The myth of 'one drink.' *Behavior Research and Therapy, 110:*119–123, 1972.

Sobell, M. B., and Sobell, L. C.: Individualized behavior therapy for alcoholics. *Behavior Therapy, 4:*49–72, 1973.

Wallace, J.: 'Alcoholism and treatment' revisited. *World Alcohol Project, 1:*3–18, 1979.

Part VIII

Alcoholism Counselors

Alcoholism Counselor Burnout:

An Overview

Interest in various reactions to job-related stress among members of the helping professions has increased rapidly within recent years. A number of articles have documented the concern with poor morale among nurses (Storlie, 1979; Shubin, 1978; Shubin, 1979; Hay & Oken, 1972; Simon & Whiteley, 1977). Armstrong (1977) has studied stress-related behaviors among child abuse case workers. Daly (1979), Pines & Maslach (1979), Costello & Zalkind (1963), and Freudenberger (1975) have examined problems among workers in a variety of work contexts—mental health clinics, free clinics, methadone clinics, social service agencies, and therapeutic communities. With regard to alcoholism workers, Gottheil (1975) and Valle (1979) have contributed observations on the problem of lowered morale in alcoholism treatment organizations. These studies all point to the existence of a possible syndrome called "burnout" among members of the helping professions.

BURNOUT IN PERSPECTIVE

Any discussion of "burnout" must necessarily begin with recognition of the limits of the metaphor and a caution against reification. "Burnout," "flameout," or, as German rocket scientists put it, *brennschluss*, refers to the cessation of burning in a jet or rocket engine due to a stoppage or exhaustion of fuel. Obviously, the metaphor can be misleading. Human service workers are not rockets. Nor do they travel along computerized trajectories, have complicated electronic circuitry, deliver payloads, or run out of fuel. Such workers are complex biological, psychosocial, and spiritual creatures with definite aims and purposes operating within complex physical, psychosocial, and political-legal organizational contexts. Lacking in order, cohesiveness, coherence, and rationality, it is often the case that these organizational contexts constitute sources of work-related stress rather than supportive systems for goal accomplishment.

Human "burnout," then, is far more complex than the deceptively simple aerospace metaphor implies. The problem does not lie within individual counselors nor within the difficult clients with whom counselors must deal. Rather, the problem seems to inhere in systems as a whole—in the numerous transactions between and among individuals and their environments that make up treating organizations. In short, "burnout," is *multifactored* and involves factors at all levels—individual, interpersonal, group, and organizational.

Defining Burnout

In defining burnout, one must take care to distinguish job-related stress reactions from general problems of mental health and adjustment in members of helping professions. Problems that have their origins outside the work situation may indeed complicate the lives of professional helpers but these cannot enter into a definition of occupational burnout. Burnout is most appropriately construed as a job-related phenomenon. Daly (1979) has offered a useful definition: . . . "burnout might be defined as a reaction to job-related stress that varies in nature with the intensity and duration of the stress itself. It may be manifested in workers becoming emotionally detached from their jobs and may ultimately lead them to leave their jobs altogether."

Maslach (1976) defines burnout similarly to Daly as a reaction to job-related stress that results in the worker's becoming emotionally detached from clients, treating clients in a dehumanizing way, and becoming less effective on the job.

Stages of Burnout

A fullblown state of burnout does not appear suddenly but develops slowly over time. The stages of burnout may follow a course described in general stress reactions by Costello and Zalkind (1963). According to Costello and Zalkind, environmental stressors interact with aspects of the individual personalities to produce tension levels of varying intensity and duration. Three stages of tension reaction may be identified as follows:

1. The Alarm State
2. The Resistance State
3. The Exhaustion State

The *Alarm State* is a normal reaction to stress that is found among individuals suddenly confronted with a difficult situation. This is the state in which the body's energy and defenses are mobilized to deal with a threat of some kind. The individual shows increased striving in order to deal with the situation and maintain effective performance and goal accomplishment. If, however, the situation remains unresolved, frustration arises. Continuous frustration may lead to the *resistance state*. It is at this point that the individual enters early phases of burnout. Virtually all of the person's energies and defenses are being exerted to deal with stress and task accomplishment becomes secondary in importance. A downward spiral is established with decreased task performance resulting in even more stress, further efforts to manage stress, higher frustration levels, growing feelings of inadequacy, loss of self-esteem, and depression. Finally, the individual's adaptive capacities breakdown altogether and the final stage of burnout is ushered in—the *exhaustion state*. At this terminal point, the individual may show a fullblown depression, withdrawal from clients and colleagues, and an attitude characterized by rage, anxiety, helplessness, hopelessness, cynicism, and despair.

SYMPTOMS OF BURNOUT

Armstrong (1977) has provided an analysis of symptoms of burnout among caseworkers:

1. high resistance to going to work every day (dragging your feet);
2. somatic symptoms, the nagging cold, frequent bouts with a virus or flu;
3. feeling tired and exhausted all day, frequent clock watching to see how late it is, usually accompanied by tiredness after work;
4. postponing client contacts, resisting client phone calls and office visits;
5. stereotyping clients, "here goes the same old story;"
6. an inability to concentrate or listen to what the client is saying;
7. feeling intolerant of client's anger, an inability to understand and interpret client's anger;
8. driving the long way to a client's home, driving around the block before entering the client's home;

9. feeling immobilized, "there is nothing I can do to help these people;"
10. excessive anxiety about investigating a new client referral or making a home visit;
11. walking through K-Mart frequently in the afternoon in between home visits;
12. problems sleeping at night, tossing and turning, feeling restless;
13. cynicism regarding clients, an emerging blaming attitude, "these clients create their own problems."

Daly (1979) describes the following as typical of burnout:

1. The worker makes a sharp distinction between his or her personal and professional selves by, for example, not discussing work at home.
2. The worker minimizes his or her involvement with clients by keeping physically distant from them or by sharply curtailing the interviews.
3. The worker becomes a petty bureaucrat, going strictly by the book and viewing clients as cases rather than as people" (Daly, 1979, p.375).

Freudenberger (1975) sees considerable psychosomatic symptoms in burnout: ". . . there is a feeling of exhaustion and fatigue; inability to shake a cold, feeling physically run down; suffering from frequent headaches and gastro-intestinal disturbances; and these symptoms may be accompanied by a loss of weight, sleeplessness, depression, and shortness of breath. In short, one becomes psychosomatically susceptible to one or more ailments" (Freudenberger, 1975, p. 3).

Factors in Burnout

As mentioned previously, burnout cannot be approached from a single level of analysis. In order to locate factors responsible, one must examine events at the following levels: the individual, interpersonal, group, organizational, and systems. In the following, problems at each of these levels are discussed.

Individual Factors

Individual differences that exist independently of a particular job context may create differential susceptibility to burnout among professional workers. Differences in frustration tolerance, ego strength, physical health and illness, energy levels, skills in stress management, willingness to accept direction and supervision, adaptability, flexibility, and general mental health do exist among professional helpers and these differences may interact with features of various work environments to increase the likelihood of burnout. The worker who is generally dissatisfied, in poor health and physical condition, holds rigid, inflexible, and dogmatic attitudes, and possesses few organizational behavior skills is not likely to survive long in even the most benign of organizational environments. Neither is the worker who is chronically distrustful of others, low in self-esteem, resistant to feedback, pessimistic, and doubtful of his abilities. Stable and enduring *personality traits* interacting with *situational* factors on the job may predispose given individuals to burnout.

Expectations toward the job and towards others on the job are further individual factors that may be related to burnout. The alcoholism counselor, for example, who expects all of his clients to achieve immediate abstinence and to maintain it without relapse is obviously setting himself up for frustration and possible eventual burnout. Counselors who expect other professionals to hold attitudes toward treatment similar to their own and to behave similarly toward clients may feel threatened in contexts where diversity is the rule and innovation actively pursued. Expectations toward such things as advancement, working conditions, recognition and reward, salaries, and so forth may also contribute to burnout by impacting negatively on job satisfaction.

In alcoholism counseling, a professional's own recovery may either facilitate or impede the recovery of others. If the recovered counselor is keenly aware of possible counter-transference effects and utilizes his own recovery selectively and appropriately, then personal recovery can be a source of strength and wisdom in the treatment situation. If, however, the recovered counselor persists in projecting aspects of his own experience and recovery on his clients, then counseling can become a frustrating, disappointing, and painful experience for the counselor as well as the client. Clients will surely resist such projections onto them and will either leave treatment or become appropriately argumentative and negative in the counseling situation. In either case, job satisfaction for the counselor is not a likely outcome.

Educational level and expectations developed in either graduate school or other advanced training contexts may be related to burnout. If graduate instruction continues to be as unrealistic as it now appears to be for professional helpers generally, one can expect people to enter the job market with very little idea of what various jobs actually entail and the less than ideal conditions under which they will work. Pines and Maslach (1978) comment on the unrealistic nature of graduate training as follows:

"Our results indicated that the more highly educated staff members tend to enter the mental health field to find self-fulfillment. They come with high expectations of themselves, their jobs, and the patients. They are not prepared for finding themselves a small part of a bureaucratic machine in what may be a mundane and uneventful job that lacks opportunity for self-expression. They develop negative expectations and become very pessimistic about the effectiveness of their work. Thus we think it is crucial that any advanced psychiatric or other clinical training program should include at least one course that will prepare mental health professionals for the tremendous emotional stresses they will encounter in their work."

Armstrong (1977) has also discussed the relationships among education, unrealistic expectations, and job dissatisfaction:

"Education is also an important characteristic that tends to be associated with turnover and burnout (job dissatisfaction). Those who are highly educated tend to change jobs more often than their peers with less education. The explanation for this phenomenon appears to be the type of education that social workers receive in masters programs of social work. Many social workers are trained to define problems with a psychoanalytic framework, others are trained in various other theories of human behavior, with an emphasis on therapeutic techniques. Workers so trained are quickly disillusioned with the agency and themselves when working with abuse or neglect clients. Contrary to what they had expected, abuse/neglect families' primary needs require that workers focus on getting families' food, solving housing problems and advocating with other agencies on the families' behalf. These efforts require different kinds of skills. Most social workers want to do therapy, and most agencies can't afford that luxury; there are too many clients to allow "one-to-one" therapy. Furthermore, clients don't always make the great leaps in self awareness or drastically change their life patterns quickly. In fact, clients often resent the social worker's intrusion into their life. Progress is slow, and often unappreciated by a worker who has higher expectations."

In general, then, individual differences among counselors can interact with situational factors to produce differential susceptibility to burnout.

INTERPERSONAL/GROUP FACTORS

Counselors do not exist and work in social vacuums. For the most part, they carry out their functions as members of a complex social ecology. This complex social ecology involves numerous transactions between and among individuals in dyads, triads, and increasingly larger groups.

In treatment organizations characterized by considerable explicit and implicit conflict over purposes and procedures, high levels of stress are usually noted. Such organizations typically show interpersonal transactions characterized by distrust, overt or covert hostility, deception, duplicity, guardedness, defensiveness, and game-playing rather than open, trusting, non-defensive, and authentic communications and interactions.

It is possible to construe interpersonal transactions as leading to positive actions and outcomes or to negative actions and outcomes. This ratio of positive to negative interpersonal exchanges may very well be associated with burnout. While a degree of conflict can be healthy in organizations, when conflict reaches a level where the ratio of positive to negative exchanges is low, the probability of individual staff burnout increases.

There are three types of interpersonal transactions that may be related to burnout: 1) counselor-patient, 2) counselor-staff and 3) counselor-patient-staff. Let's discuss these separately.

In some cases, *counselor-patient transactions* may yield high levels of stress and lead eventually to burnout. These cases may involve particular characteristics of specific alcoholic subpopulations. For example, late stage chronic alcoholics, unmotivated, and resistant to change, may pose difficult problems for counselors poorly prepared for their jobs in terms of attitudinal and technical factors. For counselors working with this population, the high relapse rate and painfully slow progress may give rise to counselor self-perceptions of failure and inadequacy. As these counselor self-perceptions become intense, counselor-patient transactions turn toward negative actions and outcomes. Some counselors respond to the stress generated by increasingly negative transactions with their patients by becoming increasingly punitive, rigid, dogmatic, and authoritarian. Others cope by withdrawing, isolating themselves, and adopting a passive attitude towards their clients. In either case, the counselor has adopted a rejecting attitude toward his clients. It is not uncommon for the counselor to begin rejecting self in the process since he will, at some level, perceive such rejection of others as a defensive projection of attitudes toward self. Eventually, however, such disowning projection may result in considerable paranoid-like behavior and thinking on the counselor's part or in massive depression.

Counselor-staff interactions may involve exchanges between staff members at the same level or at different levels. These exchanges may be formal or informal and may involve communications with others in similar or dissimilar organizational roles. At the level of counselor to counselor interactions, difficulties may develop between recovered counselors and counselors who have not personally experienced alcoholism. In organizations where recovered counselors are in the majority, non-alcoholic counselors may face serious problems concerned with the maintenance of self-esteem and organizational credibility, position, power, and influence. In organizations where recovered alcoholics are in the minority, the obverse obtains and recovered people may feel unappreciated, powerless, and unable to influence treatment policy.

Communications across disciplines may involve counselors in formal organizational power struggles they are not likely to win. Consider the following report of an interchange between a counselor and the medical unit of his center:

"My patient had been on antabuse five times and every time he either stopped taking it and then drank or he drank on top of it. The doctor ordered antabuse again when the patient came back in for treatment. Now, I know this guy and I knew he would drink again on antabuse. I told the doctor but the doctor told me that it wasn't my business to prescribe medications. He put my patient back on antabuse. I went to my office, slammed the door, and kicked the filing cabinet."

Counselor-patient-staff triads constitute the third type of interpersonal transactions that may involve all concerned in increasing levels of stress. In this case, counselor and other staff may behave in contradictory ways toward the same patients and send overt or covert contradictory messages to the patient and to one another. When two staff members disagree overtly about the patient and hold contradictory attitudes towards him, the alcoholic patient may use the staff conflict to manipulate his treatment to his own ends. When the staff conflict is *covert* and unrecognized the alcoholic patient may begin to act out in the treatment setting.

But while covert staff disagreement is uncomfortable for the patient, it introduces a further source of stress for the involved counselors. Sustained, unresolved conflict between two staff members may lead one or both to symptoms of burnout. And equally important, the conflict may radiate outward from the principals to involve other organizational members.

Group transactions may operate between and among political coalitions within the treatment organization. While some degree of coalition formation is common across organizations of all kinds and is not necessarily negative, organizations that come to rely almost exclusively upon political modes of intra-organizational problem-solving and problem-resolution are likely to show high levels of stress. High stress levels are associated with such things as guarded interactions, lack of authentic communication, rigid controls over feelings, refusal to share information, distancing among members, competitiveness, fear, game playing, and overt or covert sabotage by members of one coalition vis-a-vis members of others. Alcoholism counselors, particularly those most idealistic, sensitive, and dedicated to treatment rather than political objectives, experience high levels of stress in such organizations and begin to experience their work situation as unnecessarily complex, difficult, and, in time, meaningless and absurd.

Political coalitions in alcoholism treatment organizations may stabilize around issues involving a host of things, e.g., conceptions of alcoholism, approaches to treatment, goals for treatment, admission policies, and so forth. They may also form around structural and disciplinary lines, e.g., recovered versus non-recovered, professional versus non-professional, behavioral versus psychodynamic, medical versus non-medical, psychiatric versus A.A., etc. If mechanisms other than political ones are not discovered to resolve these issues and structural conflicts around which political coalitions form, organizational life is likely to be characterized by considerable conflict, turmoil, stress, and dissatisfaction. Eventual dysfunctional organizational behavior can be expected with typical signs of burnout appearing earliest in the most talented, dedicated, and idealistic members of the staff.

MANAGEMENT/FORMAL ORGANIZATIONAL FACTORS

As we have seen, burnout of counselors cannot be accounted for by focussing only upon individual persons. The management of the treatment organization and its formal organizational structures and processes must be considered as well.

Supervision. Factors related to supervision of counselors are critical concerns in understanding burnout. In far too many instances, supervision has been conceived along professional versus non-professional lines. Alcoholism counselors have in the past been considered non-professionals and assigned to psychologists, social workers, psychiatrists, and, in some cases, medical doctors for "supervision." In many of these instances, alcoholism counselors feel that they are more experienced, knowledgeable, and competent with regard to alcoholism and its treatment than supervisors whose only real qualification for supervision is an advanced degree.

Aside from the question of who should supervise whom in alcoholism treatment, the quality of supervision in many programs does not appear adequate. In some instances, supervisors fail to supervise at all, permitting counselors to go it on their own even when feedback, guidance, and direction are clearly needed.

Supervisors may also fail to be sensitive to the needs of frontline alcoholism counselors. A supervisor who understands the enormous demands placed upon alcoholism counselors by difficult tasks, situations, and patients, is a valuable ally of the counselor and may make timely interventions to offset otherwise unbearable conditions. Advising a counselor to take some days off, arrange "time outs" during a busy counseling day, give up a particular difficult patient to another counselor, and switch job assignments are important options often overlooked by supervisors. Providing recognition, support, reinforcement, and encouragement are other supervisory activities that may make all the difference in the world to counselors struggling under the burden of large case loads, difficult patients, and demanding work conditions.

The personality of the supervisor is still another factor to be considered in examining the link between supervision and burnout. Supervisors with high needs for power and control and who see the supervisory situation as a chance to exercise these needs are not likely to have satisfied workers. Nor is the supervisor whose obsessive preoccupations with trivial detail render the work situation an exercise in compulsivity rather than in creative engagement with the important demands of the work.

Supervisors with unresolved conflicts relating to alcoholism and alcoholismic behaviors may introduce these into their transactions with counselors. These conflicts may center around negative attitudes toward alcoholics or may relate to behavioral patterns frequently found among particular alcoholic populations, e.g., acting out, impulsive behavior, irresponsibility, antisocial behavior, self-centeredness, narcissism, grandiosity, and so forth.

Differential skill in interpersonal communication among supervisors is still another factor possibly related to burnout. Supervisors who cannot communicate clearly and directly, who are unresponsive to feelings, and whose verbal messages are contradicted by their actions can be a major source of job-related stress for counselors. Particularly important is the supervisor's skill in giving feedback that facilitates change and growth rather than increasing counselor self-perceptions of inadequacy, general incompetency and low self-worth.

FORMAL ORGANIZATIONAL AND SYSTEMS FACTORS.

Just as alcoholism counselors do not exist and work in social vacuums, neither do supervisors. The behavior of both supervisors and counselors is determined in part by events at the level of the formal organization and system.

At the organizational level, tight control over information and decision-making at top levels has been shown repeatedly to be associated with poor employee morale, weak commitment, and less than enthusiastic work performance. Increased sharing of important information and participation in decision-making, under most circumstances, is associated with increased understanding of organizational events on the part of workers, stronger organizational commitment, greater willingness to carry out decisions in which they have had a voice, and higher job satisfaction.

The alcoholism movement, generally in this country has been characterized by level organizational structures, high individual participation, and democratic principles. Administrators must be cognizant of these ideals and principles since expectations developed in extra-organizational alcoholism contexts are routinely brought into the formal organization by alcoholism workers. Few talented, gifted, and sensitive alcoholism workers will adapt easily to treatment organizations designed along lines of classical bureaucratic theory. But this needless and wasteful mismatch between individual characteristics and organizational design need not continue. In the private sector, well-developed alternatives to classical bureaucratic organizational structures do exist, e.g., the matrix and project organizations. The application of these or other alternative organizational models to alcoholism treatment organizations remains to be explored.

In addition to factors related to organizational structure, other management/administrative behaviors seem related to counselor burnout. Elaborate rule systems in the form of thick "policy and procedures manuals," inefficient and cumbersome quality assurance review mechanisms, and excessive paperwork are very real factors involved in poor employee morale and possibly in burnout. Counselors complain that while some amount of paperwork is unavoidable, much of it seems redundant, inappropriate, and probably unnecessary. Most important, counselors see such organizational maintenance work as diverting time and energy away from their primary mission—treating alcoholic patients.

Excessive management/administrative rule-making raises other concerns for counselors. Rules may be made by management/

administration but these must be enforced by frontline personnel. Counselors often complain that compulsive rule structures are unreasonable, that they force disagreements between patients and themselves where none need exist, and lead to severe role conflict in the counselor position. That is, the counselor is being asked to play two incompatible and incongruent roles—"therapist" and "enforcer." These incompatible roles generate stress which can develop into burnout.

Management/administration awareness of the demands of various tasks in the alcoholism treatment organization can be an invaluable tool in avoiding burnout. Simply because a worker does a particularly difficult and demanding job well does not mean that the worker should stay in that job forever. Job rotation and job reassignment should be routine practices in alcoholism treatment organizations. In multiple service component organizations, people should rotate through various services, e.g., detox units, in-take, rehabilitation units, and so forth. Where different subpopulations exist in the organization, efforts should be made by management to give counselors varied experience through routine reassignment.

Other management/administrative behaviors associated with such things as performance evaluations, pay raises, leave requests, work schedules, performance rewards, and so forth may not serve to raise employee morale but may serve to keep it from *lowering*. That is, factors of this kind may be morale *maintenance* factors or "prevention factors" useful in preventing drops in employee morale.

Finally, one must examine the broader system in which a particular alcoholism treatment agency rests if a complete picture of counselor burnout is to be drawn. Chaotic and unpredictable behavior on the part of funding sources introduces great uncertainty into the treatment organization that, if left unresolved over long enough periods, can be an enormously significant factor in burnout. Alcoholism workers need a sense of continuity, orderliness, reasonable certainty, and sufficient predictability in their careers and work environments if burnout is to be prevented.

REFERENCES

Armstrong, K.L. "How Can We Avoid Burnout?" Paper presented at the Second Annual National Conference on Child Abuse and Neglect. Houston, Texas. April 17–20, 1977.

Costello, T.W. and Zalkind, S.S. *Psychology in Administration: A Research Orientation.* Englewood Cliffs, N.J. Prentice Hall, 1963, p. 125–129.

Daley, M.R. "Burnout: Smoldering Problem in Protective Services". *National Association of Social Workers*, 1979, p. 375–379.

Freudenberger, H.J. "The Staff Burn-out Syndrome." Drug Abuse Council, Inc. Publication SS-7, Wash: 1975.

Gottheil, E. "Poor Morale in Treatment Personnel." *Alcohol Health and Research World.* Spring 1975, p. 21–25.

Hay, D. and Oken, D. "The Psychological Stress of Intensive Care Unit Nursing." *Psychosomatic Medicine, 34,* Mar.–Apr., 1972, p. 109–118.

Maslach, C. "Burned-out." *Human Behavior,* Sept. 1976, p. 16–22.

Pines, A. and Maslach, C. "Characteristics of Staff Burnout in Mental Health Settings." *Hospital and Community Psychiatry.* Vol. 29, No. 4, April 1978. p. 233–237.

Pines, A. and Maslach, C. "Staff Burnout: Can It Be Avoided?" *Innovations.* Summer 1979, p. 40.

Shubin, S. "Rx for stress—your stress." *Nursing 79,* Vol. 9, January 1979, p. 52–55.

Shubin, S. "Burnout: The Professional Hazard You Face In Nursing." *Nursing 78,* Vol. 8, July 1978, p. 22–27.

Simon, N.M. and Whitely, S. "Psychiatric Consultations With MICU Nurses." *Heart Lung,* Vol. 6, May–June 1977, p. 497–504.

Storlie, F.J. "Burnout: The Elaboration Of A Concept." *American Journal of Nursing.* December, 1979, p. 2108–2111.

Valle, S.K. "Burnout: Occupational Hazard For Counselors." *Alcohol Health and Research World.* Vol. 3, No. 3, Spring 1979, p. 10–14.

Part IX
Columns and Editorials

Sobriety Is More Than
Not Drinking

People who know very little about alcoholics often confuse the meaning of the words "dry" and "sober." To these people, sober simply means that somebody has stopped drinking. They say that they or somebody they know have "gone on the wagon." And when they start to drink again, they have "fallen off the wagon."

But to be dry is not necessarily to be sober. Dryness is a condition in which the alcoholic is not drinking alcohol. Without any further changes in the alcoholic, to be dry is to be in a rather unpleasant, uncomfortable state. To be dry and dry alone can be a miserable time filled with craving for alcohol, lots of unhappiness, resentments, bitter memories, and sorrow. At best, dryness is a transitional state on the way to being sober. But what is sober? What does it mean to say that one has achieved sobriety?

Among many recovered alcoholics, sobriety is much more than simply not drinking alcohol. Sobriety is, in effect, a change of consciousness as well as behavior. To describe what is meant by sobriety, we have to use words like "balance," "wholeness," "serenity," "fulfillment" and "gratitude." Sober people have come to grips with themselves above all else. They do not blame others, but take responsibility for their own situations and happiness. As the character in the comic strip *Pogo* put it—"we have met the enemy and they are us!"

Sober people are people in whom a heightened sense of gratitude is readily apparent. Instead of railing against the things they don't have, they give thanks for what they do have. In effect, sober people are people who have not only had a spiritual awakening but are well on the path toward spiritual transformation. With sobriety comes compassion, love, sensitivity to others and their needs, and awareness. Instead of pessimism, cynicism, and despair, sobriety means optimism, a positive attitude, and hope for tomorrow.

371

When I try to explain the meaning of sobriety to people unfamiliar with recovery from alcoholism, I use the following: **S** stands for sanity rather than insanity; **O** stands for order rather than chaos; **B** stands for beautiful; **R** is reasonable; **I** is interesting; **E** is enthusiastic; **T** is tender (loving); **Y** is young. In short, sober people are sane, orderly, beautiful, reasonable, interesting, enthusiastic, tender, and forever young. And the way to develop these things is to first stop drinking alcohol and then go to work on ourselves. Nobody gets sober without paying some dues. But as many of us have found out, the dues are worth it.

Cocaine and Sudden Death

The recent cocaine caused deaths of two young, robust American athletes, both of whom were in excellent health, should give users pause. Cocaine is not an innocent drug. It is dangerous. And it is particularly dangerous to the heart.

Cocaine is a powerful central nervous system stimulant. In its various freebase forms including crack and rock, its effects are sudden and very powerful. The drug causes immediate rushes of the brain neurotransmitter chemicals, dopamine and noradrenaline. The effects on the heart of this massive stimulation can be lethal. Cocaine causes the heart to race and the blood pressure to rise. It can induce very dangerous changes in the electrical activity of the heart, triggering off abnormal patterns of beating called arrhythmias. When the arrhythmias arise in the lower portion of the heart (the ventricles), the affected person can literally drop dead without warning. Without question, sudden cardiac death has now been linked to cocaine use. Sudden death can occur for people with essentially healthy hearts, but risks are increased greatly in people who have some known or unknown underlying cardiac abnormality.

Cocaine has another dangerous effect on the heart and its arteries. Because of its highly stimulating properties, cocaine can cause the main arteries of the heart to go into spasms. When the coronary artery goes into spasm, the person will experience chest pain not unlike the chest pain that people with advanced coronary artery disease experience. These chest pains are called *angina* and indicate that the heart is being starved for richly oxygenated blood. In effect, because of cocaine-induced spasms of the major coronary arteries, blood flow to the heart itself is greatly reduced. The resulting pain is nature's way of sounding alarms and giving warnings. If we want to go on living and avoid the high risks of heart attack, we had better leave cocaine and all other stimulating drugs alone.

Considering everything cocaine can do to the human heart, isn't it better to get high naturally than on this chemical? Let's fill our hearts with love not with cocaine!

Hope, Love and Faith: Foundations of Sobriety

Despite the many words that have been written about recovery from alcoholism, a meaningful and fulfilling sobriety may rest on a much smaller number of pillars. Hope is surely one of these supports, and so are love and faith.

Hope is often mentioned but rarely defined. What do we really mean when we say we have hope? Actually, hope is a mixture of two things: a reasonable desire for some outcome and at least some small but realistic expectation that the desired outcome can be achieved. For alcoholics, it is perfectly in order to have hope. Provided that we do what we are supposed to do, sobriety is within the reach of each of us. To want to be sober is a reasonable desire and to expect to achieve and maintain sobriety, provided we do what we must do, is a reasonable expectation.

Love, too, is a foundation for the recovering person. Love is a power—a higher power if you will—that can do extraordinary things in our lives. With love in our hearts for each other, for ourselves, and for life, we are often at our very best. And while many of us blush at the mention of love as a great power working in the world, we sense that it is tangible and real since we have seen the negative power of its opposite at work. Hate is a power we are quick to recognize and acknowledge. We know that hate is a force in the world with which we must contend in ourselves and in others. Alcoholics cannot stay sober long with rage in their hearts toward themselves or toward others. Nor can they enjoy a contented sobriety while harboring resentments toward others. If we are to stay sober, resentment must give way to respect and caring attitudes toward ourselves and others.

Faith is the third pillar of sobriety. In its broadest meaning, faith is trust in somebody or something. For recovering alcoholics, faith in

375

376 JOHN WALLACE: WRITINGS

some power greater than self is usually implied. For some persons, this power greater than self may be a recognized religious figure. Christ, God, Yahweh, Buddha, and Shiva are examples of higher powers to which humans for many centuries have turned for guidance and comfort. Some alcoholics may turn to these in sobriety as higher powers for themselves. Other alcoholics, however, may choose to search for higher powers other than those from organized religions. An A.A. group can be a power greater than self. Some persons appear to be comfortable with a higher power as the creative force or energy of the universe. Love itself may be thought of as a higher power to which we may turn for guidance in our everyday lives. Indeed, for many persons, religious or not, God is love. In any case, spiritual development is the key here and not forced identification with any religious precept.

In a very real sense, staying sober is very much about these three things: hope, love, and faith. When we admitted to being powerless over alcohol, we found hope not hopelessness. We became open to love as a guiding force in our lives and we understood that faith as trust in a power outside ourselves would give us all the support and power we would need to build sober lives of meaning and fulfillment.

A Letter To A Recovering Family

Sometimes I like to imagine myself writing letters rather than giving lectures, writing books, or composing columns for newsletters. It's more personal to write letters than to lecture. So . . . Dear Recovering Family:

"How are you? I'm well and happy and hope you are too. I've been thinking about you a lot, and want to share some thoughts with you.

First off, we have to get one thing straight. Nobody in this family is going to get well until the blaming stops. Alcoholism, you see, is a disease of blaming. Alcoholics blame their families for their drinking, and families blame the alcoholics for all their unhappiness. The truth is never quite so simple. Alcoholics have a disease called alcoholism which they are not responsible for developing. Once sober, of course, they are responsible for doing something about their illness. Families, on the other hand, are not to be blamed for causing alcoholism in their members. Families do not cause this disease anymore than they cause measles, whooping cough, or tennis elbow. As modern scientific research is showing, alcoholism is a genetically influenced disease of the chemistry of the brain.

But while families are not to be blamed, they must stop blaming the alcoholic in their midst for all their troubles, woes, and problems. Alcoholics in a family can cause a lot of heartache, but they don't cause all the heartache. Spouses and children of alcoholics have issues of their own they will have to admit to and deal with if they are to recover too.

Along with stopping the blaming, we must try to forgive each other. While we can't forget all that may have happened during the drinking years, we can forgive a lot of it. In fact, we had better forgive a lot of it if we intend to live together in peace, joy, and fulfillment. It's good to remember that forgiveness isn't a one-way street. It isn't only a matter of family members forgiving their alcoholics. Alcoholics have to practice forgiveness too. Resentments aren't good for family members, but for alcoholics, they can be lethal.

If there is one generalization that can be made about people in families, it might be this: we all seem to want the same things. Underneath our seeming differences and our surface disagreements, we all are usually pleading for respect, attention, consideration, and support. We want credit for jobs well done, recognition for trying hard to do right by each other, and love for nothing more than being who we are. Only families can give these things to each other consistently and unselfishly. And when they don't, most of us sense disappointment, sorrow, frustration, and loss. So let's get this one straight: The best way to get what you want in the family is to give it yourself. It usually comes back to you many times over. And if you have faith in this simple proposition, you'll usually get "same day service" to boot!

Finally, let's try harder to be more generous with each other. Above all else, let's resolve to be more generous with ourselves. Let's give of each other to each other more fully and more consistently.

Stress, Alcoholism, and Relapse

Hardly anybody goes through life without experiencing the unpleasant situations that give rise to stress. Tight schedules, urgent deadlines, missed airplanes, crying babies, loud radios, cars that break down, demanding bosses, a troubled marriage—the list is endless. But while the sources of stress are varied and many, their impact on our bodies is the same. When the stress alarm goes off in our minds, we prepare to fight or run. Our hearts speed up, blood pressure rises, muscles tighten, and we overproduce substances called catecholamines.

For alcoholics trying to stay sober, stress and its unpleasant effects can be dangerous. If we get going too fast, we may start thinking that a drink or two might be just what we need to calm down. But alcohol is a poor tranquilizer since its initial warmth and good feeling quickly give way to anxiety and discomfort. In effect, the more we drink to relax, the more we have to drink to relax!

Alcoholics need to be "inoculated" against stress, but alcohol isn't the ideal inoculation, and Valium, Librium, Marijuana, Morphine, and Percodan won't work either. Let's face it. We have to find other ways to cope with stress.

Fortunately, alternatives to chemicals are readily available. Diet, exercise, meditation, AA meetings, and learning the relaxation response can all help. As far as diet is concerned, a sensible course in recovery is to stay away from all stimulants. Avoid coffee, especially late at night so sleep can be refreshing and natural. Cut back on smoking or better yet, quit it altogether. Cigarettes are not only insomnia promoting, they are hard on the lungs, heart, and coronary arteries. Tea, some colas, and chocolate are stimulants that we should avoid if we wish to relax. And, of course, "upper" drugs like Amphetamines and Cocaine are things we simply must avoid.

A great deal of recent research is showing that exercise is not only good for physical health, it is great for mental health too. Running moderate distances five times a week helps reduce mild feelings of depression. Regular workouts can help the body to cope with sudden stress. Well-conditioned people, for example, will react more calmly to an emergency situation than will healthy, but untrained, persons.

With regard to exercise, however, a caution is in order. Some people react to intense physical exercise with panic and anxiety. This is because their bodies produce too much lactate during exercise, or they seem to be very sensitive to the lactate produced. In these cases, exercise should always be moderate and well-controlled. Light activities such as walking and easy swimming should be practiced for panic-prone lactate sensitive persons.

If a person is able to sit still and meditate, this activity may be useful in preparing one to cope with stress. But not all people can meditate. For some, an active form of meditation like jogging may be preferable. To engage in jogging meditation, try the following: keep up a gentle, regular pace; take long breaths in through the nose and short blowing breaths out through the mouth; relax the muscles of the body rather than tighten them; swing the arms loosely; think good thoughts!

Remember to treat your body kindly. Give it plenty of rest, sunlight in moderate amounts, fresh fruits and vegetables, and try a massage and sauna now and then to make yourself feel good all over.

Meetings of AA will also make you feel good all over. In fact, if you are seeking the perfect inoculation against stress-related relapse, put AA meetings on the top of your list of things to do.

The Hidden Menace of Designer Drugs

Alcoholics who turn to other drugs rather than trying to stay completely sober are playing a dangerous game. Substituting drugs for alcohol rarely, if ever, works. Typically, the alcoholic is led right back to his or her drug of choice—alcohol. Moreover, by adding drugs to an alcohol problem, the active alcoholic is risking exposure to the dangerous condition of drug synergy. Because of drug synergy, a couple of drinks plus a couple of Valiums amounts to far more than a mere sum of the parts. Drugs and alcohol taken together can multiply their individual effects and produce a lethal combination.

Aside from the obvious legal risks involved with illicit drugs, there are other hazards. Dirty needles can result in hepatitis or, even worse, AIDS. In some areas of the country, half of all new cases of AIDS are appearing in intravenous drug users. Drugs have serious side effects which can involve our brains, hearts, livers, and other vital organs.

To this long list of troubles that go with drugs, there is a new menace: improperly made drugs by amateur chemists. These so-called "designer drugs" were introduced to beat the laws of most states concerning the definitions of various controlled substances. By playing with the molecular structure of a drug like heroin, a chemist can produce a slightly altered new drug that escapes the technical-legal definition of heroin, but truly is heroin! But there are dangers in producing designer drugs.

In California recently, a designer drug producer mixed up a batch of synthetic "heroin." Unfortunately, his chemistry was sloppy and he produced a substance called MPTP. In the brain, MPTP is converted to MPP^+, a very dangerous chemical similar to the herbicide, **Paraquat.** This MPP^+ chemical attacks a part of the brain called the Substantia Nigra and destroys it. When this part of the brain is destroyed, the person experiences the symptoms of the dreaded neurological disorder Parkinson's Disease. Addicts who had taken this designer drug began showing up at medical clinics with the classic symptoms of Parkinson's Disease. Most were so badly crippled that they were literally frozen and could barely walk or control their movements. Tragically, this disease is permanent. Once the Substantia Nigra is destroyed, it does not regenerate. All that can be done for these poor unfortunate victims is to try to relieve their symptoms with medications.

It turns out that designer drugs are no laughing matter. Sobriety—complete, total sobriety from all but authorized necessary medications—is our only solution.

Controlled Drinking Is Not
For Alcoholics

The belief that alcoholics could control their drinking if they really wanted to is one of those irrational pieces of nonsense that just won't go away for good. Somebody is always trying to prove it to be true. Study after study loudly proclaims that "new" evidence for moderate drinking among alcoholics has been uncovered. Even though these are eventually shown to be nonsense, the damage done can be tragic. More than a few alcoholics have listened to these siren songs of the possibility of happy controlled drinking and gone to their graves as a result.

We alcoholics need straight talk and straight facts from straight people. Theoretical possibilities or people shooting words into the blue are not for us. In the interests of some straight talk, let's consider a few facts.

FACT: *If you don't drink alcohol, you can't get drunk.* It is amazing how many people fail to appreciate this simple truism. It is ironic that most of those who haven't quite grasped this elementary fact are university professors who advertise themselves as "experts in addiction."

FACT: *Alcoholics don't get well by drinking alcohol. They get well by not drinking alcohol.* I have never known a person to relapse back into active alcoholism by not picking up a drink. On the other hand, every alcoholic I have known who has tried controlled drinking relapsed back into active alcoholism.

FACT: *All of the major studies purporting to show successful controlled drinking among alcoholics have been discredited scientifically.* Every major study claiming to show successful controlled drinking among more than a tiny minority of alcoholics has been shown to be invalid, scientifically inadequate, or false.

FACT: *The recent scientific research does not support controlled drinking*

384 JOHN WALLACE: WRITINGS

for alcoholics at all. None of the recent scientific research on this question has provided support for the controlled drinking position. A recent article, for example, in the *New England Journal of Medicine* by Dr. Helzer and his colleagues reported that of 1,289 diagnosed alcoholics followed over a 5 to 7 year period, over 99% of the males studied were unable to do moderate drinking even when "moderate" was liberally defined as up to 7 drinks a day.

FACT: *Reports of successful controlled drinking among alcoholics must be taken with a grain of salt and regarded as probably untrue until definitely proven otherwise in a legitimate court of science.* We alcoholics need to be on our guard. Newspapers, television reports, magazine stories, and so forth must be viewed with great skepticism.

In the final analysis, we alcoholics must remain true to one source, and that is *ourselves.* We must have the courage to look at our pasts honestly. There we will find the evidence we need to decide the question for ourselves. I believe when we look at our past drinking honestly, we alcoholics will come to an inescapable conclusion:

If we could have controlled our drinking, we would have, but we couldn't and we didn't. Why should things suddenly be very different now and in the future when the best predictor of our future behavior is our past behavior?

Sobriety is the answer. Complete, continuous, total, and sweet sobriety from alcohol and all other unauthorized psychoactive chemicals. Anything short of this is not only utter nonsense, but very dangerous utter nonsense.

Letting Go

Unhappy people often complain that there are no answers for their particular problems. They have searched and searched but to no avail. Answers continue to elude them.

It is often the case, however, that there are no shortage of answers. There is more likely a shortage of people willing to listen to the answers rather than a shortage of answers. In any meeting of Alcoholics Anonymous, for example, the answers are literally bouncing off the walls and falling from the ceilings like manna from above. People sharing their experience, strength, and hope with each other usually come up with a lot of relevant solutions to a host of problems. What amazes me is not that there are no answers to life's inevitable problems but why some people are so determined not to hear answers or see solutions even when these are practically banging on their front doors!

One answer that recovering alcoholic people must hear concerns letting go. Virtually every relapse I have been able to look into carefully shows the same self-defeating pattern. This is a determined refusal to let go of the three biggest killers of the bright dream of recovery: persons, places and things. The recovering alcoholic who stays overinvested in another person is at risk for relapse whether or not he or she knows it. Similarly, the recovering alcoholic who has overinvested self in places and things is flirting with disaster. A degree of detachment is the key to continued spiritual growth and to satisfaction in sobriety. Members of Al-Anon know what it means to survive through detachment. Release with love is the message of this wonderful program for those who live near or with alcoholics.

But perhaps we alcoholics need to hear this message of loving detachment too. It is fine to love the people in our lives as long as we remember that loving is not controlling, dominating, and binding people to us. Love is letting go! And it is fine to love the things of the world, to enjoy them and take pleasure from them. But when we find ourselves becoming prisoners of our possessions, then it is time to remind ourselves to let go of these too. As far as places are concerned, we need to remember that our sobriety is not dependent on a particular house, town, city or even country. Sobriety like happiness and security is an inside job. Without that deep sense that all is well inside of us, external props won't keep us on the beam.

But doesn't detachment imply a lot of negative qualities like isolation, reserve, separateness, and disconnectedness? Not at all. One can be very much involved in a loving relationship yet maintain a realization of the necessity for detachment. And one can love the house of his or her dreams while being willing to let it go if the time comes when this must happen. Detachment from persons, places, and things does not mean that we must stop being delighted by the people of the world and the things of the world. Enjoy people, places, and things but don't let these define your worth, limit your happiness, or alter the direction of your spiritual becoming. Life is so much sweeter when we have mastered the gentle art of letting go.

Realistic Expectations About Recovery

What can we expect of recovery from alcoholism? Will sobriety bring us complete, total, and continuous happiness? Can we look forward to lives devoid of sorrow, pain, and suffering? Will we never again be disappointed, frustrated, and emotionally uncomfortable? Of course not. Recovery is a process, not a fixed thing. Nothing in life stays the same and recovery is no exception.

Simply because we are sober is no guarantee that all our problems will go away for good. Like all human beings, alcoholics and chemically dependent people suffer. People disappoint us, jobs turn out to be nonfulfilling, and life may hand us a hard blow that would floor anybody. Let's face it, the slings and arrows of outrageous fortune will come our way whether we are sober or not. To expect otherwise is completely unrealistic and these unrealistic expectations may land us in more trouble than we might experience if we were to keep our expectations realistic. Here are a few thoughts about expectations that may help.

1. Try to adopt reasonable and realistic expectations about yourself, your life and others with whom you get involved.

2. Without being a pessimist, try to bear in mind that suffering is a part of life and that you will probably experience your share of sorrow too.

3. You can't control other people, so don't even try. People may love us for a time and then stop loving us. They may turn away from us, reject us, and disappoint us in other ways. But other people are going to do what they are going to do, and in matters of love, we have no control. We can't force somebody to love us, to not leave us, or never to cause us pain and sorrow!

4. It is not what actually happens to us in life that is so important,

it is what we choose to tell ourselves about what is happening that is critical. We can tell ourselves to give up in a given situation and to become depressed, moody, and cynical. Or we can take the same situation and tell ourselves to learn something important from it, pick ourselves up, dust ourselves off, and go about our business reasonably optimistic and happy. Choice is the key here.

5. Finally, it is good to remind ourselves of several things about suffering. The first is that all suffering will eventually diminish over time and will not last forever. We may grieve for a period, but if we don't pick up a drink, the suffering will cease or reduce to a level that is bearable.

Secondly, when you find yourself hurting, try to have faith that your suffering has meaning, that you will someday come to understand why you had to go through this and why you had to hurt like you did. Blind suffering is probably the most unbearable thing we can face in life, but suffering in which we can find meaning can not only be borne but can actually help us.

It is important to remember always the following: There is no experience in life, negative or positive, which when properly analyzed cannot be used as a stepping stone to further growth.

Life will be good to us in sobriety, but it can also be awful. Keeping a realistic attitude toward both the good times and bad times in recovery will help us to stay sober and to lead constructive, productive lives.

When More Is Not Enough

Father Joseph Martin tells the story of the alcoholic marooned on an island who found a genie in a bottle washed up on the beach. As a reward for freeing the genie, the alcoholic gets three wishes for anything in the world. He uses his first wish by asking for a bottle full of whiskey that never empties. No matter how many drinks are taken from it, the bottle fills right back up. The genie grants this wish and then asks the alcoholic for his other wishes. Without a moment's hesitation, the alcoholic responds "give me two more bottles just like the first one!"

The alcoholic in Father Martin's story is in the grip of a powerful psychology: The Psychology of More. This ultimately self-defeating psychology involves a pattern of events that drives many alcoholics to despair and self-destruction. More, more, more. The pressure is constant. More money, more success, more fame, more sex, more things, more love, more respect, more fun, more everything! And, of course, more, more, more of everything often leads to more trouble with alcohol and drugs.

The incessant search for more usually results in frustration since nobody can have it all. Frustration usually leads to a painful obsession with self. Everything comes to center on what the "Big I" wants and not what "We" want. Typically, frustrated and self-centered people are ungrateful people; they have no gratitude no matter how much they get. An attitude of ingratitude can quickly turn to cynicism, despair, resentments, and ultimately to drinking or taking drugs. As the singer Peggy Lee plaintively asks in one of her hits, "Is that all there is?"

How can we avoid the unhappy outcomes associated with the Psychology of More? The answer is simple although putting it into practice is very difficult. Instead of feeding the fires of discontent, we must cultivate an attitude of gratitude. Instead of being ruled by the

Psychology of More, we can begin to learn the attitudes, beliefs, and values of the Psychology of Enough. Instead of demanding more, more, more of everything, we can honestly come to say, "no thanks, I've had enough!"

Recovery, People, Places, and Things

It is always interesting to hear active alcoholics talk about what is happening in their lives that makes them pick up a drink. Invariably, it is something outside themselves. The drinking is somebody else's fault. Active alcoholics get drunk because of husbands, wives, bosses, children, relatives, lovers, and neighbors; and if other people are not a fault, then situations are to blame. Alcoholics have claimed to get drunk because of cars that wouldn't run, high pressure jobs, boring jobs, wedding celebrations, business entertaining, full moons, and so forth. Because . . . Because . . . Because . . . The excuses of alcoholism are endless, the rationalizations varied and creative, and the blaming incessant. The pointing finger is always turned outward toward the world and never back upon self.

One particularly dangerous set of excuses for drinking involve our emotional reactions. Not only can we justify our drinking because of our "bad feelings", other people will often support us in doing so. We get so depressed, we have to drink, or our fear is insurmountable without a drink in our hands. Anger makes us drink. And how can we stay sober when our lives are so miserable? Usually, our "bad feelings" are invariably the result of actions of other people—never our own.

Recovering alcoholics with some years of sobriety behind them have discovered a fundamental rule for staying sober. It goes like this: while there are many excuses for an alcoholic to pick up drink, there are no valid reasons for doing so. Other people do not make us drink. Situations do not make us drink. Our feelings do not make us drink. We are responsible for our drinking and sobriety—not them.

Of course it feels unbearable to walk about in a depression or angry at the world. And going through a divorce can hurt badly. But it is one thing to hurt and quite another thing to drink at the hurt.

391

In sobriety, we need to learn how to separate our sorrows, disappointments, losses, and suffering from drinking alcohol or taking drugs. We need to learn alternative ways to cope with the inevitable negative happenings of life. For some recovering people, this may mean seeking out a professional therapist at some point in their recoveries. Others may find solace in discussions with their sponsors, in the Twelve Steps of Alcoholics Anonymous, or in quiet moments alone with their Higher Powers.

In effect, we do have choice. We can exercise responsibility. We need not be passive victims of people and events outside of ourselves, and we need not be driven and tossed about by our emotional reactions to people, places, and things.

Here is a simple but effective way to remind yourself of your choices when things get tough. Put your drinking problem in your right hand. Put your life problems, feelings, and troubles in your left hand. Don't ever shake hands with yourself!

The message is clear: we do have to work on our living problems while we are recovering from alcoholism, but we do not have to drink at these unless we choose to do so.

Studies In Brain Chemistry Confirm Disease Concept Of Alcoholism

Those who have believed in the usefulness of a disease concept of alcoholism should be gratified to know that recent scientific work is now fully supporting their belief. Within the last decade, the search for the causes of alcoholism have centered on the brain. Intensive efforts are now underway in laboratories around the world and new knowledge about the neurochemistry of alcoholism and other chemical dependencies is rapidly accumulating.

Much of this recent research fervor has centered around substances called neurotransmitters. These chemicals are the basis of the brain's information processing system. Released into the synapse or gap that separates one brain cell (neuron) from another, these neurotransmitter substances enable the brain's fifteen billion neurons to communicate with one another by binding to highly specific receptors on the surfaces of adjacent neurons.

Neurotransmitters are synthesized in the brain from various amino acid precursors. For example, the neurotransmitter, serotonin, is synthesized from the precursor L-tryptophan, an amino acid found in milk, bananas, and other foods. Serotonin has figured prominently in several decades of research on insomnia, depression, and serious mental illness. In 1954, it was independently shown to have some similarity to the psychoactive chemical, LSD.

Another neurotransmitter, dopamine, is synthesized in the brain from the amino acid precursor, L-tyrosine. Deficiencies of dopamine in the brain have been shown to be related in a striking manner to the neurological disorder, Parkinson's Disease.

In alcoholism and other chemical dependence, investigators in Europe, Australia, the Soviet Union, and the United States, are now in a heated-up race to unlock the biological puzzles that underlie these problems. We now know, for example, that the neurotransmitter, noradrenaline, plays a central role in certain withdrawal symptoms in opiate narcotic addiction and possibly alcoholism as well. Moreover, we now know that the brain actually synthesizes its own opiate-like chemicals and deficiencies in these opiate neurotransmitter substances may be linked to the origins of such addictions as heroin, morphine, percodan, and other opiate narcotic dependencies.

In alcohol research, attention has centered on serotonin, dopamine, B-endorphins, and noradrenaline. Very recent studies in animals have shown that synthesis of serotonin in the brain increases with chronic alcohol consumption and falls in withdrawal. Other studies on serotonin have indicated that alcohol may affect the normal metabolism of this brain chemical.

Many studies, too numerous to mention here in detail, have implicated B-endorphins, noradrenaline, and dopamine in alcoholism. Deficiencies in B-endorphins in alcoholics are currently actively being investigated with several studies now demonstrating such deficiencies. These studies are of particular interest because B-endorphin is one of the natural opiate-like substances produced by the brain and B-endorphin has been shown to bind to the brain's morphine receptors. B-endorphin is a contraction of two words: Endogenous (inner) and Morphine. The term literally means the brain's inner morphine, or the morphine produced in the brain itself.

Finally, it is important to mention still another line of brain research: TIQs. The term TIQ refers to a family of products formed in the brain when people drink alcohol. These substances are formed from different aldehydes (including acetaldehyde which is the first metabolic product of alcohol in the body). These aldehydes condense with the various neurotransmitters discussed previously and produce the various TIQs. For example, acetaldehyde plus dopamine produces a TIQ called Salsolinol. Other aldehydes plus dopamine produce TIQs.

All of these TIQ substances have now been shown to produce alcohol addiction in animals when infused directly into their brains. Monkeys infused with TIQs develop what appears to be irreversible preference for very high quantities of strong ethanol concentrations (the human equivalent of two quarts of 80-proof liquor a day in some cases)!

Are TIQs the basis of human alcoholism? We don't know for sure, but we can be certain of one thing—with research findings this hot on the disease concept of alcoholism, we can expect rigorous scientific research on the brain's chemistry to not only speed up but shove rapidly into overdrive. Vigorous pursuit of the underlying biological factors in the disease of alcoholism will characterize the coming decade.

Smoke Gets In Our Eyes:

Professional Denial Of Smoking

In 1978, Luce and Sweitzer writing in the *New England Journal of Medicine* estimated that 25% of the total economic costs of illness in America were attributable to alcohol abuse and smoking. Approximately $17 billion of these costs were associated with smoking-related diseases. Considering inflation, smoking's total economic costs are probably in excess of $35 billion a year. One state alone, Florida, has reported $848 million a year for medical care with the total costs for smoking climbing to $3.03 billion when lost wages, disability payments, and indirect costs are included. In Florida, smoking is responsible for 7,893 fatal heart attacks and other diseases of the circulatory system, 6,067 deaths from cancer, and 3,100 deaths from respiratory disease each year. Eight out of ten cases of lung cancer are smoking-related as are many cases of bladder, head, and neck cancer.

In light of these statistics, it is now clear that alcoholism and chemical dependence treatment programs must take the necessary steps to deal with this addiction that is too frequently swept under the rug of denial.

In most treatment centers, approximately 90% of the patients smoke heavily. Moreover, many staff, especially recovering staff, also smoke heavily. It doesn't make sense to help people to recover from alcoholism only to fall victim to heart and lung diseases some years later.

The issue of smoking by patients in alcoholism treatment usually gets cast in black or white terms. Should patients be allowed to smoke? Should we stop them from smoking? Typically, the answers to these questions are variants of, "you can't expect people to give up everything at once." Unfortunately, this response to the smoking issue usually shuts off further inquiry.

In reality, there are many things that can be tried in alcoholism and chemical dependence treatment facilities if we really want to do something about smoking. First of all, we can seek agreement among staff that smoking is an addiction like any other addiction. Moreover, it is a costly addiction in terms of costs to both the individual and society. Accordingly, we should encourage smoking staff to become nonsmoking role models. Treatment organizations which can afford to do so, may wish to offer financial help to counselors and other professional staff who are willing to enroll in smoking cessation programs. Patients who see smoking staff trying to quit may be more open to quitting themselves.

As a part of general consciousness raising about smoking, discussions of nicotine and its effects should be included in all lectures concerned with drugs. Moreover, the personal and social costs of smoking should be a part of the lecture series. The health consequences of smoking should be emphasized within a general goal of wellness as one important outcome of alcoholism and chemical dependence treatment.

Smoking should be allowed in only a few designated areas and these should-be chosen to minimize the effects of sidestream smoke on nonsmokers. Smoking should not be permitted in group therapy settings, lectures, inhouse Alcoholic Anonymous (AA) meeting rooms, staff meetings, treatment planning conferences, and so forth.

For patients who express an interest in quitting smoking during treatment, encouragement and support should be given. Literature on stopping smoking should be available, self-help support groups encouraged, and specific techniques taught by staff familiar with smoking cessation programs. Dietary advice and exercise activities should be made available to paitents who wish to quit smoking but fear weight gain.

For patients who wish to quit smoking but are apprehensive about doing so during primary treatment, aftercare plans could include a target date at some point following treatment when smoking cessation efforts will commence. Such aftercare plans should also include what the patient intends to do about smoking and where and with whom he or she intends to do it.

Given the catastrophic outcomes possible for patients who are already experiencing smoking-related illnesses such as heart disease, lung diseases of various kinds, and circulatory problems, treatment staffs must refuse to enter into the denial systems of their patients. Just as we should not enable alcoholics to kill themselves with alcohol, we must not become enablers of cigarette smokers poised on the brink of fatal heart attacks, strokes, and lung diseases. With these patients, we must take a firm no smoking position and counsel abstinence.

The alcoholism and chemical dependence treatment field has for too long refused to acknowledge the negative consequences of smoking for recovering alcoholics and addicts. We can no longer rationalize smoking, minimize its deleterious effects on health, or deny its tragic outcomes. The time has come for us to exercise the courage to change the things we can by working toward a goal of smoke free recovering people.

Minding Ourselves

Becoming aware of ourselves is the single most important aspect of our recoveries. And staying aware of ourselves runs a close second. Awareness is the key. Without it we spin our webs in darkness not knowing what we are about, or we are like dry leaves blown here and there by strong forces over which we have no control. Without awareness, we *react* to situations. With awareness, we *respond* with choice and deliberation.

Minding ourselves is a nice phrase. To me, it is a reminder that some part of our minds has to do the important work of watching over the rest of our minds. Otherwise, we remain in states of mindlessness, and states of mindlessness are dangerous for recovering people trying to stay sober. Mindlessness was the state we were in when we reached for our tenth drink of the evening, smoked yet another joint, or snorted more cocaine up our noses. Fortunately, a moment of clarity permitted us to glimpse the reality of our situation and to begin the long climb out of alcoholism.

While drinking, then, we were in a state of mindlessness. Sobriety, however, demands of us a new state, a state of *mindfulness*. What is mindfulness? And why should we value it?

Mindfulness is a state of self-awareness in which we strive to be aware of all aspects of ourselves. A mindful person is first of all aware of what he or she is doing. Instead of acting in blind and unthinking ways, a mindful person sees his or her actions and their consequences. He or she can see how these actions are affecting other people. A mindful person is constantly aware of what he may be putting into his body and permits only those things to come in that promote health and inner harmony. Similarly, a mindful person is aware of who or what he is letting into his life. People and activities that promote psychological well-being, mental health, and spritiual satisfaction are encouraged. On the other hand, people who get between us and our

401

higher powers, make us feel crazy, and cause us to suffer great emotional pain are to be avoided.

Mindfulness requires us to pay close attention to ourselves and to our loved ones. Our motivations, intentions, attitudes, beliefs, values, feelings, and actions must become familiar territory to us. Knowing who we are, what we want, what we value, how we are feeling, and what we are doing are the keys to a contented, quality sobriety. As a famous philosopher is said to have remarked: "An unexamined life is not worth living." I suppose for recovering alcoholic and chemically dependent people, the message is even simpler: An unexamined life is not possible. Without some degree of awareness and self-examination, it is not likely that we can survive at all.

INDEX